Shalom Rav Haggada

OU PRESS
מגיד
MAGGID

SHALOM RAV HAGGADA

Commentary by Rabbi Shalom Rosner

Compiled and edited by Marc Lesnick

OU Press
Maggid Books

Shalom Rav Haggada

First Edition, 2023

Maggid Books
An imprint of Koren Publishers Jerusalem Ltd.

POB 8531, New Milford, CT 06776-8531, USA
& POB 4044, Jerusalem 9104001, Israel

www.korenpub.com

The publication of this book was made possible through the generous support of *The Jewish Book Trust.*

ISBN 978-1-59264-617-3, *hardcover*

Printed and bound in Israel

Dedication from Rabbi Shalom Rosner

לעילוי נשמת

חנה שרה בת הרב מיכל שמעון ע״ה

This Haggada is dedicated to the memory of my mother a"h who returned her soul to her Creator during the preparation of this work.

My mother's unconditional love for each child, grandchild, and great-grandchild was no more evident than it was each Pesah, as she basked in the nachas of spending time with her family. She, along with my father, yb"l, brought the entire family together, to relax together, to experience together, and to celebrate together. The Haggada Shel Pesah is a most appropriate way to memorialize her commitment, loyalty, and love for all of us.

May her memory be a blessing,
and may we continue her legacy for generations.

This Haggada is dedicated to our dear parents

Rabbi David and Eileen Lesnick
Shaya and Rhona Bar-Chama

Each of whom has served as a role model
for us and our children as individuals dedicated
to Torah, Avoda and Gemilut Hasadim.

And to our dear children
who help make our Seder memorable

Ariel and Rinat, Ori, Noam and Shachar
Adena and Netanel Weil
Sarit and Yonatan and Zohar Kurtzman
Rami and Achinoam
Amichai

Each of whom continues to bring us tremendous nahat.

Tamar and Marc Lesnick

BUILDERS

In honor of our dear friend and personal role model
Marc Lesnick
May you continue to demonstrate תורה עם דרך ארץ
and flourish in all your endeavors.

And in honor of our distinguished teacher and exceptional leader
Rabbi Shalom Rosner
May you continue to spread Torah to כלל ישראל,
and may Tamar and you continue to lead the community with unparalleled dignity and devotion.

We are truly fortunate to have you in our lives.

Jan & Orit Wimpfheimer and family

BUILDERS

In fond memory of

***Moishe Wein** a"h*

My brilliant and dedicated Shas chavrusa
who devoted his life to helping Jewish teens.

Dr. Robert Schulman

BUILDERS

״שיר למעלות אשא עיני אל ההרים מאין יבא עזרי״
ר׳ שמואל ברבי נחמן פתח: שיר למעלות אשא עיני אל ההרים,
אל תקרי אל ההרים אלא אל ההורים.

לעילוי נשמת אבינו

אהרן אשר זעליג בן יעקב יצחק ז״ל

George Saks *z"l*

He lived a life of **תורה, עבודה, וגמילות חסדים**
setting an example for his children, grandchildren, great-grandson, and all who knew him. He loved to prepare for and lead the Seder and share divrei Torah about the Haggada with his family.

ת.נ.צ.ב.ה

משפחת סאקס

BENEFACTORS

Mazal tov to Rabbi Rosner for this beautiful addition
to the Shalom Rav series.
May Hashem continue to send you the chachma and strength to deliver
so many beautiful shiurim for Klal Yisrael for many years to come!

Moishe and Devora Smith

PILLARS

We would like to express our gratitude to HaShem
for the many brachos He has bestowed upon us.

שבח והודיה לקב״ה
כאשר זכינו לסדר אותו, כן נזכה לעשותו
לשנה הבאה בירושלים הבנויה

Meir and Shandee Fuchs

״שמע בני מוסר אביך ואל תטש תורת אמך״
משלי א:ח

In honor of our esteemed parents

Rabbi David and Felice Paley
Dr. Howard and Miriam Fruchter

Sarah and Jonathan Paley

In loving memory of our parents

ר׳ משה ב״ר בן ציון שלאכטער
יהודית לביאה בת ר׳ שמעון שלאכטער
ר׳ אברהם מנחם בן ר׳ אליהו מאיר גודמן

for continuing **והגדת לבנך**

Harry & Brigitte Schlachter

PATRONS

In memory of

Rav Avraham Aryeh ben R' Yaakov Hacohen
Rav Yitzchak Zalman ben Rav Avraham Shlomo

Our beloved fathers who led inspiring seders

In honor of Rabbi Rosner and in appreciation of
all the Torah I have learned from him.

Charles and Naomi Meisels

We are privileged to support the Shalom Rav Haggada
In memory of

Dr Milton and Beatrice Kook *z"l*

Dr Arthur and Linda Kook and Family

In honor of **Miriam and Irv Klavan** *and* **Joelle and Bill Zimbalist**
by their children, grandchildren and great-grandchildren.

Sara and Simmy Zimbalist

With Hakarat HaTov to Rav Rosner for all the Torah
you have taught us online and in person!
May you go מחיל אל חיל*!*

Kalman and Rochel Ausubel

In honor of our parents

Gladys and Robert Wolff
Susan and Robert Schulman

and in gratitude for all they have done for our families

Tzippy and Josh

PATRONS

לעילוי נשמת

ישראל בן שמעון
זיסיל בת יצחק
שמואל בן ישראל צבי

Sandy and Nechie Braun

Dedicated in honour of

Josy & Sara Orenstein

Community Builders and Pillars of Torah and Chessed
But above all, good friends

Family Wulwick, London

In honor of our children,
and with gratitude to those who have been and continue to be
instrumental in their Jewish education and in fostering their love of Torah

Nicole and Raanan Agus

L'iluy nishmat our beloved aunt,

June Robinson
יהודית רחל בת ישראל יקותיאל

Naomi & Zvi Nachman & family

לעילוי נשמת

שמעון מרדכי בן יהודה לייב
וזוגתו **הינדא מלכה בת זעליג**

Hilary & Colin Wingate

PATRONS

"והגדת לבנך..."

In honor of our parents
Phyllis and Jack Rubel, and Suzanne and Fred** (z"l) **Bodoff,
who continue to be role models for us, and in honor of our children
***Temima, Aliza, Yossi and Chana**, who continue to inspire us every day.*
In deep appreciation to Rabbi Rosner for all of his Torah and guidance.

Tova and Daniel Rubel

In honor of our dear friends and neighbors,
Rabbi Shalom and Dr. Tamar Rosner,
with whom we and our children dance on Rechov Sitvanit each
ליל הסדר *– the highlight of our chag!*
כאשר זכינו... כן נזכה לעשותו...לשנה הבאה בירושלים
Wishing us all many years of continued **ברכה, הצלחה** *and friendship.*

Chani and Jason Schwartz and family

In memory of our dear parents, grandparents, and great-grandparents

Shmuel and Keila Jakubovicz

Chanie and Mark (Moshe), Yitzi & Adina & Rafi, Avi & Leah,
Benyamin, Shuee, Ariel, Zevi and Akiva Jacobs

In honor of our dear mother, grandmother,
great-grandmother, and great-great-grandmother

Goldie Cantor, עמו"ש

for always bringing us together for Pesach and making the Seder
such a special place for us all to connect so meaningfully as a family.

With much love forever,
The Lustman, Ben-Dat, Sokol, Cantor, Sobol, Fisher,
Bendat-Appell, Ross, Pelc, Hanono, and Harris Families

FRIENDS

Gershon & Bayla Tokayer
Ellen & Richard Gertler
Debbie & Moish Drelich
Ira & Eileen Greenspun
Rachel & Gary Berger
Morris & Caroline Massel
Rich & Jenny Gans
Rachel & Mordechai Book and family
Terry & Aaron Friedman
Steven E. Plotnick
Gladys & Robert Wolff
Lisa & David Schlussel
L'zecher nishmas Dr. Irving Buterman, Yisroel Zev ben Yosef Menachem
Bracha & Dovid Schreiber
Dovid & Faygie Meisels and family
Susan, Michael, Simcha Nachman, Elchanan Yosef, and Tuvia Leib Geller
Rivki & Aytan Himelstein
In memory of Chaya Slava bas Rav Shmuel
Ira & Isabella Wiznitzer
Rachel & Gary Berger, New Rochelle NY
Davida & Gary Stadtmauer and family
Adina & Lawrence Burian
Steven & Michelle Farbman
Mr. & Mrs. Eli A. & Barbara Safdieh
Loni & Heshie Reich
L'zecher nishmat דליה שרה בת אברהם ודבורה *– Dahlia Fuerst Kaplan*
Jason & Bruria Rozen and family
לעלוי נשמת אטה בת אלכסנדר זיסקינד
Debbie & Michael Hamlin and family
Alison & Chaim Basch
Marc & Liraz Spear
Anonymous
Amy & Shalom Schwartz and family
Adena & Dov Goldman and family
Sara & Gil Simchi
Karen & Michael Raskas and family
Gila & Motti Friedman
Alyssa & Mark Tenenbaum and family

Asher Zelig Weiss
Kagan st. 8
Jerusalem

אשר זעליג וייס
כגן 8
פעיה"ק ירושלים ת"ו

בס"ד

5 Menachem Av 5782

Hundreds of interpretations have been written on the Haggada Shel Pesach, and each year new interpretations are added to them, but this Haggada "Shalom Rav" from the precious Torah teachings of Rav Shalom Rosner, the Rav of the Nofi HaShemesh community, is special. This interpretation is based on the shiurim of Rabbi Rosner, who is well known for his wonderful Daf Yomi shiurim and his original ideas that inspire the hearts to Torah and Emunah.

The Haggada was compiled and edited by my dear friend Rabbi Shai (Marc) Lesnick in a beautiful manner, for the benefit of the many for whom English is their primary language.

I bless the author HaRav Hagaon that he will merit many more opportunities to spread Torah, magnify its glory and enlighten many.

With profound friendship,

אשר זעליג וייס
גאב"ד
וראש ישיבת
"דרכי תורה"
פעיה"ק ירושלים ת"ו

אשר זעליג וייס
כגן 8
פעיה"ק ירושלם ת"ו

ה' מנ"א תשפ"ב

פירושים למאות נכתבו על הגדה של פסח ובכל שנה ושנה מתווספים עליהם פירושים חדשים, אך הגדה זו "שלום רב" מהגיגי תורתו של הרה"ג המצויין ר' שלום רזנר שליט"א רב קהילת נופי השמש מיוחד הוא. פירוש זה מבוסס על דרשותיו ומאמריו של הרב רזנר המפורסם בשיעורו הנפלא על הדף היומי, וברעיונותיו המקוריים להלהיב לב שומעיו לתורה ולאמונה.

הספר נכתב ונערך ע"י תלמידי יקירי הרב שי לזניק נ"י בטוב טעם ודעת בשפה האנגלית לתועלת הרבים ששפה זו שגורה על לשונם.

ברכתי להרה"ג המחבר שליט"א שיזכה עוד רבות להגדיל תורה ולהאדירה בתפארת ורבים יאותו לאורו.

באהבה וביקר

אשר וייס

אשר זעליג וייס
גאב"ד
וראש ישיבת
"דרכי תורה"
פעיה"ק ירושלים ת"ו

CONTENTS

Preface

After making available a collection of Rav Rosner's thoughts on the *parasha* in the two-volume work *Shalom Rav,* I am very excited to be able to facilitate the printing of Rav Rosner's inspirational insights on the Haggada.

The thoughts Rav Rosner shares come from a wide spectrum of sources that include *Rishonim, Aharonim,* Hasidic masters, contemporary *rabbanim,* and scholars with an assortment of *hashkafot* (philosophies). I have personally been inspired by many of these *divrei Torah.* I have used Rav Rosner's material at our family Seder as well as at various *shiurim* I have given in our community, and the feedback has been phenomenal. This is what prompted me to compile and print these pearls of wisdom – so that they can be enjoyed by many.

Rav Rosner has given a Haggada *shiur* annually since 2003. These *shiurim,* which serve as a basis for most of the material included in this book, can be accessed on the websites www.yutorah.org and www.outorah.org.

This Haggada is organized in a user-friendly manner so that its insightful and inspiring messages may be read and shared at the Seder. In addition to the explanations that appear below the text of the Haggada, there are short essays that relate to Pesah and the Seder night. It is suggested to read these in advance so that these thoughts can be shared at the Seder and throughout the holiday.

◂ What is

What is most important, though, is to prepare for the Seder itself. The more one prepares, the greater the experience for all present. Hopefully, this Haggada will provide material that is pertinent and useful in triggering engaging conversation at the Seder.

I owe a tremendous debt of gratitude to several individuals, without whom this endeavor would not have been possible. First and foremost, I would like to thank my wife Tamar, who has encouraged and supported the effort to compile this Haggada commentary. She is my true partner in life, my *ezer kenegdo*. Her patience and understanding allowed me to spend evenings, weekends, and free time completing this project.

I have a tremendous appreciation for all of my children, with whom I have shared many of these *divrei Torah*, and who have helped make each Seder night a most memorable and enjoyable occasion. I have learned a tremendous amount from the approach of each of my children and their interpretations of the Haggada. Most recently, in order to encourage participation, we started assigning specific sections to each attendee of the Seder. This empowers each individual to prepare and participate. I highly recommend this approach. We have also shifted to discussing the Haggada in the living room rather than around the dining room table. The change of location has had a positive impact, and we have found the relaxing atmosphere to be most conducive to discussion.

I want to thank Miriam Schlussel, who assisted with transcribing Rav Rosner's *shiurim* that were used as a basis for this Haggada. I would also like to thank Matthew Miller, Rabbi Reuven Ziegler, Aryeh Grossman, Ita Olesker, Caryn Meltz, Rina Ben-Gal, Debbie Ismailoff, Tani Bayer, and Sabrina Lightstone for their support and uncompromising efforts in ensuring that this Haggada be presented in the most professional manner.

My utmost gratitude is to my parents, who made my Seder experience as a child unforgettable. I learned a tremendous amount of Torah from my father, not only on Seder night, but always. The love and appreciation that I have for Torah was imbued in me by him.

◂ In addition

In addition to running a business, my father utilizes every free moment to learn and transmit Torah through organized *shiurim* and discussion after shul and on the avenue. On my way to work, I listen to *shiurim* by Rav Rosner and Rav Weiss, and on my way home from work, I learn Torah with my father over the telephone. May Hashem grant my father many more happy and healthy years so that he may continue to spread Torah and *hesed*!

Since the publication of *Shalom Rav* (on the *parasha*), I have been spending a lot more time engaging in Torah discussions with my mother as well. I very much enjoy our discussions and her insightful perspectives. May Hashem grant my mother many more happy and healthy years so that she too can continue to share Torah with others.

I want to thank my in-laws, who enjoy sharing *divrei Torah* with us at the Shabbat table and who generously gift *sefarim* to all members of our family. They have instilled within us a great appreciation for learning.

After my parents, the person from whom I have learned the most Torah is Rav Rosner. By sharing his Torah with my family, Rav Rosner has had a positive impact on myself and on my children. I experience such *nahat* from my children when I hear them repeating Rav Rosner's *divrei Torah*. I am indebted to Rav Rosner for allowing me to publish ideas from his *shiurim* on the Haggada, and I truly appreciate this opportunity to make these inspiring *divrei Torah* accessible to many. I thank Rav Rosner for all the time he has invested in reviewing the drafts, checking the sources, and enabling this work to be published.

It is my hope that all who use this Haggada will enjoy it, share its content with others, and be inspired by it. *Hag kasher vesame'ah*!

Marc Lesnick
Beit Shemesh, Av 5782

Introduction

There is no more glorious night in the Jewish calendar than Seder night. It is a night when families gather together to recite and to remember, to educate and to experience, to uplift and to uphold. It is a night filled with mitzvot, in both deed and word, that is geared to uplift us all to a better spiritual place. The vehicle which guides our journey is the Haggada, the text which probably has more commentaries than any other book in our library. The Haggada and its commentaries allow each Jew around the table, young and old, seasoned scholar and layman, to participate in creating the experience of reenacting *yetzi'at Mitzrayim*.

There are two different types of commentaries within our tradition, those that "zoom in" and those that "zoom out." For example, the *Maggid Mishneh* and *Kesef Mishneh* commentaries on the *Mishneh Torah* of the Rambam are "zoom in" types, delving into understanding the words of the Rambam and discovering which earlier sources his writings are based on. The classic commentaries on the *Shulhan Arukh*, on the other hand, are of the "zoom out" variety, generally using the text as a springboard to present new issues and related situations. We have tried, throughout this work, to employ both approaches, one that stimulates questions which flow from the text and enables one to delve deeper into the classical sources, and one that uses the Haggada as a springboard to discuss ethical and spiritual messages. Our *tefilla* is that the words found

◂ in this

in this commentary help foster discussion, curiosity, and above all, learning and feelings of closeness to Hashem.

The Seder night is built on the principle of *hakarat hatov,* as can be seen in many of the practices throughout the evening; we are called *Yehudim* based on this basic and defining principle. The Chofetz Chaim was once overhead in his study talking to Hashem: "What have I done for You? You have given me the *zekhut* to write the *Mishna Berura, Shemiras HaLashon, Chofetz Chaim,* and more, but what have I done for You?" It is truly a *zekhut* to be able to share Torah with Jews, both in person and virtually, and now, through the pages of this Haggada. *Ma ashiv LaShem kol tagmulohi alai.* I continue to try to be a committed servant and act as a conduit for bringing some of the endless *divrei Hashem* to His people.

This work, as well as the previously published *Shalom Rav on the Torah,* would never have seen the light of day were it not for the diligent and all-encompassing work of my dear friend Marc Lesnick. He listened over and over again to hundreds of hours of my Haggada *shiurim* and committed some of those thoughts to paper. It is not an easy feat to take "*Torah Shebe'al Peh*" and format it as "*Torah Shebikhtav,*" but he did just that with finesse, precision, and an immense love of Torah. He and his wife Tamar should merit all the *berakhot* promised to those who are involved in Jewish communal service, and we should be able to continue to publish many more *sefarim* together.

The thoughts in these pages were culled from twenty years' worth of Haggada *shiurim* which I merited to transmit in my position as *rav* of Congregation Bais Ephraim Yitzchak (2002–2008) and later as *rav* of Kehillat Nofei Hashemesh (2008–present). These two shuls are overflowing with members who love Torah, Jews, and spiritual growth. I thank all of their members for allowing me to share these words of Torah with them. I also want to express gratitude to the OU and the entire staff at OU Torah for their amazing work archiving, organizing, and disseminating countless hours of Torah to the Jewish people worldwide.

◂ All of the

All of the Torah which I have been privileged to share is not my own. I try to be a conduit from my rebbeim to the *tzibbur*. Yeshiva University was my spiritual home for twenty years, and my rebbeim helped shape my way in Torah and mitzvot. I sat at the feet of Mori VeRabi Rav Michael Rosensweig for seven years, gaining from his mastery of *kol haTorah kula*, as well as his daily *hatmada* and the bond he created with all his students. Rav Herschel Schachter, Rav Mordechai Willig, Rav Mayer Twersky, Rav Yonasan Sacks, and Rav Yitzchak Cohen continue to be my guiding lights each and every day, through their Torah and their leadership of our community. Rav Yechezkel Yakovson, former *rosh yeshiva* of Yeshivat Sha'alvim, helped model for me what it means to be an *ohev Torah* and an *ohev Eretz Yisrael*. Most recently, I feel a tremendous debt of gratitude to Rav Asher Weiss, who has been a mentor to me both personally and through his numerous *shiurim* and *seforim*. May Hashem grant all my rebbeim *arikhut yamim veshanim*.

Teaching at Yeshivat Kerem B'Yavneh for the past five years under the leadership of Roshei Yeshiva Rav Gavriel Saraf and Rav Ahron Friedman, has been a demanding yet exhilarating experience. The students are inquisitive, hardworking, and have forced me to always be more prepared than I have ever been. May the yeshiva keep producing students who are a *kiddush Hashem* in all fields and areas of life.

Matthew Miller, Rabbi Reuven Ziegler, and the team at Maggid Books have been a pleasure to work with, and I hope that our teamwork can continue for a very long time, in both the English and Hebrew realms.

My first rebbi was my father, who learned Rambam (his favorite) with me each Friday night from when I was very young. He continues to be a guiding light in my life, blending Torah values and learning, along with a constant focus on using every minute each day. My mother, *a"h*, who returned her soul to the Creator on Rosh Hodesh Av, during the preparation of this Haggada, was the matriarch of our family. She was our rock, our symbol of loyalty and

◂ commitment

commitment, our source of love and comfort, and our lighthouse that lit up the way through every situation in life. Her *hokhmat hayim* and spiritual legacy will continue to guide us for generations. My in-laws, Dr. Robert and Dr. Susan Schulman, treat me like a son, supporting and caring for me at every stage of life. Their recent aliya to our neighborhood allows them to be a daily part of our children's lives. May Hashem give them both many years of good health, *simcha,* and *nahat* from all of their progeny.

To my life partner, Tamar, thank you for everything. Hashem has blessed us with so many *berakhot.* Our *tefilla* is that He enable us to continue to serve His people in His land for many years to come. May He allow us to guide our amazing children Yehoshua, Avigayil, Avraham, Michael, Naama, Eliyahu, and Chananya to follow in His path and to fulfill His will.

May we merit, along with all of Am Yisrael, to bring the *korban pesah* and celebrate this glorious evening in Yerushalayim, speedily in our days.

Shalom Rosner
Beit Shemesh, Av 5782

SEDER BEDIKAT HAMETZ

On the eve of the fourteenth of Nisan at nightfall, one is to search for hametz. The custom is to hide ten pieces of bread throughout the house and to search with a candle and feather (Rema 432:2; Mishna Berura 13). If one plans to travel for Pesah and will not be home on the eve of the fourteenth of Nisan to conduct Bedikat Hametz in their home, it should be done at an earlier date without a blessing.

בָּרוּךְ Blessed are You, Lord our God, King of the Universe,
who has made us holy through His commandments,
and has commanded us about the removal of leaven.

After completing the search, the following declaration is made to nullify any remaining hametz that may be in one's possession. (Any hametz that you intend to use until the next morning is not included in this declaration and should be nullified in the morning during Biur Hametz.)

כָּל חֲמִירָא Any type of leaven
that may still be in my possession,
that I have not seen or not removed
or that I do not know about,
let it be nullified and considered ownerless
like the dust of the earth.

SEDER BIUR HAMETZ

On the morning of the fourteenth of Nisan, all the remaining leaven in one's possession is burned. After burning the leaven (prior to an hour before midday), one should nullify the leaven and recite the following:

Any type of leaven that may still be in my possession,
that I may or may not have seen, found or removed,
let it be nullified and considered ownerless
like the dust of the earth.

בדיקת חמץ

On the eve of the fourteenth of Nisan at nightfall, one is to search for hametz. The custom is to hide ten pieces of bread throughout the house and to search with a candle and feather (Rema 432:2; Mishna Berura 13). If one plans to travel for Pesah and will not be home on the eve of the fourteenth of Nisan to conduct Bedikat Hametz in their home, it should be done at an earlier date without a blessing.

בָּרוּךְ אַתָּה יהוה אֱלֹהֵינוּ מֶלֶךְ הָעוֹלָם
אֲשֶׁר קִדְּשָׁנוּ בְּמִצְוֹתָיו וְצִוָּנוּ עַל בִּעוּר חָמֵץ.

After completing the search, the following declaration is made to nullify any remaining hametz that may be in one's possession. (Any hametz that you intend to use until the next morning is not included in this declaration and should be nullified in the morning during Biur Hametz.)

כָּל חֲמִירָא וַחֲמִיעָא דְּאִכָּא בִרְשׁוּתִי
דְּלָא חֲמִתֵּהּ וּדְלָא בִעַרְתֵּהּ
לִבְטִיל וְלֶהֱוֵי הֶפְקֵר
כְּעַפְרָא דְאַרְעָא.

ביעור חמץ

On the morning of the fourteenth of Nisan, all the remaining leaven in one's possession is burned. After burning the leaven (prior to an hour before midday), one should nullify the leaven and recite the following:

כָּל חֲמִירָא וַחֲמִיעָא דְּאִכָּא בִרְשׁוּתִי
דַּחֲמִתֵּהּ וּדְלָא חֲמִתֵּהּ, דְּבִעַרְתֵּהּ וּדְלָא בִעַרְתֵּהּ
לִבְטִיל וְלֶהֱוֵי הֶפְקֵר
כְּעַפְרָא דְאַרְעָא.

CANDLE LIGHTING

Prior to sundown, the candles are lit, and then the following blessing is recited (on Friday night, add the words in brackets):

בָּרוּךְ Blessed are You, LORD our God, King of the Universe, who has made us holy through His commandments, and has commanded us to light (the Shabbat light and) the festival light.

בָּרוּךְ Blessed are You, LORD our God, King of the Universe, who has given us life, sustained us, and brought us to this time.

THE SEDER PLATE

The most common practice of arranging the Seder plate is that of the Arizal:

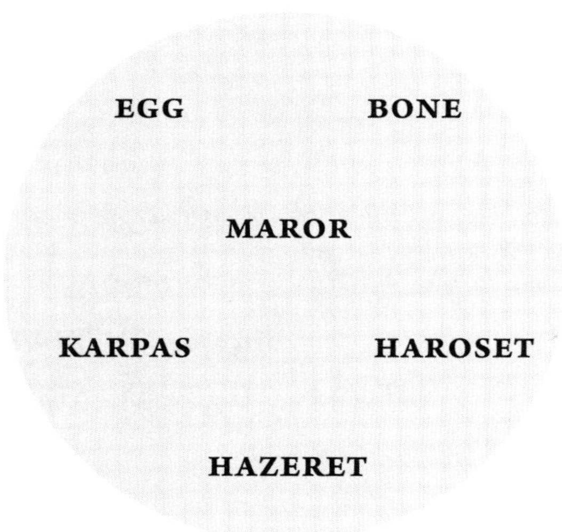

הדלקת נרות

Prior to sundown, the candles are lit, and then the following blessing is recited (on Friday night, add the words in brackets):

בָּרוּךְ אַתָּה יְהֹוָה, אֱלֹהֵינוּ מֶלֶךְ הָעוֹלָם
אֲשֶׁר קִדְּשָׁנוּ בְּמִצְוֹתָיו וְצִוָּנוּ
לְהַדְלִיק נֵר שֶׁל (שַׁבָּת וְשֶׁל) יוֹם טוֹב.

בָּרוּךְ אַתָּה יהוה אֱלֹהֵינוּ מֶלֶךְ הָעוֹלָם
שֶׁהֶחֱיָנוּ וְקִיְּמָנוּ וְהִגִּיעָנוּ לַזְּמַן הַזֶּה.

קערת הסדר

The most common practice of arranging the Seder plate is that of the Arizal:

THE ORDER OF THE SEDER:

1. *Kadesh* – Kiddush
2. *Urhatz* – Wash the hands without a blessing prior to dipping the *karpas*
3. *Karpas* – Eat a vegetable after dipping it in salt water
4. *Yahatz* – Break the middle matza and reserve a larger portion for the afikomen
5. *Maggid* – Recite the story of the Exodus from Egypt
6. *Rahtza* – Wash the hands with a blessing prior to eating matza
7. *Motzi Matza* – Recite blessing of *Hamotzi* and eat the matza
8. *Matza* – the special blessing over matza
9. *Maror* – Eat the bitter herbs
10. *Korekh* – Eat the matza and bitter herbs together
11. *Shulhan Orekh* – Enjoy the main meal
12. *Tzafun* – Eat the afikomen
13. *Barekh* – Recite Grace After Meals
14. *Hallel* – Continue with the remainder of *Hallel*
15. *Nirtza* – Conclude the Haggada with songs of inspiration

Reflections on Pesah and the Haggada

BOARD THE PLANE

Every year I like to begin the *Shabbat HaGadol* lecture with an idea expressed by Rav Shimshon Pincus (*Haggada Tiferet Shimshon*, p. 1).

Imagine two separate individuals that prepare to depart on a trip by plane. One individual packs his bags, has them checked in at the curbside of the airport, and proceeds to the gate. He buys a cup of coffee and sits patiently, reading a newspaper. As the steward announces that boarding has begun, the individual peers out the window, admiring the various aircraft adjacent to the terminal. As the steward announces, "Last call for boarding," this individual remains mesmerized, oblivious to the fact that the gate is closing. A moment later, he witnesses the departing flight lifting above the horizon.

The second individual performs the same preparation and goes through all the same motions, but with one difference: He actually boards the plane!

As we spend days and perhaps even weeks cleaning, shopping, and preparing *divrei Torah* for the night of the Seder, we need to make sure that we not only get ready for the flight, but that we actually board the plane on this monumental night. We need to ensure that all the preparations culminate in a meaningful and enjoyable Seder.

It is said that the Hatam Sofer's son-in-law was warned not to look at his father-in-law at the Seder. The son-in-law did not fully understand the warning until he personally experienced a Seder with the Hatam Sofer. The Hatam Sofer was so illuminated that it hurt one's eyes to look in his direction. Clearly, we need to prepare for this most special of nights.

RETELLING (*SIPPUR*) AND REMEMBERING (*ZEKHIRA*) GO HAND IN HAND

Rav Chaim Soloveitchik (*Emek Berakha Haggada*, p. 1) distinguishes between the mitzva of *zekhirat yetzi'at Mitzrayim* (remembering the Exodus from Egypt) and *sippur yetzi'at Mitzrayim* (retelling the story of the Exodus from Egypt). Remembering the Exodus is something that we fulfill on a daily basis. We mention *yetzi'at Mitzrayim* each morning and evening in the third paragraph of the *Shema*. However, retelling the intricacies of the event, along with questions and answers – this we perform once a year at the Seder.

Notwithstanding that one can distinguish between remembering, which requires one to merely mention the Exodus, and retelling the story in full, perhaps they in fact work in tandem. Rav Yosef Dov Soloveitchik (Rav Chaim's grandson) in his *sefer Me'afela Le'Or Gadol*, 2005, suggests that if we had a mitzva to merely remember *yetzi'at Mitzrayim* in a cursory manner every day, the memory would not have a lasting impact (p. 31). That's why we need to spend one night a year delving into the intricacies of the event. This is what enables the remembrance to work for a whole year. Similarly, if we limit our focus to merely one night, it wouldn't last either. We need a combination of daily remembering backed up by an annual, extended retelling in order to reinforce its significance.

Rav Asher Weiss (*On Mo'adim*, vol. 3, ch. 15) compared this phenomenon to that of a telephone speed dial. It takes time and effort to input the phone numbers of one's family, friends, and business associates, but once they are saved in the phone, one can push a single button and use speed dial to quickly call a number. Seder night is equivalent to the initial insertion of all the contact information. We spend time and effort exploring the details of what transpired when we experienced the Exodus. Then, during the rest of the year, all we need to do is just mention *yetzi'at Mitzrayim*, and it brings up our memory of the story we discussed in more detail at the Seder.

There are other examples of how we can use both an extended and abridged style in order to commemorate an event. For instance, on Tisha Be'Av, we experience twenty-four hours of mourning the destruction of the *Beit HaMikdash*. Yet there are smaller symbolic acts we perform on occasion to remind us of the

◂ destruction,

destruction, such as leaving an unfinished portion of a wall opposite the front door (Bava Batra 60b) or reciting *Al Naharot Bavel* prior to *Birkat HaMazon* (*minhag* instituted by the Shla). We can be reminded of the destruction of the *Beit HaMikdash* on occasion, so long as we experience an extensive mourning once a year.

Similarly, the combination of the daily remembrance coupled with the annual, in-depth discussion of *yetzi'at Mitzrayim* at the Seder is the winning formula to ensure that this momentous event is embedded in our hearts and minds.

ONE NATION – SPANNING GENERATIONS

In the Haggada, we state that tonight, we are to feel as if we left Egypt:

בְּכָל דּוֹר וָדוֹר
חַיָּב אָדָם לִרְאוֹת אֶת עַצְמוֹ כְּאִלּוּ הוּא יָצָא מִמִּצְרָיִם

Generation by generation,
each person must see himself
as if he himself had come out of Egypt.

How is one to fulfill the imperative of feeling as if one participated in the Exodus from Egypt?

The Brisker Rav expresses that this is the most challenging mitzva of the entire year. What strategies, then, can we utilize in order to succeed in fulfilling this sublime command?

Rav Shimon Schwab in his *sefer Maayan Beit Hasho'eiva* (p. 155) offers an interesting insight to help us comprehend what it means to feel as if we personally participated in the Exodus.

Consider the human body. When a baby is born, the baby has hands, feet, toes, and fingers. What happens when the child matures? The child's body parts grow alongside the development of the child's mind. The hands of a person at the age of ten, twenty, or fifty are the same hands that person has always had, though they have grown larger and encountered more experiences. The hands are attached to the same person, just in a different form.

Rav Schwab posits that all of Klal Yisrael are *guf ehad* – one single entity. *Kol Yisrael areivim zeh lazeh* (each Jew is responsible for the other, is a guarantor for the other) is an idea not relevant only to the present nation, but to all generations, going all the way back to *yetzi'at Mitzrayim* and Avraham and Sarah. Therefore, when we state that we left Mitzrayim, we refer to our ancestors, who are like our hands at an earlier stage of our lives. Our predecessors and ourselves are one single entity, and leaving Mitzrayim is to be viewed as if it were our leaving Mitzrayim at an earlier phase of our development, as one nation, spanning generations.

Perhaps that is also the deeper reason of why, when the wicked son asks, *ma ha'avoda hazot lakhem* (what is this practice of yours) – he defeats the whole purpose of the evening. We are supposed to feel as if *we* left Egypt. We are one people – another link in the chain of the tradition. By the wicked son excluding himself from our history, he removes himself from the historic link to our people. Our future is connected to our past.

Tonight, we must re-experience the Exodus that we previously endured through our ancestors.

BALANCING PERSONAL AND COMMUNAL RESPONSIBILITY

Pesah is referred to as the celebration of the creation of our nation. It is a time when families join together at the Seder and, when the *Beit HaMikdash* stood, they partook of the *Korban Pesah*. It is also a time when the nation gathered and will gather together in Jerusalem. Yet, as we unite, we must not forget the significance of each individual. We ought to strike and maintain a balance between the individual and the group or the *tzibbur*.

This holds true in many areas. Regarding Torah, we have to focus on the larger picture but also on each separate mitzva. The Or

HaHayim on *Parashat Ekev* (*Devarim* 8:1) expresses this idea in the way he interprets the *pasuk Kol hamitzva*. The Torah should have selected the plural term *kol hamitzvot* to depict all of the mitzvot in the Torah. Why was the singular term "mitzva" chosen? The Or HaHayim suggests that Moshe knew that there is a dangerous attitude some may have while serving Hashem that can lead one down an erroneous path. One may focus on a particular mitzva that speaks to them, like *tzedaka*, learning, or *oneg Shabbat*, and let other less "appealing" mitzvot fall by the wayside. We need to have a bird's-eye perspective that encompasses all of the mitzvot. Imagine if a patient informed the doctor that his pinky was bruised and he could not bend it and the doctor's response was: "Don't worry, you have nine other healthy fingers." The fact that the patient's finger is injured impacts his entire body. The focus needs to be on the whole package, not just on an individual mitzva. That is why Moshe uses the singular *kol hamitzva*. *Avodat Hashem* is a package deal. At the same time, we have to focus on our performance of each mitzva, recognizing the special opportunity that each one presents.

The Rambam, at the beginning of *Hilkhot Berakhot*, describes three types of blessings: *shevah* (praise), *nehenin* (pleasure), and *mitzva* (performance of a commandment). The Rambam inserts a seemingly superfluous word, linking two of these blessings. He states, "*keshem*" – just as we are obligated to make a *berakha* prior to enjoying a food or beverage, so too we are to recite a blessing prior to the performance of a mitzva. Rav Yosef Dov Soloveitchik is troubled by the use of the word *keshem* (just as). What exactly is the connection between these two distinct blessings? In the sixth chapter of *Masekhet Berakhot* (35a), we learn that the blessing recited prior to eating is a *matir* – it serves to permit one to partake of a meal. Without such a blessing, one would be viewed as "stealing" for not recognizing that one's food is provided by God.

Is the Rambam's intention to compare the blessing on performing a mitzva to the blessing on partaking of food, such that both serve as a *matir*? What does a blessing prior to the

◂ performance

performance of a mitzva permit? The Rav explains that when one shakes a *lulav* or eats a piece of matza, they perform a physical act. How does that physical act evolve into a mitzva? How do we close the gap between the infinite and finite? Isn't it presumptuous to even dream of using this physical act to achieve closeness to the Master of the world?

That is the purpose of a *birkat hamitzva*. Once we recognize that we are serving Hashem in this manner because He instructed us to do so – once we recognize the Commander of our commandments – that turns waving a palm branch into *netilat lulav* and fulfilling the mitzva of the four species. Each and every mitzva presents this opportunity.

In life as well, we need to strike this same balance. Each of us has a unique purpose in life. We each have different goals and ways to sanctify God's name. We were born in this era to fulfill a specific obligation. As Rav Kook expresses (*Siddur Olot HaRaaya*) in connection with the prayer *Elokai ad shelo notzarti eini kedai* that we recite on the *yamim nora'im,* we state that until one was created he had no purpose. Now that he was created, if he does not fulfill that purpose (*takhlis*) it is as if he were never created. We must do our best to maximize our potential and fulfill our duty. Yet we cannot solely focus on ourselves. We are part of a larger picture.

We are all familiar with the simple understanding of the sin of the golden calf (*het ha'egel*), where Moshe Rabbenu threw down the *luhot*. Yet, the *Yalkut* offers a very different explanation. It states that when Moshe descended with the first set of *luhot* and he saw the *egel,* the letters flew heavenward, and the *luhot* became extremely heavy and Moshe dropped them. What does this mean? Furthermore, later in the *parasha* Hashem tells Moshe to carry the *luhot* up Har Sinai. Why was Moshe then able to carry the *luhot* all the way up the mountain, and they were not too heavy? Rav Yosef Dov Soloveitchik explains that it all depends on one's state of mind. When he saw the *het ha'egel,* Moshe was downtrodden. His mission had failed, and that was reflected in his strength and ability to

◂ hold the

hold the *luhot*. When he was commanded to take the second set of *luhot*, he was energized and excited that Am Yisrael was granted a second chance, and he now had a purpose and a mission to fulfill.

In the Brisk milieu, when Moshe descended with the first set of *luhot*, having witnessed the nation indulging in idolatry, he was passive – a *heftza* – but when he sought God's forgiveness and was granted a second chance to transmit the *luhot*, he became a *gavra* – with a purpose and active role. It's all about one's mentality.

We all have a mission in life. When we awake each morning, the first prayer we recite is *Modeh Ani*. At the end of that sentence we state, "*Rabba emunatekha*." Many *baalei musar* ask: Shouldn't it have stated, "*Rabba emunati*," "I have faith in You, God"? What is actually stated is, "You have faith in me." In other words – I am being granted another day of life because You, God, have faith in me. If that is so, then I have the confidence to persevere and fulfill my mission for today.

This is all regarding the individual. But we also must recognize our second dimension, our being a small part of a greater whole, that whole being Am Yisrael.

To help clarify what it means to be connected to others, I am reminded of something I was told by Rav Yehiel, an elderly man who sat behind me in a shul in Boro Park. He learned in Radin with the Hafetz Hayim. He once told me that the Hafetz Hayim always cried when he heard of a *simha* or *tzara* (sad occasion) of a fellow Jew. He felt as if he were in the other person's shoes. He truly shared their happiness and sadness. He was ecstatic for their *simha* and deeply saddened by their tragedy. He was truly part of the *Am*.

In the introduction to his *sefer Shaarei Yosher*, Rav Shimon Shkop discusses how we define ourselves and the need to expand our definition of *ani* (me). On the surface, focusing upon oneself seems to conflict with focusing on another, yet upon deeper reflection, one should unite the two. We start alone and focus on ourselves. Then once we get married, the "I" turns into "we." It

◂ expands

expands further when we have children and establish a family. It then extends to our shul, school, community, country, and to our entire nation. Hashem demands more from us so that we include those around us.

We see then that both in the world of Torah and mitzvot, as well as in the world of our personal *avodat Hashem,* we need to recognize the *klal* and *prat,* the general and the specific, the singular individual as well as the global and communal.

As we celebrate Pesah and the formation of our nation, may we reflect on our personal mission and what we can do to maximize our personal potential and improve the lives of those around us.

WHY THE TITLE "HAGGADA"?

VEHIGADETA LEVINKHA

The book we use to guide us through the Seder is referred to as the Haggada. Why has this book merited this title? The term *vehigadeta levinkha* – to tell your children – is utilized in the response we are to provide to the son who does not know how to ask (*she'eino yode'a lishol*). Yet the verb *amira,* to tell, is connoted in our response to the other three sons.[1] Since the term *amira* is utilized in connection with three of the four sons, perhaps it would have been more appropriate to refer to the Seder guidebook as *ha'amira* rather than Haggada.

Rav Yerachmiel Kram, in his *Haggada Talmudo Biyado* (p. 50), explains that the only *pasuk* in the Torah that refers directly to the night of the Seder is *Vehigadeta levinkha* ("Tell your son"). All the other *pesukim* are more general and represent the questions of the sons that are asked throughout the year. Therefore, *she'eino yode'a lishol* ("the one who does not know how to ask") is connected to the Seder by the *pasuk Vehigadeta levinkha bayom hahu leimor.*

1. To the *hakham,* it states *atah emor lo;* to the *rasha, hak'hei et shinav ve'amar lo;* the *tam, ve'amarta eilav.* Only with respect to the *she'eino yode'a lishol,* it states *vehigadeta levinkha.*

◂ It also

It also relates to a specific day – *bayom hahu* (the Seder night). In sum, this shows that even if a child does not ask, we are obligated to transmit to him our history of *yetzi'at Mitzrayim.*

That is why we call it Haggada, since the phrase *vehigadeta levinkha* describes our obligation specifically on this evening.

Still, we may ask, why is that word most appropriate? Maybe we can glean an answer based on Rashi. In a different context, Rashi asks in *Parashat Yitro* (*Shemot* 19:3): What is the difference between *amira* and *aggada*? *Amira*, explains Rashi, is soft-spoken. In contrast, *haggada* is a more serious expression which goes into depth. The *pasuk* states: *Ko tomar lebeit Yaakov, vetaged livnei Yisrael.* In the *pasuk,* Moshe is directed to instruct the men and women, yet the term used when instructing the women (*beit Yaakov*) is *tomar,* which refers to a softer language. When instructing the men (*bnei Yisrael*) the term used is *taged* (from Haggada), which is a harsher manner of speaking. This does not mean the language should have a negative connotation. Rather, *haggada* is meant to be an intense, lasting experience. That is why the term Haggada is most suited for this mitzva of telling *yetzi'at Mitzrayim.*

REVELATION

Here's an additional thought with respect to the term Haggada. The Gra believes that to best comprehend a word, one should study the first time the word appears in the Torah. The word Haggada first appears after Adam and Hava eat from the forbidden tree. Hashem asks Adam,

...וַיֹּאמֶר מִי הִגִּיד לְךָ כִּי עֵירֹם אָתָּה? (בראשית ג:יא)

> And [God] said [to Adam]: Who revealed to you that you are naked?... (*Bereshit* 3:11)

The term *higid,* to reveal, is used here to highlight something that was previously unknown. Only after eating the forbidden fruit did

Adam have a revelation that he was unclothed. This connects to our obligation on Seder night. We are to inquire and explore our history and our customs on this night. We are to gain a deeper understanding and comprehend new ideas that were previously unknown to us. It behooves us to prepare and encourage others to raise new insights that are engaging and meaningful at the Seder. That is the true meaning of Haggada.

TESTIMONY

Another explanation as to the use of the word Haggada is offered by Rav Yosef Dov Soloveitchik. The Torah itself uses the term Haggada with respect to the requirement to transmit to our children the historical events surrounding the Exodus from Egypt, as is stated: *vehigadeta levinkha.* Rav Soloveitchik suggests that perhaps it is also related to another area in the Torah where a similar term is used: *haggadat eidut* (testifying). What is *haggadat eidut*? It is when I relate something that I witnessed or experienced. When a person provides testimony in court, it is based on his personal experience and not on hearsay. Haggada means I saw it, I felt it, I witnessed it! On this night, we are to feel as if we participated in the Exodus, as it is said, *Bekhol dor vador, hayav adam lirot et atzmo, ke'ilu hu yatza miMitzrayim.* We have to feel as if we've become free. That is what we are to experience at the Seder. We should be transmitting the story as if we experienced it firsthand, similar to the requirement of *haggadat eidut,* which requires eyewitness testimony.

SIPPUR – INSCRIBE

There's another word, another element, we can focus on as well. In the Haggada, the term *lesaper* is used to describe the transmission of the story of the Exodus. וְכָל הַמַּרְבֶּה לְסַפֵּר בִּיצִיאַת מִצְרַיִם הֲרֵי זֶה מְשֻׁבָּח, "The more one tells of the coming out of Egypt, the more admirable it is."

Rav Yosef Dov Soloveitchik in *Haggada: The Night That*

◂ *Unites*

Unites (Aaron Goldscheider, 2014, p.38) suggests that there is a special meaning to this word. *Sippur* is derived from the words *sofer* and *sefer*. What does a scribe do? He writes on a parchment, on a *klaf*, something that's meant to last. Whenever we're *mesaper*, we're *sofrim*! We are scribes, and we are writing into the hearts of all who will be attending our Seder.

When a *sofer* writes a *sefer*, he creates something that has permanence, something that will serve future generations, even beyond the time that he is physically present. At the Seder, every parent and grandparent creates a *sefer* by being *mesaper* (transmitting the story). We are each a scribe. We are engraving the messages of tradition on the hearts and minds of each child. If we can succeed in telling our story through the Haggada – feeling as if we experienced it – we can be that *sofer* who will create something that will last for generations.

Moshe was called the Great Scribe because he inscribed the Torah on the hearts of all of Am Yisrael. May we be able to properly and successfully transmit the tradition and engrave the Torah into the hearts of our children.

A NIGHT OF EXPRESSING APPRECIATION

Seder Night can be summed up in two words: *hakarat hatov*, expressing appreciation. Perhaps that is why in the Haggada, when we cite *pesukim* related to *yetzi'at Mitzrayim*, we refer to *pesukim* in *Parashat Ki Tavo* that are recited during the ceremony of *Mikra Bikkurim* (offering of the first fruits) rather than from *Shemot*, where the description of the story is recorded originally. Bringing *bikkurim* exemplifies one's gratitude to Hashem for having provided produce. Retelling the story of *yetzi'at Mitzrayim* is also an example of expressing gratitude to Hashem, which is what we are to do this evening.

Rav Yitzchak Zilberstein once observed a certain *rosh yeshiva* standing outside of a hospital, looking up at a sign containing names

◂ of all the

of all the different wards. He was mumbling to himself. Rav Zilberstein asked what he was doing. The *rosh yeshiva* replied: "When I come to the hospital, I look at all the signs, and I thank Hashem for my health and for keeping me out of the cardiology ward, the oncology ward, the emergency room, and all the other departments of the hospital."

So often, we don't focus on gratitude. We just live our lives and go through our daily routine. Only when there is a problem and we lose something do we start to appreciate what we had. Pesah is about recognizing what Hashem does for us even while we have everything.

At the Seder, it would be a meaningful exercise to go around the table and have each participant state something for which they are thankful. Health, special talent, being together, milestones achieved, because that's what this night is all about, gratitude and appreciation.

THE SOURCE OF HAKARAT HATOV

> **וַיֹּאמֶר יהוה אֶל־מֹשֶׁה אֱמֹר אֶל־אַהֲרֹן קַח מַטְּךָ וּנְטֵה־יָדְךָ עַל־מֵימֵי מִצְרַיִם עַל־נַהֲרֹתָם ׀ עַל־יְאֹרֵיהֶם וְעַל־אַגְמֵיהֶם וְעַל כָּל־מִקְוֵה מֵימֵיהֶם וְיִהְיוּ־דָם וְהָיָה דָם בְּכָל־אֶרֶץ מִצְרַיִם וּבָעֵצִים וּבָאֲבָנִים.** (שמות ז:יט)
>
> And Hashem said unto Moshe: "Tell Aharon: Take your staff and stretch out your hand over the waters of Egypt, over their rivers, over their canals, and over their ponds, and over all their reservoirs of water, that they may turn into blood; and there shall be blood throughout all the land of Egypt, even inside vessels of wood and of stone." (*Shemot* 7:19)

Hashem commanded Moshe to tell Aharon to initiate the plague of blood. Rashi explains that the reason Moshe didn't bring the

◂ first three

first three plagues is because of the *hakarat hatov* he had for the water and earth which had protected him when he was an infant! The water protected Moshe when his mother left him in a basket in the Nile, and the earth covered up the corpse of the Egyptian he had killed as an adult. Hitting the water or earth to bring about a plague wouldn't have been an appropriate display of *hakarat hatov* on Moshe's part.

Rabbi Bernard Weinberger, in his *sefer Shemen HaTov – Al HaMo'adim* (p. 268) asks a simple question based on a gemara in Bava Kama (92b). The gemara cites the source for gratitude as being from a *pasuk* in *Parashat Ki Tetzeh*: "Do not despise the Egyptian, for you were a stranger in his land" (*Devarim* 23:8). In other words, we owe the Egyptians *hakarat hatov* because they hosted us.

The Shemen HaTov cites the Hatam Sofer, who asks why the gemara uses the *pasuk* in *Parashat Ki Tetzeh* as the source for *hakarat hatov* and not these *pesukim* in *Shemot*, which are much earlier in the Torah, where Moshe displayed *hakarat hatov* to the water and earth. The Hatam Sofer answers that *Hazal* chose this *pasuk* because the Egyptians seem the least likely to have deserved any *hakarat hatov*. They enslaved us! They threw our babies into the Nile! Yet despite all that, we still owe them *hakarat hatov* because they did do something about which we could be minutely positive.

A Jew finds something to be grateful for even in a situation that seems completely terrible. Even though the Egyptians were wicked, we can't disregard the tiny amount of good they gave us. We have to find the good within the bad. Most things in life are multifaceted; therefore, we can't define any one event by just one aspect of it. Even in Egypt, we can find a small bit of positivity.

Further, in a situation in which we fail to find the good, we have to fall back on our belief that all is from HaKadosh Barukh Hu. We believe that Hashem has a divine plan; therefore, all that happens is for our best.

That is why *hakarat hatov* is learned from the *pasuk* in *Devarim* and not from *Shemot*. We are taught about this *midda*

◂ specifically

specifically in a place where there doesn't appear to be anything good or deserving of *hakarat hatov*. It's easy to feel *hakarat hatov* in a situation where the *tov* is obvious; it's a much greater level to feel appreciation in the darkest times.

The Shemen HaTov adds at the beginning of *Parashat Emor* that perhaps the words of *Hazal, lehazhir gedolim al ketanim* – "To admonish the older about the minors" – refers to taking care to not look at the big picture alone, but to also recognize the small details and see all the different levels of each experience.

Rav Avigdor Nebenzahl points out that an underlying theme of the first five *parashot* of the book of *Shemot* is *hakarat hatov*, that is, "gratitude and acknowledgment of a benefactor" (*Sihot Al Sefer Shemot*, p. 13). Sometimes it can be very hard to recognize and acknowledge all the good that has been bestowed upon us. We often have great excuses to justify why we don't owe any debt of gratitude to someone who has been kind to us. "They owed me." "I paid for it." "It was not big deal for them." "It wasn't even that helpful." "I didn't ask for help." "They had ulterior motives." These are just a few of the ways a person can justify a lack of gratitude.

Nevertheless, *hakarat hatov* is one of the cornerstones of our faith, and we witness it in several dimensions in the beginning of the book of *Shemot*.

First, we are introduced to the *midda* of *kefui tova* – the "denial of goodness" that Pharaoh exhibited. The Torah says:

וַיָּקׇם מֶלֶךְ־חָדָשׁ עַל־מִצְרָיִם אֲשֶׁר לֹא־יָדַע אֶת־יוֹסֵף.
(שמות א:ח)

> A new king arose over Egypt who did not know Yosef. (*Shemot* 1:8)

Whether or not it was the same Pharaoh who had ruled during the time of Yosef, this ruler was extraordinarily ungrateful to Yosef, who had saved the country in its time of distress.

◂ This attribute

This attribute of *kefui tova* toward people ultimately leads to having the *midda* of *kefui tova* toward Hashem. Soon after Pharaoh rejected the goodness of Yosef and his people, he said:

מִי יהוה אֲשֶׁר אֶשְׁמַע בְּקֹלוֹ לְשַׁלַּח אֶת־יִשְׂרָאֵל. (שמות ה:ב)

Who is Hashem that I should heed His voice to let Israel out? (*Shemot* 5:2)

In contrast to Pharaoh, the *midda* of *hakarat hatov* is exemplified many times by Moshe Rabbenu. From the first plague, we learn of Moshe's strong *midda* of recognizing the good done to him when he refrained from striking the water or the land because the dirt and the water had previously saved him. Moshe was saved by the water as a baby when he was placed in a basket on the Nile. He was saved by the earth when it covered the Egyptian guard he killed for striking a Jewish slave.

Further, the Torah notes the reward dogs received because they did not bark when we left Egypt. God commands us to throw them dead animal carcasses for their benefit.

וּבָשָׂר בַּשָּׂדֶה טְרֵפָה לֹא תֹאכֵלוּ לַכֶּלֶב תַּשְׁלִכוּן אֹתוֹ. (שמות כב:ל)

You shall not eat dead animals lying in the field; rather, you shall cast it to the dogs. (*Shemot* 22:30)

There's further complexity to this concept of *hakarat hatov*. One can understand that it behooves us to show appreciation to a person who provided us with a benefit, but water and soil are inanimate objects. The water and soil that Moshe refrained from striking were not even the same water and soil that rescued him! Water flows continually, and the earth that hid the body of the Egyptian killed by Moshe was not the same earth that he would have had to hit.

◂ Similarly,

Similarly, the dogs that we feed with our non-kosher carcasses are not the same dogs that remained silent when we left Egypt.

Why must we show them *hakarat hatov*?

Rav Nebenzahl explains that we offer thanks not because the provider needs the appreciation, but rather, because the recipient ought to recognize his dependency on the assistance of another. The Hebrew word for thanks, *hodaya,* is also the word for "admission," that is, the confession of having a debt. One who gives thanks expresses their dependency on others.

Perhaps this is why it is difficult to say thank you.

The same theme can be found in the *Sefer HaHinukh,* which explains (mitzva 33, *Kibud Av Va'Eim)*:

> **וכשיקבע זאת המדה בנפשו יעלה ממנה להכיר טובת האל ברוך הוא...**
>
> When this trait becomes engrained in a person, it will lead one to recognize the good that Hashem has bestowed upon all.

Showing appreciation to others leads one to appreciate all that Hashem has provided to him. Rav Nebenzahl cites a story about Rabbi Yisrael Zev Gustman, the *rosh yeshiva* of Yeshivat Netzah Yisrael. Rabbi Gustman, at the age of eighteen, served on the *beit din* of Rabbi Hayim Ozer Grodzinski in Vilna. During the Holocaust, Rabbi Gustman hid in the bushes and forests to avoid the Nazis. Years later, he was seen watering the plants at his yeshiva in Jerusalem. When asked why he was doing this trivial task, he responded that it was his way of showing his appreciation to the bushes that saved his life in Vilna. Even though those were not the same bushes, he felt obligated to express his appreciation to the same species, even in a different geography, thus exemplifying the *midda* of *hakarat hatov*.

◂ We have

We have to realize that the *midda* of *hakarat hatov* is a fundamental principle in Judaism. We are known as *Yehudim*, a word whose root is also *hodaya*. We must make gratitude an integral part of who we are.

WHY IS THERE NO BLESSING ON THE RECITATION OF THE HAGGADA?

Why don't we recite a *berakha* on the recitation of the Haggada? After all, the recitation of the Haggada is the way we fulfill the mitzva of *sippur yetzi'at Mitzrayim*, and we usually recite a *Birkat HaMitzva* prior to performing a mitzva.

We will suggest six explanations:

Kiddush: This is recited at the beginning of the Seder, includes a reference to the holiday, and also serves as the blessing on *sippur yetzi'at Mitzrayim* (Rif, quoted in *Sefer Abudraham*).

The *Berakha of Asher Ge'alanu:* This references the salvation that is recited later in the Haggada and thus serves as the blessing over *Sippur Yetzi'at Mitzrayim* (*Shibolei HaLeket*, Pesah Seder, *siman* 218). But there is a problem with this: The *berakha* appears much later, after we have already spent over an hour engaging in *sippur yetzi'at Mitzrayim*. We should have recited the *berakha* earlier in the Seder, based on the general rule of *over le'asiyatan* that requires us to recite a blessing immediately preceding the performance of the mitzva!

Perhaps we can suggest that since we are supposed to feel as if we are experiencing the Exodus for the first time our status is similar to a convert. Our nation was formed this very evening, and we are thus evolving throughout the night. A convert does not recite a *berakha* until after he immerses in a *mikve*, even though typically blessings are recited prior to the performance of a mitzva. This is due to the fact that one cannot recite a *berakha* before becoming a Jew. Similarly, we cannot recite a *berakha* at the beginning of the

◂ Seder because

Seder because we first have to experience the process of becoming a nation.

Birkhot HaTorah: The Ponovitcher Rav (cited in *Rivavot Efraim*, 2:129) suggests that since *sippur* is a form of Talmud Torah, it is connected to the *Birkhot HaTorah* which we recited earlier in the day in our morning prayers.

Infinite: One recites a *berakha* only on a mitzva with a finite requirement. Since there is no *shiur* (limit) or any way to quantify this mitzva, no *berakha* is recited. *Kol hamarbeh lesaper hareh zeh meshubah*. The more one retells the story, the more one is praiseworthy (Rashba, cited in *Sefer Abudraham*).

Spontaneous Praise: It is preferable to engage in *sippur* and express our gratitude to Hashem for our Exodus from Egypt in an authentic manner rather than out of an obligation. For example, if a child recites a blessing of *barukh ata… al mitzvat kibud av* before bringing a parent a drink of water, the parent could be upset that the child is acting out of the obligation of *kibud* rather than out of love. We do not recite a blessing prior to fulfilling the mitzva of *kibud av va'eim* because it would be formalizing it, making it seem that we do not respect our parents out of love and appreciation. It is a similar idea with *sippur yetzi'at Mitzrayim*.

Hashem took us out of Egypt. He saved us from slavery and potential total annihilation. Wouldn't it be natural to recall such an event out of *appreciation*? Making a *berakha* would dilute the natural outpouring of emotion that one should experience when recalling such a meaningful and remarkable event. For the same reason, we do not preface the recitation of *Hallel* at the Seder with a *berakha*. This reflects a natural instinct to offer praise and joy for having experienced the Exodus (*Rabbi Lau Haggada*, citing Sefat Emet, p. 23).

◂ *Berakha*

***Berakha* on a *Berakha*:** The Netivot (Rav Yaakov MiLisa, *Maaseh Nissim Haggada*, p. 23) suggests that one does not recite a *berakha* on a *berakha* or on a mitzva performed in the context of saying a *berakha*. Since the Haggada is already structured within four other *berakhot*, there is no need to introduce it with a blessing. For the same reason, we don't recite a *berakha* on *Birkat HaMazon* (which is a biblical obligation) because it in itself is a *berakha*.

UNDERSTANDING *HUKAT HAPESAH*

Dovid HaMelekh requested: יְהִי־לִבִּי תָמִים בְּחֻקֶּיךָ – "May my heart be perfect in your statutes" (*Tehillim* 119:80). The Midrash explains that the word "statutes" is in the plural form to reflect two statutes (*hukim*). First, the *korban pesah*: It is written "*Zot hukat haPesah*" (*Shemot* 12:43) – "This is the statute of the *korban pesah*." Second, "*Zot hukat haTorah*" (*Bemidbar* 19:2) is the statute of the *para aduma*.

What is the connection between the *para aduma* and the *korban pesah*?

Why did Dovid HaMelekh pray that his heart be sincere in the fulfillment of both of these statutes specifically?

Rav Asher Weiss offers an explanation. In the Midrash, there is not a comparison of these two different statutes, but rather, a contrasting. On the Seder night, we are encouraged to ask questions. Those people that are learned delve into an understanding of every nuance in the Haggada. We also do specific acts in order to trigger questions from our children (*Minhat Asher Al HaTorah: Vayikra, Bemidbar, Devarim*, p. 180, and *Rav Asher Weiss on the Haggada*, p. 309). Thus, the *korban pesah* is a symbol for asking questions: asking, searching, studying. For what other mitzva do we have to state the reason for doing it? We keep saying, *Al shum ma* – "For what reason?" We have to go above and beyond in order to understand and internalize the message and customs of Pesah.

On the other hand, the mitzva of *hukat para aduma* is a

mystery. Even Shlomo HaMelekh admitted he does not fully understand the reasoning behind the intricacies of the statute of *para aduma* (*Kohelet* 7:23).

So these are the two approaches to mitzvot. *Hukat haPesah* involves striving to understand, searching, and yearning. *Para* requires us to accept what HaKadosh Barukh Hu dictates we must do.

When are we meant to ask and investigate, and when are we meant to humbly accept Hashem's commandments?

Rav Asher Weiss suggests we learn the answer to this question from Avraham Avinu. When asked to sacrifice his son Yitzhak, Avraham acts without questioning. He wakes up early in the morning and sets out on his journey. Yet after Avraham binds his son and lifts a knife to slaughter him, an angel calls out to Avraham instructing him to cease and desist.

At this point, according to the Midrash (*Bereshit Rabba* 56:8, quoted in Rashi, *Bereshit* 22:12), Avraham begins to question. First Hashem says, "Yitzhak will be your heir," and then He says, "Kill your son." Now Hashem is commanding me, "Don't kill him." What is the meaning of all this?

However, why didn't Avraham question Hashem's request immediately?

So long as Avraham Avinu had a responsibility to act, he asked no questions. He focused on fulfilling a command. Only after he is instructed to spare his son and no longer has an obligation to complete an action, he inquires more deeply in order to better comprehend Hashem's intentions.

Perhaps that is also the explanation as to why Bnei Yisrael received two crowns for stating *naaseh venishma*. The gemara (Shabbat 88a) tells us that 600,000 angels descended and placed two crowns on the head of each individual at Har Sinai, one crown for having stated *naaseh* and the second for stating *nishma*. Why did we get two crowns? Bnei Yisrael did one great thing: We said *naaseh* before *nishma*. Why did we get a second crown for *nishma*?

◂ The *Minhat*

The *Minhat Asher* explains that yes, the first thing they did was *naaseh,* that is, *hukat hapara.* We accepted the commandments unconditionally. Then, there was the *hukat haPesah,* and this involved searching, yearning, and trying to understand the messages of the mitzvot. That's also what Bnei Yisrael committed to do.

Throughout the year we observe *hukat hapara*: obedience and unconditional fulfillment of Hashem's commandments. For one night of the year, it's time to try to fulfill the *hukat haPesah,* and that is on the night of the Seder. There's no other night of the year that we have more questions and more discussion.

Let's do all we can to fulfill this *hok* and engage in stimulating discussion around the intricacies of the Haggada, enhancing this special night for all present at our Seder.

LESSONS OF THE *KORBAN PESAH*

There are many lessons to be learned from the laws of the *korban pesah.* We will explore several.

SEFER HAHINUKH: ROYALTY

The Torah commands that the *korban pesah* be eaten in the house and not be taken outside.

בְּבַיִת אֶחָד יֵאָכֵל לֹא־תוֹצִיא מִן־הַבַּיִת מִן־הַבָּשָׂר חוּצָה
וְעֶצֶם לֹא תִשְׁבְּרוּ־בוֹ. (שמות יב:מו)

> In one house shall it be eaten; you shall not remove any of the meat out of the house, nor shall you break a bone thereof. (*Shemot* 12:41)

What is the reason behind this prohibition? The *Sefer HaHinukh* (mitzva 20) suggests that because we eat the *korban pesah* as a symbol of our freedom, we must eat it in the way that royalty would eat – inside the home. Royals don't eat outside on the run. Kings

◂ eat at home,

eat at home, while sitting, and in a relaxed manner. Their time is theirs. They don't leave in the middle of their meal. Since we are like royalty on the night of Pesah, we must act like it.

For the same reason we are also prohibited from breaking the bones of the *korban pesah*. We are to eat it in a civilized and dignified manner.

MESHEKH HOKHMA: DISCIPLINE

With respect to the preparation of the original *korban pesah* in Egypt, the Torah dictates:

> דַּבְּרוּ אֶל־כָּל־עֲדַת יִשְׂרָאֵל לֵאמֹר בֶּעָשֹׂר לַחֹדֶשׁ הַזֶּה וְיִקְחוּ לָהֶם אִישׁ שֶׂה לְבֵית־אָבֹת שֶׂה לַבָּיִת. (שמות יב:ג)
>
> Speak unto all the congregation of Israel, saying: On the tenth day of this month they shall take to them every man a lamb, according to their fathers' houses, a lamb for a household. (*Shemot* 12:3)

Hashem commanded Bnei Yisrael to bring sheep into their homes on the tenth of Nisan, four days before they would be redeemed. Why was a four-day waiting period necessary?

The *Meshekh Hokhma* (*Shemot* 12:3) explains that Hashem wanted to take us out of Egypt in an orderly and disciplined way. He didn't want us to escape in a wild mob. Obviously, after 210 years of forced labor, all of Klal Yisrael just wanted to get out. Additionally, the entire Egyptian nation was on the verge of civil war, desperate for Pharaoh to release Bnei Yisrael so as not to lose all their firstborn. Would anyone have said anything if Bnei Yisrael had left? The Egyptians would probably have been thrilled; nobody would have wanted to stop Bnei Yisrael from leaving.

For this reason, Hashem commanded the four-day waiting period. The sheep would be tied for four nights, bleating the whole time, and the Egyptians would have to suffer the pain of witnessing

◂ their "gods"

their "gods" tied up to Bnei Yisrael's bedposts, and then watch as they were roasted.

That was the purpose of the four days: HaKadosh Barukh Hu wanted to show the world that Bnei Yisrael could leave at that very moment, but didn't because they were waiting to be told when to do so by Hashem. They were disciplined and orderly rather than spontaneous and disorganized. Yiddishkeit is not only about following the dictates of the Torah, but is also about being organized and disciplined.

Perhaps this is also why Bnei Yisrael were commanded to eat the *korban pesah* whole, without any broken bones, so that it was done in a neat and orderly fashion, not in an animalistic way. Additionally, on several occasions, the Gemara (Shabbat 114a) dictates that a *talmid hakham* has to act properly and dress immaculately so as not to appear disheveled. It is essential that all we do is viewed by others in a positive light, so to create a *kiddush Hashem.*

RAV AHRON SOLOVEICHIK

Rav Ahron Soloveichik (*Logic of the Heart, Logic of the Mind,* p. 138) expands on this idea of orderliness, linking it to the moment of liberation from Egypt. Most often, when there's a change of leadership in a country, anarchy results and utter chaos reigns. There are several reasons why this is so: There is confusion and fear of the unknown, and moral laws fall by the wayside as people are delighted with their newfound freedom. The pent-up emotions of the people come to the forefront, and often in their anger over their pain, they hurt others.

During the Exodus from Egypt, although there was a change in rulership, says Rav Soloveichik, the usual chaos that follows the collapse of a regime was blatantly missing. When we left Egypt, there was perfect order. We did not leave a second earlier than we were told to. We left as a nation, in calm quiet, because while we may had been liberated, we were not yet free. When a Jew experiences physical freedom, it does not mean that he no longer has moral and ethical standards to uphold.

◂ *Hazal*

Hazal tell us that the only truly free person is one who engages in Torah (Avot 6:2). The more we subjugate ourselves to HaKadosh Barukh Hu, the more we appreciate life. It's only when we don't have the proper appreciation of halakha that we feel chained down to the Torah. Judaism, however, through its restrictions and laws, guides us to a meaningful and truly free life.

The halakhot of the *korban pesah* were a message to Bnei Yisrael regarding their newfound freedom. Chaos had no part in their redemption; they were told exactly where to be on that night. They were instructed to stay put in their homes and not to congregate in public places. Everyone was to remain in their house and be accounted for, eating exactly what Hashem told them to eat. Only when Hashem would tell them to go would they get up and leave.

OZNAYIM LATORAH: UNIFICATION

Rabbi Zalman Sorotzkin (*Oznayim LaTorah*) offers yet another lesson to be learned from the laws of the *korban pesah.*

It took a long time for Bnei Yisrael to become a nation. There was a lot of divisiveness before we finally unified. Every single sibling relationship in the Torah, from Kayin and Hevel through to the tribes, was rife with discord, which is why we ended up in Egypt. Egypt served to purify us and heal us from this conflict that was so ingrained in us. We had to go through the pain of Egyptian servitude *together* in order to feel unity, a unity that was a necessary achievement in our becoming a nation.

The *korban pesah* was the first national *korban,* the defining *korban* of the Jewish nation, the *korban* that bound Bnei Yisrael together. It is the only *korban* in which every single Jew must partake. This serves as a lesson that we are all in it together. The *korban pesah* was all about unity. Even if a person could eat an entire lamb himself, he was not allowed to do so with the *korban pesah;* it had to be shared. The commandment was to eat it in groups, and no one was allowed to leave his group.

◂ The main

The main message of the *korban pesah* is a message of unity. At least once a year, the community would have to sit together, and if any conflict occurred, they were forced to resolve it. No one could leave. This command was meant to accustom Bnei Yisrael to a life of unity and love.

WHY *SHIRA* NOW – AT THE SPLITTING OF THE SEA?

What was it about the Splitting of the Sea that prompted Bnei Yisrael to sing? Why did they not sing at any earlier point, and specifically after any of the awe-inspiring plagues? We sing their very *shira* every single morning following the words *vayaaminu ba-Hashem uveMoshe avdo*, "They had faith in Hashem and His servant Moshe." This intensifies the question: Did Bnei Yisrael only begin having faith in Hashem after the Splitting of the Sea?

Rabbi Zalman Melamed (*LaZeman HaZeh*, p. 60), founder of the Beit El yeshiva, answers this question with a concept that is relevant up to this day. There is a corrupt mentality that existed then and unfortunately still exists. Some of Bnei Yisrael felt that Hashem was dealing too harshly with the Egyptians. They were worried that the Egyptians would worsen things for them after each plague Hashem dealt them. Somehow, they forgot about their infants who had been tossed into the sea. They chose to forget about the baths Pharaoh took in Israelite blood. They erroneously viewed the Egyptians as victims and themselves as aggressors, despite the very obvious falsehood of that belief. These members of Bnei Yisrael worried that the whole world would think negatively of them for treating their oppressors so harshly.

When a member of Bnei Yisrael chooses to side with their oppressors and defend them, no miracle is great enough. This point is relevant even today, unfortunately. Throughout history, we have been made to feel like we are the aggressor and our enemy is the victim.

What can be done to drive out this mentality? Hashem had to push the reset button on us. Hashem performed a miracle that

◂ was like

was like an electric shock – it froze the entire world for a few seconds, and then we rebooted. The Splitting of the Sea left no doubts for anyone. No one had any choice but to believe.

The Mekhilta (*Parashat Beshallah*) describes this concept very well with a *mashal*. A dove was being chased by a predatory bird. It finally found a crevice in a rock to hide in, but then it saw a snake lying in wait there. On one side, the dove was being chased by a predatory bird, and on the other side, it was trapped by a snake. Bnei Yisrael was that dove during the Splitting of the Sea. The Egyptians' cruelty was undeniable at that moment when Hashem performed the Splitting of the Sea, the greatest divine revelation that had ever occurred. At that moment, everyone was shocked into believing.

The *Sefer HaHinukh* (mitzva 173) explains that the idea of a *mikve* is that when we emerge from the water, it is as if we are recreated as a totally new person. It is compared to a baby emerging from the amniotic fluid of its mother's womb. The baby is created when it leaves that water and exits the womb.

This is what happened at the Splitting of the Sea. Bnei Yisrael were reborn as they emerged from the water. At that point, they no longer pitied their killers, and they recognized their misplaced pity. As the Gemara (Yoma 22b) tells us: "One who has mercy on the cruel will end up being cruel to those who deserve mercy." We learn this from Shaul who had mercy on Amalek and later massacred the entire city of Nov.

We are a merciful nation, but we must realize who our enemy is and not have misplaced mercy. This was what the *shira* by the sea was about. It was the moment when every single member of Bnei Yisrael recognized the extent of Hashem's greatness and couldn't hold themselves back from singing His praises.

Another explanation is offered by Rav Yosef Dov Soloveitchik in *Mo'adei HaRav* (pp. 70–168). The Rav raises a question as to why Bnei Yisrael sang praises at *Yam Suf* and not when they left Mitzrayim. The Rav explained that the two events, that at Har

◂ Sinai and

Sinai and that at Har HaMoriah are distinguishable. Har Sinai was infused with *kedusha* (holiness) when Hashem rested above it and transmitted the Torah to us at that location. Yet it did not possess an eternal *kedusha*. Har HaMoriah, on the other hand, the location upon which the *Beit HaMikdash* was built, has eternal *kedusha*. Why the difference? The Rav explains: Man is required to partake in something in order for it to be infused with eternal *kedusha*. At Har Sinai, man was passive. At Har HaMoriah, man was active. Avraham sacrificed there, Yaakov slept there, and for generations, *korbanot* were offered there. Once man participates, *kedusha* is eternal! Man was also active at Keriat Yam Suf. The nation had to immerse themselves in the sea in order for it to split, so that they could cross through the water to the other side. It was this activism that infused the event with a higher level of *kedusha* that warranted *shira* (praise).

THREE HOLIDAYS AS A UNIT

Rav Asher Weiss in his Haggada (p. 132) asks, why is it that in *mussaf leshalosh regalim* we include a reference to all three *mo'adim*? On Pesah, why not just focus on Pesah – why mention Sukkot and Shavuot as well?

Rav Weiss explains that really, each of the holidays represent another stage of an *avoda* that we perform. First, in order to engage in *avodat Hashem* (worshipping the Creator), we need to remove any impediments or stains that we have. This is referred to as *sur mei'ra*. This is symbolized by the holiday of Pesah, when we remove ourselves from the impurity of Mitzrayim. The second stage is the preparation (*hakhana*). This is symbolized by Sukkot, when Bnei Yisrael traveled through the desert in preparation for entering into Eretz Yisrael. Lastly, the goal of *asei tov* is symbolized by Shavuot and includes receipt of the Torah!

We need to extend the symbolism of the *hagim* to our daily lives. First, we need to rid ourselves of distractions, prepare

◂ ourselves,

ourselves, and then, actually engage in the performance of Torah and mitzvot. They all go together; they are not mutually exclusive. That is why they are referenced together in the *tefilla,* because we ought to combine all three attributes into our daily lives.

ORDER HIGHLIGHTS FREEDOM

Why do we announce the fourteen *simanim* at the beginning of the Seder?

There is a custom to start the Seder with the recitation of the fourteen *simanim,* representing the various sections of the Haggada (*Kadesh, Urhatz, Karpas, Yahatz,* etc.). We don't do this on any other holiday. We don't announce the different *yehi ratzon*'s that we will recite on Rosh HaShana evening at the beginning of our meal, nor do we have a similar custom on any other Yom Tov. Why don't we just begin the Seder? Why is it necessary to announce in advance what we will be experiencing?

We can glean an answer by looking at the end of the Seder. Following our meal, we recite חֲסַל סִדּוּר פֶּסַח כְּהִלְכָתוֹ... כַּאֲשֶׁר זָכִינוּ לְסַדֵּר אוֹתוֹ, כֵּן נִזְכֶּה לַעֲשׂוֹתוֹ, "Just as we merited organizing the evening, we should be able to sacrifice the *korban pesah* as well." The Shemen HaTov, in his Haggada (p. 175), explains that this is a sort of prayer. We left Egypt "*behipazon,*" in a hurried and unorderly fashion. Yet tonight, as we recall that event, we organize the night into fourteen sections: *Kadesh, Urhatz,* etc. These juxtaposed positions underscore that we are in fact now free and able to control our time. We are not like slaves chaotically escaping their master. To maximize the experience tonight, we carefully plan and prepare the meal and the *divrei Torah,* as well as the sequence of events that will unfold. As *Hazal* tell us, "*zerizin makdimin lemitzvot,*" "We should rush to fulfill mitzvot." However, there is no such concept as, "*zerizin makdimin bemitzvot.*" That is, once we are engaged in the mitzva, there is no rush. After all the preparation, let's relax and enjoy these monumental moments as we relive our past and transmit our tradition to future generations.

◂ MAXIMIZE

MAXIMIZE THE EXPERIENCE

Rabbi Sender, in the *Commentator's Pesah Seder Haggada* (p. 93), addresses this question. He explains as follows. When one prepares for a long trip, he receives an itinerary detailing where he's headed, with all the stops along the way, as well as the final destination. An itinerary prepares the traveler emotionally for the trip and also enables the traveler to maximize his trip. Imagine traveling to Europe without preparing an itinerary and deciding haphazardly to visit a museum that afternoon. Upon arriving to the museum without an advance reservation, one may not be granted admission. Without a preplanned itinerary, inevitably, time will be wasted and sights will be left unseen.

Similarly, tonight we are embarking on a journey. True, we are to experience the Exodus from Egypt, but just as importantly, we are to arrive at a higher spiritual destination. The best way to achieve our goal is to announce the way in which we seek to get there (like the route established by a GPS system), so we all know how we will arrive at our endpoint. Staging the evening in an organized fashion guides the participants so that expectations are clear, as well as the path and the destination.

THE "SEDER"

We inquired earlier as to the choice of the term Haggada for the book that leads us through the ceremony of the evening. What about the name of the meal itself? Why is it referred to as the "Seder"? The term Seder means order. *Talmudo Beyado* (p. 23) suggests that at the beginning, we list the *simanim,* in order to inform all present regarding the structure of the evening. This is an important lesson in education. It is important for the student to understand the structure of a *shiur.* To better absorb the material, a student should be told what questions will be raised and the structure of the lesson. This is the pedagogical nature of this night. There is a specific order to the ceremony of this night, and we lay out the structure at the beginning so everyone can understand the progression. That is why we call it the Seder – this means "the order."

SIMANIM ... OF LOST OBJECTS

The Tiferet Ish, cited in the *Maayana Shel Torah* (Alexander Friedman, *Haggada Shel Pesah*) discusses *derekh drush, "aveida hushav besimanim"* – a lost object is returned after being identified by signs particular to the item. If a person can relay a description of the unique aspects of an object, it proves his ownership of such lost item. Throughout the year, we're lost. We lose ourselves getting caught up in trivial matters. One night a year, on our national birthday, at the Seder, we provide *simanim*, which are like declarations. When we partake in these *simanim* throughout the night, we find ourselves and return to where we ought to be. On the night of Pesah, we can return to ourselves, and that's why those items are called the *simanim*, the signs. These are the signs of every Jew at the Seder.

There are only two times in the year we have a Seder: the Seder on Pesah night and Seder Yom HaKippurim (this is a reference to the Kohen Gadol's services). These are the two nights of the year that we need to find ourselves to get back to our true identities. On Yom Kippur, a Jew gets back to his true identity and uncovers his true self as an individual. On Pesah, we do so as a nation.

RECLINING AT THE SEDER

Why are we obligated to recline at the Seder? This is so fundamental that if one eats matza or drinks wine without reclining, then they have not properly fulfilled their obligation.

In *Haggada, The Night That Unites* (Aaron Goldscheider, p. 78) there is a citation from Rav Kook, explaining that when a nation is exiled from its homeland, its ability to survive is tested. Do the exiled people pray to return to their homeland? Most nations

◂ eventually

eventually conform and are integrated into other nations. The Jewish nation continuously prays to return to Israel and to rebuild our Temple. Although our land was taken from us, we retained our Torah ideals. Even though we may not have experienced full redemption, we recline in order to portray that although we are in exile, we are free because we can practice our religion and maintain our spirituality.

הגדה של פסח

THE PESAH HAGGADA

The program for the evening is announced beforehand in the following form:

קדש / ורחץ / כרפס / יחץ
מגיד / רחצה / מוציא מצה
מרור / כורך / שלחן עורך
צפון / ברך / הלל / נרצה

KIDDUSH

WASHING

KARPAS

SPLITTING

TELLING

WASHING

MOTZI MATZA

BITTER HERBS

WRAPPING

TABLE SETTING

HIDDEN

BLESSING

PRAISING

PARTING

KADESH / KIDDUSH

The first cup of wine is poured. Lift the cup with the right hand and say the following:

On Shabbat add:

quietly: And it was evening, and it was morning –
יוֹם הַשִּׁשִּׁי the sixth day. *Gen. 1*

Then the heavens and the earth were completed, *Gen. 2*
and all their array.
With the seventh day, God completed the work He had done.
He ceased on the seventh day from all the work He had done.
God blessed the seventh day and declared it holy,
because on it
He ceased from all His work He had created to do.

On other evenings Kiddush starts here:
When saying Kiddush for others, add:

Please pay attention, my masters.

Blessed are You, Lord our God, King of the Universe,
who creates the fruit of the vine.

To sanctify whatever follows it. We sanctify the *seuda*. Typically, the sanctification takes a few minutes, and then we continue on to the *seuda*. Rav Shlomo Zalman says that those two hours of reciting the Haggada are not a *hefsek* (interruption); rather, it's part of Kiddush. The extended retelling of *yetzi'at Mitzrayim* is part and parcel of sanctifying the night. It's not a matter of how much time passes. Rather, *Kiddush bemakom seuda* means, I can't do other things that have nothing to do with the *seuda*. The entire Haggada is about sanctifying the night of Pesah, and that's considered a continuation of Kiddush.

KADESH – FOR US TO SANCTIFY

We conclude the first paragraph of Kiddush on Friday night with the words *asher bara Elokim laasot*, that God "had created to do."

The last

קדש

The first cup of wine is poured. Lift the cup with the right hand and say the following:

On שבת *add:*

quietly: וַיְהִי־עֶרֶב וַיְהִי־בֹקֶר בראשית א
יוֹם הַשִּׁשִּׁי:
וַיְכֻלּוּ הַשָּׁמַיִם וְהָאָרֶץ וְכָל־צְבָאָם: בראשית ב
וַיְכַל אֱלֹהִים בַּיּוֹם הַשְּׁבִיעִי מְלַאכְתּוֹ אֲשֶׁר עָשָׂה
וַיִּשְׁבֹּת בַּיּוֹם הַשְּׁבִיעִי מִכָּל־מְלַאכְתּוֹ אֲשֶׁר עָשָׂה:
וַיְבָרֶךְ אֱלֹהִים אֶת־יוֹם הַשְּׁבִיעִי, וַיְקַדֵּשׁ אֹתוֹ
כִּי בוֹ שָׁבַת מִכָּל־מְלַאכְתּוֹ, אֲשֶׁר־בָּרָא אֱלֹהִים, לַעֲשׂוֹת:

On other evenings קידוש *starts here:*
When saying קידוש *for others, add:*

סברי מרנן

בָּרוּךְ אַתָּה יהוה אֱלֹהֵינוּ מֶלֶךְ הָעוֹלָם, בּוֹרֵא פְּרִי הַגָּפֶן.

KADESH / KIDDUSH

HALAKHIC QUESTION

Usually, we have a halakhic obligation of *Kiddush bemakom seuda*. One is obligated to recite Kiddush adjacent to where one is to partake in the Shabbat meal. In fact, there are three requirements, including the place, the time, and the content of the food. The meal should include bread, or at least an item of food upon which one recites *borei minei mezonot*. Lastly, the recitation of Kiddush should be within a certain proximity of time to the meal.

On Seder night we make Kiddush, but we don't wash for *Hamotzi* for some time. What happens to the requirement of *Kiddush bemakom seuda*?

Rav Shlomo Zalman Auerbach (cited in *Kemotze Shalal Rav Haggada)* explains as follows. What's the purpose of Kiddush usually?

On Shabbat, add the words in parentheses.

בָּרוּךְ Blessed are You, Lord our God, King of the Universe,
who has chosen us from among all peoples,
raised us above all tongues, and made us holy
through His commandments.
You have given us,
Lord our God, in love
(Shabbats for rest),
festivals for rejoicing,
holy days and seasons for joy,
(this Shabbat day and)
this day of the festival of Matzot,
the time of our freedom
(with love), a holy assembly in memory
of the Exodus from Egypt.
For You have chosen us
and sanctified us
above all peoples,
and given us as our heritage
(Your holy Shabbat in love and favor and)
Your holy festivals for joy and gladness.
Blessed are you, Lord,
who sanctifies (the Shabbat,) Israel and the festivals.

---

circumcised, why didn't he create us circumcised? Just finish the job! He created us with lungs, kidneys, and a heart; couldn't he have just taken off that extra piece of skin?

The *Sefer HaHinukh* explains that HaKadosh Barukh Hu created us up to a certain point and then wanted us to take over. We have to act in order to perfect ourselves and our world. This is also why our custom is to mention Pinhas at the beginning of every *brit*. As Rashi mentions in *Parashat Pinhas* (*Bemidbar* 25:11), God stepped aside so Pinhas could act in a way that would sanctify God's name.

This is precisely

On שבת, add the words in parentheses.

בָּרוּךְ אַתָּה יהוה אֱלֹהֵינוּ מֶלֶךְ הָעוֹלָם, אֲשֶׁר בָּחַר
בָּנוּ מִכָּל עָם, וְרוֹמְמָנוּ מִכָּל לָשׁוֹן, וְקִדְּשָׁנוּ בְּמִצְוֹתָיו
וַתִּתֶּן לָנוּ יהוה אֱלֹהֵינוּ בְּאַהֲבָה (שַׁבָּתוֹת לִמְנוּחָה
וּ)מוֹעֲדִים לְשִׂמְחָה, חַגִּים וּזְמַנִּים לְשָׂשׂוֹן, אֶת
יוֹם (הַשַּׁבָּת הַזֶּה וְאֶת יוֹם) חַג הַמַּצּוֹת הַזֶּה
זְמַן חֵרוּתֵנוּ (בְּאַהֲבָה) מִקְרָא קֹדֶשׁ
זֵכֶר לִיצִיאַת מִצְרָיִם, כִּי בָנוּ
בָחַרְתָּ וְאוֹתָנוּ קִדַּשְׁתָּ
מִכָּל הָעַמִּים, (וְשַׁבָּת)
וּמוֹעֲדֵי קָדְשֶׁךָ
(בְּאַהֲבָה וּבְרָצוֹן)
בְּשִׂמְחָה וּבְשָׂשׂוֹן הִנְחַלְתָּנוּ.
בָּרוּךְ אַתָּה יהוה, מְקַדֵּשׁ (הַשַּׁבָּת וְ)יִשְׂרָאֵל וְהַזְּמַנִּים.

The last word, *laasot* (to do) seems superfluous. The *pasuk* which is quoted from the first chapter of *Bereshit* could have ended with the statement *asher bara Elokim*, that God created. What does the word *laasot*, to do, add to the phrase?

Hashem created the entire world. As the description of the six days of creation are concluded, God tells man: I have created this world; now it is your turn to do your share, so to speak (*laasot*). Now, you take over. You be creative. Work hard to maximize your potential and achieve great accomplishments.

A similar idea is expressed by the *Sefer HaHinukh* (mitzva 2) in connection with the mitzva of *brit mila*. If God wanted us to be

On Motza'ei Shabbat, the following Havdala is added:

בָּרוּךְ Blessed are You, Lord our God,
King of the Universe,
who creates the lights of fire.

Blessed are You, Lord our God,
King of the Universe,
who distinguishes between sacred and secular,
between light and darkness,
between Israel and the nations,
between the seventh day and the six days of work.
You have made a distinction
between the holiness of the Shabbat
and the holiness of festivals, and have sanctified
the seventh day above the six days of work.
You have distinguished and sanctified
Your people Israel with Your holiness.
Blessed are You, Lord,
who distinguishes between sacred and sacred.

Those who recited the blessing Sheheheyanu at candle lighting do not repeat it here:

בָּרוּךְ Blessed are You, Lord our God,
King of the Universe,
who has given us life, sustained us,
and brought us to this time.

Drink while reclining to the left.

Now begins man's task to perfect himself and the world around him, to conduct himself in a way that will sanctify Hashem's name throughout the world.

KIDDUSH IS PERSONAL AT THE SEDER

Although every Shabbat and Yom Tov begins with Kiddush, at the Seder, there is a unique aspect to it. Not only do we drink four cups, but whereas on other occasions one may recite Kiddush on behalf of others, tonight everyone has their own cup of wine for Kiddush.

Kiddush

On מוצאי שבת*, the following* הבדלה *is added:*

בָּרוּךְ אַתָּה יהוה אֱלֹהֵינוּ מֶלֶךְ הָעוֹלָם
בּוֹרֵא מְאוֹרֵי הָאֵשׁ.

בָּרוּךְ אַתָּה יהוה אֱלֹהֵינוּ מֶלֶךְ הָעוֹלָם
הַמַּבְדִּיל בֵּין קֹדֶשׁ לְחֹל
בֵּין אוֹר לְחֹשֶׁךְ
בֵּין יִשְׂרָאֵל לָעַמִּים
בֵּין יוֹם הַשְּׁבִיעִי לְשֵׁשֶׁת יְמֵי הַמַּעֲשֶׂה
בֵּין קְדֻשַּׁת שַׁבָּת לִקְדֻשַּׁת יוֹם טוֹב הִבְדַּלְתָּ
וְאֶת יוֹם הַשְּׁבִיעִי מִשֵּׁשֶׁת יְמֵי הַמַּעֲשֶׂה קִדַּשְׁתָּ
הִבְדַּלְתָּ וְקִדַּשְׁתָּ אֶת עַמְּךָ יִשְׂרָאֵל בִּקְדֻשָּׁתֶךָ.
בָּרוּךְ אַתָּה יהוה הַמַּבְדִּיל בֵּין קֹדֶשׁ לְקֹדֶשׁ.

Those who recited the blessing שהחינו *at candle lighting do not repeat it here.*

בָּרוּךְ אַתָּה יהוה אֱלֹהֵינוּ מֶלֶךְ הָעוֹלָם
שֶׁהֶחֱיָנוּ וְקִיְּמָנוּ וְהִגִּיעָנוּ
לַזְּמַן הַזֶּה.

Drink while reclining to the left.

This is precisely congruous to a *brit mila*. Man perfects his physical body and is charged with perfecting his spiritual essence as well.

Similarly, the *Meshekh Hokhma*, at the end of *Parashat Shelah* states that the tzitzit contain strings that appear like an unfinished garment. The tzitzit remind us of the 613 mitzvot, and we are to "finish the job" by properly adhering to the *taryag* mitzvot, weaving the world around us.

That is what we say in Kiddush every Friday night. HaKadosh Barukh Hu did everything for us, all the miracles of *yetzi'at Mitzrayim*.

2. **Physical persecution** – We are beaten, severely injured, maimed, and killed with no ramifications.
3. **Social persecution** – We are second-class citizens, stripped of basic rights and human dignity.
4. **Spiritual persecution** – There are prohibitions on religious observance and forced conversion.

All four of these types of persecutions were rampant in Mitzrayim. Our possessions were confiscated, we were forced into slavery, we were treated as second-class citizens, and we lacked any spirituality, so much so that we descended to the forty-ninth level of *tuma* (impurity).

We were redeemed, and the four *leshonot hageula* address each of these four persecutions.

Vehotzeiti... mitahat sivlot Mitzrayim – *Sivlot* is a burden, in this case that we had to get our own straw and that we suffered financially, and Hashem delivered us from these burdens.

Vehitzalti etkhem, me'avodatam – Hashem saved us from physical labor.

Vegaalti etkhem bizro'a netuya – Hashem redeemed us and raised us up from where we had been socially, as second-class citizens.

And finally, *velakahti etkhem* – Hashem led us to Har Sinai to infuse us with spiritualty.

We can add one additional point. The four mitzvot that we perform when we take each of the four cups also specifically connect to these four types of persecution.

1. **First cup:** The Seder starts off with *Kadesh* (Kiddush), representing spiritual sanctification.
2. **Second cup:** We start *Maggid*, going from *avadim hayinu* to *gaal Yisrael*, when Hashem raised us up from being downtrodden.
3. **Third cup:** After the meal, we recite *Birkat HaMazon*. This represents financial stability, our ability to partake in a feast. Hashem provides us with the sustenance that we require.
4. **Fourth cup:** As we recite *shefokh hamatekha el hagoyim* after the

Kiddush is a way we sanctify our holidays, as we recite in the *Amida* prayer on the holidays – *mekadesh Yisrael vehazmanim.* It is the *beit din* (court) that determines the new month and establishes the calendar. In essence, with Kiddush, we sanctify time. By making Kiddush, we show that we are free.

A slave is not in control of his own time. His master tells him when to work and when to take a break. He cannot sanctify his time because it's out of his control. To sanctify our time is the first national mitzva that was commanded to Am Yisrael prior to their departure from Egypt: *Hahodesh hazeh lakhem rosh hodashim* (*Shemot* 12:2). Essentially, the mitzva is to take control of time and sanctify the new month.

Perhaps the deeper reason why each individual has their own cup of wine, and many have a custom of having each individual recite the Kiddush, is to reflect on the fact that each of us was granted freedom, not only by being redeemed from physical bondage but by being able to control our own time and destiny. To utilize our freedom, we must take care not to waste time. Reciting Kiddush is a way of sanctifying time, which is the first commandment we received and evidence of our being free human beings (see also *Sforno, Shemot* 12:2). May we always be able to sanctify our time and maximize the productivity of every moment.

SYMBOLISM OF THE FOUR CUPS OF WINE

The Yerushalmi in Pesahim (10:1) writes that the four cups of wine that we drink at the Seder are symbolic of the *arba leshonot of geula*: והוצאתי, והצלתי, וגאלתי, ולקחתי – *vehotzeiti, vehitzalti, vegaalti, velakahti* (*Shemot* 6:6–7).

Haggadat Maayna Shel Torah (p. 43), citing the *Binah Le'Ittim*, offers a beautiful insight. The *arba leshonot* of *geula* counter the four types of persecution that we experience in *galut* (exile) in general, and in Mitzrayim in particular.

1. **Financial persecution** – Laws are established that are antisemitic to justify appropriation of Jewish property and Jewish bank accounts. Jews cannot own assets.

worship Hashem in the *Beit HaMikdash*. This is the connection between the four references to *kos Pharaoh* and the four cups upon which we bless this night: to highlight that we are fully committed, willing, and able to dedicate ourselves as servants of Hashem.

CHOSEN PEOPLE

When reciting Kiddush we declare, "*Asher bahar banu...*" We praise God for selecting us as His chosen people. In *Haggadat Hashukei Hemed*, Rav Yitzchak Zilberstein cites an event that transpired during the Holocaust. The Klausenberg Rebbe (who lost his wife and eleven children during those years) was asked by his students how we can recite the blessing *asher bahar banu* while being oppressed and murdered. Is this a depiction of a "chosen" people? The Rebbe answered, "When I witness the atrocities which the gentiles are capable of and realize that there is no way a Jew would ever act in such a wicked fashion, the blessing *asher bahar banu* flows off my tongue, and I desire to express my appreciation for having been selected to be given a moral guidebook (the Torah) upon which to base my objective ethical behavior."

BEGIN WITH *KADESH*

Why do we start the evening with Kiddush? If this is a night on which we are especially encouraged to ask questions, why not start with the *Ma Nishtana*? The Alexander Rebbe (cited in *The Night That Unites Passover Haggadah*) suggests that we begin with Kiddush to underscore that initially we accept unconditionally, and only thereafter do we inquire. It is always important to question and delve into matters, but that is only after one has built a solid foundation of belief and trust in God. Avraham accepted God's command to sacrifice his son and inquired only later. As a people, we declared, *Naaseh venishma*. We first act, then we seek to understand. Rav Yisrael Salanter was fond of saying, "We first declare, *Ein kelokenu*" (There is no other like our God), and only thereafter do we ask the question *Mi kelokenu* (Who is like our God). Thus, at the Seder, we first praise God; only afterward do we inquire about our enslavement and salvation.

URHATZ

> meal, we start discussing the future. We ask HaKadosh Barukh Hu to take revenge on all those who have destroyed, hurt, and physically annihilated us.

This is a fresh perspective on the symbolism of the four cups and the four *leshonot hageula*.

CONNECTION OF PHARAOH'S CUP TO OUR FOUR CUPS OF WINE

The Yerushalmi in the beginning of *Arvei Pesahim* cites several reasons as to why we drink four cups of wine at the Seder. One of the more popular reasons is that it corresponds to the four stages of redemption (*vehotzeiti, vehitzalti, vegaalti, velakahti*). One of the other suggestions offered by the Yerushalmi is that it corresponds with the four times the *sar* butler spoke to Yosef and used the term "*kos* Pharaoh" (Pharaoh's cup). We can understand that both relate to four cups, but is there a deeper connection between the cups of Pharaoh and the cups over which we recite blessings at the Seder?

The *KeMotze Shalal Rav,* citing Rav Eliyahu Klatzkin (p. 51), explains as follows. The gemara in Berakhot (55b) teaches us that a dream will follow its interpretation. If so, why did Yosef provide a positive interpretation to the butler and a negative one to the baker? Maybe we can derive an answer based on another line in that same gemara, where we learn that dreams at night relate to events over which one contemplates and fantasizes during the day (*hirhurei libo*).

What does the butler state? Over and over again he repeats "Pharaoh's *kos.*" Yosef recognizes that this is an individual who is dreaming of returning to serve Pharaoh. Such a dedicated servant will regain his position. On the other hand, the baker only relates to Pharaoh once and mostly refers to the bread in the dream as his own. This is not a dedicated servant, and therefore Yosef deduced that this individual will not return to his post.

At the Seder, we ought to have the attitude of the butler, to view ourselves as *avdei Hashem,* servants of God, to yearn to be freed from our bondage and current exile and to be able to return and

URHATZ / WASHING

Water is brought to the leader.
The participants wash their hands but do not say a blessing.

---

clean ourselves and rid ourselves of our faults, and then we can sanctify ourselves. This is known as *sur mera ve'asei tov*. One cannot jump into a *mikve* holding a *sheretz* (dead insect) and expect to be purified, so to speak. However, Seder night is a rule breaker. Seder night, we just jump in! We have faults and that's okay – we can sanctify ourselves later. In this same way, usually it should be *rahatz* and only then *Kadesh,* but when it comes to the Seder, we jump in. We complete *Kadesh,* and then very quickly one has to purify himself with washing. That is why we have the *vav hahibur,* the letter *vav* that connects. As soon as possible after *Kadesh,* we wash to purify ourselves. We use the *Kadesh* to capitalize on the moment, but very quickly we have to look back and gain perspective from the Seder experience. With that, we can perfect ourselves and get the most out of the *leil haSeder.*

WHY DO WE WASH OUR HANDS BEFORE *KARPAS*?

The *Shulhan Arukh* cites that during the period when the *Beit HaMikdash* stood, people were very careful regarding the laws of purity and would wash their hands prior to partaking of a wet fruit or vegetable. Tonight, we take that precaution before we dip the *karpas* in salt water.

The Taz, who wrote a well-known commentary on the *Shulhan Arukh,* was very upset with this tradition. We are hypocrites! If we don't wash our hands before we dip vegetables all other nights of our lives, why are we so careful to adhere to the laws of purity on this night? Rav Shlomo Zalman Auerbach (cited by Rabbi Moshe Bronstein, *Haggadat Asapra Kevodkha*) suggests that HaKadosh Barukh Hu went above and beyond for us tonight, so we go above and beyond for Him. Irrespective of how we act all year long,

tonight we

ורחץ

Water is brought to the leader.
The participants wash their hands but do not say a blessing.

URHATZ / WASHING

THE CONNECTION BETWEEN THE FIRST AND SECOND *SIMANIM*

We begin the Seder with the recitation of the *simanim,* highlighting the order of events that are to unfold throughout the evening. We begin with Kiddush, followed by washing our hands without a *berakha*. We would have expected to refer to washing the hands as *rahtza,* as we in fact do with respect to washing later on, prior to the meal, with *Rahtza* preceding *Motzi Matza*. Instead, we call the first washing *urhatz,* adding a *vav*. Why? Typically, the letter *vav* depicts a connection between a word and that which preceded it. It's known in Hebrew as *vav hahibur,* the connecting letter.

Rav Avraham Schorr in *HaLekah VeHalibuv* (p. 63) suggests that perhaps the word *rahatz* can be interpreted differently. In the *tefilla* that is recited when the Torah is removed from the *aron, Berikh Shemei,* we find the phrase *bei anah rahitz*. This Aramaic statement means "we have faith in you." Applying this meaning of faith to the word *urhatz* signifies that we are first sanctifying the evening and ourselves through the recitation of Kiddush. Then, we declare that we have faith and belief that tonight is a significant night, and we are ready to begin our journey through Jewish history with our family. We have faith that the performance of our mitzvot have major effects in heaven as well as help us shape our own religious personality. That is why the *vav* appears. It connects our sanctification with our faith. Throughout the highs and lows, we maintain our *emuna* and *bitahon,* our belief and faith in the Almighty.

Rabbi Yitzchak Sender in his Haggada, *The Commentators' Seder* (p. 44) offers an alternative explanation. Usually, we first have to

KARPAS

A small quantity of radish, greens, or roots of parsley is dipped in salt water.
Say the following over the karpas,
with the intent to include the maror in the blessing:

בָּרוּךְ Blessed are You, Lord our God,
King of the Universe,
who creates the fruit of the ground.

Eat without reclining.

---

are referred to in the Talmud as *maaseh yadayim* (the work of your hands). *Yadayim* symbolizes one's accomplishments.

Netilat yadayim, then, may refer to the removal of one's hands. This symbolizes the removal of one's perception of power. We nullify ourselves before HaKadosh Barukh Hu. Before we eat, we acknowledge that all we have is gifted to us by Hashem. Before we *daven,* we need to perform this act of *netila* to highlight that Hashem is in charge.

On this night when Hashem is the *go'el,* the redeemer, and we recognize our freedom, and look around and see the beautiful table set, the first thing we must do after we make Kiddush and prior to conducting the Seder is *netilat yadayim.* We nullify ourselves before the Almighty to set the tone for the evening.

KARPAS

THE SIGNIFICANCE OF *KARPAS*

At the beginning of the Seder, we have a *minhag* of dipping *karpas* in salt water. What is *karpas*? It is a kind of vegetable. Some people have a tradition to use a potato; others use celery or another green leaf. Is it significant which vegetable is used? Apparently not.

Let us then analyze this custom. Rabbeinu Manoah, *Hilkhot Hametz U'matza* 8:2, suggests that the act of dipping the *karpas* in salt water symbolizes the time when Yosef's brothers dipped his

multicolored

כרפס

A small quantity of radish, greens, or roots of parsley is dipped in salt water. Say the following over the karpas, with the intent to include the maror in the blessing:

בָּרוּךְ אַתָּה יהוה
אֱלֹהֵינוּ מֶלֶךְ הָעוֹלָם
בּוֹרֵא פְּרִי הָאֲדָמָה.

Eat without reclining.

---

tonight we take additional measures and go the extra mile to reflect our appreciation of our Exodus from Egypt. This is not hypocritical. Rather, it exemplifies our gratitude toward our Redeemer.

THE PURPOSE OF WASHING OUR HANDS

We do a lot of handwashing in our religion. We wash our hands before eating bread and prior to praying, and the *kohanim* wash their hands before they partake in *birkat kohanim.*

There are halakhic reasons for washing our hands, but let's look at it from a hashkafic viewpoint. What does washing symbolize? We do it twice at the Seder. What is the symbol of *rehitza*?

Washing one's hands is referred to as *netilat yadayim*. What does the word *netila* mean? Most *Rishonim* suggest that the word is derived from the Aramaic word *natla,* a utensil. We refer to it as *netilat yadayim* because we use a utensil, a *kli.*

The *Tiv HaHaggada* (Rav Gamliel Rabinovitch, p. 76) offers an alternative explanation based on a *drush. Litol* means to take something, to remove something. *Netilat yadayim* is the removal of the hands. What does that mean? Throughout the Torah and in statements uttered by *Hazal,* hands represent one's power. As it is stated, *Kokhi ve'otzem yadi asa li et hahayil hazeh,* "My power and the strength of my hand have brought me this wealth" (*Devarim* 8:17). One's *yad* (hand) symbolizes one's power. One's earnings

Rav Asher Weiss develops this idea, suggesting that these three troubles of Yaakov represent something larger. Since *maaseh avot siman levanim* – the deeds of our forefathers prefigure the history of the Jewish people – these three troubles represent the three types of troubles that Klal Yisrael suffer throughout exile. The troubles that haunted Yaakov will haunt us, his descendants. According to this idea, Esav will represent those who want to annihilate us physically (just like Esav wanted to physically kill Yaakov). There are "Esavs" throughout the generations who want to obliterate the Jewish people: Hamans and Hitlers, *yemah shemam*.

The second type of trouble for Klal Yisrael is that represented by "Lavan." His goal was not to kill Yaakov. Rather, Lavan wanted to destroy Yaakov spiritually. Lavan represents our enemies who wish to do the same by having us assimilate and abandon our religious beliefs. Lavan symbolizes people like Antiochus and Stalin, *yemah shemam*.

Then, we have the troubles symbolized by those of Yosef's life. The conflict with Yosef's brothers represents the problem of *sinat hinam,* inner fighting within Klal Yisrael. That's the greatest problem and the one we still suffer from the most today. It is the trouble that we bring upon ourselves out of a lack of respect for our fellow Jew. The actions of "Esav" and "Lavan" are not in our control. We can just react to them. However, the trouble experienced by Yosef is one that we can prevent. Each and every individual has to do his part to spread *ahavat Yisrael,* so that we can bring an end to the difficulty of Yosef and the *sinat hinam* that caused our exile and prevents our redemption to this day.

Before we discuss the *geula* from Egypt at the Seder, we need to understand what brought us into exile in the first place. We dip the *karpas,* and it is not so important which vegetable we use. What is important, though, is that we understand what caused the first exile and the exile that still exists today. It was the dipping of Yosef's *karpas,* his multicolored, majestic garment into blood, due to the brother's jealousy and rivalry with him. It is that hatred between Jews that we need to avoid to achieve our salvation. May we learn our lesson and unite, so we can be worthy of a complete redemption.

DOUBLE DIPPING

multicolored coat into the blood of a goat and presented it to their father as proof that Yosef was killed. We do the symbolic act of dipping at the beginning of the Seder to set the tone, and to declare, before we tell the story of what transpired in Egypt, that we should be aware of what originally sent us into exile in Egypt: the hatred between Yaakov's sons.

Rabbi Isaac Bernstein suggests that perhaps what led Rabbeinu Manoah to this interpretation is Rashi's commentary in *Parashat Vayeshev*. When Yaakov gifts Yosef with a *ketonet passim* (multicolored garment), Rashi describes the garment as similar to the one described in *Megillat Esther*, using the terms *hur, karpas, tekhelet, ve'argaman*... In other words, it was a majestic item. We take a vegetable – the specific type is less significant – and dip it into saltwater to symbolize the brother's dipping Yosef's *karpas*, his majestic garment, into blood.

Rav Asher Weiss (*Minhat Asher Haggada*, p. 92), expands upon this idea of the entire episode of Yaakov and his sons. When Yaakov Avinu is told by his mother to "trick" his father so he could obtain the blessing of the firstborn son, Yaakov feared that Yitzhak would recognize that he was disguised as Esav. Rivka reassured him that he had nothing to fear. Rivka told him: *Alai kilelatkha beni*, "Your curse will be upon me" (*Bereshit* 27:13). The Vilna Gaon explains the meaning of her statement: Rivka was informing Yaakov that trouble will only come to him from three individuals, which are hinted to from the acronym *alai* – Esav, Lavan, and Yosef.

Only three specific troubles were going to affect Yaakov in his life: Esav, Lavan, and Yosef, represented by the *rashei teivot* of the word *alai* (עלי = עשו לבן יוסף). Later, when Yosef's brothers requested to take Binyamin to Egypt, Yaakov responds with the identical acronym *alai*, עלי, stating: עלי היו כלנה, "All these troubles have come upon me" (*Bereshit* 42:36). In other words, "I am only supposed to agonize due to three people: Esav, Lavan, and Yosef, but not Binyamin. You can't take Binyamin. This is not meant to be." That's how the Vilna Gaon understands the hint connecting the words in these two *pesukim*.

YAHATZ / SPLITTING

The middle matza is broken in two.

The bigger portion is then hidden away to serve as the afikoman with which the meal is later concluded.
The smaller portion is placed between the two whole matzot.

Long ago, when two friends had to separate, they would take a paper bill, split it in half, and each of them would retain half. When they would look into their wallet later, they would remember that they are only half of their full being. Similarly, we split the matza and put half of it away for the afikomen. The other half we keep in front of us, reminding us of our connection with Hashem.

Related to this thought, *Sefer HaIkarim* (4:45) by Rav Yosef Albo discusses the first *brit* (covenant) between Hashem and Am Yisrael, the *brit bein habetarim*. On the night of Pesah, when we were formed into a nation, *Yahatz* reminds us of the first covenant that Hashem established with Avraham Avinu.

During *brit bein habetarim,* animals were split in half, and Avraham walked between the halves. Then fire passed through them, symbolizing Hashem's passage through the territory. This illustrates that HaKadosh Barukh Hu and Avraham were two parties that became connected, and the unbreakable bond that was created between God and the Jewish nation.

At the Seder, we perform an act that is symbolic of that first covenant. We hide away the larger half to recognize Hashem. We recognize that HaKadosh Barukh Hu is the greater half, and He is *tzafun,* hidden.

WHAT'S WITH STEALING THE AFIKOMAN?

Seder night is a special event. We share *divrei Torah* and sing together. It can be an incredibly spiritually uplifting opportunity. Yet if one is to inquire of the children as to what is the highlight of the Seder, most would respond that it's the part with the afikomen! All night long,

the children

יחץ

The middle מצה is broken in two.

The bigger portion is then hidden away to serve as the אפיקומן with which the meal is later concluded.

The smaller portion is placed between the two whole מצות.

DOUBLE DIPPING

Our discussion of *yetzi'at Mitzrayim* begins and ends with an act of dipping. Initially we dip the *karpas* into salt water. Later, we dip the *maror* (bitter herbs) into the *haroset*. Rabbi Jonathan Sacks explains in his Haggada (p. 21) that there is symbolic significance in these two acts. The entire story of the Exodus began and ended with acts of dipping. As we mentioned above, it began with Yosef's brothers dipping his multicolored garment into blood, and it ended with Am Yisrael dipping bunches of hyssop into blood and daubing them on the doorframes of their houses (in preparation for the final plague of the firstborn).

Karpas is sweet and is dipped into salt and becomes somewhat sour. *Maror* is bitter and is dipped in *haroset* to sweeten the taste. These two acts remind us that freedom, which is sweet, can become sour if we use it to mistreat others. Slavery, which is bitter, is sweetened when collective suffering leads to solidarity, as a prelude to freedom. Life in general is a combination of both – it is often bittersweet, and we need to learn to adapt as it fluctuates between sour and sweet experiences.

YAHATZ / SPLITTING

WHAT'S THE MESSAGE OF *YAHATZ*?

What is the reason for splitting the matza in half?

Rav Elimelech Biderman explains in the *Be'er HaHaim,* quoting Rav Menachem Mendel of Riminov, that breaking the matza represents the creation of the covenant between Hashem and Am Yisrael.

MAGGID / TELLING

During the recital of this paragraph the seder plate is held up and the middle matza is displayed to the company.

הָא לַחְמָא עַנְיָא **THIS**

IS THE BREAD OF OPPRESSION

our fathers ate in the land of Egypt.
Let all who are hungry come in and eat;
let all who are in need come and join us for the Pesah.
Now we are here; next year in the land of Israel.
Now – slaves; next year we shall be free.

Mitzrayim, but rather on the future *geula* (redemption). We recite *shefokh hamatekha,* and *leshana haba'a b'Yerushalayim.* Like the hidden piece of matza, the future redemption is also hidden from us. We yearn for it, but have no inkling as to when it will occur.

Perhaps the message to our children is that the future is in their hands. Just as they take charge of the *Tzafun* part of the afikomen at the end of the Seder, so too, they have the power to uncover the future redemption which is currently hidden. The *geula* is dependent on their actions. They can "steal" or, rather, help determine the future. We should reveal to our children that it's up to them to unify the nation and act in a way that will merit the final redemption. They are in control of our nation's future.

MAGGID / TELLING

WHY BEGIN MAGGID WITH HA LAHMA ANYA?

We start off the *Maggid* part of the Haggada with *ha lahma anya.*

The *Haggadat Kemotze Shalal Rav* includes the following question: How we can be so happy at the Seder when we are still in *galut* (exile)? During the many difficult periods in Jewish history especially, how were people able to establish a frame of mind to fulfill

the requirement

מגיד

During the recital of this paragraph the קערה *(seder plate) is held up and the middle* מצה *is displayed to the company.*

הָא
לַחְמָא עַנְיָא

דִּי אֲכַלוּ אֲבָהָתַנָא בְּאַרְעָא דְמִצְרָיִם

כָּל דִּכְפִין יֵיתֵי וְיֵיכֻל, כָּל דִּצְרִיךְ יֵיתֵי וְיִפְסַח

הָשַׁתָּא הָכָא   לַשָּׁנָה הַבָּאָה בְּאַרְעָא דְיִשְׂרָאֵל

הָשַׁתָּא עַבְדֵי   לַשָּׁנָה הַבָּאָה בְּנֵי חוֹרִין.

---

the children pay close attention to every move the father makes so they can observe when he attempts to hide the afikomen. After the children find the afikomen, we parents have to "bargain" with them so we can have it back and complete the Seder. The kids essentially take control of the Seder. What is the purpose of this game? Wouldn't it be preferable to instill a more serious atmosphere on this holy night?

The Shemen HaTov (*Haggadat Shemen HaTov*) offers a keen insight into this charade. When we split the matza at *Yahatz,* we save the larger slice for the *Tzafun* part of the Seder. The word *Tzafun* means "hidden" (as the Kli Yakar states on the *pasuk Pnu lakhem tzafona,* "One should keep his blessings hidden and not flaunt his success," *Devarim* 2:3). We hide the larger piece of the matza and take it out to eat after we conclude our meal. Then, the second half of the Seder takes on a different element. It is not focused on *yetzi'at*

seemingly simple but intriguing question. Each of the six questions listed in the Gemara have a source in the Torah. These questions include whether one was honest in business, engaged in Torah study, had children, and more. They are all explicitly mentioned as mitzvot, and they sometimes appear more than once in the Torah. But from where comes the mitzva to anticipate salvation? Can one be a good, God-fearing Jew, perform all the mitzvot, and not believe in *Mashiah* and the final redemption?

The Smak posits that the requirement to anticipate salvation is actually part of the mitzva of belief in Hashem. We believe that HaKadosh Barukh Hu controls the world now, just as He controlled it when He took us out of Egypt. Just as He redeemed us in the past, so will He redeem us in the future.

The first of the Ten Commandments, which include the recognition that Hashem redeemed us from Egypt, is the foundation of our continued belief that Hashem will once again save us. That is the source of "*tzipita leyeshua*," the belief and faith that enables Jews throughout the generations, even during times of persecution, to celebrate our past redemption and anticipate a future salvation.

May we be able to strengthen our faith and merit the final redemption in our lifetime.

LESHANA HABA'A BE'ARA D'YISRAEL

At the beginning of the Seder, we make a declaration, "*Leshana haba'a be'ara D'Yisrael*." Why is it so important to make this statement at the beginning of the Seder? We sing it at the end as well.

Rabbi Menachem Genack (*Gan Shoshanim*, p. 53) explains that as we sit at the Seder in exile (*galut*), do we really feel free? It's difficult to achieve the feeling of being free while undergoing oppression. Throughout history, we've been downtrodden. There have been many Sedarim in which it would be challenging to experience

sovereignty.

the requirement of *ke'ilu yatzata miMitzrayim* – to experience the Seder as if they were leaving Egypt?

Perhaps the *geula* of Mitzrayim offers us hope for the future. If you think about the situation in Mitzrayim, it had seemed impossible to get out of there. Logically, redemption made no sense. There were locked gates, barbed wire, dogs, a stone wall, and a moat. If you would have asked anyone who lived at that time about leaving, you would have heard that there was never a servant who was able to escape from Egypt. And yet, it happened!

If we focus on what transpired, this will provide us with the strength to believe that it is possible to once again be redeemed.

A similar idea is expressed by the Smak, Rav Yitzhak of Korveil, one of the *Baalei HaTosafot*. He organized his own list of mitzvot which differed from the works of the Behag and the Rambam. The first (and therefore most important) mitzva that he enumerated is knowledge of God. What are the sources upon which he based this first mitzva? He cites two *pesukim*: "*Anokhi Hashem Elokekha* – I am Hashem your God," which is the first of the Ten Commandments, and "*Veyadata hayom vehashevota...* – Know today and take to heart..." (*Devarim* 4:39).

Why does the Smak reference two verses? The Smak maintains that it is not enough to believe in the Creator of the world. One must believe that the Creator is actively *involved* in the world. The *pasuk* of *Anokhi* emphasizes that God took us out of Egypt. He had, and continues to have, an active hand in history. This is a fundamental tenet of Judaism.

The next part of the Smak's explanation is truly fascinating. He quotes the Gemara that lists the six questions that each individual will be asked after having lived for 120 years and proceeding to the next world (Shabbat 31a). Question number four is, "*Tzipita leyeshua*?" Did you anticipate salvation, the *Mashiah*? The Smak asks a in the future the Jewish people will be redeemed in the final redemption (Rosh HaShana 11b). As long as we have that view, we can feel like *bnei horin*.

In a similar vein, Rav Shlomo Zalman says that on the night of Yom Kippur, we're all like *malakhim* (angels). We scream out *barukh shem kevod malkhuto le'olam va'ed*. Right after Yom Kippur ends, when we daven Maariv and we've just fasted for twenty-four hours, we are on top of the world. We were just forgiven and granted a clean slate, and we recite *barukh shem* quietly.

Rav Shlomo Zalman asks, Wouldn't it make more sense the other way around? When we just filled up on *seudat hamafseket*, with our stomachs full of food, how can we run into shul for *tefillat zaka, leil* Yom Kippur, and start screaming *barukh shem kevod*? Are we already on such a high level?

Rav Shlomo Zalman says: Don't consider the position, but the direction. On *leil* Yom Kippur when we're sitting in shul, what are we thinking about? Yom Kippur. At that time, everything's on the line. On *motza'ei Yom Kippur,* we just finished being at shul for twenty-five hours, so we're thinking about *takhlis,* such as, What am I breaking my fast on? When am I buying the stuff for the sukkah? Suddenly, we have so much on our minds. Since our direction is not as focused on *motza'ei* Yom Kippur, we say *barukh shem* quietly.

That's why at the beginning of the Seder, we say *leshana haba'a be'ara d'Yisrael:* We begin with a focus on our direction!

INVITING GUESTS AT THIS JUNCTURE?

In the paragraph of *ha lahma anya,* we state:

כָּל דִּכְפִין יֵיתֵי וְיֵכֹל, כָּל דִּצְרִיךְ יֵיתֵי וְיִפְסַח.

> Let all who are hungry come in and eat, let all who are in need come and join us for the Pesah.

Typically,

sovereignty. If one would peruse any of the *Teshuvot Mimaamakim* of Rav Oshry, which were written in the Kovno ghetto, one would be unable to comprehend how his congregation would be able to experience a true Seder Pesah. Certainly, they were not free people. The whole Seder was just a show. How can one who is starving and running for his life act like a *ben horin*?

Rabbi Genack offers a *mashal*. There is an individual who has been a prisoner in a jail for many years, and one day, he is informed that he will be released tomorrow. All of a sudden, this prisoner is ecstatic. He takes a shower and tries to look neat. He is still in jail, but he smells his freedom, knowing that he will be out tomorrow. His mentality is one of a free man already, although he is still locked up.

Then there is a different person, one who is at home, but is told that tomorrow he is being indicted and will likely be sentenced to twenty years in prison. He is still physically at home, but mentally, he is already in jail.

It's all about perspective. Our mentality in life is not dependent on our position, but on our direction. If we contemplate what we would like to achieve and where we would like to be, it is as if we are already there, or are at least gaining momentum in that direction. We could be sitting in a jail cell, but if we know we are getting out tomorrow, we begin to feel free.

Even though on the outside it appears as if we are slaves, since our destiny is to be redeemed, the spark of freedom is within us and we never feel truly hopeless.

That is what the Haggada is teaching us. Even while we are in *galut* being oppressed by our enemies, the knowledge that one day we will be redeemed enables us to hope and experience a better future, to act as *bnei horin* at all times! We know our goal. HaKadosh Barukh Hu promised, *BeNissan nigalu ubeNissan atidin lehiga'el* – in Nisan the Jewish people were redeemed from Egypt, and in Nisan

does not apply to other holidays, a special obligation to be charitable. It is known as *ma'ot hitin*. Specifically, the mitzva of matza is not complete until we have provided for others as well.

At the beginning of the Seder we recite *ha lahma anya*, highlighting the dual significance of the matza. It's not just about my eating it; it's about taking care of everybody else as well.

That is why we extend an invitation to guests immediately after being reminded of the matza.

A story is told about the Beit Halevi which highlights his concern for other's needs, in particular on Seder night. An individual asked the Beit Halevi if it was permissible to recite the blessings over four cups of milk rather than four cups of wine. After the individual left, the Beit Halevi told his gabbai to be sure to send money to that family so they can prepare food for Pesah. The gabbai asked how he knew the family required financial assistance, since the individual did not request any funds. The Beit Halevi responded, "If he is drinking milk at his Seder, that means he cannot afford to have meat at his table" (Shulamit Soloveitchik Meiselman, *The Soloveitchik Heritage: A Daughter's Memoir*, p. 57).

FOCUSING ON OTHERS

A similar idea is expressed by Rav Shalom Schwadron. If you look closely at the words in the paragraph about welcoming guests to our Seder, you'll notice that we start off with a statement about matza being "poor man's bread." Then, we state *kol ditzrikh yetei veyifsah*, "Whoever is in need can join us for the *korban pesah*." But then, all of a sudden, we're not only inviting guests to eat matza; we're offering them meat. We start off by focusing on bread, *lehem oni* – matza – and then we switch over to meat. If we really want to get people to join us, we ought to mention the steak at the beginning! So why do we start by mentioning "poor man's bread"?

Rav Schwadron

Typically, we invite guests in advance. What kind of invitation is this, to invite people once the Seder is already in process? The doors are closed and we already began the Seder, having recited Kiddush and fulfilled the first four *simanim*. Why are we extending an invitation to guests now?

Obviously, this is not an actual invitation. Rather, it is symbolic. It accentuates the fact that we are free men and women. A slave is not able to invite guests to the table. That is only within the power of his master. Tonight, we reflect on the fact that we are *bnei horin*, free people, that among other things, we are able to extend an invitation to others to join us and partake in our feast.

Related to this, there is another idea based on an interpretation offered by the Gra. There are two *pesukim* that refer to the obligation of eating matza. The first *pasuk* dictates that matza should be eaten for seven days, שבעת ימים מצות תאכלו (*Shemot* 12:15). The second *pasuk* expresses an obligation on the individual to eat matza, בערב תאכלו מצת (*Shemot* 12:18). The first *pasuk* is spelled מצות with the letter *vav* (*ketiv malei*). In the second *pasuk* that refers to the individual's obligation to eat matza, the word מצת is spelled without a *vav* (*haser*).

The meaning of these *pasukim* is this. The mitzva of eating matza has two aspects to it. On the one hand, each individual is obligated to consume matza. In addition, one must make sure others are able to afford matza, so that they too can fulfill this biblical imperative. The command "you should eat matza" is spelled without a *vav* to illustrate that one should spend less money on oneself. "Matza should be eaten" is a reference to *ma'ot hitin*, to giving *tzedaka* so that other people can partake in the mitzva of eating matza as well. This reference to matza is spelled with a *vav* and is referred to as *malei* (full) in order to highlight that one should ensure others have all that is required to fulfill this mitzva.

Based on this interpretation of the Gra, Rav Yosef Dov Soloveitchik suggests that there is a unique aspect on Pesah that

Rav Yaakov Kamenetzky (cited in *Haggadat Arzei HaLevanon*, p. 115; see also *Emet LeYaakov Parashat Bo*) addresses this question. Rav Kamenetzky asks, Why is the Talmud Yerushalmi, which was compiled in Israel by Rav Yohanan, written in Aramaic, not in Hebrew?

Furthermore, when Bnei Yisrael returned to Israel during the rebuilding of the second *Beit HaMikdash*, they continued to use the names of the Persian months. In the Torah, months don't have names; they are referred to by numbers. We count from "Nisan," referred to as the first month. The only *yahrzeit* we have in the Torah is of Aharon Hakohen which occurs on the first of the fifth month. In *Megillat Esther*, we have references to Adar and Iyar, which are Persian names for months. Why didn't Bnei Yisrael revert to referring to months by numbers after they returned during *Bayit Sheni*? Why do we still refer to months by their Persian names?

Rav Yaakov Kamenetzky explains that even when Klal Yisrael returned to rebuild the second *Beit HaMikdash*, they knew that this was not the ultimate redemption. They were lacking the *Aron HaKodesh*! The *urim vetumim* didn't light up, either. This was clearly not a complete redemption!

The reason behind using Persian names for months, and the explanation as to why the Talmud Yerushalmi was written in Aramaic, is because we are still in *galut*. These aspects are a reminder of that. Although we have come a long way, our redemption, our *geula*, is not complete.

We begin the Seder with the Aramaic *ha lahma anya* to highlight that although we were redeemed in the past, we are not fully there yet. There is a lot to pray for: *Leshana haba'a be'ara d'Yisrael.* May we be worthy of a *geula sheleima*, a complete redemption in the near future.

MA NISHTANA

Rav Schwadron explains that we should examine the focus of each sentence. The first sentence in that paragraph is about what *I* have. The next sentence is what I'm *offering to others*. When we focus on *ourselves,* we are satisfied with the basics. When it comes to *guests,* we are to go above and beyond, providing the best delicacies!

SOMETHING IS MISSING!

The *Otzrot HaTorah Haggada,* citing the Shelah HaKadosh, suggests that as we begin the Seder, we highlight that something critical is absent from our table: the *korban pesah,* which should be the centerpiece. Ever since the destruction of the *Beit HaMikdash,* it is missing.

When we used to partake in the *korban pesah,* one had to prearrange the group with whom he was to share the *korban* prior to it being slaughtered. We could not extend an invitation after commencing the *korban* process. By inviting guests during the Seder, it serves as testimony to the fact that we are in exile. We are unable to celebrate Pesah in its fullest sense, inclusive of the *korban pesah.*

Therefore, we begin the *Maggid* section with a testimony of *gnut,* a negative, declaring that we are in exile. Yet we conclude with a statement of hope: "Next year in Jerusalem!"

WHY ARAMAIC?

Why is *ha lahma anya* in Aramaic? We just started the Haggada. Why do we switch to reciting in Aramaic rather than doing so in Hebrew?

The Midrash states that during our time in Mitzrayim, we did not change our language. We remained Hebrew speakers! Why would we insert a paragraph in Aramaic precisely at the beginning of the Seder?

The seder plate and the matzot are now covered and the second cup of wine is poured. The youngest child asks the following questions:

מַה נִּשְׁתַּנָּה

WHAT MAKES

THIS NIGHT UNLIKE ALL OTHER NIGHTS,

---

from a different exit, potentially a greater distance from where you parked your donkey. Why? Though the *Beit HaMikdash* was the greatest edifice of that era, when viewed a second time from the same angle, its awesomeness may seem less apparent. The attitude of "been there, done that" might kick in. Bnei Yisrael were miraculously granted the *mann* in the desert, and after a short while they desired other sustenance. No matter how special an item, over time we take it for granted and it loses its unique character.

That's exactly why we have questions and answers at the Seder. If we would just listen to a lecture, we would get bored and doze off. Being challenged by questions keeps us on our toes and maintains our curiosity and interest. It is best to prepare challenging questions, riddles, and games to ensure that all members remain engaged throughout the Seder.

MA NISHTANA – HOME SCHOOLING

Rav Eli Sadan (*Kamah Maalot Tovot, Mekhinat Eli,* p. 62) differentiates between the method of education in school and at home. In school, ideas are communicated. In the home, *emuna* (belief) is transmitted.

Tonight is the night of transmitting *emuna*. Tonight is a night not just of the intellect, but of the heart. Tonight, our children should see us emotional and intense, connecting with our past and being upbeat about our future. Content, laws, and ideas are conveyed in

the school

The קערה *and the* מצות *are now covered and the second cup of wine is poured. The youngest child asks the following questions:*

מַה נִּשְׁתַּנָּה הַלַּיְלָה הַזֶּה מִכָּל הַלֵּילוֹת

מַה נִּשְׁתַּנָּה – MA NISHTANA

AUSPICIOUS MOMENT

Rav Elimelech Biderman (in his Haggada *Be'er HaHaim*) offers a powerful insight into the *Ma Nishtana*. The mishna on Pesahim 116a states that we pour the second cup and "here the son asks." There is a tradition that this is an auspicious time and we can ask anything we desire of HaKadosh Barukh Hu, whose heart is open at this instance.

At this point in the seder I stop and ask all present around the table to take a moment to think of something they would like to request of HaKadosh Barukh Hu, before we state the "official" four questions of the evening. It could be a meaningful moment for all present at the Seder.

WHY SO MANY QUESTIONS?

Why do we begin with the famous four questions of *Ma Nishtana*? Why not just jump right into *Sippur*, telling the story of the Exodus? Why is it preferable to package the Seder around questions?

Rav Chaim Shmulevitz (*Sihat Mussar*, maamar 66) explains that *Hazal* are very worried about the danger of *hergel*, routine, as it could cause someone to lose excitement in the performance of mitzvot. For example, there is a halakha that one is prohibited from entering and exiting the *Beit HaMikdash* from the same gate. In other words, if you entered on the north side, then you had to leave

so that every other night we eat either bread or matza,
but tonight there is only matza?

And that every other night we eat many different greens,
but tonight we will eat bitter herbs?

And that every other night we do not dip [our food] at all,
but tonight we will dip it twice?

And that every other night some sit to eat and some recline,
but tonight we are all reclining?

KORBAN TODA

Is the *Ma Nishtana* a list of several questions, or rather, a list of statements? The *Arukh HaShulhan,* based on the Rambam, reads it as a list of statements, not as questions. Therefore, the verses of *Ma Nishtana* should be expressed as, *Ma Nishtana!* – How awesome is this night! This is similar to the simple reading of *Ma rabbu maasekha Hashem* – How awesome and wondrous are Your creations!

Most commentators, however, interpret the *Ma Nishtana* as a series of questions.

In the first line of the *Ma Nishtana,* we distinguish between the Seder night and all other nights. On all other nights, we eat *hametz* and matza, but tonight, we eat only matza. Why isn't the question phrased differently? Most of us do not eat matza throughout the year. The sentence could have been more accurate, stating that on all other nights we eat just *hametz,* yet tonight, we eat matza.

The *korban pesah* has a special kind of power. According to a number of early sources such as the Zohar, the *korban pesah* is a unique type of *korban toda.* It is in the category of *kodshei kalim;* non-kohanim are allowed to eat it throughout all of Yerushalayim.

There are

שֶׁבְּכָל הַלֵּילוֹת אָנוּ אוֹכְלִין חָמֵץ וּמַצָּה
הַלַּיְלָה הַזֶּה כֻּלּוֹ מַצָּה

שֶׁבְּכָל הַלֵּילוֹת אָנוּ אוֹכְלִין שְׁאָר יְרָקוֹת
הַלַּיְלָה הַזֶּה מָרוֹר

שֶׁבְּכָל הַלֵּילוֹת אֵין אָנוּ מַטְבִּילִין אֲפִלּוּ פַּעַם אֶחָת
הַלַּיְלָה הַזֶּה שְׁתֵּי פְעָמִים

שֶׁבְּכָל הַלֵּילוֹת אָנוּ אוֹכְלִין בֵּין יוֹשְׁבִין וּבֵין מְסֻבִּין
הַלַּיְלָה הַזֶּה כֻּלָּנוּ מְסֻבִּין

---

the school from teacher to student. *Emuna*, however, is passed from father to son.

Many of the concepts in the Torah about this night are really about our children: *Arba'a banim, vehigadeta levinkha.* As we state, *anahnu maaminim bnei maaminim*, "We are believers, descendants of believers." We do not state that we are *maaminim talmidei maaminim*, "students of believers." That's because *emuna* is transmitted from parent to child, via the family. When a child turns to a parent to ask something, there's an opportunity to convey our passion, complete belief, and unequivocal faith. Seder night is about talking. It's about conversations, strengthening one's belief, one's faith, and one's love of Judaism. It is an opportunity to take what our parents embedded in us and transmit it to our children's hearts. Through questions and answers, and enlightening discussion rather than dictation, one can maximize the opportunity to transmit the excitement to the next generation.

MA NISHTANA – QUESTIONING AMBIGUITY

Abarbanel was bothered and asked: Why only four questions, and why these four?

Further, the most obvious question that should be asked is: We just poured the second cup of wine. Why didn't the child ask, "We never have two cups of wine for Kiddush. Why two cups?" Shouldn't that be the most obvious question?

The Abarbanel says that really, there's one question, and throughout the night, we are asking this one question over and over. That is, why is this night so self-contradictory? We do so many things that are the opposites of each other. We act like kings, yet at the same time, we recall being slaves. We're on top of the world, and we're at the bottom of the world.

We dip; only kings dip. We lean; only kings lean. On the other hand, we eat *maror*; only slaves eat *maror*. We eat matza, and there are many sources that say that matza is a food of servitude. The Avudraham writes that he had a friend who was captured, and they served him matza in prison because matza stays in the stomach for a long time. It's the food of slaves and captives.

Even within these symbols, there are contradictions. Matza is a bread of slaves, but it also symbolizes that we were freed so quickly that we didn't have time to let dough rise.

Why so many contradictions?

The answer is, we are celebrating our salvation, and yet to truly appreciate it, we have to comprehend the nightmare of our servitude. Therefore we start with our lowest point – from *avadim hayinu*. In order to truly celebrate our high, we have to appreciate how low we were.

These two aspects do not contradict one another, but rather facilitate a more complete appreciation of the freedom that was given.

AVADIM

There are four events that can trigger an obligation to offer a *korban toda* (and today, to make the blessing *birkat hagomel*): if someone who was ill became better, or if someone crossed the sea safely, crossed the desert, or was released from jail. We experienced each of these scenarios during our tenure in Mitzrayim and during our Exodus from Mitzrayim! Therefore, we were obligated to bring a *korban toda*.

What does a *korban toda* usually entail? It includes forty loaves, thirty hallot, *and* ten matzot.

Rav Yerucham Kram in *Talmudo BeYado* (p. 35) suggests that's exactly what we're referencing in the *Ma Nishtana*. *Sheb'khol haleilot* means that on all other nights, when we bring the *korban toda, anu okhlim hametz u'matza* (both bread and matza are part of the *korban toda*). We're not talking about any *hulin* food we eat during the year. We're making a parallel between *korban toda* and the *korban pesah*. All other nights of the year, we eat the *korban* with *hametz u'matza*. But on *leil haSeder,* this *korban toda* is accompanied solely with matza. This *korban toda* is different.

In relation to this question of why on this night do we not include bread in our *korban toda* – the parent answers that this is a qualitatively different type of *korban toda,* which is to be distinguished from all others. This is matza night.

If we could capture the essence of the whole night in a word, it's *hoda'a*. At the root, it's *toda,* thanks. That's the message. Later on in the Seder, we cite *pesukim* that relate to *yetzi'at Mitzrayim*. We quote from *Sefer Devarim,* from a paragraph that is recited when one brings his first *bikkurim* fruits to the *Beit HaMikdash,* rather than from *Sefer Shemot,* where the story is told. Why do we cite from *mikra bikkurim,* rather than from the story of *yetzi'at Mitzrayim*?

Mikra bikkurim is all about *hoda'a,* thanking Hashem for bringing us to the land of Israel and for enabling us to grow this produce. That should be the tone at the Seder.

The seder plate and the matzot are uncovered.

עֲבָדִים הָיִינוּ
WE WERE SLAVES

to Pharaoh in Egypt,
and the Lord our God brought us out of there
with a strong hand and an outstretched arm.
And if the Holy One, blessed be He,
had not brought our fathers out of Egypt –
then we, and our children, and the children of our children,
would still be enslaved to Pharaoh in Egypt.

In the responsa *Mimaamakim* (3:6) written by Rav Ephraim Oshry in the Kovno ghetto during the Holocaust, a story is told of a situation that transpired during the morning *tefilla* in the ghetto. The *hazan* began with the recitation of the morning *berakhot*, and when he got to the third *berakha*, he paused and questioned, *shelo asani aved*? Can I thank God for not enslaving me? Is there any worse situation than the oppression and servitude we are experiencing under the Nazi regime?

The congregation's silence was deafening, as other members seemed puzzled as to whether to indeed recite this blessing given their dire situation. Rav Oshry responded that so long as they have the freedom to worship God, then they are indeed free men, and the blessing should be recited.

Our enemy can usurp our physical freedom but cannot take away our faith and belief in God.

A similar idea is reflected by Natan Sharansky. After he was sentenced to prison for practicing Judaism, he turned to the judge and stated: "You think you are free, and I am going to jail? You are not free to think as you desire. You are subject to act as the KGB dictates. You are the prisoner. I, however, have my freedom to believe in my religion, and that faith is the basis of my freedom."

We may have been enslaved by Pharaoh in a physical sense, but in a spiritual realm, we were truly *avdei Hashem*!

"PHARAOH"

The קערה *and the* מצות *are uncovered.*

עֲבָדִים הָיִינוּ

לְפַרְעֹה בְּמִצְרָיִם
וַיּוֹצִיאֵנוּ יהוה אֱלֹהֵינוּ מִשָּׁם
בְּיָד חֲזָקָה וּבִזְרוֹעַ נְטוּיָה.
וְאִלּוּ לֹא הוֹצִיא הַקָּדוֹשׁ בָּרוּךְ הוּא
אֶת אֲבוֹתֵינוּ מִמִּצְרָיִם
הֲרֵי אָנוּ וּבָנֵינוּ וּבְנֵי בָנֵינוּ מְשֻׁעְבָּדִים הָיִינוּ
לְפַרְעֹה בְּמִצְרָיִם.

עֲבָדִים הָיִינוּ – AVADIM HAYINU

AVADIM LEPHARAOH AND NOT *AVDEI* PHARAOH

We use the term *avadim hayinu lePharaoh* (we were slaves to Pharaoh). Why do we not use the shorter phrase of *avdei* Pharaoh (slaves of Pharaoh), since we always refer to ourselves as being *avdei Hashem* (servants of God)?

Rav Yosef Dov Soloveitchik (*Nora'ot HaRav*) explains that there is a stark distinction between these two phrases. We relate to our bondage as "*avadim hayinu lePharaoh,*" which means that our social status was one of slavery. The term *avdei* Pharaoh would have reflected not our social standing, but our identity.

This was the hidden message behind the burning bush. After all, why was this the chosen mechanism through which God first revealed Himself to Moshe? There was a crucial lesson being conveyed. Although the bush was on fire, the fire did not consume the bush. This symbolized the status of the Jewish people. They were slaves on the outside, but not on the inside. They yearned to be free and maintained their Jewish identity. They did not identify with Pharaoh, with his culture or his society – they were not *avdei* Pharaoh. Rather, they were forced into physical servitude – *avadim hayinu lePharaoh*.

And even were we all wise,
all intelligent,
all aged and all knowledgeable in the Torah,
still the command would be upon us
to tell of the coming out of Egypt;
and the more one tells of the coming out of Egypt,
the more admirable it is.

Further, wisdom is a gift that should be used properly, as highlighted by the lesson derived below.

In *Parashat Ki Tisa*, Hashem tells Moshe that he has selected Betzalel to assist with the construction of the *Mishkan*. The *pasuk* states, *Re'ei karati beshem Betzalel*, "See – I designated Betzalel" (*Shemot* 31:1). Rav Moshe Feinstein inquires, where did Hashem previously designate Betzalel? We do not find a previous *pasuk* that articulates any such delegation.

Rav Feinstein explains that if Betzalel possessed special talent with respect to architecture, then obviously he was gifted with such characteristics in order to use them for the good of society and to fulfill *ratzon Hashem*, the will of God. He was allotted this skill so that he could contribute to the building of the *Mishkan*.

Each individual has specific skills. Some individuals have the ability to sing or sculpt, while others have the power of persuasion, or the ability to organize or manage. No matter what talent one enjoys, one is to direct that talent toward doing the will of Hashem, and to recognize that he was gifted with a specific ability in order to utilize it for a specific purpose.

There is an event that is recorded in *I Melakhim* 21 with respect to the vineyard of Navot, and it illustrates the importance of utilizing one's strengths in order to serve Hashem.

Navot had a vineyard that was located next to King Ahav's vacation home. King Ahav wanted to acquire Navot's vineyard, but Navot refused to sell it because it was a property that he inherited from his ancestors. Ahav returned to the palace upset. His evil wife,

Queen Jezebel,

וַאֲפִלּוּ
כֻּלָּנוּ חֲכָמִים, כֻּלָּנוּ נְבוֹנִים, כֻּלָּנוּ זְקֵנִים
כֻּלָּנוּ יוֹדְעִים אֶת הַתּוֹרָה
מִצְוָה עָלֵינוּ לְסַפֵּר בִּיצִיאַת מִצְרַיִם
וְכָל הַמַּרְבֶּה לְסַפֵּר בִּיצִיאַת מִצְרַיִם הֲרֵי זֶה מְשֻׁבָּח.

"PHARAOH" – WHY NOT DISCLOSE HIS REAL NAME?

Rabbi Norman Lamm (*The Royal Table*, p. 35) notes: Isn't it interesting that in the Torah, Pharaoh's name is not mentioned? Pharaoh is the name of his position, like President or Prime Minister. Why are we not informed of Pharaoh's actual name?

Rabbi Lamm offers the following explanation. If Pharaoh's name would have been written in the Torah, historians and psychologists would speculate about him. They would analyze his childhood, suggesting probable reasons for his atrocious behavior. He was weaned too early or too late. He had a harsh father, or his mother was too over-protective. These are all excuses as to why he was such a terrible person.

The Torah is silent as to his name, highlighting that no matter one's upbringing, a person, especially a leader, is to be judged by his or her actions and must be accountable for their conduct. The explanations and the causes of a person's behavior may be of legitimate concern to a therapist treating a political monster, but to the masses of his victims, they are of no consequence whatsoever.

And so, he is known Pharaoh, no matter who he was. He will be judged for what he did. There are no legitimate excuses for his immoral and unethical behavior.

KULANU HAKHAMIM – USE WISDOM PROPERLY

At this point in the Haggada, we are told that no matter how wise one may be, every individual is still obligated to engage in the retelling of the Exodus from Egypt.

praising God's greatness, it goes without saying that if we start using our own words, we can go on forever.

In regard to the telling of the Exodus from Egypt on the Seder night, isn't *kol hamarbeh lesaper harei zeh meshubah* – the ideal to extend praise – contrary to Rabbi Hanina's statement, *kol hamosif gorei'a*? If we apply the warning of Rabbi Hanina, then there should be an exact script of what to recite and we should not add to it, lest we be accused of belittling God's greatness.

Second, the Meshekh Hokhma (*Behukotai* 26:4) cites two seemingly opposing statements in the *gemara*. In Massekhet Berakhot (4b), we are told that one who recites *Ashrei* every single day is considered a *ben olam haba*. Elsewhere, the Gemara (Shabbat 118b) claims that one who recites *Hallel hagadol* (*hodu l'Hashem ki tov*…) every single day is a blasphemer. What's the difference between reciting *Ashrei* and *Hallel*? They are both chapters in *Tehillim*.

The Meshekh Hokhma explains that *Ashrei* illustrates God's greatness through the natural realm (*teva*). He feeds us all, He is good to all, and He fulfills the requests of those that fear Him. In contrast, *Hallel hagadol* reveals God's greatness through miracles, *nissim*. One who recites *Hallel hagadol* daily acknowledges that God is responsible for the miracles in his life, but that the day-to-day natural events may be left to mother nature or circumstance. It is blasphemy to place a limitation on God's control of the world, not to view Him as the source of all existence.

That brings us back to the same question regarding *kol hamarbeh lesaper*, the more one extends the retelling, the more one is praiseworthy: How can we spend so much time discussing the miracles like the *makot* and *yetzi'at Mitzrayim*? Wouldn't that be similar to one who focuses on *Hallel* rather than *Ashrei*?

The Ketav Sofer (cited in the *Maayana Shel Torah*) explains that when one refers to past events, this is when it is problematic to focus on miracles alone. However, at the Seder, we are actually reliving the redemption and are to experience the event as if we are currently participating in the Exodus from Egypt, *ke'ilu yatza miMitzrayim*. When someone experiences a miracle with his own eyes, there is no limit to the gratitude that one may express to Hashem.

MAASEH B'REBBI

Queen Jezebel, devised a plan whereby Navot was falsely accused of treason and sentenced to death. Ahav then took over Navot's vineyard, an act for which he and his descendants were later punished.

One can understand why Ahav was punished, but why did Navot, a seemingly innocent bystander, have to be killed? The Yalkut Shimoni explains based on a *pasuk* in *Mishlei* (3:9): *Kabed et Hashem mehonekha,* "Honor Hashem from your valuables."

If one is gifted with a good voice, he should use it to serve as a *hazan,* a cantor. Likewise, Navot had a beautiful voice and used to go to Yerushalayim – and not the Temple built by Yeravam in the North – to sing in the *Beit HaMikdash.* All of Klal Yisrael looked forward to hearing his enchanting voice.

One year, Navot decided not to go to Yerushalayim. This is derived from the *pasuk* that states, "Navot the Jezreelite had a vineyard, which was in Jezreel" (*I Melakhim* 23:1). Why the repetition of Jezreel? If Navot is from Jezreel, then it is clear that the vineyard is likely located there as well! *Hazal* explain that Navot decided to remain in Jezreel rather than go up to Jerusalem during the festivals. For this, he was punished. That year Navot did not utilize his skill and his gifted voice to serve Hashem. Not exercising his potential led to devastating consequences.

THE MORE THE MERRIER – WHEN RELIVING IT

At the end of *Avadim Hayinu,* we state, *Kol hamarbeh lesaper beyetzi'at Mitzrayim, harei zeh meshubah,* the more one extends the retelling of the Exodus from Egypt, the more it is praiseworthy.

There are two questions with respect to this statement.

First, there is a *gemara* in Berakhot (33) that describes a situation that transpired in Rav Hanina's shul. The *hazan* was reciting the repetition of the *Amida* and inserted several descriptions of God, in addition to the standard descriptions that appear in the siddur (*hagadol, hagibor, vehanora,* which are derived from a biblical source).

Rabbi Hanina was very upset with the *hazan*'s rendition. When it comes to praising God, sometimes, *kol hamosif gorei'a* (supplementing with new ideas can detract from the praise). When it comes to

מַעֲשֶׂה

ONCE,

Rabbi Eliezer and Rabbi Yehoshua and Rabbi Elazar ben Azarya

It was not a usual Seder, but a secretive planning session. Maybe the students participated in the Seder until midnight, at which time it concluded and discussions among the Sages were initiated. The *talmidim* were likely waiting outside for instructions as to whether to fight or to concede to the Romans.

The student's statement of *higia zeman keriat Shema shel Shaharit* ("The time to recite the morning *Shema* has arrived") could be a reference to being willing to sacrifice their lives for their own redemption, as *keriat Shema* is symbolic of self-sacrifice. As stated in Berakhot 61b, Rabbi Akiva derives from the term *bekhol nafshekha*, "with all your soul," that one should serve Hashem even if required to sacrifice one's life. Witnessing that the discussion among their Rabbis was extending into the morning hours, the *talmidim* wanted to reassure their *rabbanim* that they were ready and willing to adhere to their directive, even if it would lead to sacrificing oneself *al kiddush Hashem*, to sanctify God's name. As is seen, understanding the historical context sheds light on the potential meaning of this scene.

SEEKING COMFORT

With historical context in mind, given that these *rabbanim* lived soon after the destruction of the *Beit HaMikdash*, imagine how depressing it must have been to experience the first Seder after the destruction of the Temple. The main object is missing from the Seder plate, that is, the *korban pesah*! How could one celebrate Pesah with its main event lacking?

Rav Yechiel Michel Epstein (*Haggadat Leil Shimurim*, p. 33) explains that these *rabbanim* gathered together in Bnei Brak for their

Seder.

מַעֲשֶׂה
בְּרַבִּי אֱלִיעֶזֶר וְרַבִּי יְהוֹשֻׁעַ וְרַבִּי אֶלְעָזָר בֶּן עֲזַרְיָה

מַעֲשֶׂה בְּרַבִּי – MAASEH B'REBBI

HISTORICAL PERSPECTIVE

The gathering of great *Tanna'im* for the Pesah Seder in the time of Rabbi Akiva gives rise to a number of questions.

First, why did they gather in Bnei Brak, Rabbi Akiva's town? Rabbi Akiva was not the eldest of the Rabbis. What were they all doing there?

Second, why weren't their students with them? It would make sense that the great Rabbis would want to have their students participate, or at least listen to the pearls of wisdom they are sharing with each other at the Seder. In fact, the students were not even in the room, as they entered to tell the Rabbis when it was time to recite *keriat Shema.*

Third, it seems like the students barged in, like it was an emergency to inform the Rabbis of the time of day. What was so pressing?

Rabbi Lau in his *Haggada Around the Seder Table* (p. 24), as well as many other commentators, express the importance of knowing the historical background of this Seder. These great sages lived immediately following the destruction of the *Beit HaMikdash*. During this period, the Jewish people were contemplating whether to join forces with Bar Kokhba to rebel against the Romans or to submit to them.

Rabbi Lau conjectures that Rabbi Akiva must have thought that Seder night, when we were freed from Egyptian bondage, would be an appropriate night to consider alternative ways to obtain freedom from the Romans. He invited his peers, the leading Sages of the time, to discuss what should be done for the future of the nation. This may have been why the students were not present in the room.

and Rabbi Akiva and Rabbi Tarfon
reclined [for the seder] in Bnei Brak.
And they told of the Exodus from Egypt all that night;
until their students came in and said,
"Teachers –
the time for saying the *Shema* of the morning has come."

ALL ENCOMPASSING

The *Otzrot HaTorah,* citing the Hida, explores what this paragraph is seeking to convey to us. Everyone is obligated to recite the Haggada. What is so unique about these *rabbanim* who had the Seder with Rabbi Akiva? Granted, they stayed awake all night, but perhaps there is an additional idea that we can derive from their story.

The Hida offers a keen insight. These five rabbis had one thing in common. None of their ancestors were included in *shibud Mitzrayim,* meaning they had not been enslaved in Egypt. Three of them were *kohanim,* one was a *levi,* and one descended from *geirim* (converts). Rav Elazar ben Azarya was a *kohen,* Rebbi Tarfon was also a *kohen,* Rebbi Yehoshua was a *levi,* Rebbi Elazar was a *kohen,* and Rebbi Akiva was a *ben geirim.* Even these rabbis, who one might have thought were exempt from partaking in *sippur yetzi'at Mitzrayim,* are included in the obligation of the Seder and maximized the experience! In fact, the word וכל stands for *kohanim, levi'im, ve'geirim.*

SYMBOLISM OF DAYLIGHT

As daylight appeared, the students interrupted their rebbeim to inform them that it was almost time to recite the morning *Shema, keriat Shema shel Shaharit.* What time was it? It appears it was sunrise. If so, then according to most opinions they still had three halakhic hours to recite *keriat Shema.* What's the rush?

Rav Avraham Schorr (*HaLekah VeHalibuv,* p. 93) suggests that perhaps there is a symbolic meaning to *higia zeman keriat Shema shel Shaharit,* and we shouldn't take it literally. He quotes a thought from

the Eglei Tal.

וְרַבִּי עֲקִיבָא וְרַבִּי טַרְפוֹן
שֶׁהָיוּ מְסֻבִּין בִּבְנֵי בְרַק
וְהָיוּ מְסַפְּרִים בִּיצִיאַת מִצְרַיִם כָּל אוֹתוֹ הַלַּיְלָה
עַד שֶׁבָּאוּ תַלְמִידֵיהֶם וְאָמְרוּ לָהֶם
רַבּוֹתֵינוּ
הִגִּיעַ זְמַן קְרִיאַת שְׁמַע שֶׁל שַׁחֲרִית.

Seder. Where were their families? Why were the *talmidim* not present? Again, the students only entered in the morning.

These Rabbis sought guidance and comfort, so they went to visit Rabbi Akiva, who resided in Bnei Brak, because he was the eternal optimist. We are told at the end of Makot (24b) that when several rabbis witnessed jackals walking on the ruins of the *Beit HaMikdash*, they cried, yet Rabbi Akiva laughed!

The rabbis were puzzled. How could Rabbi Akiva laugh when animals are pacing upon the land where our Holy Temple stood? Rabbi Akiva explained that this is the fulfillment of the destruction depicted in the prophecy of Mikha (alternatively, Uria – *see Tosafot,* ibid.). Rabbi Akiva explained, "Now I am certain that just as Mikha's prophecy of destruction was fulfilled, so too the prophecy of Zekharya, that the redemption will one day follow, and elders and children will again reside peacefully in Jerusalem will surely be fulfilled as well." Rabbi Akiva is the one who declared upon losing his donkey, rooster, and candle that "everything that the Merciful One does, He does for the best" (Berakhot 60b). Rabbi Akiva is the one who, at the age of forty, started to learn the aleph-bet! (Avot DeRabbi Natan, chapter 6).

At this difficult time, the Sages sought reassurance and encouragement from Rabbi Akiva, so that they could return to their families and students and portray optimism for the future. The students' statement of *higia zeman keriat Shema shel Shaharit* symbolized their acceptance that there is light at the end of the tunnel.

Rabbi Elazar ben Azarya said: *Berakhot 12b*
It is as if I am seventy years old,
and I did not merit to find the command
to speak of the Exodus from Egypt at night –
until Ben Zoma interpreted:

One side is picturesque, but the other side is full of loose strings without any apparent charm. As Hashem sews history, we see one side of the tapestry. Hashem knows how the loose strings will end up creating a stunning result on the other side. Seeing this is beyond our grasp, even as we experience chaos.

Keriat Shema shel Shaharit is an even higher level of faith. We recite it when it is bright and we have clarity. This is when times are good, and still, we express our appreciation.

The students witnessed their rebbeim engage in discussion about *yetzi'at Mitzrayim* all night. Imagine the aura there. They understood that their rebbeim had achieved a level of clarity and feeling close to HaKadosh Barukh Hu, feeling that everything fits in perfectly and there's no darkness. Once they achieved this feat, it was time to recite the *keriat Shema* of Shaharit, symbolizing clear reliance and unadulterated faith in the Almighty.

אָמַר רַבִּי אֶלְעָזָר בֶּן עֲזַרְיָה – AMAR RAV ELAZAR BEN AZARYAH

SIGNIFICANCE OF REMEMBERING

We recite the third paragraph of *keriat Shema* primarily for the reference in the last sentence: *Anokhi Hashem Elokekha, asher hotzeitikha me'eretz Mitzrayim.* "I am the God who took you out of Egypt."

This paragraph is the only one included in the Seder that relates not to the mitzva of *sippur*, telling over the story, but rather to *zekhirat yetzi'at Mitzrayim*, remembering the Exodus, which we fulfill every single day and night of our lives.

The *Haggada Lekah Tov* (Rav Yaakov Yisrael HaCohen Byfus,

p. 29) cites

אָמַר רַבִּי אֶלְעָזָר בֶּן עֲזַרְיָה ברכות יב:
הֲרֵי אֲנִי כְּבֶן שִׁבְעִים שָׁנָה
וְלֹא זָכִיתִי שֶׁתֵּאָמֵר יְצִיאַת מִצְרַיִם בַּלֵּילוֹת
עַד שֶׁדְּרָשָׁהּ בֶּן זוֹמָא

---

the Eglei Tal. In his introduction to his *sefer,* the Eglei Tal discusses the concept of a *tvul yom,* day of immersion. A *tvul yom* is somebody who was impure and immersed in a *mikve,* but does not achieve full purity, *tahara,* until nightfall. Why is this so? He immersed in a *mikve* hours earlier and performed no additional ritual. Why does the appearance of darkness suddenly change his impure status?

The Eglei Tal explains that the individual was impure at the start of the day and this impression remains with him throughout the day. Beginnings are critical, and they impact what follows. If one starts the day in an impure state, this affects one's disposition for the entire day. Therefore, one has to wait until nightfall to change his status from impure to a state of purity.

Returning to the previous question, why is it so critical to recite *keriat Shema* in the morning? It was recited at night, just a few hours earlier. The impact of the recitation of the *Shema* and *kabbalat ol malkhut shamayim,* acceptance of the yoke of heaven, lasts all day. But when it is a new day, we need to infuse that day with holiness again.

Based on this concept, Rav Schorr suggests as follows. Perhaps there are different symbols for, and purposes of, the *keriat Shema* of Maariv and of Shaharit. *Kabbalat ol malkhut shamayim* at night symbolizes *emuna* during dark times, *ve'emunatkha baleilot.* Just as nights are dark, there are dark periods of Jewish history. *Keriat Shema shel arvit* symbolizes our faith in Hashem, even though we don't understand why we sometimes suffer.

Rav Yosef Dov Soloveitchik once offered an allegory with respect to man's lack of understanding of God's ways (*Divrei Hagut VeHaarakha – Kol Dodi Dofek,* p. 11). Imagine a beautiful tapestry.

It is written,

"SO THAT YOU REMEMBER
THE DAY OF YOUR EXODUS FROM EGYPT
ALL THE DAYS OF YOUR LIFE." *Deut. 16*

"The days of your life" would mean in the days;
"all the days of your life" includes the nights.

But the sages say,

"The days of your life" would mean only in this world;
"all the days of your life" brings in the time of the Messiah.

God provides us with an abundance of the most valuable items, like bread, water, and air, yet we overlook their significance.

The most defining event in our history is *yetzi'at Mitzrayim*, when our nation was born. That's our bread and water, and that's why there are so many mitzvot connected to that event.

What is the litmus test to determine value? If you have nothing, and you'd pay a lot of money for something, what would you buy? Bread and water. That's how you determine the basics and the necessities. *Yetzi'at Mitzrayim* is the necessity, the defining moment of our nation. That is why we spend Seder night discussing it, and that is why we are to remember it each and every day.

SYMBOLISM OF A WHITE BEARD

Rabbi Elazar ben Azarya said, "It is as if I am seventy years old." A more detailed description of the way in which Rabbi Elazar ben Azarya became the *rosh yeshiva* is detailed in Berakhot 27b. Rabbi Gamliel had been removed from the post, and they offered Rabbi Elazar ben Azarya the position. At the time, he was only eighteen years old. He consulted with his wife, who warned him that he too can be replaced any day. Rabbi Elazar ben Azarya responded, "Better to be a glass cup for one day than an earthen cup all my life." His wife then told him, "But you don't have a white beard" (a nicer way of stating that he seems young for the task). Miraculously, he grew a white

beard

שֶׁנֶּאֱמַר

לְמַעַן תִּזְכֹּר אֶת־יוֹם צֵאתְךָ מֵאֶרֶץ מִצְרַיִם דברים טז
כֹּל יְמֵי חַיֶּיךָ:
יְמֵי חַיֶּיךָ הַיָּמִים
כֹּל יְמֵי חַיֶּיךָ הַלֵּילוֹת.
וַחֲכָמִים אוֹמְרִים
יְמֵי חַיֶּיךָ הָעוֹלָם הַזֶּה
כֹּל יְמֵי חַיֶּיךָ לְהָבִיא לִימוֹת הַמָּשִׁיחַ.

---

p. 29) cites the Sabba of Kelm who offers an insightful idea. *Zekhira* is mentioned here to underscore the importance of remembering and appreciating *yetzi'at Mitzrayim*. Yet why are there so many mitzvot connected to remembering the Exodus? There are at least ten, maybe more mitzvot. Kiddush, tefillin, Shabbat, Yom Tov… what is the reason for the emphasis on the Exodus? There is no other event that is mentioned nearly as much in the Torah. What is it about *yetzi'at Mitzrayim* that makes it such a primary focus, not just at the Seder, but throughout the Torah and with respect to numerous mitzvot? (See Ramban, end of *Parashat Bo*.)

Reb Simha Zissel of Kelm explains by way of a parable. If we think about our world, we can discern two types of valuable items. One type is gold and silver and another type is bread and water. If someone isn't focused, they might get a misimpression of which one is more valuable. Someone could think, gold and silver are expensive, and water you can get for free! But deep down, we know that's not true. We know that bread and water are essential. Without bread and water, one cannot survive. Yet we take bread and water for granted and place greater value on gold and silver.

What about air? What if you could only breathe in certain places in the world? Since air surrounds us, we take it for granted. Yet again, that is something that one cannot live without. Sometimes

BEING ENLIGHTENED BY TORAH

There's one phrase that seems superfluous in Rav Elazar ben Azarya's statement. He declared, *harei ani ke'ven shivim shana,* it is as if I am seventy years old… *velo zakhiti,* and I did not merit, *ad shedarash Ben Zoma,* until Ben Zoma explained. What is the meaning of the phrase *velo zakhiti,* I did not merit? What does it add to the description of Rav Elazar ben Azarya's previous lack of understanding?

The *Barukh She'amar* (Rav Barukh Halevi Epstein) suggests that this teaches us that every time we hear something in Torah – if we figure out something new, or if we hear the answer to a question that has been bothering us for a long time – we need to appreciate that we have gained insight and clarity with respect to Torah.

It sounds as if Ben Zoma was a young man. He doesn't even go by a first name, but is referred to as the son of his father. He may have been younger than Rav Elazar ben Azarya, and yet, Rav Elazar ben Azarya felt privileged to learn something new from this lad.

We have to be passionate about Torah, recognize its truth, and cherish every insight. We should truly internalize that it is a *zekhut,* a privilege, to gain a clear understanding of the Torah. When we have difficulty comprehending a *gemara* or *Tosafot,* and then afterward it all becomes clear to us, it is an exciting experience, and a *zekhut* to have been gifted the privilege of that perception.

CONSIDER IMPACT ON A SPOUSE

There is an additional insight that we can learn from what transpired with Rav Elazar ben Azarya. As we mentioned earlier, the paragraph in the Haggada starts in the middle of his story. In Berakhot 27b, we are informed that when he was offered the role of *rosh yeshiva* in place of Rabbi Gamliel, rather than accept the position instantly, his immediate response was, "I have to ask my wife." Why would he need to do that? This was likely his dream position that he had yearned for all his life.

The answer

beard overnight! That's why he stated, *Harei ani ke'ven shivim shana*, it is as if I am seventy years old – based on appearance, not actual years.

Rav Pincus in his Haggada discusses the symbolism of one's hair turning white as they age. We were created in a manner in which our hair is naturally darker in our youth and whiter as we mature. Everything about our body has a purpose and is to teach us something. The Gemara (Ketubot 5b) explains that we have earlobes so we can bend them over our ears to protect against hearing *lashon hara*. Also, our fingers are shaped like pegs so we can put them in our ears to prevent hearing gossip.

Rav Pincus asks, why does our hair turn white? Black and white are symbolic. Imagine you have a child who has a bunch of colored crayons and colors with all of them on the same spot. The spot turns black. Why? Because black is a combination of all the colors. When you mix multiple colors, the combination ends up dark. White is the opposite. It's clean and transparent.

When we are young, we are influenced by many things and can be pulled in all directions. We have family responsibilities, education, careers, financial obligations, community commitments, and more. As we get older, things become clearer. The white symbolizes that as we get closer to 120, there's more clarity. HaKadosh Barukh Hu even gives us a little hint: He turns our hair white. There's only one thing that starts motivating us, and that's *din veheshbon*.

That's the deeper meaning of *harei ani ke'ven shivim shana*. HaKadosh Barukh Hu has us in mind, and as we get older, He reminds us that there's only one thing that should be pulling us, and that is to come closer to Him. He reminds us to prioritize and focus on the right area.

Rav Avigdor Miller, in his later years, stopped attending *semahot*. When asked why he stopped attending weddings, he replied, "I'm too busy studying for finals." He had one thing on his mind: Before whom he will soon stand at the end of his life. He viewed the world through white lenses.

בָּרוּךְ הַמָּקוֹם

Blessed is the Omnipresent –
blessed is He.
Blessed is the One
who gave His people Israel, the Torah –
blessed is He.

---

the father provides the child with a vast amount of knowledge at a young age. Perhaps that is what is meant by receiving *arikhut yamim*, a long life as a reward for fulfilling *kibud av.* One gains the years of knowledge of his father.

Now we can understand why Rav Elazar ben Azarya states that it is as if he is seventy years old. By internalizing all the Torah his father transmitted to him, at the age of eighteen he absorbed the knowledge his father obtained over a seventy-year period.

בָּרוּךְ הַמָּקוֹם בָּרוּךְ הוּא – BARUKH HAMAKOM BARUKH HU

MEANING OF *HAMAKOM*

There are several titles that we use to refer to the Creator. Just before the section depicting the four sons, the title *Hamakom* is used. Why is this word specifically selected?

Rav Shimon Schwab in *Maayan Beit Hasho'eiva*, p. 460 (as well as Rav Yosef Dov Soloveitchik, *Harerei Kedem*, vol. 2, p. 215) suggests that the term *Hamakom* is always used when one feels distant from God. For example, if visitors bless a mourner, they depart stating, *Hamakom yenahem etkhem,* may the mourner be comforted by God. Perhaps this is to provide the mourner, who just experienced a great loss, with the assurance that he's not alone.

Similarly, the term *Hamakom* is used when referencing our brethren who are suffering: *Ahenu kol beit Yisrael… ha'omdim batzara uveshivya, Hamakom yenahem, Hamakom* will comfort you.

What is the common denominator of all these times when we refer to Hashem as *Hamakom*?

Generally,

בָּרוּךְ הַמָּקוֹם
בָּרוּךְ הוּא
בָּרוּךְ שֶׁנָּתַן תּוֹרָה לְעַמּוֹ יִשְׂרָאֵל
בָּרוּךְ הוּא

The answer is that he understood that to become *rosh yeshiva* would have a profound impact on his family, and in particular his wife. He would not be home early to bathe the children. He may have to host students in his home. He would not have as much time to assist with chores around the house.

Rather than only consider the glory the position will bring to his career and future, he contemplated the potential adverse effects it may have on his wife and wanted to ensure that she approved of it as well.

This is such a significant message for all of us. No matter how important a certain promotion or career advancement may be, even in the spiritual realm, we need to be certain that others around us, in particular our spouse and family, are on board with the potential changes that such an event will trigger in their lives.

LIKE A SEVENTY-YEAR-OLD

The gemara in Yevamot 16a depicts three great sages, Rav Yehoshua, Rav Elazar ben Azarya, and Rabbi Akiva, who visit Rav Duma ben Hurkenus who was blind. Rav Yehoshua informs Rav Duma ben Hurkenus of Rav Elazar ben Azarya's presence. Rav Duma is excited to learn that his close friend Azarya had a child that is a scholar. Why was he so excited about the fact that his friend had a son that was a *talmid hakham*? The Ben Yehoyada citing the Ohel Yaakov (Dubna Maggid) suggests that if one has a child that follows in the father's footsteps and grasps everything his father teaches him, then he is considered to have essentially gained those years of his father. By transmitting the knowledge that he accumulated over a lifetime,

כְּנֶגֶד אַרְבָּעָה בָנִים

The Torah relates
to four types of sons –
one who is wise,
one who is wicked,
one with a simple nature,
and one who does not know how to ask.

The Beit Halevi offers a tremendous insight. In most fields of knowledge in the world, there are different materials for people at different levels. Beginners, intermediates, and advanced students do not study the same data. A first-grader will learn addition and subtraction, a high school student will study geometry, and a college student will seek to master calculus. When you fully comprehend one topic, you move on the next phase.

With respect to Torah, levels are not like that at all. The magic of the Torah is that the very same Rashi the first-grader is learning to read, the *gadol hador* is interpreting as well. That is the meaning of *keneged arba'a banim dibra Torah*. The Torah is for everyone! No matter how elementary or advanced one is, it is the same exact text that is being studied.

There is a story told about Rabbi Yehezkel Levenstein that highlights the significance of appreciating Torah. Years ago, in order to attract customers, banks gave out gifts when people opened accounts. One of Rabbi Levenstein's *talmidim* told him that he had received a toaster from a bank as a gift, and he demonstrated how it works. You insert the bread here, push this button, and after a few minutes, the toasted bread pops up. The rabbi nodded, indicating that he understood how to operate the new electronic device.

The rabbi then noticed a large booklet that was in the box with the toaster and inquired about what it was. His *talmid* explained that it was the user manual which described how to use the toaster, included warnings about misusing the toaster, and gave suggestions about

what could.

כְּנֶגֶד אַרְבָּעָה בָנִים דִּבְּרָה תוֹרָה
אֶחָד חָכָם
וְאֶחָד רָשָׁע
וְאֶחָד תָּם
וְאֶחָד שֶׁאֵינוֹ יוֹדֵעַ לִשְׁאוֹל

Generally, it refers to when we experience *hester panim,* when we experience God in a hidden manner. When somebody is going through a difficult situation, a loss of a relative or oppression from an enemy, they feel lost and alone. It is at this juncture that we refer to God as *Hamakom,* which means place. Hashem is omnipresent and fills the void in times when we experience emptiness. As the Kotzker Rebbe declared, "Where's God? Wherever you let Him in."

As we start the section in the Haggada where the four sons are featured, we may remember our challenges in raising our own children. We look around the table and ask ourselves, are we doing a good job at parenting? Are we providing our children with the tools they need to succeed? One child has learning disabilities; will we be able to get him or her through school? What about those that are not fortunate enough to have a child at the table? Or maybe the children themselves feel distant and not connected to Torah. At this point, one may feel somewhat alone or distanced due to their troubles.

It is at this very moment that we are reassured that Hashem, *Hamakom,* is with us as we experience difficulties in life. It is also a time to be grateful for the amazing community of which we have been blessed to be a part.

כְּנֶגֶד אַרְבָּעָה בָנִים – KENEGED ARBA'A BANIM...

"KENEGED" – RELEVANT TO ALL

What does the word *keneged* mean?

The
WISE SON
what does he say?
"What are the testimonies, the statutes and laws, *Deut. 6*
that the Lord our God commanded you?"
And you must tell him the laws of Pesah:
"After eating the Pesah offering
one does not eat anything more."

---

who raise questions. What's the correct method of transmission? Is it *mesora*, to accept what is being transmitted to us from the previous generation? Or are we to ask questions and, in a sense, cast doubt on what we are being told?

On this night more than on any other night, we cling to our tradition. What kind of *maror* does one use? What vegetable is used for *karpas*? Celery, potato, lettuce? Does everyone make their own Kiddush? Is Kiddush recited while standing or sitting? Do you get up to wash your hands or is a bowl of water brought to the table? At the Seder, so much of what we do is *minhag avoteinu*, the tradition that was transmitted to us by our father and grandfather.

On the other hand, it is a night to question and to delve, to wonder and to ponder. Everybody has questions, and Judaism encourages questions. The pages of the Talmud are filled with questions. How do we explain the juxtaposition of *barukh Hamakom* followed by the four sons that question? Judaism offers a balance between acceptance of tradition and questioning in order to better understand our tradition.

You could have two opposite types of religions. On one extreme it declares: this is the tradition. Don't ask, don't talk, just do it! And don't ask questions. Everything's a *hok*. You could also have a religion that questions everything, and if you feel like it, you do it, and if you don't feel great about something or don't fully comprehend it, you do

not have

חָכָם

מַה הוּא אוֹמֵר

דברים ו

מָה הָעֵדֹת וְהַחֻקִּים וְהַמִּשְׁפָּטִים
אֲשֶׁר צִוָּה יהוה אֱלֹהֵינוּ אֶתְכֶם:
וְאַף אַתָּה אֱמָר לוֹ כְּהִלְכוֹת הַפֶּסַח
אֵין מַפְטִירִין אַחַר הַפֶּסַח אֲפִיקוֹמָן.

---

what could be wrong if the toaster is not working properly. These instructions, moreover, appeared in several different languages.

The rabbi began dancing in joy and explained that if this simple toaster, which just requires one to push a button, comes with a detailed instruction manual, then certainly HaKadosh Barukh Hu had to provide us with an instruction manual on how to act in this world which is infinitely more complicated.

If only we really understood that the Torah is that manual, and that if we follow its instructions – what a perfect world this would be! The Torah relates to each of us, no matter whether we are wise, wicked, simple, or unable to ask.

TRANSMITTING TRADITION

Another explanation offered for the juxtaposition of the four sons with *barukh Hamakom* is offered by Rabbi Lamm (*The Royal Table*, p. 36). We start the paragraph by stating *barukh Hamakom barukh Hu, barukh shenatan Torah le'amo Yisrael* (Blessed is God, Blessed is He; blessed is the One who gave the Torah to His people Israel). We praise Hashem, recognizing that He gave the gift of the Torah to the Jewish nation. Torah symbolizes *mesora,* tradition, which we transmit from generation to generation.

Following the recitation of this praise, we have the four children

The
WICKED SON
what does he say?
"What is this service to you?" *Ex. 12*
"To you," he says, not to him.
When he sets himself apart from the community,
he denies the very core of our beliefs.
And you must set his teeth on edge and tell him,
"Because of this *Ex. 13*
the Lord acted for me when I came out of Egypt."
"For *me*," and not for *him*;
had he been there he would not have been redeemed.

---

needs. In that chapter, he suggests that perhaps the four sons are not four separate individuals, but rather, stand for four stages of development in every human being. After all, Judaism does not usually believe in labelling individuals.

We all start out as infants when we are dependent on others to feed, bathe, and care for our every need. We have no consciousness of ourselves as individuals. We do not ask for anything as we are too young to speak. This is essentially the stage of *eino yode'a lishol,* one who does not know to ask.

In the second phase in our lives, we begin to gain independence. We start to crawl, walk, and explore the world around us. We are curious and begin to inquire. *Ma zot*? What is this and what is that? This is the *tam,* the simple son phase.

The third phase is when a child feels he can do it all. "I can do it by myself." They do not want to listen, and at times they act mischievously. There is a feeling of pride and resentment. That is the phase of *rasha,* wickedness.

The final stage is when one becomes intellectually honest, a *hakham,* and is able to feel and express gratitude to parents and others for all they do for them.

These four,

רָשָׁע

מָה הוּא אוֹמֵר

שמות יב מָה הָעֲבֹדָה הַזֹּאת לָכֶם:

לָכֶם וְלֹא לוֹ

וּלְפִי שֶׁהוֹצִיא אֶת עַצְמוֹ מִן הַכְּלָל

כָּפַר בָּעִקָּר

וְאַף אַתָּה הַקְהֵה אֶת שִׁנָּיו, וֶאֱמָר לוֹ

שמות יג בַּעֲבוּר זֶה עָשָׂה יהוה לִי בְּצֵאתִי מִמִּצְרָיִם:

לִי וְלֹא לוֹ

אִלּוּ הָיָה שָׁם, לֹא הָיָה נִגְאָל.

---

not have to perform that act. We try to strike a balance. As Rabbi Norman Lamm *z"l* so eloquently states (*The Royal Table*, p. 37): "First, let us never be perturbed by questions. They are characteristic of an alert and intelligent mind. As Jews, we welcome not only questions of inquiry, but also those of challenge.... Indeed, the questioning of tradition, is itself a tradition."

Questioning is fine, and in fact encouraged, so long as there is an underlying understanding and acceptance of the God-given Torah. As Rabbi Yisrael Salanter said, we first admit *ein keilokeinu,* "there is none like our God." Only after can we ask, *mi keilokeinu,* "who is like our God?" First we express our appreciation for the God-given Torah, *barukh shenatan Torah*. Then we can delve into the questions that arise from the acceptance and practice of the Torah as articulated by the four sons.

FOUR SONS, OR FOUR STAGES OF ONE'S LIFE

In Rav Ahron Soloveichik's *sefer Logic of the Heart, Logic of the Mind* (p. 23), he has an entire chapter devoted to children with special

The
SIMPLE-NATURED SON
what does he say?
"What is this?" *Ex. 13*

And you must tell him,
"With a strong hand the Lord *Ibid.*
brought us out of Egypt,
from the grip of slavery."

---

potential Moshe Rabbenu. Every child should be looked at as the next *gadol hador*, the next unbelievable man or woman who will change the destiny of Klal Yisrael! Our mentality with regard to our children should be that each one has the ability to become a great person in the future, and we should provide them with the proper tools to enable them to fulfill their potential.

A WISE ANSWER TO A WISE QUESTION

The wise son inquires, *ma ha'eidut vehahukim*? What are all the rules and regulations?

Rav Moshe Feinstein in his Haggada (p. 132) points out that the four questions reflect four distinct *pesukim* that appear in the Torah. However, in the Haggada, the response to each son's question is not always consistent with the response in the Torah.

The *pasuk* attributed to the wise son is:

> כִּי־יִשְׁאָלְךָ בִנְךָ מָחָר לֵאמֹר מָה הָעֵדֹת וְהַחֻקִּים וְהַמִּשְׁפָּטִים... וְאָמַרְתָּ לְבִנְךָ עֲבָדִים הָיִינוּ לְפַרְעֹה בְּמִצְרָיִם... (דברים ו:כ)
>
> When your son will ask you tomorrow, What are the testimonies and statutes... You shall say to your son, we were slaves to Pharaoh in Egypt... (*Devarim* 6:20)

Yet the

תָּם

מַה הוּא אוֹמֵר

שמות יג מַה־זֹּאת

וְאָמַרְתָּ אֵלָיו

שם בְּחֹזֶק יָד הוֹצִיאָנוּ יהוה מִמִּצְרַיִם

מִבֵּית עֲבָדִים:

These four, explains Rav Ahron, are not mutually exclusive. They are overlapping, and we have aspects of each within us. There are times where we are cynical like the *rasha* and times where we act wisely like the *hakham*. There are times when we are indifferent like the *tam*, and times when we have no clue like the *eino yode'a lishol*. We need to ensure that all aspects of our personalities, at all stages of our development, are in sync with our understanding and appreciation of our religion.

We all have a bit of each son within us. What is important is which personality is more manifest as we mature as individuals.

EACH CHILD HAS TREMENDOUS POTENTIAL

As we approach the four sons, we should contemplate the way in which we educate our youth. A halakha quoted in the Rema (YD 81:7) states that a Jewish child should not nurse from an Egyptian woman. The reason given is that Moshe Rabbenu would not nurse from an Egyptian woman, because the mouth that would speak directly with the *Shekhina* could not be fed by an Egyptian source. However, is this applicable to anyone other than Moshe Rabbenu?! If not, then why is this halakha quoted in the *Shulhan Arukh*? It is unlikely that other children will reach that level.

Yet Rav Yaakov Kaminetzky, in his *sefer Emet LeYaakov* (*Shemot*), suggests that every one of our children needs to be treated as a

And the

ONE WHO DOES NOT KNOW HOW TO ASK

you must open [the story] for him,
as it is said:

> "And you shall tell your child Ex. 13
> on that day,
> 'Because of this the Lord acted for me
> when I came out of Egypt.'"

---

throughout the generations, then even if it may not make total sense to me yet, if my forefathers kept this tradition, I will do so as well.

Now we understand the answer the Torah offers the wise son. Only after you understand the history of *avadim hayinu* which led to *matan Torah,* only then can you fully comprehend the beauty of the halakhot, of all of the customs and regulations of our religion. First, build the foundation and then, delve into the details.

THE DIFFERENCE BETWEEN THE WISE AND WICKED SON

One of the most famous questions asked with respect to the four sons is, what is the real difference between the inquiry of the wise son compared to the inquiry of the wicked son?

The Haggada tells us that the wicked son excludes himself, but actually, both seem to exclude themselves. The wise son uses the term *etkhem* and the wicked son uses the term *lakhem,* both of which are translated as "you."

We will offer a few explanations.

Rav Asher Weiss in *Haggadat Minhat Asher* (p. 85) suggests that the distinction lies not in the act of exclusion, but with respect to other terminology. The wise son inquires about the laws, the rules and regulations that were commanded with respect to the *korban pesah.* The wicked son, however, is not interested in the details.

Quite the

וְשֶׁאֵינוֹ יוֹדֵעַ לִשְׁאוֹל

אַתְּ פְּתַח לוֹ
שֶׁנֶּאֱמַר
וְהִגַּדְתָּ לְבִנְךָ שמות יג
בַּיּוֹם הַהוּא לֵאמֹר
בַּעֲבוּר זֶה עָשָׂה יהוה לִי
בְּצֵאתִי מִמִּצְרָיִם:

Yet the response offered in the Haggada is:

> וְאַף אַתָּה אֱמָר לוֹ כְּהִלְכוֹת הַפֶּסַח, אֵין מַפְטִירִין אַחַר הַפֶּסַח אֲפִיקוֹמָן.
> And you must tell him the laws of Pesah: "After eating the Pesah offering one does not eat anything more."

Why is the *pasuk,* which serves as the source of the question posed by the wise son, followed by the response in the Torah, *avadim hayinu lePharaoh beMitzrayim,* "we were slaves to Pharaoh in Egypt"? How does that answer his question?

The wise son wants to understand halakha to understand the relevant laws and customs. Why is the response in the Torah a lesson in Jewish history, that *avadim hayinu* (we were slaves)?

Rav Moshe explains that in order to properly learn Torah, one must have the proper perspective about the *mesora* and our chain of transmission. People less connected to Judaism reject certain practices because they do not seem relevant or logical. If there's no backbone, no foundation of *emuna,* faith, of believing in Jewish history, that we are a chain in the link that has passed along our tradition from the times of Moshe Rabbenu, then one may feel as if they can reject a custom or rule. If I believe in Jewish authenticity

Hazal tell us that only after Avraham is told to halt his knife and spare the child does he inquire as to why God requested this in the first place. There is a time to ask, but first, one acts out of trust and faith. (See more on this topic in the introduction, "Understanding *Hukat HaPesah.*")

The *hakham* inquires, *ma ha'eidut vehahukim?* What are the rules and regulations? He is trying to understand it, to appreciate it. He first performs the rituals, and only after completing them, he inquires to gain a better understanding.

The *rasha*'s attitude is, what is this *avoda* that you are performing? I don't understand it! I don't like it! It does not make sense to me, so I will not do it. That's not called commitment.

I once heard an idea related to this, in connection to the Sifri on *Parashat Vezot Haberakha*. The Sifri says that HaKadosh Barukh Hu approached all the nations of the world offering them the Torah prior to approaching Am Yisrael. Each nation asked what was written in the Torah. Hashem explained to each, it includes "do not kill," "do not steal," "do not covet." After learning of the contents of the Torah, each nation rejected it. When Hashem approached Am Yisrael, they responded, *naaseh venishma*. They accepted it without inquiring as to its contents.

A question is asked: Why didn't Hashem tell the other nations about the more attractive mitzvot? If God would have told them about love your neighbor as you love yourself or about the mitzva of charity, they may have been more open to accepting the Torah. Why did Hashem share only restrictions that they would consider difficult to accept?

The answer is that once the other nations inquired as to what is written in the Torah, Hashem concluded that they did not deserve the Torah, and did not want to make it attractive to them. A commitment cannot be based on "we'll accept it if it appeals to us." The nations should have agreed to accept the Torah because it was divinely written, no matter what it contained.

Once Am Yisrael agreed unequivocally and unconditionally to accept the Torah by stating *naaseh venishma*, Hashem knew these were

His chosen

Quite the opposite. He questions all this *avoda*. What is all this commotion that revolves around the *korban pesah*? Who needs all this?

The wicked son says, I can be a good Jew by feeling close to God in my heart. I do not need to labor and invest a great deal of effort in the performance of all these commandments. That is not what our religion is all about.

Feelings are great, but the performance of specific actions are a prerequisite to the fulfillment of our obligations as a Jew. We are servants of God. Our commitment cannot be expressed solely in our thoughts. It must be implemented in action.

Panim Yafot

A related idea is offered by the *Panim Yafot,* the Baal Haflaah, whose commentary on the Haggada appears at the end of *Sefer Shemot.*

He suggests that perhaps the difference between the *hakham* and *rasha* is related to the uniqueness of *naaseh venishma.*

What is the definition of a servant? Someone who does the will of his master even without understanding why.

The most famous example of this is the *Akeda*. Hashem asked Avraham Avinu to sacrifice his son. Avraham Avinu likely thought to himself, "Wait a second, last week Hashem told me, this is the son from whom you will build a great nation. This is the son who will yield so many children like the stars and the sand; you will be unable to count them. Did I hear correctly? Did He just tell me to sacrifice this son?"

What was Avraham's response? Avraham didn't say a word and just followed orders: *vayashkeim Avraham baboker*. Avraham woke up in the morning, which means he was able to sleep the night before. If we have a difficult day coming up we can't sleep the night before. Yet Avraham was content with his decision to follow God's instructions even if it did not make sense to him, and even if it meant losing the son for whom he waited 100 years!

The *hakham* asks, what can I do for God? He wants to understand the relevant rules so that he can better serve his Creator. The wise son has the attitude of JFK who so famously declared, "Ask not what your country can do for you; ask what you can do for your country." In short, be a provider, not a recipient.

Unfortunately, many people reject religion because they determine that it will not bring them any benefit nor personal satisfaction. They have the attitude of "what's in it for me?"

The better perspective is to show appreciation to our Creator for having granted us everything we have, and to ask ourselves what more we can do to demonstrate gratitude.

Including God's Name

Rav Melech Schachter once shared an alternative explanation with me. The *hakham* inserts one word which is lacking from the *rasha*'s statement. Which word is that? The *hakham* mentions Hashem.

What's the significance?

When you mention someone's name, you're highlighting their importance. When someone's name is singled out, it provides them with a certain level of respect and recognition.

Two proofs that he offered as evidence of this point are as follows. In the episode of the spies, Rashi cites a *gemara* in Sota 35a that explains what transpired when Kalev began to defend Moshe. To gain the people's attention, Kalev initiates his speech with the following statement: "You know what this individual, ben Amram, did for us?"

Everybody responded, you tell us! Everybody thought he would say something negative.

Instead, Kalev responded, "You know what he did? He gave us the *mann*, the *be'er*, wonderful things."

Why did the people think Kalev would say something derogatory about Moshe Rabbenu? It was the way Kalev introduced his thought. He stated, *vehi zu bilvad asah lanu, ben Amram* (You think this is the only thing ben Amram has done to us?).

The listeners thought he meant it in a negative way because he did not say Moshe. He said "ben Amram." He didn't reference Moshe

by name,

His chosen people. We had communicated, do not know what's in it, but we trust you. That is the proper attitude of a servant of God.

This is essentially the same way the *hakham* is acting. He engages in the performance of mitzvot because he has full faith and belief in God. Only afterwards does he gain a deeper understanding of the regulations.

Rhetorical Question?

Rabbi Lord Jonathan Sacks *z"l*, in his Haggada (p. 39), points out that in the Torah, the *hakham*'s statement is prefaced with the words *ki yishalkha binkha*, when your son will *ask* you. The preface to the *rasha*'s statement in the Torah is *vehaya ki yomru aleikhem*, when your sons will *state*. The *rasha* is *not* inquiring. Rather, he is making a statement. At times, people ask questions without being interested in receiving a response. The question is rhetorical, or being asked simply to ridicule.

That's what the *rasha* is doing. He's not truly asking anything. What is this *avoda*, this foolishness? It is a burden. Not the activities with which a "free man" should busy himself! His statement is preceded with the words "will state," not "will ask." He's not asking; he is making a declaration!

However, freedom is not to do what you like. It's to do what you ought. This is incomprehensible to the *rasha*. That is why we do not provide the *rasha* with an answer. We just inform him that he would not have merited being saved. He is not asking a serious question and is not seeking an answer, so we do not bother providing him with one.

Responsibility vs. Privilege

Rabbi Norman Lamm (*The Royal Table*, p. 41) distinguishes between the comment of the wise son, which portrays responsibility, and that of the wicked son, which depicts privilege. The *rasha* inquires, what's in it for me? What does Judaism offer me? Does it make me feel good? Do I understand it easily? Will it be inspiring to me? That type of attitude of "what's in it for me" is of the wicked son. Instead, what should be asked is, what does the world expect of me?

Mind, p. 87) interprets the term ההוא גברא, "that person." This phrase is often used in the Talmud to self-depict a person who transgresses. By referring to himself in the third person, it is as if the transgressor was not himself. In contrast, when referring to oneself in a positive manner the term אנא, "I," is used.

She'eino yode'a lishol, at petah lo

Why do we use a *lashon nekeva,* the feminine gender *"at,"* in reference to addressing the child who does not know how to ask?

Rav Zilberstein in *Haggadat Hashukei Hemed* suggests that in our generation, in order to have a positive influence on those less connected to Judaism, we need to take a soft approach. This is symbolized by the use of the feminine gender, as the mother is usually the more sympathetic and sensitive parent.

Rav Yitzchak Zilberstein cites an interaction that he experienced once as he exited a *shiur*. He encountered an Israeli soldier, a paratrooper. The Rav saw from his negative glance that he was anti-religious. Rav Zilberstein thought to himself, how can I connect with this lost soul?

He then approached the soldier and said, "I am so jealous of you." Puzzled, the soldier asked why. The Rav explained that Rabbenu Yonah in *Shaarei Teshuva* writes that one's transgressions are forgiven at death: *mita mekhaperet al kol avonot.*

The Rav continued: Near-death situations also trigger fear, and lead one to realize that in certain situations, one can only rely on the mercy of the Almighty. Surely, as you jump out of a plane or face action in combat, you experience such life-threatening situations. What was it like? You achieved forgiveness in those moments. For that, I am envious of you!

The soldier smiled and asked the Rav when he would be giving his next *shiur*.

At times, the best way to pierce a skeptic is not through might, but with sensitivity. *At petah lo!* That's the attitude we ought to have in our generation.

YAKHOL

by name, showing that he doesn't give him respect. That's how Kalev got everybody's attention and got people to think, just for a moment, that he was on their side.

The second proof that illustrates how not using a name shows disrespect is from the *haftara* of *Mahar Hodesh*, the story of Yonatan and Shaul at a Rosh Hodesh feast. Shaul HaMelekh asks his son Yonatan about Dovid's whereabouts, but refers to him as Ben Yishai. The two go back and forth, with Shaul referring to Ben Yishai and Yonatan referring to his dear friend by his first name, Dovid.

The *hakham* mentions *shem Hashem*, God's name. When you mention a name, it shows an affinity, respect, and identification. That's the stark difference between the statement of the *hakham* and the *rasha*: an intentional and significant omission of God's name.

Defanging the Rasha

It seems quite harsh to direct a father to knock out his son's teeth. This cannot be meant to be taken literally! Rabbi Immanuel Bernstein (*Darkness to Destiny*, p. 56) emphasizes that a parent can never lose faith in a child. A parent cannot make the mistake of identifying the child with his words or deeds. Bad behavior is a product of other factors, perhaps exposure to bad influences or lack of understanding.

In this regard, "knocking out his teeth" is symbolic of seeing beyond his words to reach the root of the child, which is good. Change his speech. Debate with him. Yet recognize that he is not evil; rather, it is his misconception and the way in which he depicts his ideas that is wrong.

It is interesting to note that the *gematria* (numerical value) of the word *rasha* is 570 (ר = 200, ש = 300, ע = 70). If you subtract his teeth (שניו = 366), you are left with 204, which is the numerical value of… צדיק, a righteous individual.

The response to the *rasha* is in the third person, אלו היה שם, perhaps to highlight that this behavior is not becoming of him. Similarly, Rav Ahron Soloveichik (*Logic of the Heart, Logic of the*

וְהִגַּדְתָּ לְבִנְךָ

"AND YOU SHALL TELL YOUR CHILD" –

One might have thought
this meant from the beginning of the month.
And so it says, "on that day."
Had it said only "on that day,"
one might have thought [the obligation] applied during the day.
And so it also says, "Because of this" –
"because of *this*" can only be said
when matza and bitter herbs are there before you.

---

ability to inculcate the values and traditions that are transmitted on this momentous night.

SERVING HASHEM UNDER ALL CIRCUMSTANCES

You might think the mitzva of *sippur yetzi'at Mitzrayim* is from Rosh Hodesh. However, the Haggada tells us: *Talmud lomar bayom hahu,* "And so it says, 'on that day'" – the mitzva is only when there's matza and *maror* in front of us.

There is a beautiful *drush* quoted in the *Be'er HaHaim,* Rav Elimelech Biderman's Haggada.

Yakhol me'Rosh Hodesh: I might think I only have to serve Hashem when I'm feeling *hit'hadshut,* when I'm feeling newness or excitement. That is, at the beginning of something, on opening day, so to speak. I'm so into it on the first day of a new job, and even kids are excited on the first day of school. There's something special about beginnings. I might think I have to serve Hashem when there's *hit'hadshut,* but no, I must do so every day.

Yakhol mi'beod Yom. I might not feel *hit'hadshut,* freshness, on a daily basis, but I always need clarity, to maintain the brightness of daylight. *Lehagid baboker hasdekha.* I must praise God each morning.

Talmud Lomar, baavur zeh...besha'a sheyesh mata u'maror munahim lefanekha, "So it says, 'Because of this'...when matza and *maror* are there before you."

We have

וְהִגַּדְתָּ לְבִנְךָ

יָכוֹל מֵרֹאשׁ חֹדֶשׁ
תַּלְמוּד לוֹמַר: בַּיּוֹם הַהוּא.
אִי בַּיּוֹם הַהוּא יָכוֹל מִבְּעוֹד יוֹם
תַּלְמוּד לוֹמַר: בַּעֲבוּר זֶה.
בַּעֲבוּר זֶה לֹא אָמַרְתִּי
אֶלָּא בְּשָׁעָה שֶׁיֵּשׁ מַצָּה וּמָרוֹר מֻנָּחִים לְפָנֶיךָ.

יָכוֹל מֵרֹאשׁ חֹדֶשׁ – YAKHOL MEROSH HODESH

SEEING IS BELIEVING

Yakhol me'Rosh Hodesh? We may have thought that one should begin telling the story of the Exodus two weeks before the start of Pesah, since one is required to learn the laws of each holiday thirty days prior. Yet we are taught to tell the story *bayom hahu*, on that day. In fact, not only on that day, but specifically, when matza and *maror* are visibly before us.

Rabbi Israel Meir Lau (*Haggada Around the Seder Table*) explains that a picture is worth a thousand words. Human beings are visual learners. When we see something in front of us, it makes a big a difference.

Why is there something called "show and tell" in the younger grades? Because when something is in front of us, it makes more of an impression. When we have the props, so to speak, the matza, *maror*, and dips, we have a much more powerful learning tool. *Hazal* identified that the most prudent manner to convey the message is to have the *heftza shel mitzva* in front of us, thus utilizing visual aids to tell the story.

That is why it is specifically when we have all the props on our table that we engage in *sippur yetzi'at Mitzrayim*. They facilitate our

מִתְּחִלָּה

IN THE BEGINNING,

our ancestors were idol worshippers.

The doctor replies, the first patient happens to be sick, but you? Your father had this illness and your grandfather had this illness as well. It seems to pass from generation to generation, so I need to root it out. You have to be treated differently because I know where you're from, and I know where you have to get to.

Mit'hila ovdei avoda zara hayu avoteinu. HaKadosh Barukh Hu knows our forefathers, and He knows where we are going. HaKadosh Barukh Hu knew that in order to be able to become Am Yisrael, to be a light unto the nations, we needed to be purified. We needed to go through a *shibud* Mitzrayim in order to gain the proper perspective.

We recognize that HaKadosh Barukh Hu was in charge of the whole process. He put us in Egypt because he knew it was in our DNA to have negative inclinations. We acknowledge it was all for our benefit.

MODERN FORMS OF *AVODA ZARA*

There is a dispute in the Gemara (Pesahim 116a) regarding how to interpret the idea of *mat'hil begnut umesayem beshevah*. The Gemara explains the statement in the mishna that declares that we should begin the Haggada with the negative aspects and complete it on a positive note.

Which negative aspects should we recall? Rav and Shmuel argue as to whether the negative aspects of the exile relate to our physical bondage in Egypt or to the spiritual bondage into which we fell. In actuality, we tell both.

We start with the Seder with *avadim hayinu*. We were enslaved. Then, we reference that we were idol worshippers, *ovdei avoda zara*.

When we

מִתְּחִלָּה
עוֹבְדֵי עֲבוֹדָה זָרָה הָיוּ אֲבוֹתֵינוּ

We have to serve Hashem also when there's no *hit'hadshut* and when there's no *yom,* but rather only darkness, even when we have the matza and the *maror* mixed together. Throughout history, we conducted the Seder when our nation was under tremendous oppression and we felt far from being a free people. Sometimes we have to host a Seder when people are in pain, having recently lost a close relative, and the Seder brings back many family memories.

That is the meaning of *besha'a sheyesh matza u'maror lefanekha,* that we fulfill the mitzvot not just in happy and exciting times. In every situation we have to serve Hashem.

מִתְּחִלָּה עוֹבְדֵי עֲבוֹדָה זָרָה – MIT'HILA OVDEI AVODA ZARA

NECESSARY PROCESS

We thank Hashem for taking us out of Mitzrayim, yet if you think about it, He is the one who put us there in the first place! He sent us down to Mitzrayim, so why are we so thankful? Shouldn't it be obvious that He is the one to redeem us as well?

Rav Shlomo Kluger in his *Haggada Imrei Shefer* explains as follows. Our forefathers were idol worshippers. In this paragraph, we acknowledge that in order to totally cleanse ourselves from idolatry and form a nation, the entire enslavement in Mitzrayim was a necessary step in the process.

Rav Kluger provides an allegory. Two individuals with the same symptoms visit a doctor. To one person, the doctor provides a certain medication, and to the other, he prescribes a much stronger dosage. The second patient says, I don't understand. We have the same symptoms, so why did you give me a stronger dosage?

BUT NOW

the Omnipresent has drawn us close in His service;
as it is said:
"Yehoshua said to all the people, *Josh. 24*
'This is what the LORD God of Israel has said:
Beyond the river your ancestors always dwelled –
Terah the father of Avraham, the father of Nahor –
and they served other gods.
But I took your father Avraham from beyond the river,
and I led him all the way across the land of Canaan,
and I multiplied his offspring and gave him Yitzhak.
And to Yitzhak I gave Yaakov and Esav,
and I gave Esav Mount Seir as an inheritance,

WHILE YAAKOV AND HIS CHILDREN WENT DOWN TO EGYPT.'"

If I value pleasing my boss or clients over all else, that is a form of *avoda zara*! *Avoda zara* can also be addiction to certain forms of social media. All of these objects detract from our focus on the Almighty and on the performance of mitzvot, and as such, may be labeled as a modern iteration of idolatry.

We have to realize that we serve only one being, and that's God. Therefore, *mit'hila,* we used to serve *avoda zara,* but *akhshav,* now, at our Seder, when we have the right focus, let's abandon these forms of idolatry and *keirvanu Hamakom le'avodato,* let us focus on HaKadosh Barukh Hu.

Let us contemplate what distracts us and consider how to minimize the noise that diverts our attention, so our focus can be directed toward properly serving our Creator.

BARUKH SHOMER

וְעַכְשָׁו

קֵרְבָנוּ הַמָּקוֹם לַעֲבוֹדָתוֹ, שֶׁנֶּאֱמַר

וַיֹּאמֶר יְהוֹשֻׁעַ אֶל־כָּל־הָעָם, כֹּה־אָמַר יהוה אֱלֹהֵי יִשְׂרָאֵל יהושע כד

בְּעֵבֶר הַנָּהָר יָשְׁבוּ אֲבוֹתֵיכֶם מֵעוֹלָם

תֶּרַח אֲבִי אַבְרָהָם וַאֲבִי נָחוֹר, וַיַּעַבְדוּ אֱלֹהִים אֲחֵרִים:

וָאֶקַּח אֶת־אֲבִיכֶם אֶת־אַבְרָהָם מֵעֵבֶר הַנָּהָר

וָאוֹלֵךְ אוֹתוֹ בְּכָל־אֶרֶץ כְּנָעַן

וָאַרְבֶּ אֶת־זַרְעוֹ, וָאֶתֶּן־לוֹ אֶת־יִצְחָק:

וָאֶתֵּן לְיִצְחָק אֶת־יַעֲקֹב וְאֶת־עֵשָׂו

וָאֶתֵּן לְעֵשָׂו אֶת־הַר שֵׂעִיר לָרֶשֶׁת אוֹתוֹ

וְיַעֲקֹב וּבָנָיו יָרְדוּ מִצְרָיִם:

When we relate to the fact that we were idolaters, we state *ovdei avoda zara hayu avoteinu, ve'akhshav keirvanu Hamakom le'avodato.* Back then, we worshipped idols, but now God brought us closer to Him, so we can worship Him.

The Lubavitcher Rebbe offers an important insight with respect to this statement. Why do we insert the word *ve'akhshav,* "now"? Why now? It has been thousands of years since we were idolators. *Hazal* tell us that the Great Assembly removed the evil inclination for idolatry (Sanhedrin 64). Why, then, the reference to the present time?

The unfortunate truth is that *avoda zara* remains a huge threat today, albeit in a different form. Today, we may not worship stone figures or celestial beings, but we do at times place infinite value in *avoda zara,* that is, in foreign forms. These objects may take the shape of currency, luxury items, or even our workplace.

BLESSED IS THE ONE WHO HAS KEPT HIS PROMISE TO ISRAEL –
blessed is He.
For the Holy One calculated the end
and fulfilled what He had spoken
to our father Avraham in the Covenant between the Pieces.

Rabbi Zalman Sorotzkin (*Oznayim LaTorah*) answers that only now in the twenty-first century do we understand this *pasuk* and *Hazal*. We did not understand it for thousands of years. Only now, after the Holocaust, is it clear to us.

There have been major controversies over the past decades about German reparations. One side abhors the idea of taking money from the Germans, as the Germans do not deserve to feel like money can cleanse them of their sins. Money cannot forgive the evil committed, and we will not allow them to feel absolved from the atrocities they committed. We cannot possibly put a monetary value on our fellow brethren who were murdered in cold blood.

The other camp believes that the Germans did enough injustice by murdering millions of Jews; they do not deserve to profit off of us as well. "Absolutely not," they say, "but at least give us our money back!"

The issue is a very murky one, yet this debate is not a new one. This is exactly what Bnei Yisrael felt as they were leaving Egypt. After 210 years of subjugation, some Jews felt that the least they deserved was the Egyptians' valuables, while the other side wanted nothing from the Egyptians. The issue was very unclear.

Hashem, therefore, requested of Bnei Yisrael to take the Egyptians' valuables. He did not use an objective, flat-out command. Instead, He requested it as a favor because there were many who wanted nothing from these murderers of their families.

Hashem saw that it would be hard for many of Bnei Yisrael to take anything from the Egyptians, as if taking Egyptian money was

putting

בָּרוּךְ שׁוֹמֵר הַבְטָחָתוֹ לְיִשְׂרָאֵל
בָּרוּךְ הוּא
שֶׁהַקָּדוֹשׁ בָּרוּךְ הוּא חִשַּׁב אֶת הַקֵּץ
לַעֲשׂוֹת כְּמָה שֶׁאָמַר לְאַבְרָהָם אָבִינוּ בִּבְרִית בֵּין הַבְּתָרִים

בָּרוּךְ שׁוֹמֵר – BARUKH SHOMER...

BORROWING MONEY FROM THE ENEMY

> דַּבֶּר־נָא בְּאָזְנֵי הָעָם וְיִשְׁאֲלוּ אִישׁ מֵאֵת רֵעֵהוּ וְאִשָּׁה מֵאֵת רְעוּתָהּ כְּלֵי־כֶסֶף וּכְלֵי זָהָב: (שמות יא:ב)
>
> Speak now in the ears of the people and let them ask every man of his friend and every woman of her friend jewels of silver and jewels of gold. (*Shemot* 11:2)

Why did Hashem use the word *na*, please, when telling Moshe to instruct Bnei Yisrael to take gold and silver vessels from the Egyptians before leaving Egypt?

Rashi explains that the term *na* connotes a request. He phrased it as a request so that Avraham would not claim that Hashem fulfilled only part of the *brit bein habetarim*: He kept His promise to enslave them, but His promise that they leave with riches, He did not fulfill. Hashem requested that Bnei Yisrael not forget to leave Egypt with these valuable items, so that Avraham would not have a complaint against only Him.

Now, this begs a basic question: Wouldn't Hashem keep His word anyway? Would Hashem really not have fulfilled the promise in its entirety if not for Avraham's potential complaint?

Additionally, the word *na* seems to suggest that Bnei Yisrael did not *want* to take the valuables, and that Hashem had to convince them to take the wealth. Why is that?

As it is said:
"He said to Avram, 'Know that your descendants will be strangers in a land not their own, and they will be enslaved and oppressed for four hundred years; but know that I shall judge the nation that enslaves them, *Gen. 15*

AND THEN THEY WILL LEAVE WITH GREAT WEALTH.'"

Pharaoh's whole plan had been to dehumanize Bnei Yisrael, to convince everyone that the blood of Israel was cheap, but Hashem showed the Egyptians what kind of people we really are, the most refined nation, the only nation who would feed its own captors. Ultimately, at the time of the Exodus from Egypt, Bnei Yisrael had won favor in their eyes. From their perspective, Bnei Yisrael had indeed become "friends."

In truth, the whole purpose of the plagues was to bring the Egyptians to recognize Hashem, and that Am Yisrael is His chosen nation. The mellowing of their negative feelings was a fulfillment of that purpose.

THE TEACHING STAFF

The Midrash tells us that magic was so rampant in Egypt that any Egyptian child could turn a stick into a snake (Menahot 85b). In that case, why did Hashem command Moshe and Aharon to perform something that even a five-year-old Egyptian could do?

The *Be'er Yosef* (*Shemot*, p. 208) quotes this question from the Midrash with an additional famous question from the Rambam's *Hilkhot Teshuva* 6:5. Why were the Egyptians punished for enslaving Bnei Yisrael if it was preordained that they would be in a land that was not theirs and be subjugated by its ruling? Hashem told Avraham about this at the *brit bein habetarim*. Why was Egypt punished for simply following Hashem's orders?

The Raavad ↰

שֶׁנֶּאֱמַר

בראשית טו וַיֹּאמֶר לְאַבְרָם יָדֹעַ תֵּדַע כִּי־גֵר יִהְיֶה זַרְעֲךָ בְּאֶרֶץ לֹא לָהֶם
וַעֲבָדוּם וְעִנּוּ אֹתָם אַרְבַּע מֵאוֹת שָׁנָה׃
וְגַם אֶת־הַגּוֹי אֲשֶׁר יַעֲבֹדוּ דָּן אָנֹכִי
וְאַחֲרֵי־כֵן יֵצְאוּ בִּרְכֻשׁ גָּדוֹל׃

---

putting a price on their murdered babies. He couldn't force them to do it. Instead, He just requested it, in the name of Avraham Avinu.

The Netziv (*Haamek Davar, Shemot* 11:2) questions the wording of the *pasuk*. Why does the Torah say, *me'et re'ehu*, "from his friend"? The Netziv asks, were Bnei Yisrael and the Egyptians friends? "From his master," "from his persecutor" maybe…but "friend"?

The Netziv points out that earlier, the Torah uses a different description for the Egyptians, referring to "each woman will ask of her *neighbor*" (*Shemot* 3:22). The Torah does not use the term "friend" at that point.

The Netziv explains that initially, the Egyptians were definitely not friends with the Jews. Far from it! However, during the twelve months that the plagues took place, the Egyptians developed somewhat of a relationship with the Jewish people. They did not exactly become friends, but due to the miraculous display of the plagues, the Egyptians slowly started changing their tune.

During the plague of wild animals, some Egyptians actually sought refuge in Goshen. They saw the writing on the wall, so to speak, and over the course of the plagues, the unpleasant relationship between the Egyptians and Bnei Yisrael started to wane.

An element that furthered this positive change occurred during the plague of darkness. One might wonder how the Egyptians didn't starve during the three days of darkness which froze them in their places. The only reason they did not is because Bnei Yisrael came and fed them. Unbelievable!

The matzot are covered and the wine cup is raised.

וְהִיא שֶׁעָמְדָה

AND THIS

[promise] is what has stood
by our ancestors and us;
for it was not only one man who rose up to destroy us:
in every single generation people rise up to destroy us –

וְהִיא שֶׁעָמְדָה – VEHI SHE'AMDA

EVERY GENERATION?

Rav Aharon Kotler asks, what does this mean: *Ela shebekhol dor vador omdim aleinu lekhaloteinu,* "In every single generation people rise up to destroy us"? Was there *never* a generation in which the nations of the world didn't want to kill us? Hasn't there been at least a couple of years of respite from this hatred of Am Yisrael?

Rav Kotler says, you have to look at the next paragraph to understand this concept. *Vehi she'amda* is followed by the paragraph of *tzei ulemad ma bikeish Lavan haArami laasot leYaakov Avinu,* go out and learn what Lavan desired to do to Yaakov our forefather. Do you know what Lavan did to Yaakov? Pharaoh sought to kill the male Jews, but Lavan wanted to destroy *all* of Judaism.

Were the years that Yaakov spent with Lavan really so terrible? Yaakov had four wives, eleven children, worked hard, and earned a living. What was so terrible? Even though on the surface it appeared as if all was well, deep down Lavan wished he could destroy Yaakov.

We need to learn from the experience with Lavan. Even when things appear all right, in each generation, nations seek to annihilate us, *omdim aleinu lekhaloteinu*. Even in generations where there appears to be tranquility, other nations either plot unsuccessfully against us, or seek to annihilate us not through physical means, but rather, by doing all they can to degrade our spirituality.

VEHAKADOSH

The מצות are covered and the wine cup is raised.

וְהִיא

שֶׁעָמְדָה לַאֲבוֹתֵינוּ וְלָנוּ
שֶׁלֹּא אֶחָד בִּלְבָד עָמַד עָלֵינוּ לְכַלּוֹתֵנוּ
אֶלָּא שֶׁבְּכָל דּוֹר וָדוֹר עוֹמְדִים עָלֵינוּ לְכַלּוֹתֵנוּ

The Raavad and Ramban answer that while Hashem allowed the Egyptians to subjugate Bnei Yisrael, He had not given permission for the Egyptians to torture and murder them. The Egyptians went far beyond what God had decreed, and that's why they were held responsible for their actions.

Since the Egyptians knew about this decree and felt justified in torturing Bnei Yisrael, it was very possible that they did not believe that Hashem was going to punish them. Therefore, Hashem told Moshe and Aharon to take their staff and turn it into a snake.

A staff is something with no inherent power. Its power is completely dependent on the power of its wielder. It is merely a means used to achieve a result. It's a tool. Hashem, therefore, wanted to hint to the Egyptians that while they were supposed to be Hashem's "tool" and follow His commands, they still acted independently, like a snake does. Their terrible actions had nothing to do with what Hashem wanted them to do.

The *Be'er Yosef* adds that if the Egyptians had not gone beyond Hashem's decree and added to the torture, they would not have been punished for enslaving Bnei Yisrael. That's what the staff was meant to teach them: they were only supposed to be the staff of Hashem and not do more. Like the snake, they did what they wanted to do, beyond Hashem's decree.

BUT THE HOLY ONE, BLESSED BE HE, SAVES US FROM THEIR HANDS.

The wine cup is put down and the matzot are uncovered.

Many nations ruled over us and yet no longer exist. We have outlived our enemies solely because it is God's desire. *Am levadad yishkon*: we're alone, we've always been alone, but we have a friend upstairs. *VeHaKadosh Barukh Hu matzilenu miyadam*. The hardship, ironically, leads us to the revelation that God loves us and protects us.

Famously, Mark Twain, a non-Jewish American nineteenth-century writer, wrote an essay "Concerning the Jews" and makes this same amazing observation with respect to the survival of the Jewish nation:

> *He has made a marvelous fight in this world, in all the ages; and has done it with his hands tied behind him. He could be vain of himself, and be excused for it. The* Egyptian, *the* Babylonian, *and the* Persian *rose, filled the planet with sound and splendor, then faded to dream-stuff and passed away; the* Greek *and the* Roman *followed, and made a vast noise, and they are gone; other peoples have sprung up and held their torch high for a time, but it burned out, and they sit in twilight now, or have vanished. The Jew saw them all, beat them all, and is now what he always was, exhibiting no decadence, no infirmities of age, no weakening of his parts, no slowing of his energies, no dulling of his alert and aggressive mind. All things are mortal but the Jew; all other forces pass, but he remains. What is the secret of his immortality?*

We recognize this reality from the inside and thank Hashem for it at this point in the Seder.

VEHI SHE'AMDA

וְהַקָּדוֹשׁ בָּרוּךְ הוּא מַצִּילֵנוּ מִיָּדָם

The wine cup is put down and the מצות *are uncovered.*

וְהַקָּדוֹשׁ בָּרוּךְ הוּא מַצִּילֵנוּ מִיָּדָם –
VEHAKADOSH BARUKH HU MATZILENU MIYADAM

PORTRAYAL OF HIS LOVE

The Avudraham in his *Seder Haggada* posits that the way HaKadosh Barukh Hu shows that He still loves us is by at times inflicting us with hardship. He states:

> **להראות השגחתו בישראל מקים להם בכל דור ודור אויבים ומציל אותם מידם.**
>
> To portray His protection over Israel, in every generation He creates enemies of Israel and saves us from their hands.

If we would be on cruise control all the time, nothing happening to us, just another nation on planet Earth with nobody bothering us, how would we know HaKadosh Barukh Hu loves us?

It is the salvations that remind us that we have a special relationship with Him.

Rav Yaakov Emden says that the greatest miracle in the history of the world is that the Jewish people have survived throughout it all. This a greater miracle than even *yetzi'a*t *Mitzrayim* or the Splitting of the Sea! It is a constant miracle.

In virtually every generation, other nations blame us for their issues. We are everyone's scapegoat. Yet notwithstanding their desire to annihilate us, the Almighty one above protects us and ensures our survival.

I once heard another idea about *vehi* from Rav Rafael Pelcovitz, based on the words of the *Meshekh Hokhma* at the beginning of *Parashat Vaera*. When we recite *vehi she'amda,* our custom is to lift up our cups of wine. The reference of *vehi,* "this," is to the cup of wine that we lift.

Wine holds a special position in rabbinic literature. The Rabbis targeted wine more than any other food or beverage in terms of setting boundaries between ourselves and the non-Jewish world around us. It is the rabbinical directives, *mitzvot d'rabbanan,* like those of *yein nesekh,* that kept us separate and distinct from our enemies.

Yein nesekh, the prohibition of drinking wine handled by a non-Jew, and other halakhot such as *pat akum* and *bishul akum,* prohibitions of eating baked and cooked items of non-Jews, are all to protect us from getting too close to other nations, and God forbid, intermarrying.

Historically, whenever there was a group of Jews who threw away the *takanot* and *gezerot d'rabbanan,* the following generation generally disappeared as Jews. In their infinite wisdom, our Rabbis understood the boundaries that needed to be implemented to protect us from assimilation.

At the Seder, we raise our cups in tribute to those edicts, and affirm that indeed it is those regulations that have protected the authenticity of the Jewish nation throughout the generations.

FOR LACK OF UNITY

The Sefat Emet, quoted in the *Asapra Kevodkha, al pi drush* offers a beautiful explanation of the underlying meaning of this paragraph. By inserting a few commas, we uncover a deeper understanding.

Shelo ehad,

VEHI SHE'AMDA – WHAT IS THE *VEHI*?

How are we to interpret the term *vehi*, "and this"?

The simple answer is that it relates to the previous paragraph which discussed the *brit bein habetarim*. Hashem is keeping His promise that He made to Avraham Avinu, and that promise is the secret of our survival.

The *Haggada Migdolei Yerushalayim* focuses on the last line of that paragraph: *ve'aharei khen yetzu birkhush gadol*, "after this, they went out with great wealth." On the simple level, this describes the great wealth that we accumulated when we left Egypt, but perhaps there is a deeper understanding.

What are the *real* assets of a Jew? At the end of our lives, we do not focus on how large our houses are, or how many funds remain in our bank accounts. Rather, what is important to us is our Torah and mitzvot. *Lo bemoto yikakh hakol, lo yered aharav kevodo*, "They will take nothing with them in death; their esteem will not descend with them" (*Tehillim* 49:18) – when one passes on, he does not take his assets with him.

After experiencing *yetzi'at Mitzrayim*, our most valuable asset was the spiritual heights that we achieved through the process and our connection to HaKadosh Barukh Hu. That's the meaning of *vehi*. This connection, this *emuna*, is *vehi she'amda*. This uncompromising commitment to and reliance on HaKadosh Barukh Hu are the assets that help us through exiles and constant oppression.

This is also alluded to in the letters of *vehi*, which is spelled *vav, hei, yud, alef*. The letter *vav* alludes to six volumes of Mishna; *hei*, five books of the *Humash*; *yud*, ten *dibrot*, and *alef*, the one above, Hashem. That is the *vehi she'amda* that has carried us throughout our history.

Moshe, in naming his son Gershom, was thanking Hashem for helping him hold onto his identity in Midian when he was surrounded by pagans. He was thanking Hashem for helping him retain his feeling of being a *ger* and not assimilating into those impure surroundings.

Moshe easily could have been elected an official in Midian. He was charismatic, powerful, and smart. Yet he chose not to assimilate. Rather, he stayed separate as an outsider, so he could stay loyal to Hashem and not succumb to the temptations around him.

Therefore, says Rav Moshe, he named his first son Gershom. It was only because Moshe maintained his identity and loyalty to Hashem throughout his sojourn in Midian that he could retroactively thank Hashem for saving him from Pharaoh.

Had Moshe been saved from Pharaoh's hand only to succumb to the impurities of Midian, his salvation would have been for naught. Only because he remained apart from everyone in Midian, he became able to look back and see that it had been worthwhile to save him. Thus, he named his second son Eliezer.

This is also the message to those who left Mitzrayim. If Hashem saw fit to redeem them, then they must act to fulfill the trust that had been bestowed upon them.

The message for our generation, the generation immediately following the greatest tragedy in the history of our nation, is evident. We have to ask ourselves: Why were we chosen to carry the torch out of the ashes of the Holocaust?

If we are strong in our observance of mitzvot throughout this exile, then the salvation was indeed worthwhile. The test is the generation after the tragedy. If we remain loyal to our heritage, then retroactively, we can say we have been worthy of such a miracle as having been saved.

Shelo ehad, the fact that we're not one, we're not united, *bilvad,* for that reason alone we have experienced so many atrocities. *Omdim aleinu lekhaloteinu,* due to the fact that there are rifts within the Jewish nation, this is why our enemies are victorious over us.

Hashem cannot tolerate the inner fighting within Am Yisrael just as a parent despises hostility among his or her children. Let us each do our share to spread tolerance and respect our differences, so we can unite as a people and merit a complete redemption.

LESSONS FROM THE NAMES OF MOSHE'S CHILDREN

As we approach the climax of *Maggid* and start singing our praises of God, we must recognize the awesome responsibility that befalls all those who are redeemed and merit salvation.

This is echoed in the insightful words of Rav Moshe Feinstein (*Darash Moshe,* p. 120). We are informed that Moshe Rabbenu had two sons, Gershom and Eliezer. Why did Moshe name his sons outside of the chronological order of the events which are referenced by the names? The event for which he named Eliezer, when he was saved from Pharaoh's sword after he killed an Egyptian, happened before that of Gershom, when he became a stranger in the foreign land of Midian. Chronologically speaking, Moshe should have named his first son Eliezer, and then his second son Gershom.

Even more astonishing is why Moshe would want to memorialize the event that led to the naming of Gershom. He was living in a strange land, away from Klal Yisrael, and surrounded by temptation. Wouldn't he want to forget that time? Instead, he named his son after it!

צֵא וּלְמַד

GO [to the verse]

AND LEARN

what Lavan the Aramean
sought to do to our father Yaakov:
Pharaoh condemned only the boys to death,
but Lavan sought to uproot everything,

as it is written:

"AN ARAMEAN SOUGHT MY FATHER'S DEATH, *Deut. 26*
AND HE WENT DOWN TO EGYPT
AND RESIDED THERE,
JUST A HANDFUL OF SOULS;
AND THERE HE BECAME A NATION –
LARGE, MIGHTY, AND GREAT."

Now we can understand the segue of the preceding paragraph. *Ve'HaKadosh Barukh Hu matzilenu miyadam. Tzei ulemad,* go learn the Lavan story. Yaakov did not realize it, and we may not realize it either: While in *galut,* the seeds of *geula* are being sowed.

WHAT WAS SO TERRIBLE ABOUT LAVAN?

We are told that Lavan was worse than Pharaoh. What acts did he perform that were so terrible?

Kill the messenger: In order to explain Lavan's actions, Maharal Diskin cites a *gemara* (Nazir 12a) that declares how if a man appoints a messenger to betroth a women on his behalf without specifying a particular woman, and the messenger dies before the man is informed of whether or not the messenger fulfilled his mission and which woman he spoke with, the man who sent the messenger is forbidden to marry.

The reason

צֵא וּלְמַד

מַה בִּקֵּשׁ לָבָן הָאֲרַמִּי
לַעֲשׂוֹת לְיַעֲקֹב אָבִינוּ
שֶׁפַּרְעֹה לֹא גָזַר
אֶלָּא עַל הַזְּכָרִים
וְלָבָן בִּקֵּשׁ לַעֲקֹר אֶת הַכֹּל

שֶׁנֶּאֱמַר

דברים כו אֲרַמִּי אֹבֵד אָבִי
וַיֵּרֶד מִצְרַיְמָה, וַיָּגָר שָׁם בִּמְתֵי מְעָט
וַיְהִי־שָׁם לְגוֹי גָּדוֹל עָצוּם וָרָב

צֵא וּלְמַד – TZEI ULEMAD

RECOGNIZING THE *GEULA*

What's the connection between this paragraph and the previous one? The last line of the previous paragraph is *ve'HaKadosh Barukh Hu matzilenu miyadam*. Then we say *tzei ulemad,* go out and learn.

The Lekah Tov, quoting from Rav Yehezkel Levenstein, suggests that in life, we often lack the ability to fully comprehend what we experience. We do not realize that the *geula* is transpiring before our very eyes. Often, we may feel it is just the opposite.

Yaakov Avinu escapes his brother and arrives at the home of Lavan. Yaakov must have feared the worst. How would things turn out while under the auspices of Lavan? He likely did not fathom the birth of a nation, the beginning of the twelve tribes. The seeds of the *geula* may be planted even while one feels buried in exile!

"AND HE WENT DOWN TO EGYPT" –
Compelled by what had been spoken.

"AND RESIDED THERE" –
From this, learn that our father Yaakov went down
not to be absorbed into Egypt,
but only to reside there for a time.
As it is said:
"They said to Pharaoh, *Gen. 47*
'We have come to *reside* in this land,
for there is no pasture for your servants' flocks,
for the famine is heavy in the land of Canaan;
and now, if you please,
let your servants dwell in the land of Goshen.'"

---

daughters, the children are my children" (Bereshit 31:43). Your kids are my kids! With that statement, Lavan was trying to blur the lines between Am Yisrael and the other nations. That would have been it! We would not have been able to survive with blurred lines. Losing our Jewish identity would lead to assimilation, and the end of the Jewish people.

LEAVING ONE'S COMFORT ZONE

The Lubavitcher Rebbe asks in his Haggada, why is it necessary to include the word *tzei,* go out? It would have sufficed to just state *lemad,* learn. What does the word *tzei* add?

In the Haggada, the statement precedes a section of quotes and interpretations of *pesukim* from the Torah. The Lubavitcher Rebbe explains that the word *tzei* is hinting to us that we should have a certain attitude when we learn Torah. At times, one hears a halakha *shiur* or learns a new law and reacts negatively, saying: What I have been doing is correct. This new idea must be a stringency. I can

ignore it.

וַיֵּרֶד מִצְרַיְמָה
אָנוּס עַל פִּי הַדִּבּוּר

וַיָּגָר שָׁם
מְלַמֵּד שֶׁלֹּא יָרַד יַעֲקֹב אָבִינוּ
לְהִשְׁתַּקֵּעַ בְּמִצְרַיִם, אֶלָּא לָגוּר שָׁם
שֶׁנֶּאֱמַר
וַיֹּאמְרוּ אֶל־פַּרְעֹה בראשית מז
לָגוּר בָּאָרֶץ בָּאנוּ
כִּי־אֵין מִרְעֶה לַצֹּאן אֲשֶׁר לַעֲבָדֶיךָ
כִּי־כָבֵד הָרָעָב בְּאֶרֶץ כְּנָעַן
וְעַתָּה יֵשְׁבוּ־נָא עֲבָדֶיךָ בְּאֶרֶץ גֹּשֶׁן׃

The reason for this restriction is that, since we do not know who the messenger betrothed on behalf of this individual, we fear that he may in the future marry his betrothed's sister, which would be entering into a prohibited relationship.

The midrash tells us that Lavan sought to poison Eliezer, the messenger Avraham sent to find a wife for Yitzhak. The cup of poison Lavan designated for Eliezer was switched with the cup of Betuel, Lavan's father. Had Lavan been successful in poisoning Eliezer, Yitzhak would have been prohibited to marry, since the messenger would have been killed before Avraham would have known whether or not a women was in fact selected. This would have prevented Am Yisrael from coming into being.

Assimilation: The Imrei Emet, one of the Gerer rebbes, offers the following explanation. After Yaakov abruptly leaves Lavan's home and is chased by Lavan, Lavan asks Yaakov, why are you running away? *Habanot benotai, vehabanim bnai,* "The daughters are my

"JUST A HANDFUL OF SOULS" –
As it is said:
"Your ancestors were but seventy souls *Deut. 10*
when they went down to Egypt –
and now the LORD has made you
as many as the sky has stars."

"AND THERE HE BECAME A NATION" –
From this, learn that Israel was distinct there.

"LARGE, MIGHTY" –
As it is said:
"And the children of Israel were fertile, *Ex. 1*
and they swarmed,
and grew *more and more numerous*
and strong, and the land was filled with them."

---

her rabbi to inquire as to whether this was an extra stringency or an actual requirement. After she was told it is in fact a halakhic requirement, she immediately requested that all of their utensils be immersed in a local *mikve,* despite the hardship. She acted in a noble fashion, allowing halakha to shape her life and implementing a *tzei ulemad* approach. She acted upon what she learned immediately.

Bikkurim

Rav Yosef Dov Soloveitchik, in *Harerei Kedem* (vol. 2, p. 219), emphasizes that the selection of *Arami Oved Avi* (from *Parashat Ki Tavo*), which is recited when one brings *bikkurim* (first fruits) to the *Beit HaMikdash,* is included in the Haggada as it is an expression of gratitude, *hakarat hatov.*

The Mishna

בִּמְתֵי מְעָט

כְּמָה שֶׁנֶּאֱמַר
דברים י בְּשִׁבְעִים נֶפֶשׁ יָרְדוּ אֲבֹתֶיךָ מִצְרָיְמָה
וְעַתָּה שָׂמְךָ יהוה אֱלֹהֶיךָ
כְּכוֹכְבֵי הַשָּׁמַיִם לָרֹב:

וַיְהִי־שָׁם לְגוֹי

מְלַמֵּד שֶׁהָיוּ יִשְׂרָאֵל מְצֻיָּנִים שָׁם

גָּדוֹל עָצוּם

כְּמָה שֶׁנֶּאֱמַר
שמות א וּבְנֵי יִשְׂרָאֵל פָּרוּ וַיִּשְׁרְצוּ וַיִּרְבּוּ
וַיַּעַצְמוּ בִּמְאֹד מְאֹד
וַתִּמָּלֵא הָאָרֶץ אֹתָם:

---

ignore it. However, we must be honest with ourselves regarding our *avodat Hashem*.

We all have preconceived notions of what we think is correct and what we think "should be" the halakha. *Tzei ulemad,* whenever we learn something, we have to *go out* of our comfort zone, leaving behind our assumptions and preconceived notions, and have an open heart and mind to seek the truth.

About twenty years ago, I gave a *shiur* on the topic of *tevilat keilim,* the requirement to immerse dishes made by a non-Jew in a *mikve*. One of my students informed me that the next day, all day, he was busy immersing all of his family's dishes, pots, cutlery, and so forth into a *mikve*. Apparently, he told his mother what we had learned and his mother, who was unfamiliar with this halakha, contacted

"AND GREAT" –

As it is said:

"I let you *grow wild* like meadow plants, *Ezek. 16*
and you grew and matured and came forth in all your glory,
your breasts full and your hair grown,
and you were naked and exposed."

Some add:

"And I passed by you *Ibid.*
and saw you wallowing in your own blood –
and I said to you, 'In your blood, live!'
and I said, 'In your blood, live!'"

---

week on which certain holidays will fall on a given year based on the days of Pesah. For example, the first day of Pesah (א) falls on the same day as ת – Tisha Be'Av. The second day of Pesah (ב) falls on the same day as ש – Shavuot. The third day of Pesah (ג) falls on the same day as ר – Rosh HaShana. Using this methodology there is a connection between Seder night and Tisha Be'Av. This was the date of the transgression of the spies.

Rav Yohanan (Taanit 28a) declares that on this night (the Ninth of Av) we cried for no reason, therefore God gave us something serious to cry about. This is why we emphasize the act of bringing *bikkurim* on this night – to try to rectify the lack of gratitude and recognition that we exhibited long ago.

This idea can help us understand another peculiarity found in the Haggada. Earlier, in *Ha Lahma Anya,* we state: *Leshana haba'a be'ara D'Yisrael* – "Next year in Israel." Usually, we reference "next year in Jerusalem." Tonight we refer to the land of Israel as a whole, perhaps due to the connection between the Seder and the spies, highlighting our appreciation of the entire land of Israel, not just a connection to Jerusalem.

וָרָב

כְּמָה שֶׁנֶּאֱמַר

יחזקאל טז
רְבָבָה כְּצֶמַח הַשָּׂדֶה נְתַתִּיךְ
וַתִּרְבִּי וַתִּגְדְּלִי, וַתָּבֹאִי בַּעֲדִי עֲדָיִים
שָׁדַיִם נָכֹנוּ וּשְׂעָרֵךְ צִמֵּחַ, וְאַתְּ עֵרֹם וְעֶרְיָה:

Some add:

שם
וָאֶעֱבֹר עָלַיִךְ וָאֶרְאֵךְ מִתְבּוֹסֶסֶת בְּדָמָיִךְ
וָאֹמַר לָךְ בְּדָמַיִךְ חֲיִי וָאֹמַר לָךְ בְּדָמַיִךְ חֲיִי:

The Mishna in *Bikkurim* (3:1) states: "How should one separate the first fruits? A person descends to his field, sees a fig tree, a cluster [of grapes], or a pomegranate tree that has budded, and ties them with a reed."

Why does the Mishna single out the fruits of these three species: figs, grapes, and pomegranates? It is fascinating to note that these are identical to the three fruits that were brought back by the spies, as is stated in *Bemidbar* 13:23 – "They came to the Eshkol Ravine and there they cut down a vine branch, and on it one cluster of grapes, which they carried on a pole between two men."

In *Hidushei HaGarmaz* (Rav Menachem Ziemba, *siman* 50), the Arizal is cited as suggesting that the imperative of *Bikkurim* is a *tikkun* (correction) for the transgression of the spies. The Torah lists the same fruits that the spies rejected as examples of why we should express our gratitude for the land of Israel. One can suggest that there is a further connection between the transgression of the spies and Seder night. The *Shulhan Arukh* (RH 428:3) claims that by utilizing the *atbash* code (א"ת ב"ש) – a parallelism between the first and last letters of the alphabet – one can derive the day of the

"AND THE EGYPTIANS DEALT CRUELLY WITH US AND OPPRESSED US, AND IMPOSED HARD LABOR ON US." *Deut. 26*

"THE EGYPTIANS DEALT CRUELLY WITH US" –
As it is said:
"We must act wisely against [this people], *Ex. 1*
in case it grows great,
and when we are called to war
they may join our enemies,
fight against us,
and rise up to leave the land."

---

regarding Onkelos, what was "Yosef's decree" that the new king "did not uphold"?

The *Be'er Yosef* explains that Pharaoh had one goal: to subjugate, enslave, and torture Bnei Yisrael. The problem with his plan, though, was the positive feelings of his nation toward Yosef's family and descendants. After all, Yosef had saved them from starvation. How could Pharaoh convince his people to hate Bnei Yisrael and agree that his plan was of national importance? Yosef undoubtedly went down in history as a great person, but now Pharaoh wanted to repay his goodness with evil.

Pharaoh's first step was to uproot the laws Yosef established. When Yosef ruled Egypt during the years of famine, he sold food to the Egyptians, and as they ran out of money and then all possessions that they could use to purchase food, Yosef compelled the Egyptians to sell themselves as slaves to Pharaoh.

Additionally, Yosef forced them to uproot themselves and move to different parts of the land to show that they did not own the land,

but that

דברים כו

וַיָּרֵעוּ אֹתָנוּ הַמִּצְרִים
וַיְעַנּוּנוּ
וַיִּתְּנוּ עָלֵינוּ עֲבֹדָה קָשָׁה:

וַיָּרֵעוּ אֹתָנוּ הַמִּצְרִים
כְּמָה שֶׁנֶּאֱמַר
שמות א
הָבָה נִתְחַכְּמָה לוֹ פֶּן־יִרְבֶּה
וְהָיָה כִּי־תִקְרֶאנָה מִלְחָמָה
וְנוֹסַף גַּם־הוּא עַל־שֹׂנְאֵינוּ
וְנִלְחַם־בָּנוּ
וְעָלָה מִן־הָאָרֶץ:

וַיָּרֵעוּ אֹתָנוּ הַמִּצְרִים – VAYARE'U OTANU HAMITZRIM

ANTISEMITIC TACTICS

How was Pharaoh able to convince the Egyptians to turn against the Jewish people even after Yosef was loved by all? They owed everything to Yosef, who had navigated them through a harsh famine and saved their lives.

The *Be'er Yosef* (*Shemot*, p. 180) offers an insight based on a *pasuk* in *Sefer Shemot*. We are told that a "new" king arose in Egypt. Rashi explains based on a *gemara* in Sota 11a that the "new king" might have been either a new king literally, or in fact the same old king whose decrees were "renewed." Onkelos translates the verse as follows: "A new king arose over Egypt who did not uphold Yosef's decree" (*Shemot* 1:8).

What is Rashi referring to when he describes the decrees as being "renewed"? The decrees were presumably *new*, not *renewed*! And

"AND OPPRESSED US" –
As it is said:
"They placed taskmasters over [the people] Ex. 1
to *oppress* them under their burdens;
they built store cities for Pharaoh:
Pithom and Raamses."

"AND IMPOSED HARD LABOR ON US" –
As it is said:
"The Egyptians enslaved the children of Israel Ex. 1
with *heavy labor.*"

"foreigners," were again given the status of second-class citizens, eventually becoming the slaves.

Based on this, says the *Be'er Yosef,* we can understand the next *pasuk* in a more profound way.

וַיֹּאמֶר אֶל־עַמּוֹ הִנֵּה עַם בְּנֵי יִשְׂרָאֵל רַב וְעָצוּם מִמֶּנּוּ. (שמות א:ט)

> He told his nation that the people of Israel are more plentiful and mightier than us. (*Shemot* 1:9)

In this *pasuk,* the word *rav* can mean "numerous" or "master." Pharaoh meant that Bnei Yisrael had been the masters over the Egyptians for long enough. It was time to turn the table.

Now we can also understand an interesting passage in the Haggada. In the *tzei ulemad* section, each word of the four *pesukim* recited when bringing *bikkurim* (*Devarim* 26:5–8) is expounded upon. The Haggada, based on the *Sifrei,* explains the phrase *vayare'u otanu haMitzrim,* the Egyptians were evil to us, by quoting our *pasuk* about Pharaoh strategizing to outsmart Bnei Yisrael.

How does

וַיְעַנּוּנוּ

כְּמָה שֶׁנֶּאֱמַר
וַיָּשִׂימוּ עָלָיו שָׂרֵי מִסִּים שמות א
לְמַעַן עַנֹּתוֹ בְּסִבְלֹתָם
וַיִּבֶן עָרֵי מִסְכְּנוֹת לְפַרְעֹה
אֶת־פִּתֹם וְאֶת־רַעַמְסֵס:

וַיִּתְּנוּ עָלֵינוּ עֲבֹדָה קָשָׁה

כְּמָה שֶׁנֶּאֱמַר
וַיַּעֲבִדוּ מִצְרַיִם אֶת־בְּנֵי יִשְׂרָאֵל בְּפָרֶךְ: שמות א

---

but that all land was owned by Pharaoh. The only people this law did not apply to were Bnei Yisrael who lived in Goshen. Thus, the natives became strangers, and the strangers became natives (see *Shemot* 47:19). This was all part of Yosef's plan to allow his family to settle in Egypt undisturbed by the Egyptians.

Now, Pharaoh stood up and incited his nation against the Israelites, telling them that Yosef's intentions were purely for his own benefit and that of his family. We are the real Egyptians, he claimed, and it's time for things to revert to what they were before Yosef came into power. You are an Egyptian if you were born here, and only you truly belong here! Anyone else is a stranger and has no rights here!

This is how the *Be'er Yosef* understands the word *nit'hadshu*, renewed. In order to be able to carry out his wicked plan against Klal Yisrael and to subjugate them, Pharaoh used flattery, telling his nation that none of them were really slaves. He "renewed" the law by making Bnei Yisrael the slaves, instead of the Egyptians. The law was not purely new, but it was reversed: Egyptians became free and could own land as they had previously, and Bnei Yisrael, the

"AND WE CRIED OUT TO THE LORD, *Deut. 26*
GOD OF OUR ANCESTORS,
AND THE LORD HEARD OUR VOICE,
AND HE SAW OUR OPPRESSION
AND OUR LABOR AND SLAVERY."

"AND WE CRIED OUT TO THE LORD,
GOD OF OUR ANCESTORS" –
As it is said:
"It came to be, as a long time passed, *Ex. 2*
that the king of Egypt died,
and the children of Israel
groaned under the burden of work,
and they *cried out,*
and their plea rose to God from amid the work."

That was Pharaoh's plan. That was where it all started. He made us appear as a subhuman. Following this statement, Pharaoh offers the "final solution" to the Jewish problem: they will multiply and overtake us unless we take drastic measures to prevent it. Let's slaughter their newborn babies to cease their ability to further proliferate.

This strategy has been emulated by antisemitic leaders throughout history: first demonize and dehumanize the Jewish people, then strip them of property and rights, and in the last stage, attack, enslave, and eradicate them. This is how *Hazal* understood *vayare'u otanu.*

MAKING US DESPAIR

The literal interpretation of the phrase *vayarei'u otanu hamitzrim* is that the Egyptians were evil to us. Rav Avraham Schorr (*HaLekah VeHalibuv*) offers a deeper explanation. *vayarei'u* refers to the Egyptian's making us feel bad about ourselves. They made us lose our feeling of self-worth. They wanted us to feel distraught and

despair

דברים כו

וַנִּצְעַק אֶל־יהוה אֱלֹהֵי אֲבֹתֵינוּ
וַיִּשְׁמַע יהוה אֶת־קֹלֵנוּ
וַיַּרְא אֶת־עָנְיֵנוּ וְאֶת־עֲמָלֵנוּ וְאֶת־לַחֲצֵנוּ:

וַנִּצְעַק אֶל־יהוה אֱלֹהֵי אֲבֹתֵינוּ
כְּמָה שֶׁנֶּאֱמַר

שמות ב

וַיְהִי בַיָּמִים הָרַבִּים הָהֵם
וַיָּמָת מֶלֶךְ מִצְרַיִם
וַיֵּאָנְחוּ בְנֵי־יִשְׂרָאֵל מִן־הָעֲבֹדָה
וַיִּזְעָקוּ
וַתַּעַל שַׁוְעָתָם אֶל־הָאֱלֹהִים מִן־הָעֲבֹדָה:

How does this prove anything? This *pasuk* does not explain how the Egyptians were evil to us; rather, it describes their fears of the evil that *we* might do to *them*.

Rabbi Immanuel Bernstein (*Darkness to Destiny: The Haggada Experience*, p. 82) says in the name of the Beit HaLevi on *Parashat Shemot* that the Haggada does not interpret *vayare'u otanu hamitzrim* to mean "the Egyptians were evil to us." Rather, he says that it means "the Egyptians made us out to be evil." The Beit Halevi explains that our enemies seek to portray us as evil in every generation.

How do you wipe out a nation? It's not politically correct to order extermination of human beings. It just doesn't work. Yet if I'm able to create a sense that they're not really human beings, that they're really coming from the devil, and they're really a leech on society, then yes, I could kill leeches. Our enemies throughout history have tried to dehumanize us, to say that we do not have a right to live. Hitler utilized this strategy to justify inhumane acts.

"AND THE LORD HEARD OUR VOICE" –

As it is said:
"And God *heard* their groans, Ex. 2
and God remembered His covenant
with Avraham, Yitzhak, and Yaakov."

"AND HE SAW OUR OPPRESSION" –

The separation of husband from wife,
as it is said:
"And God saw the children of Israel, Ex. 2
and God knew."

"AND OUR LABOR" –

[The killing of] the sons,
as it is said:
"Throw every boy who is born into the river, Ex. 1
and the girls let live."

---

an object. The Kotzker homiletically extends this verse to one who is in a state of depression or despair. He places the comma in a different place and declares: *ye'ush, shelo midaat*. If somebody gives up hope, it's because *shelo midaat*: he is not thinking properly! Thus we must never despair.

וְאֶת־עֲמָלֵנוּ – VE'ET AMALENU

REWARD FOR SAVING INFANTS

As the *pesukim* continue, we *darshen* the trials and tribulations we experienced in Mitzrayim. The Haggada references *et amalenu, eilu habanim*. This refers to the sons, as it states: *kol haben hayilod haye'orah tashlikhuhu*, throw all the male infants into the river.

The Beit Halevi

וַיִּשְׁמַע יהוה אֶת־קֹלֵנוּ

כְּמָה שֶׁנֶּאֱמַר
וַיִּשְׁמַע אֱלֹהִים אֶת־נַאֲקָתָם שמות ב
וַיִּזְכֹּר אֱלֹהִים אֶת־בְּרִיתוֹ
אֶת־אַבְרָהָם אֶת־יִצְחָק וְאֶת־יַעֲקֹב:

וַיַּרְא אֶת־עָנְיֵנוּ

זוֹ פְּרִישׁוּת דֶּרֶךְ אֶרֶץ
כְּמָה שֶׁנֶּאֱמַר
וַיַּרְא אֱלֹהִים אֶת־בְּנֵי יִשְׂרָאֵל שמות ב
וַיֵּדַע אֱלֹהִים:

וְאֶת־עֲמָלֵנוּ

אֵלּוּ הַבָּנִים
כְּמָה שֶׁנֶּאֱמַר
כָּל־הַבֵּן הַיִּלּוֹד, הַיְאֹרָה תַּשְׁלִיכֻהוּ שמות א
וְכָל־הַבַּת תְּחַיּוּן:

---

despair: *ye'ush*. You are a slave. You have no independence and never will have a meaningful life.

In *Pirkei Avot* (2:13) we are taught, *al tehi rasha bifnei atzmekha,* do not view yourself negatively. The great Hasidic Rebbe the Kotzker once said that we need to avoid falling into a state of *ye'ush shelo midaat*: unintentional despair. He alluded to a halakhic statement in Bava Metzia 21b, relating to the despair one expresses after losing

"AND SLAVERY" –
The forced labor that was pressed down on them,
as it is said:
"I have seen the *slavery* *Ex. 3*
that Egypt forced upon you."

"AND THE LORD BROUGHT US OUT OF EGYPT *Deut. 26*
WITH A STRONG HAND
AND AN OUTSTRETCHED ARM,
IN AN AWESOME HAPPENING,
WITH SIGNS AND WITH WONDERS."

The Beit Halevi says, what was Pharaoh trying to accomplish by killing only the boys? He did not want to destroy the Jewish people per se, as the descendants of the Jewish mothers would remain Jewish. However, there would be no more *kohanim, levi'im,* or *yisraelim.* There would be no more *malkhut,* which all flow from the father. Had Pharaoh been successful, the essence of Judaism would have been wiped out, although there would still be "Jews" from Jewish mothers.

That's why Shifra and Puah were granted *batei kehuna* and *batei levia.* That's the *midda keneged midda.* They saved the *yichus* and the *malkhut* because that's what's passed through the males. These women saved the patrilineal aspects of Judaism.

LO AL

וְאֶת־לַחֲצֵנוּ

זֶה הַדְּחַק
כְּמָה שֶׁנֶּאֱמַר
שמות ג וְגַם־רָאִיתִי אֶת־הַלַּחַץ
אֲשֶׁר מִצְרַיִם לֹחֲצִים אֹתָם׃

דברים כו **וַיּוֹצִאֵנוּ יהוה מִמִּצְרַיִם**
בְּיָד חֲזָקָה וּבִזְרֹעַ נְטוּיָה
וּבְמֹרָא גָּדֹל
וּבְאֹתוֹת וּבְמֹפְתִים׃

The Beit Halevi quotes a Rashi (*Shemot* 1:21) that relates to the boys who were meant to be killed. The midwives Shifra and Puah devised a plan to prevent the murder of the infants. In return, they were rewarded with *batei kehuna* and *batei levia,* houses of *kohanim* and *levi'im*. The Beit Halevi asks, how is being granted children that are *kohanim* and *levi'im* related, *midda keneged midda,* to their pious acts of saving the lives of the children?

The Beit Halevi explains: if somebody has a Jewish mother, they're Jewish. That means that Judaism is a religion of matrilineal descent. Yet *yichus,* whether one is a *kohen, levi,* or *yisrael,* that goes by the father. If a Jew has a mother who is a *bat kohen,* but his father is a *yisrael,* he is a *yisrael*. The father determines the *shevet* as well.

"AND THE LORD BROUGHT US OUT OF EGYPT" –
Not through an angel,
not through a seraph,
not through any emissary.
No, it was the Holy One, His glory, His own presence.
As it is said:
"I shall pass through the land of Egypt on that night; *Ex. 12*
I shall kill every firstborn son in the land of Egypt,
man and beast,
and I shall pass judgment on all the gods of Egypt:
I am the Lord."
"I shall pass through
the land of Egypt on that night" – I and no angel.
"I shall kill every firstborn son in
the land of Egypt" – I and no seraph.
"And I shall pass judgment on all
the gods of Egypt" – I and no emissary.
"I am the Lord" – It is I and no other.

---

the following: God must be a *kohen,* since it states *veyik'hu li teruma,* that *teruma* should be taken for Him as is done for *kohanim*. If so, how could he have buried Moshe and become impure? The response provided in the Gemara is that for first-degree relatives, a *kohen* is allowed to become impure, and we are considered God's children, as is stated, *banim atem LeHashem.*

The *Nahalat Yaakov,* the commentary on *Masekhet Semahot,* then comments, how did Hashem perform the plague of the death of the firstborn? The midrash says that He performed the plague Himself, not through an angel. So how did Hashem "impurify himself"? Hashem was killing Egyptians who are not considered *banim atem LeHashem,* first degree relatives from which *kohanim* would be prohibited.

Due to the connection between the chapter regarding a person on his death-bed and the section regarding whether *makat bekhorot*

וַיּוֹצִאֵנוּ יהוה מִמִּצְרַיִם.

לֹא עַל יְדֵי מַלְאָךְ
וְלֹא עַל יְדֵי שָׂרָף
וְלֹא עַל יְדֵי שָׁלִיחַ
אֶלָּא הַקָּדוֹשׁ בָּרוּךְ הוּא בִּכְבוֹדוֹ וּבְעַצְמוֹ
שֶׁנֶּאֱמַר
שמות יב וְעָבַרְתִּי בְאֶרֶץ־מִצְרַיִם בַּלַּיְלָה הַזֶּה
וְהִכֵּיתִי כָל־בְּכוֹר בְּאֶרֶץ מִצְרַיִם
מֵאָדָם וְעַד־בְּהֵמָה
וּבְכָל־אֱלֹהֵי מִצְרַיִם אֶעֱשֶׂה שְׁפָטִים
אֲנִי יהוה:

וְעָבַרְתִּי בְאֶרֶץ־מִצְרַיִם	אֲנִי וְלֹא מַלְאָךְ
וְהִכֵּיתִי כָל־בְּכוֹר	אֲנִי וְלֹא שָׂרָף
וּבְכָל־אֱלֹהֵי מִצְרַיִם אֶעֱשֶׂה שְׁפָטִים	אֲנִי וְלֹא הַשָּׁלִיחַ
אֲנִי יהוה	אֲנִי הוּא וְלֹא אַחֵר

לֹא עַל יְדֵי מַלְאָךְ – LO AL YEDEI MALAKH

***MAKAT BEKHOROT* – TWO-STAGE PROCESS**

At the beginning of *Masekhet Semahot* there is a *baraita* that describes *makat bekhorot*. Hashem smote the firstborn men at midnight, but they didn't die until the morning. Why is this *baraita* placed at the beginning of *Masekhet Semahot,* which deals mainly with the laws and customs of mourning?

The first line of the *masekhet* discusses a *goses,* a person on his deathbed, who is yet considered a live person until he actually dies. What is the connection between the *baraita* relating to the plague of the firstborn and this first line that deals with a *goses*?

There is a *gemara* in *Masekhet Sanhedrin* 39 where a heretic asked

"WITH A STRONG HAND" –
This refers to the pestilence,
as it is said:
"You shall see the *hand* of the LORD *Ex. 9*
among your cattle in the field,
among your horses and donkeys and camels,
in the herd and in the flock,
bringing harsh, heavy pestilence."

"AND AN OUTSTRETCHED ARM" –
This refers to the sword,
as it is said:
"And His sword was drawn in His hand, *1 Chron. 21*
stretched out over Jerusalem."

"IN AN AWESOME HAPPENING" –
This refers to the revelation of His Presence,
as it is said:
"Has any god ever tried to come *Deut. 4*
and take a nation out of the midst of another,
with trials
and with signs
and wonders,
in war
and with a strong hand,
with an outstretched arm,
inspiring *great awe,*
as the LORD your God has done all this
for you in Egypt, before your eyes?"

---

the morning. Hashem carried out the infliction Himself, but did not "become impure" since the firstborn did not die at that moment, but only the following morning.

בְּיָד חֲזָקָה

זוֹ הַדֶּבֶר
כְּמָה שֶׁנֶּאֱמַר
הִנֵּה יַד־יהוה שמות ט
הוֹיָה בְּמִקְנְךָ אֲשֶׁר בַּשָּׂדֶה
בַּסּוּסִים בַּחֲמֹרִים בַּגְּמַלִּים
בַּבָּקָר וּבַצֹּאן
דֶּבֶר כָּבֵד מְאֹד:

וּבִזְרֹעַ נְטוּיָה

זוֹ הַחֶרֶב
כְּמָה שֶׁנֶּאֱמַר
וְחַרְבּוֹ שְׁלוּפָה בְּיָדוֹ דברי הימים א׳ כא
נְטוּיָה עַל־יְרוּשָׁלָיִם:

וּבְמֹרָא גָּדֹל

זֶה גִּלּוּי שְׁכִינָה
כְּמָה שֶׁנֶּאֱמַר
אוֹ הֲנִסָּה אֱלֹהִים לָבוֹא לָקַחַת לוֹ גוֹי מִקֶּרֶב גּוֹי דברים ד
בְּמַסֹּת בְּאֹתֹת וּבְמוֹפְתִים וּבְמִלְחָמָה
וּבְיָד חֲזָקָה, וּבִזְרוֹעַ נְטוּיָה
וּבְמוֹרָאִים גְּדֹלִים
כְּכֹל אֲשֶׁר־עָשָׂה לָכֶם יהוה אֱלֹהֵיכֶם בְּמִצְרַיִם לְעֵינֶיךָ:

---

occurred at night or in the morning, we can derive a viable explanation. There was a two-stage process with respect to *makat bekhorot.* Hashem inflicted the Egyptians at night, but they only perished in

"WITH SIGNS" –

This refers to the staff,
as it is said:
"Take this staff in your hand, *Ex. 4*
and with it you shall perform the *signs*."

"AND WITH WONDERS" –

This refers to the blood,
as it is said:
"I shall make *wonders* *Joel 3*
in the sky and on the earth –

A drop of wine is spilled from the cup as each wonder is mentioned:

**BLOOD, AND FIRE,
AND PILLARS OF SMOKE."**

דָּבָר אַחֵר Another interpretation:

"With a strong hand" –	Two.
"And an outstretched arm" –	Two.
"In an awesome happening" –	Two.
"With signs" –	Two.
"And with wonders" –	Two.

וּבְאֹתוֹת

זֶה הַמַּטֶּה
כְּמָה שֶׁנֶּאֱמַר
וְאֶת־הַמַּטֶּה הַזֶּה תִּקַּח בְּיָדֶךָ שמות ד
אֲשֶׁר תַּעֲשֶׂה־בּוֹ אֶת־הָאֹתֹת:

וּבְמֹפְתִים

זֶה הַדָּם
כְּמָה שֶׁנֶּאֱמַר
וְנָתַתִּי מוֹפְתִים יואל ג
בַּשָּׁמַיִם וּבָאָרֶץ

A drop of wine is spilled from the cup as each wonder is mentioned:

דָּם וָאֵשׁ וְתִימְרוֹת עָשָׁן:

דָּבָר אַחֵר

בְּיָד חֲזָקָה שְׁתַּיִם
וּבִזְרֹעַ נְטוּיָה שְׁתַּיִם
וּבְמֹרָא גָּדֹל שְׁתַּיִם
וּבְאֹתוֹת שְׁתַּיִם
וּבְמֹפְתִים שְׁתַּיִם

THESE WERE THE TEN PLAGUES
that the Holy One brought
upon Egypt,
and these are they –

A drop of wine is spilled from the cup as each plague, and each of the acronyms, Detzakh, Adash and Be'ahav, is mentioned:

BLOOD	FROGS
LICE	WILD ANIMALS
PESTILENCE	BOILS
HAIL	LOCUSTS

DARKNESS
THE STRIKING DOWN OF THE FIRSTBORN.

Rabbi Yehuda grouped these under acronyms –
DETZAKH, ADASH, BE'AHAV.

---

a single punishment. He explains that a person can sin so gravely that his *teshuva* is withheld and is not accepted by Hashem. Pharaoh reached this level of grave sin, so Hashem hardened his heart, preventing him from doing *teshuva* and thus ensuring that all of the plagues would come to pass (Rambam, *Hakdama LeMasekhet Avot: Shemona Perakim*, *perek* 8, and *Hilkhot Teshuva* 6:3).

Sforno (*Shemot* 7:3) has a different insight, stating that Pharaoh had the free will to do *teshuva* all the way up until the plague of the death of the firstborn.

Hashem wants humans to do *teshuva*, as it says, "'By My life,' says Hashem, 'I do not want the wicked to die, but for the wicked to repent from his ways and live!'" (*Yehezkel* 33:11). Hashem therefore increased His miracles and wonders in Egypt so the Egyptians

would return

אֵלּוּ עֶשֶׂר מַכּוֹת
שֶׁהֵבִיא הַקָּדוֹשׁ בָּרוּךְ הוּא
עַל הַמִּצְרִים בְּמִצְרַיִם
וְאֵלּוּ הֵן

A drop of wine is spilled from the cup as each plague, and each of the acronyms, דְּצַ"ךְ, עֲדַ"שׁ *and* בְּאַחַ"ב, *is mentioned:*

דָּם צְפַרְדֵּעַ
כִּנִּים עָרוֹב
דֶּבֶר שְׁחִין
בָּרָד אַרְבֶּה
חֹשֶׁךְ מַכַּת בְּכוֹרוֹת.

רַבִּי יְהוּדָה הָיָה נוֹתֵן בָּהֶם סִימָנִים
דְּצַ"ךְ עֲדַ"שׁ בְּאַחַ"ב

אֵלּוּ עֶשֶׂר מַכּוֹת – ELU ESER MAKOT

THE PURPOSE OF THE PLAGUES

וַאֲנִי אַקְשֶׁה אֶת־לֵב פַּרְעֹה וְהִרְבֵּיתִי אֶת־אֹתֹתַי וְאֶת־מוֹפְתַי בְּאֶרֶץ מִצְרָיִם. (שמות ז:ג)

And I will harden Pharaoh's heart and multiply My signs and My wonders in the land of Egypt. (*Shemot* 7:3)

Commentators have different understandings of the purpose of the plagues. The Rambam maintains that all of the plagues formed to recognize the various ways of fulfilling this custom, each way filled with meaning and symbolism.

The most common reason we pour out some wine is to symbolize the concept of *binfol oyvekha al tismah*, "Do not rejoice when your enemy falls" (*Mishlei* 24:17). Even when our enemies are getting punished, we should not celebrate. We drink a cup of wine, but we pour some out to lessen our happiness.

Rav Schachter in his Haggada states that this *pasuk*, *binfol oyvekha*, which is in *Mishlei*, also appears in *Pirkei Avot* when Shmuel Hakatan said, *binfol oyvekha al tismah* (*Avot* 4:19). This is the only *pasuk* in *Avot* that is phrased as a statement by an individual. Why is this cited as his statement if it is already a verse in *Mishlei*?

The answer is that Shmuel Hakatan lived *binfol oyvekha al tismah*. This was his essence. His every motion was governed by the service of God, and for him, nothing was personal or self-motivated.

This is why Shmuel Hakatan was the only one who was fit to write the *berakha* of *velamalshinim*, the nineteenth *berakha* requesting that the slanderers who generate so much trouble for Jews be punished. He was the only one who could write it *lishma*. He received no personal satisfaction by his enemy falling, even though it was someone who was endangering Am Yisrael. His only satisfaction was that there would be no more desecration of Hashem's name.

Rav Schachter suggests we should all try to develop this attitude. We should keep in mind that wanting our enemies to suffer is a highly improper character trait, even when it comes to non-Jewish enemies who persecuted us for so many years. We do not drink *lehaim* to their demise. Instead, we drink *lehaim* to our own freedom.

Rabbi Oelbaum, in a commentary on Rambam's *Hilkhot Teshuva*, writes that is why we celebrate Purim a day after our military victory, when we rested from the war, and not on the day we actually won the war. We're celebrating the day of peace because we can go back to serving HaKadosh Barukh Hu. We do not celebrate the enemies' loss, rather our freedom to once again freely worship our Master.

TZEFARDE'A

would return to him. Accordingly, the plagues were not only for Bnei Yisrael, but also for the Egyptians, to bring them to *teshuva*.

According to Sforno's approach, how can we explain the hardening of Pharaoh's heart? How was he expected to do *teshuva* if his heart had been hardened by Hashem against just that?

Sforno explains that *teshuva* can take one of two forms: *teshuva* out of fear and *teshuva* out of recognition of Hashem. There is no doubt, Sforno says, that if Hashem hadn't hardened Pharaoh's heart, leveling the playing field a little bit, Pharaoh would have sent Bnei Yisrael out earlier, not because of any feelings of humility or repentance, but only to alleviate his own suffering. Yet this would have gone against the purpose of the plagues, so Hashem hardened Pharaoh's heart.

Nevertheless, the possibility of doing real *teshuva* out of true recognition of Hashem remained opened to Pharaoh until the end. If Pharaoh would have wanted to humble himself and do *teshuva*, nothing would have stood in his way.

Thus, the hardening of Pharaoh's heart, according to Sforno, did not remove his ability to do *teshuva*. It removed the possibility that he would repent out of fear of suffering, but left open the option of doing sincere *teshuva*.

MAKOT – PLAGUES

Many have a *minhag* of spilling out a bit of the wine while reciting the ten *makot*.

There are different variations on the *minhag*. Some use the pinky because they want to take out only a little bit. Others use the fourth finger, which is the finger associated with *kemitza*, the *avoda* of the *korban minha*.

A third custom is to use the second finger because it is *etzba elokim*. Some people prefer not to stick any fingers into their cup and just tip their cup and spill some wine from the side. It is fascinating

Rav Shimshon Pincus (*Tiferet Shimshon*, p. 61) takes this one step further and says that when we react out of anger, we're ultimately hurting ourselves. Every time we react in anger, hoping it will affect someone else, it really boomerangs and we just hurt ourselves. This is the reality of every situation of anger. The Egyptians were angry and reacted in anger, which only made the situation worse.

If we stop and do not retaliate when we're angry, the situation will usually calm down. Reacting and responding to a situation tends to escalate and worsen it. Every time we feel ourselves getting angry, we should remember the Egyptians hitting the frog, and realize that it is only logical to stop before we get out of control.

Rav Pincus suggests that this reality applies to all of the plagues: If the Egyptians would have just let us go, they could have stopped getting hit by plagues and spared themselves a lot of pain. Each time they hit us, they were in actuality hitting themselves! They brought the plagues upon themselves through their stubbornness and poor *middot*.

This is true for all of us. We have to realize that everything is sent our way for a purpose, and that if we react in anger, we're just hurting ourselves.

A story is told of a rabbi who kept what he referred to as an "anger jacket." Whenever he would get angry, he would put on this anger jacket. He kept this anger jacket on the third floor of his house. By the time he climbed three flights and reached his anger jacket, a few minutes had passed, and he realized he was no longer as angry as he had initially been.

We need to take a deep breath and calm down rather than immediately react, to ensure that we do not overreact, or say or do something that we may regret later.

In a correspondence between the Rambam and Rav Ovadia the *ger*, the Rambam addresses a debate that Rav Ovadia had with his rabbi about the status of Muslims (*Iggeret LeRav Ovadia Hager, Birkat Moshe*, p. 233).

The Rambam writes that Muslims are not idolaters because even if they believe in a false prophet, they do not believe in a false God.

Moreover,

צְפַרְדֵּעַ – *TZEFARDE'A* (FROGS)

ANGER MISMANAGEMENT

> וַיֹּאמֶר יהוה אֶל־מֹשֶׁה אֱמֹר אֶל־אַהֲרֹן נְטֵה אֶת־יָדְךָ בְּמַטֶּךָ עַל־הַנְּהָרֹת עַל־הַיְאֹרִים וְעַל־הָאֲגַמִּים וְהַעַל אֶת־הַצְפַרְדְּעִים עַל־אֶרֶץ מִצְרָיִם.
> (שמות ח:א–ב)
>
> Hashem said to Moshe: "Speak to Aharon: Stretch out your hand that holds your staff over the rivers, the canals, and the pools, and cause frogs to climb up and out onto the land of Egypt." So Aharon stretched out his hand over the waters of Egypt, and frogs climbed up and covered the Egyptian land. (*Shemot* 8:1–2)

Rashi points out that this pasuk switches from the plural *hatzefarde'im,* the frogs, to the singular *hatzefarde'a,* the frog. He quotes *Hazal,* who explain this discrepancy:

> צפרדע אחת היתה והיו מכין אותה והיא מתזת נחילים נחילים.
>
> There was one big frog, and every time the Egyptians hit it, it split and multiplied.

Rabbi Yaakov Yisrael Kanievsky, also known as the Steipler (*Birkat Peretz,* p. 28), asks a question: If the frog multiplied each time the Egyptians beat it, why did they continue to do so? It completely defies logic! They saw the consequences of their actions, so why didn't they just stop?

The Steipler explains that we see from here the power of anger. A person can become so angry that he begins to act irrationally. Then, despite the reality that stares him in the face, he cannot control his reaction. The Egyptians saw that it wasn't helping to hit the frog, but their anger made them unable to think straight and control themselves. And so, they kept on hitting!

Perhaps that it what is being alluded to in the *pasuk*:

> **וּמָלְאוּ בָּתֵּי מִצְרַיִם אֶת־הֶעָרֹב וְגַם הָאֲדָמָה אֲשֶׁר־הֵם עָלֶיהָ.** (שמות ח:יז)
>
> The houses of the Egyptians shall be full of swarms of animals, as well as the land upon which they appear. (*Shemot* 8:17)

The *pasuk* states that the homes will be full of the animals, and then adds, "as well as the land upon which they appear." This means that animals that came from different geographies required their specific habitat to survive, and they came along with a piece of their natural surroundings.

Another example that highlights a supernatural detail within a large plague is expressed in the *pasuk*:

> **הִנְנִי מַמְטִיר כָּעֵת מָחָר בָּרָד כָּבֵד מְאֹד אֲשֶׁר לֹא־הָיָה כָמֹהוּ בְּמִצְרַיִם לְמִן־הַיּוֹם הִוָּסְדָה וְעַד־עָתָּה.** (שמות ט:יח)
>
> Behold, tomorrow, about this time, I will cause it to rain a very grievous hail, such as that which has not been in Egypt, from the day it was founded even until now. (*Shemot* 9:18)

In connection with the plague of hail, Rashi explains that the words "tomorrow, about this time" teach us that Moshe made a scratch on the wall, creating a sort of sundial, and said that when the sun would reach that line on the wall, the plague of hail would begin. Why did he only draw this scratch on the wall for this one plague?

The Be'er Yosef explains that within the answer to this question lies the miracle: Since when is the sun out during a hailstorm? It was sunny and balmy in Egypt while the hail came down! During the storm, the sundial Moshe referenced was being utilized. This wasn't a typical hailstorm, but rather a miraculous plague from God.

These two examples highlight the supernatural aspects of the plague, clearly depicting the hand of Hashem and His miraculous ways.

Moreover, said the Rambam, Rav Ovadia should know that anyone who got angry at him over his past was in fact an idolater, as *Hazal* tell us, "View anyone who gets angry as an idolater." They will have to do *teshuva* for idolatry, says the Rambam, something Rav Ovadia who had converted to Judaism would not have to do!

From this letter, we see clearly that when a person is angry, they are considered an idolater, as they worship themselves in their anger.

The Rambam in *Hilkhot De'ot* (2:3) notes that though Hashem desires that we follow the middle path, there are two exceptions to this principle when we must go to the opposite extreme: the tendencies toward anger and arrogance. These traits must be annihilated completely. Let us learn from the words of the Rambam and the Steipler and refrain from exhibiting anger.

עָרוֹב – *AROV* (WILD ANIMALS)

LESSONS FROM THE NAME OF A PLAGUE

The Torah assigns names to most plagues and those titles describe their effect. The plague of *dam* was blood, *tzefarde'a* was frogs, and so on. Yet then we get to the plague of wild animals, and the Torah names the plague *arov,* which means "mixture."

Why didn't the Torah call it *hayot ra'ot,* "wild animals"? Instead, the Torah describes just an element of the plague: that it was a mixture of animals. What is so significant about that detail of mixing, such that the Torah actually refers to the plague by that name?

The Be'er Yosef (*Shemot,* p. 214) explains that the mixture of animals itself highlights the miraculous nature of this plague. As we know, all animals require a specific climate to survive. A polar bear, a camel, and a crocodile all need completely different climates. How did all these animals get to Egypt and survive there? It was actually a major part of the miracle: Hashem created the specific climates around each animal so that they could all exist in Egypt. That was the greatness of the plague of *arov*: the mixture itself.

> by the sword; there remained not so much as one of them. (*Shofetim* 4:16)

In these two places, *Hazal* explain that *ad ehad* means that nothing was left except for one. Regarding the Splitting of the Sea, this would mean that only one survivor remained from the Egyptians, and that was Pharaoh. With regards to the war against Sisera, everyone died except for one person: Sisera.

Here, too, says the Malbim, it must be that the *pasuk* intends that not a single animal died except for one. The Malbim suggests that the one animal that died belonged to a blasphemer, the son of an Israelite woman and an Egyptian man.

> וַיֵּצֵא בֶּן־אִשָּׁה יִשְׂרְאֵלִית וְהוּא בֶּן־אִישׁ מִצְרִי בְּתוֹךְ בְּנֵי יִשְׂרָאֵל וַיִּנָּצוּ בַּמַּחֲנֶה בֶּן הַיִּשְׂרְאֵלִית וְאִישׁ הַיִּשְׂרְאֵלִי: וַיִּקֹּב בֶּן־הָאִשָּׁה הַיִּשְׂרְאֵלִית אֶת־הַשֵּׁם וַיְקַלֵּל וַיָּבִיאוּ אֹתוֹ אֶל־מֹשֶׁה וְשֵׁם אִמּוֹ שְׁלֹמִית בַּת־דִּבְרִי לְמַטֵּה־דָן. (ויקרא כד:י–יא)
>
> And the son of an Israelite woman, whose father was an Egyptian, went out among the children of Israel; and a fight broke out in the camp between the son of the Israelite woman and a man of Israel. And the son of the Israelite woman blasphemed the Name and cursed; and they brought him unto Moshe. And his mother's name was Shelomit, the daughter of Divri, of the tribe of Dan. (*Vayikra* 24:10–11)

Pharaoh saw that every single animal belonging to the Egyptians died, which was a clear sign of the hand of Hashem. Yet when he realized that the animals of one Israelite died, he chose to focus on that one non-Egyptian death as proof that it was all a coincidence and not the hand of God.

When a person doesn't want to believe, then the greatest act of God can stare him in the face, and he will choose not to see it. Similarly, when Hashem told Moshe that the plague of the death of the firstborn would occur at midnight, Hashem used the term

דֶּבֶר – *DEVER* (PESTILENCE)

ONLY ONE

וַיַּעַשׂ יהוה אֶת־הַדָּבָר הַזֶּה מִמָּחֳרָת וַיָּמָת כֹּל מִקְנֵה מִצְרָיִם וּמִמִּקְנֵה בְנֵי־יִשְׂרָאֵל לֹא־מֵת אֶחָד: וַיִּשְׁלַח פַּרְעֹה וְהִנֵּה לֹא־מֵת מִמִּקְנֵה יִשְׂרָאֵל עַד־אֶחָד וַיִּכְבַּד לֵב פַּרְעֹה וְלֹא שִׁלַּח אֶת־הָעָם. (שמות ט:ו-ז)

And Hashem did that thing on the morrow, and all the cattle of Egypt died; but of the cattle of the children of Israel, not one died. And Pharaoh sent, and behold, there was not so much as one of the cattle of the Israelites dead. Yet the heart of Pharaoh was stubborn, and he did not let the people go. (*Shemot* 9:6–7)

The Malbim (*Al HaTorah, Shemot* 9:6) comments on the wording of these *pesukim* and points out a change in the language used to express that none of the flocks of Bnei Yisrael died. The first *pasuk* says *lo meit ehad*, "not one died," and the second says *lo meit… ad ehad*. What does *ad ehad* mean? What does this odd extra word signify?

The Malbim cites two other *pesukim* where *ad ehad* appears. The first is at the Splitting of the Sea:

וַיָּשֻׁבוּ הַמַּיִם וַיְכַסּוּ אֶת־הָרֶכֶב וְאֶת־הַפָּרָשִׁים לְכֹל חֵיל פַּרְעֹה הַבָּאִים אַחֲרֵיהֶם בַּיָּם לֹא־נִשְׁאַר בָּהֶם עַד־אֶחָד. (שמות יד:כח)

And the waters returned, covering the chariots, the horsemen, and all the host of Pharaoh that went in after them into the sea; there remained not so much as one of them. (*Shemot* 14:28)

The other is at the war of Bnei Yisrael against Sisera, at the beginning of *Sefer Shofetim*:

וּבָרָק רָדַף אַחֲרֵי הָרֶכֶב וְאַחֲרֵי הַמַּחֲנֶה עַד חֲרֹשֶׁת הַגּוֹיִם וַיִּפֹּל כָּל־מַחֲנֵה סִיסְרָא לְפִי־חֶרֶב לֹא נִשְׁאַר עַד־אֶחָד. (שופטים ד:טז)

And Barak chased after the chariots and after the camp, until the location of the nation, and all of Sisera's camp fell

Essentially, the Torah is telling us that indifference, not putting one's heart into his service, is the cardinal sin of mankind. The opposite of awe is apathy. As we are told in *Sefer Devarim* (28:47), great infliction will befall us because we did not serve Hashem *besimha u'vetuv levav.* We did not serve God happily and wholeheartedly. We may have fulfilled the commandments, but we did not fulfill them with feeling.

We need to understand what we are doing and focus on our actions, so that we can perform mitzvot with the proper intention and understanding, as a people who are *yarei Shamayim.*

מַכַּת בְּכוֹרוֹת – *MAKAT BEKHOROT* (FIRSTBORN)

We are commanded to perform several mitzvot in commemoration of *makat bekhorot,* the plague of the firstborn. This includes *pidyon haben,* the redemption of the firstborn son, as well as *pidyon behema tehora,* redemption of a firstborn offspring of a kosher animal, and *pidyon hamor,* redemption of the firstborn offspring of a donkey.

Why are we obligated to redeem the firstborn offspring of a donkey, which is a non-kosher animal? The *Meshekh Hokhma* (*Shemot* 13:13) quotes the Yerushalmi (*Shekalim*), which states, "You sold Rachel's firstborn for twenty silver coins; you shall contribute five shekel for your firstborn donkey." This mitzva is connected to the sin of the sale of Yosef. Yet this seems a bit strange. If this is a punishment, then why are Yosef's offspring, the tribes of Efraim and Menashe, required to contribute five *shekalim* to redeem their firstborn donkeys, and to whom do they donate those proceeds? To the tribe of Levi, who was responsible for the sale of their forefather Yosef?

What exactly is the connection between *makat bekhorot and mekhirat Yosef,* and what is the message for us?

The *Meshekh Hokhma* explains that we do not only thank HaKadosh Barukh Hu for our salvation, but we thank Hashem for the entire process. We may not comprehend it at the time, but the challenging experiences prior to our salvation are but a piece in the puzzle.

Hashem informed Avraham Avinu that his children were destined to be enslaved in Egypt and will leave with riches. While experiencing slave labor, it is difficult to fathom that it is a necessary *bahatzot,* at midnight. When Moshe transmitted the message, he said, *kahatzot,* meaning, approximately at midnight (Berakhot 3a). Why the change? For a similar reason. People who want to disbelieve will say, hey, on my watch, it happened at 12:01, so God was wrong since it didn't occur at midnight.

The Ramban brings an example of this attitude from *Parashat Beshallah.* The *pasuk* says: "Moshe stretched out his hand over the Reed Sea, and Hashem brought eastern winds, and He made the sea into dry land and the waters split" (*Shemot* 14:21). The Splitting of the Sea was the greatest revelation of Hashem that Am Yisrael ever experienced, yet what did the Egyptians say? Simply, wow, what a huge tide, that's incredible. I've never seen such a thing before.

The Ramban (*Shemot* 14:21) explains that Hashem made the eastern winds blow to give the Egyptians, and the world, the opportunity to attribute the Splitting of the Sea to a natural phenomenon. Hashem gave them the *option* to believe that it was the wind that had split the sea and not God Himself. If someone has such an attitude, that he refuses to attribute anything to the hand of God, then he can even experience the Splitting of the Sea and it will not make any impression on him!

בָּרָד – *BARAD* (HAIL)

Rabbi Lamm (*The Royal Table,* p. 63) notes the Torah as stating that by the time the plague of hail came, some Egyptians were ready to listen to God. These Egyptians are referred to as *hayarei et dvar Hashem,* those who feared God. They brought their animals inside in order to protect them from the imminent hail. The other group of Egyptians who were disbelievers are referred to as *velo shot libo,* those who did not put their hearts to it. This group left their animals outside.

Rabbi Lamm asks, what's the opposite of *yarei Hashem*? It should be those who hate God! Either you fear God, or you hate God. Yet what terminology is used in this case? Those who fear God vs. those who just *do not care.* The opposite of a *yarei Shamayim* is somebody who is apathetic to his religion, somebody who goes through the motions and performs mitzvot by rote.

רַבִּי יוֹסֵי הַגְּלִילִי

RABBI Yossei HaGelili says: How can you know
that the Egyptians were struck with ten plagues in Egypt
and another fifty at the sea?
For in Egypt it is said,
"The astrologers said to Pharaoh, 'This is the *finger* of God,'" Ex. 8
while at the sea it is said,
"When Israel saw the great *hand* Ex. 14
the Lord raised against the Egyptians,
the people feared the Lord,
and they believed in the Lord and in His servant Moshe."
If a finger struck
them with ten plagues,
conclude from this that

THEY WERE STRUCK WITH TEN PLAGUES IN EGYPT
AND WITH FIFTY PLAGUES AT THE SEA.

וַיַּאֲמִינוּ בַּיהוה וּבְמֹשֶׁה עַבְדּוֹ – VAYAAMINU BAHASHEM U'VEMOSHE AVDO

WHY WAS MOSHE SELECTED?

At the end of this paragraph, we witness the only time Moshe Rabbenu is mentioned in the Haggada: "And they believed in Hashem and in His servant Moshe."

What is so special about Moshe Rabbenu that he was selected to be the leader of Am Yisrael? The Torah does not explicitly specify anything about Moshe's leadership qualities. In fact, quite the contrary. We are told that Moshe had a speech impediment, something that may be considered a handicap for an orator.

Perhaps the text *alludes* to Moshe's unique qualities which made him the appropriate choice as a leader.

Rabbi Lau

רַבִּי יוֹסֵי הַגְּלִילִי אוֹמֵר

מִנַּיִן אַתָּה אוֹמֵר
שֶׁלָּקוּ הַמִּצְרִים בְּמִצְרַיִם עֶשֶׂר מַכּוֹת
וְעַל הַיָּם לָקוּ חֲמִשִּׁים מַכּוֹת
בְּמִצְרַיִם מַה הוּא אוֹמֵר
וַיֹּאמְרוּ הַחַרְטֻמִּם אֶל־פַּרְעֹה, אֶצְבַּע אֱלֹהִים הִוא: שמות ח
וְעַל הַיָּם מַה הוּא אוֹמֵר
וַיַּרְא יִשְׂרָאֵל אֶת־הַיָּד הַגְּדֹלָה אֲשֶׁר עָשָׂה יהוה בְּמִצְרַיִם שמות יד
וַיִּירְאוּ הָעָם אֶת־יהוה
וַיַּאֲמִינוּ בַּיהוה וּבְמֹשֶׁה עַבְדּוֹ:
כַּמָּה לָקוּ בְּאֶצְבַּע
עֶשֶׂר מַכּוֹת.
אֱמֹר מֵעַתָּה

בְּמִצְרַיִם לָקוּ עֶשֶׂר מַכּוֹת
וְעַל הַיָּם לָקוּ חֲמִשִּׁים מַכּוֹת.

---

step toward the creation of a nation. Therefore, as we recall the end of the process, *makat bekhorot,* we are also to recall what got us to Egypt in the first place. It was the sale of Yosef by his brothers.

In fact, when the tribes journeyed to Egypt, the Torah emphasized several times how donkeys were utilized to carry their goods to Mitzrayim (*Bereshit* 42:24; 43:18; 44:3, 13; 45:23). We perform the mitzva of *pidyon hamor* to recall *makat bekhorot,* as the donkey was used to facilitate the descent of our people to Egypt, and *makot bekhorot* was also the final plague that led to our salvation. This completes the circle of events, fulfilling Hashem's divine plan.

Rabbi Eliezer says: How can you know
that each and every plague
the Holy One brought upon the Egyptians in Egypt
was in fact made up of four plagues?
For it is said,
"His fury was sent down upon them, *Ps. 78*
great anger, rage, and distress,
a company of messengers of destruction."
"Great anger" – one,
"rage" – two,
"distress" – three,
"a company of messengers of destruction" – four.
Conclude from this that
THEY WERE STRUCK WITH FORTY PLAGUES IN EGYPT
AND WITH TWO HUNDRED PLAGUES AT THE SEA.

Moshe showed compassion to the oppressed. He did not distinguish between a dispute among a Jew and a non-Jew, a dispute between Jews, or a dispute between non-Jews.

Rav Meir Yechiel, known as the Ostrovtzer Rav, and Rav Chaim Ozer Grodzinski, known as the Ahi'ezer, were once traveling together and each asked the other to share a *dvar Torah*. The Ahi'ezer asked the Ostrovtzer to go first, since he was a *gavra raba,* a great individual. The Ostrovtzer responded: A *gavra raba* is demonstrated not by one who interprets Torah in a powerful manner, but rather by one who relieves the suffering of another. This is clearly depicted in the Talmud.

The *gemara* in Makot 22b states in the name of Rava, "How foolish people are who stand out of respect for a *sefer Torah,* but do not stand out of respect for a *gavra raba.*" Rava goes on to prove that Rabbis should be respected, since the Torah dictates that a person may be judged to receive forty lashes, while the Rabbis limited the number of lashes to thirty-nine. This shows their power of interpretation.

We may

רַבִּי אֱלִיעֶזֶר אוֹמֵר מִנַּיִן שֶׁכָּל מַכָּה וּמַכָּה
שֶׁהֵבִיא הַקָּדוֹשׁ בָּרוּךְ הוּא עַל הַמִּצְרִים בְּמִצְרַיִם
הָיְתָה שֶׁל אַרְבַּע מַכּוֹת, שֶׁנֶּאֱמַר: יְשַׁלַּח־בָּם חֲרוֹן אַפּוֹ תהלים עח
עֶבְרָה וָזַעַם וְצָרָה, מִשְׁלַחַת מַלְאֲכֵי רָעִים:

עֶבְרָה אַחַת
וָזַעַם שְׁתַּיִם
וְצָרָה שָׁלוֹשׁ
מִשְׁלַחַת מַלְאֲכֵי רָעִים אַרְבַּע
אֱמֹר מֵעַתָּה
בְּמִצְרַיִם לָקוּ אַרְבָּעִים מַכּוֹת
וְעַל הַיָּם לָקוּ מָאתַיִם מַכּוֹת.

Rabbi Lau in his Haggada points out that the first three interactions that Moshe has with others portray Moshe's true personality. Moshe is present at three disputes, and rather than act as a passive bystander he leaps into action to protect the underdog.

First, we are told that Moshe left the palace in Egypt to assist his brothers that were being oppressed by the Egyptians. When he witnessed an Egyptian whipping a Jew, Moshe defended the Jew. He could not bear to see the suffering of his people.

Second, we are informed that Moshe witnessed two Jews quarreling and interceded by asking, how can you raise your hand to hit your fellow Jew?

Third, when Moshe arrived in Midian, when we might have expected that he behave as a fugitive and maintain a low profile, Moshe defends Yitro's daughters from the other shepherds and assists with feeding their cattle.

What do we learn about Moshe's personality from these scenarios? He could not stand idly by when injustice was being committed.

Rabbi Akiva says: How can you know
that each and every plague
the Holy One brought upon the Egyptians in Egypt
was in fact made up of five plagues?
For it is said,
"His fury was sent down upon them, Ps. 78
great anger, rage, and distress,
a company of messengers of destruction."
"His fury" – one,
"great anger" – two,
"rage" – three,
"distress" – four,
"a company of messengers of destruction" – five.
Conclude from this that
THEY WERE STRUCK WITH FIFTY PLAGUES IN EGYPT
AND WITH TWO HUNDRED AND FIFTY PLAGUES
AT THE SEA.

A Jewish leader is someone who gets involved, who tries to alleviate the suffering of others no matter who they might be. He seeks to make the world around him a better place. He does the right thing even when it is not in accordance with the popular opinion.

We should emulate Moshe Rabbenu, to see the pain of suffering of others and to do everything we can to improve their predicament. We cannot remain as mere bystanders, but rather take responsibility and action in order to achieve justice and a better world.

Moshe had many names, but he is best known by the name Moshe, which he was called for the simple reason that he was lifted out of the water as a child, *min hamayim mishituhu*. Water represents conformity. It takes the shape of the container into which it is poured. Moshe was pulled *out* from the water. That's Moshe. Someone who was not afraid to swim against the current, so that justice can prevail.

רַבִּי עֲקִיבָא אוֹמֵר מִנַּיִן שֶׁכָּל מַכָּה וּמַכָּה
שֶׁהֵבִיא הַקָּדוֹשׁ בָּרוּךְ הוּא עַל הַמִּצְרִים בְּמִצְרַיִם
הָיְתָה שֶׁל חָמֵשׁ מַכּוֹת, שֶׁנֶּאֱמַר: יְשַׁלַּח־בָּם תהלים עח
חֲרוֹן אַפּוֹ, עֶבְרָה וָזַעַם וְצָרָה, מִשְׁלַחַת מַלְאֲכֵי רָעִים:

חֲרוֹן אַפּוֹ	אַחַת
עֶבְרָה	שְׁתַּיִם
וָזַעַם	שָׁלוֹשׁ
וְצָרָה	אַרְבַּע
מִשְׁלַחַת מַלְאֲכֵי רָעִים	חָמֵשׁ

אֱמֹר מֵעַתָּה
בְּמִצְרַיִם לָקוּ חֲמִשִּׁים מַכּוֹת
וְעַל הַיָּם לָקוּ חֲמִשִּׁים וּמָאתַיִם מַכּוֹת.

We may ask why Rava did not offer as proof an earlier *pasuk* where we see a parallel of the strength of the rabbinic interpretation. The Torah dictates that one should count fifty days between Pesah and Shavuot and the Rabbis determined to count only forty-nine days. This, too, would be illustrative of how the Rabbis were able to reduce by one number a biblical directive. Why quote from *Sefer Devarim* when you can quote from an earlier appearance in *Sefer Vayikra*?

The Ostrovtzer Rav offered the following explanation. To be considered a *gavra raba,* a great individual, it is not just about the power of interpretation. Rather, one has to be concerned with minimizing the pain of another individual. This is exemplified by the idea of reducing the lashes, but not by reducing the counting of the *omer*.

What made Moshe Rabbenu a *gavra raba*? Moshe witnessed another's suffering and he had to get involved. He felt the pain of others even without having a personal relationship with them.

כַּמָּה מַעֲלוֹת טוֹבוֹת

HOW MUCH GOOD, LAYER UPON LAYER, THE OMNIPRESENT HAS DONE FOR US:

Had He brought us out of Egypt
without bringing judgment upon
[our oppressors],
that would have been enough for us.

Had He brought judgment upon them
but not upon their gods,
that would have been enough for us.

Had He brought judgment upon their gods
without killing their firstborn sons,
that would have been enough for us.

We can best explain by using a parable. When a child comes home from school with a painting, a parent can compliment the child for having created such a beautiful painting. However, if the parent specifies the details that he or she appreciates about the painting, the sharp colors and realistic images, the child appreciates the recognition to a greater degree.

Similarly, when a guest thanks the host for specific items, stating that the soup was stupendous or the salad scrumptious, it means a lot more to the host than a vague "thanks for the great meal."

The more detailed the compliment, the more sincere it will be perceived.

In *Dayeinu*, we thank Hashem for specifics: the *mann*, the Shabbat, the Splitting of the Sea. Every single act is appreciated. A vague "thanks for everything" would not adequately portray our deep appreciation of every single *hesed* Hashem performed on our behalf.

An alternative

כַּמָּה מַעֲלוֹת טוֹבוֹת לַמָּקוֹם עָלֵינוּ

אִלּוּ הוֹצִיאָנוּ מִמִּצְרַיִם
וְלֹא עָשָׂה בָהֶם שְׁפָטִים דַּיֵּנוּ

אִלּוּ עָשָׂה בָהֶם שְׁפָטִים
וְלֹא עָשָׂה בֵאלֹהֵיהֶם דַּיֵּנוּ

אִלּוּ עָשָׂה בֵאלֹהֵיהֶם
וְלֹא הָרַג אֶת בְּכוֹרֵיהֶם דַּיֵּנוּ

MOSHE – FIRST TO RECITE THE HAGGADA

Why is Moshe's name absent from the Haggada other than this one reference?

Rabbi Pelcovitz offers an explanation. Who was the first Jew in history to fulfill the mitzva of *vehigadeta levinkha,* to tell the story of *yetzi'at Mitzrayim* to his children? It was none other than Moshe Rabbenu. He was the only one in that generation whose children were not in Mitzrayim. They joined later on with their mother and grandfather Yitro. Therefore, Moshe was the first individual to fulfill the mitzva of *vehigadeta levinkha*.

When retelling the story, Moshe surely would not mention his own name. Thus, each year when we fulfill this mitzva, we mimic the first one who did so. In that way, we give him the honor which he did not give himself.

דַּיֵּנוּ – *DAYEINU*

Why so many *dayeinus*?

Had He killed their firstborn sons
without giving us their wealth,
that would have been enough for us.

Had He given us their wealth
without splitting the sea for us,
that would have been enough for us.

---

wanted to give us merit. There are so many different types of personalities in our nation. Although we have to fulfill each and every mitzva, some people relate to certain mitzvot more than others, and through fulfilling those mitzvot, can feel totally connected to Hashem.

A night person connects to staying up all night and learning on Shavuot. An outdoorsman relates to Sukkot. A person who likes wine looks forward to Purim. Each of the holidays has its unique angle as well, and individuals may relate to them in their own ways.

WE THANK HASHEM FOR THE *MANN*

The *gemara* in *Masekhet Yoma* (75) states that the *mann* tasted like whatever one desired.

Rav Shimon Schwab related being in Radin in the 1930s when the Hafetz Hayim asked his students the following question: If one ate *mann* without contemplating a specific delicacy, then what was its taste?

Nobody offered an answer. The Hafetz Hayim went on to explain: If one is not thinking of a particular food item while eating the *mann*, then it did not have any taste. It was the blandest, tasteless thing. Why? Because all spiritual items are a function of what you invest in it. A *gemara* can be sweet or bland. It all depends on how I approach it. If I want to learn, the *gemara* will be delicious. If I'm not in the mood to learn, it will be boring.

This was the *mann*. If we realized and appreciated it as a gift from Hashem, it was delicious. Likewise, having a positive attitude when approaching everything in life, especially a spiritual encounter, will provide added sweetening.

ILU KARA

אִלּוּ הָרַג אֶת בְּכוֹרֵיהֶם
וְלֹא נָתַן לָנוּ אֶת מָמוֹנָם דַּיֵּנוּ

אִלּוּ נָתַן לָנוּ אֶת מָמוֹנָם
וְלֹא קָרַע לָנוּ אֶת הַיָּם דַּיֵּנוּ

An alternative explanation is offered by Rav Moshe Feinstein (*Haggadat Arzei Levanon*). Rav Moshe explains that all humans are different. We're all inspired by different events. Some are inspired by a *shiur,* some by a *kumzitz,* and others through conducting acts of *hesed*. Therefore, in *Dayeinu,* we list all the events that occurred so everybody can be inspired by what resonates with them. Some people get inspired by the *makot,* some by Keriat Yam Suf, and some by the *mann*. We list them all.

A similar concept appears in connection with Shabbat. In the introduction to Rabbi Mordechai Willig's *Am Mordechai: Shabbat* (p. 11), Rabbi Yaakov Kamenetsky's explanation of a line in the Friday night *zemirot, Kol Mekadesh Shevi'i,* is translated as follows: Whoever sanctifies Shabbat as befits him, whoever keeps Shabbat correctly without desecrating it, he receives a great reward, each individual in accordance with his camp and flag, *ish al diglo*.

What do the "flags" have to do with the sanctification of Shabbat? Rabbi Willig explains that the line relates to an individual who observes Shabbat as befits him. The Shabbat experience resonates in a different manner for each individual. As long as we are careful not to desecrate Shabbat and we are bound by observance, there may be different nuances in each individual's Shabbat. As long as one is careful not to desecrate it, then one can experience it in a personal way.

One person may appreciate the singing, another the *shiurim,* and a third the *cholent,* all "as befits him"! Each person can wave his Shabbat flag as the tribes did in the desert, as long as there is the unifying factor of avoiding any desecration.

The *gemara* at the end of *Masekhet Makot* explains the reason why we were given 613 commandments: רצה הקב"ה לזכות את ישראל, God

Had He split the sea for us
but not brought us through it dry,
that would have been enough for us.

Had He brought us through [the sea] dry
without drowning our enemies in it,
that would have been enough for us.

Had He drowned our enemies in it
without providing for our needs
for forty years in the desert,
that would have been enough for us.

Had He provided for our needs
for forty years in the desert,
without feeding us with manna,
that would have been enough for us.

---

placing their trust in God and creating an unbreakable bond with Hashem that merited the miracles that followed.

Rav Asher Weiss cites a similar idea in the name of Rav Shimshon Raphael Hirsch. The *pasuk* states that Hashem will redeem us "as an eagle awakens its nest, hovering over its fledglings, it spreads its wings, taking them and carrying them on its pinions" (*Devarim* 32:11). In contrast to other birds, the eagle carries its offspring on its wings that protect them from danger below. How does the eagle place his offspring on its wings? It cannot lift them up and place them on its wings. Each of the offspring need to take a step onto the wing.

Similarly, Bnei Yisrael must make the first move, and then Hashem will follow, as is stated, *shuvu eilai ve'ashuva aleikhem,* first you return to Me, then I will return to you.

Perhaps this is the meaning of this statement in *dayeinu*. The level of *emuna* that we achieved at that moment, *dayeinu,* that would have been enough! The closeness we felt to HaKadosh Barukh Hu, at such an exalted level, would have been enough.

ILU HE'EKHILANU,

אִלּוּ קָרַע לָנוּ אֶת הַיָּם
וְלֹא הֶעֱבִירָנוּ בְּתוֹכוֹ בֶּחָרָבָה דַּיֵּנוּ

אִלּוּ הֶעֱבִירָנוּ בְּתוֹכוֹ בֶּחָרָבָה
וְלֹא שִׁקַּע צָרֵינוּ בְּתוֹכוֹ דַּיֵּנוּ

אִלּוּ שִׁקַּע צָרֵינוּ בְּתוֹכוֹ
וְלֹא סִפֵּק צָרְכֵּנוּ בַּמִּדְבָּר
אַרְבָּעִים שָׁנָה דַּיֵּנוּ

אִלּוּ סִפֵּק צָרְכֵּנוּ בַּמִּדְבָּר אַרְבָּעִים שָׁנָה
וְלֹא הֶאֱכִילָנוּ אֶת הַמָּן דַּיֵּנוּ

אִלּוּ קָרַע לָנוּ אֶת הַיָּם – *ILU KARA LANU ET HAYAM...*

If He would have split the sea, but not led us through it on dry land, *dayeinu*.

How are we to understand this perplexing line of *Dayeinu*? What purpose would there be in splitting the sea and not even taking us through?

The Ohr HaHaim HaKadosh posits it this way. Imagine the scene. Bnei Yisrael are at the edge of the sea and surrounded on all sides. The *yam*, the Egyptians, and the desert. They are trapped. Bnei Yisrael turn to Moshe pleading for help. Moshe turns to Hashem for assistance, and Hashem's response is, *ma titzak eilai*, what are you calling out to me for?

The Ohr HaHaim HaKadosh asks (*Shemot* 14:15), what does a Jew do during a time of *tzara*? If we do not turn to request Hashem's assistance, to whom are we to turn?

The Ohr HaHaim suggests that Hashem was essentially telling Moshe, I will assist, but you have to take the first step. Do something to exemplify your belief and unequivocal faith in Me!

As Bnei Yisrael marched forward, they exhibited this very *emuna*,

Had He fed us with manna
without giving us Shabbat,
that would have been enough for us.

Had He given us Shabbat
without drawing us close
around Mount Sinai,
that would have been enough for us.

Had He drawn us close around Mount Sinai
without giving us the Torah,
that would have been enough for us.

Had He given us the Torah
without bringing us to the land of Israel,
that would have been enough for us.

Had He brought us to the land of Israel
without building for us
the House He chose
that would have been enough for us.

---

we need to also realize Hashem's role in our everyday lives. The Ramban (*Shemot* 13:16) teaches us that really, there is no such thing as nature. Rather, it is a system of constant miracles to which we are *already* accustomed, and thus, not shocked by. In other words, we must believe in God's constant involvement in our lives.

This was the message of Yitro when he stated *barukh Hashem*. His praise was not only about Shabbat, but also regarding *maaseh Bereshit,* the major miracles. We're talking about *mann,* bread, and water too! Basic sustenance. That's also something. We have to recognize that the provision of our sustenance is also from the hand of God.

Even though it's *gashmiyut,* Rav Moshe says, thank Hashem for *gashmiyut*! Thank Hashem for a pillow at night. Thank Hashem for running water. For all the "little" things.

AL AHAT KAMA

אִלּוּ הֶאֱכִילָנוּ אֶת הַמָּן
וְלֹא נָתַן לָנוּ אֶת הַשַּׁבָּת דַּיֵּנוּ

אִלּוּ נָתַן לָנוּ אֶת הַשַּׁבָּת
וְלֹא קֵרְבָנוּ לִפְנֵי הַר סִינַי דַּיֵּנוּ

אִלּוּ קֵרְבָנוּ לִפְנֵי הַר סִינַי
וְלֹא נָתַן לָנוּ אֶת הַתּוֹרָה דַּיֵּנוּ

אִלּוּ נָתַן לָנוּ אֶת הַתּוֹרָה
וְלֹא הִכְנִיסָנוּ לְאֶרֶץ יִשְׂרָאֵל דַּיֵּנוּ

אִלּוּ הִכְנִיסָנוּ לְאֶרֶץ יִשְׂרָאֵל
וְלֹא בָנָה לָנוּ אֶת
בֵּית הַבְּחִירָה דַּיֵּנוּ

אִלּוּ הֶאֱכִילָנוּ אֶת הַמָּן – *ILU HE'EKHILANU ET HAMANN...*

What's the connection between the *mann* and Shabbat?

Mann was a miracle through which God provided us with sustenance, but it pales in comparison to Creation which is represented by Shabbat. In *Dayeinu* we are stating that a small miracle would have sufficed.

The Mekhilta tells us that the first person in history to state the words *barukh Hashem* was Yitro.

Rav Moshe Feinstein asks, how is it that after experiencing all of the miracles in Egypt and Yam Suf, Bnei Yisrael never expressed those very words, recognizing the hand of God?

Rav Moshe explains that, so often in life, we recognize extraordinary miraculous events, yet we seem to ignore the mundane happenings, the daily, natural course of life.

Of course, we must offer praise to Hashem for the miracles. Yet

עַל אַחַת כַּמָּה וְכַמָּה

HOW MANY
AND MANIFOLD THEN,
THE OMNIPRESENT'S KINDNESSES
ARE TO US –

for He brought us out of Egypt
and brought judgment upon
[our oppressors]
and upon their gods,
and He killed their firstborn sons
and gave us their wealth,
and He split the sea for us
and brought us through it on dry land
and drowned our enemies there,
and He provided for our needs
for forty years in the desert
and fed us manna,
and He gave us Shabbat,
and He drew us close
around Mount Sinai
and gave us the Torah,
and He brought us to the land of Israel
and built for us the House He chose,

SO WE COULD FIND ATONEMENT [THERE]
FOR ALL OUR SINS.

---

to recognizing Hashem's goodness, doubled and repeated. What is the meaning of this phrase that multiples God's acts of goodness?

Rav Pam explains that once we begin to comprehend all that Hashem has done for us, we begin to uncover more and more. As a

mashal,

עַל אַחַת כַּמָּה וְכַמָּה
טוֹבָה כְּפוּלָה וּמְכֻפֶּלֶת
לַמָּקוֹם עָלֵינוּ

שֶׁהוֹצִיאָנוּ מִמִּצְרַיִם
וְעָשָׂה בָהֶם שְׁפָטִים
וְעָשָׂה בֵאלֹהֵיהֶם
וְהָרַג בְּכוֹרֵיהֶם
וְנָתַן לָנוּ אֶת מָמוֹנָם
וְקָרַע לָנוּ אֶת הַיָּם
וְהֶעֱבִירָנוּ בְתוֹכוֹ בֶּחָרָבָה
וְשִׁקַּע צָרֵינוּ בְּתוֹכוֹ
וְסִפֵּק צָרְכֵּנוּ בַּמִּדְבָּר אַרְבָּעִים שָׁנָה
וְהֶאֱכִילָנוּ אֶת הַמָּן
וְנָתַן לָנוּ אֶת הַשַּׁבָּת
וְקֵרְבָנוּ לִפְנֵי הַר סִינַי
וְנָתַן לָנוּ אֶת הַתּוֹרָה
וְהִכְנִיסָנוּ לְאֶרֶץ יִשְׂרָאֵל
וּבָנָה לָנוּ אֶת בֵּית הַבְּחִירָה

לְכַפֵּר עַל כָּל עֲוֹנוֹתֵינוּ.

עַל אַחַת כַּמָּה וְכַמָּה – AL AHAT KAMA VEKHAMA

After we sing the *dayeinu* song, there is a summary which states: *Al ehat kama vekhama tova kefula umekhupelet,* "How many and manifold are the Omnipresent's kindnesses..." This is a reference

רַבָּן גַּמְלִיאֵל Rabban Gamliel would say:
Anyone who does not say these three things on Pesah
has not fulfilled his obligation, and these are they:

PESAH, MATZA AND BITTER HERBS.

The meaning is that one should not miss out on the performance of a single mitzva. *Shelo mahmitzin et hamitzvot.* Not only does one have to rush while baking matza to ensure that the dough does not rise and become invalid, so too, one should not procrastinate in the performance of mitzvot.

Rav Shalom Schwadron in his Haggada expands upon this idea. He warns against one idea in particular. At times, we prepare to engage in a mitzva, but then once we partake in the mitzva our excitement is diminished. For example, one labors for weeks to clean the house for Pesah and cook for the holiday, but then, he doses off during the Seder.

Preparation is essential, but we must maintain our focus and enthusiasm while we engage in the mitzvot as well. *Ushemartem et hamitzvot.* Let's take care in preparing as well as performing mitzvot with vigor.

PESAH, MATZA, AND *MAROR*

Rav Yosef Nechemia Kornitzer, the last Rav in Cracow, informs us that at the Seder we are to express *hallel* and *hoda'a* to HaKadosh Barukh Hu.

There are three reasons why it might be hard for someone to say thank you or offer gratitude to another.

1. **"I deserve it."** We may not offer gratitude to others because we feel we already deserve the act that was performed for us. *Magia li.* You know who I am? Of course, they *had* to do it for me.

On Pesah,

רַבָּן גַּמְלִיאֵל הָיָה אוֹמֵר
כָּל שֶׁלֹּא אָמַר שְׁלוֹשָׁה דְבָרִים אֵלּוּ בַּפֶּסַח
לֹא יָצָא יְדֵי חוֹבָתוֹ וְאֵלּוּ הֵן

פֶּסַח מַצָּה וּמָרוֹר

mashal, when we stargaze, at first we notice just a few stars. As one adjusts a telescope, more stars become visible until the entire sky seems to be totally covered with stars.

The more we recognize the *hesed* that Hashem has bestowed upon us, the more we realize that it is truly endless.

This is the true purpose of *Dayeinu*. Whatever we began to perceive is only an iota of all the goodness Hashem has performed for us. Thus, we break down each phase of the Exodus and begin to grasp all the acts of goodness that transpired. At the Seder, we spend time deciphering all the hidden acts that may not be readily apparent.

This is a time to begin to comprehend *hasdei Hashem* in our everyday lives as well, appreciating every little thing!

RABBAN GAMLIEL ... *PESAH, MATZA, MAROR*

USHEMARTEM ET HAMITZVOT

One of the three quintessential symbols at the Seder is the matza. *Hazal* states that one should not just read the word in the *pasuk* (*Shemot* 12:17) as *ushemartem et hamatzot*, referring to matza, but rather as *ushemartem et hamitzvot*, referring to the commandments. In Hebrew, the spelling of matzot and mitzvot is identical: **מצות** (Rashi, *Shemot* 12:17, citing the Mekhilta).

The
PESAH
is what our ancestors would eat while the Temple stood:
and what does it recall?
It recalls the Holy One's
passing over (*Pasah*) the houses of our ancestors in Egypt,
as it is said:
"You shall say: *Ex. 12*
'It is a Pesah offering for the Lord,
for He passed over the houses of the children of Israel in Egypt
while He struck the Egyptians,
but saved those in our homes' –
and the people bowed and prostrated themselves."

The matzot are now lifted:
THIS MATZA
that we eat:
what does it recall?
It recalls the dough of our ancestors,
which did not have time to rise
before the King, King of kings, the Holy One, blessed be He,
revealed Himself and redeemed them,

---

korban pesah. This was our only merit. Therefore, we owe a debt of gratitude.

2. **"No big deal."** We may minimize the act performed for us. We may think, it wasn't so difficult, and they were doing it anyway, and so on.

פֶּסַח

שֶׁהָיוּ אֲבוֹתֵינוּ אוֹכְלִים בִּזְמַן שֶׁבֵּית הַמִּקְדָּשׁ הָיָה קַיָּם
עַל שׁוּם מָה
עַל שׁוּם שֶׁפָּסַח הַקָּדוֹשׁ בָּרוּךְ הוּא
עַל בָּתֵּי אֲבוֹתֵינוּ בְּמִצְרַיִם
שֶׁנֶּאֱמַר
וַאֲמַרְתֶּם זֶבַח־פֶּסַח הוּא לַיהוה שמות יב
אֲשֶׁר פָּסַח עַל־בָּתֵּי בְנֵי־יִשְׂרָאֵל בְּמִצְרַיִם
בְּנָגְפּוֹ אֶת־מִצְרַיִם וְאֶת־בָּתֵּינוּ הִצִּיל
וַיִּקֹּד הָעָם וַיִּשְׁתַּחֲווּ:

The מצות *are now lifted:*

מַצָּה זוֹ

שֶׁאָנוּ אוֹכְלִים, עַל שׁוּם מָה
עַל שׁוּם שֶׁלֹּא הִסְפִּיק בְּצֵקָם שֶׁל אֲבוֹתֵינוּ לְהַחֲמִיץ
עַד שֶׁנִּגְלָה עֲלֵיהֶם מֶלֶךְ מַלְכֵי הַמְּלָכִים
הַקָּדוֹשׁ בָּרוּךְ הוּא, וּגְאָלָם

On Pesah, we recognize that when we were slaves, we had zero *zekhuyot*. Hashem allowed us to earn some merit. We needed to do *something* to merit leaving Mitzrayim. For this reason, we were commanded to slaughter and partake in the

as it is said:
"They baked the dough that they had brought out of Egypt *Ex. 12*
into unleavened cakes, for it had not risen,
for they were cast out of Egypt and could not delay,
and they made no provision for the way."

The bitter herbs are now lifted:

THESE BITTER HERBS

that we eat:
what do they recall?
They recall the bitterness that the Egyptians imposed
on the lives of our ancestors in Egypt,
as it is said:
"They embittered their lives with hard labor, *Ex. 1*
with clay and with bricks
and with all field labors, with all the work
with which they enslaved them – hard labor."

---

times beforehand. That is the *maror*. It helps us remember our bitter times as slaves.

Rav Yosef Nechemia says, *pesah*, matza, and *maror* are the three mitzvot that counter any type of claim that could justify not being able to offer our complete gratitude to Hashem for taking us out of Mitzrayim.

שֶׁנֶּאֱמַר
וַיֹּאפוּ אֶת־הַבָּצֵק אֲשֶׁר הוֹצִיאוּ מִמִּצְרַיִם שמות יב
עֻגֹת מַצּוֹת, כִּי לֹא חָמֵץ
כִּי־גֹרְשׁוּ מִמִּצְרַיִם, וְלֹא יָכְלוּ לְהִתְמַהְמֵהַּ
וְגַם־צֵדָה לֹא־עָשׂוּ לָהֶם:

The bitter herbs are now lifted:

מָרוֹר זֶה

שֶׁאָנוּ אוֹכְלִים עַל שׁוּם מָה
עַל שׁוּם שֶׁמֵּרְרוּ הַמִּצְרִים אֶת חַיֵּי אֲבוֹתֵינוּ בְּמִצְרַיִם
שֶׁנֶּאֱמַר
וַיְמָרְרוּ אֶת־חַיֵּיהֶם בַּעֲבֹדָה קָשָׁה, בְּחֹמֶר וּבִלְבֵנִים שמות א
וּבְכָל־עֲבֹדָה בַּשָּׂדֶה
אֵת כָּל־עֲבֹדָתָם אֲשֶׁר־עָבְדוּ בָהֶם בְּפָרֶךְ:

---

and so on. To counter this, we recognize the matza which we ate on our way out of Egypt. We left with flour and water which didn't even rise. It was just basic sustenance, yet we are still ecstatic and offer our appreciation.

3. **"Forget the tough times."** We may not remember what it was like before we were helped. We may not focus on the tough

בְּכָל דּוֹר וָדוֹר

GENERATION BY GENERATION,

each person must see himself
as if he himself had come out of Egypt, *Pesahim 119b*
as it is said:
"And you shall tell your child on that day, *Ex. 13*
'Because of this the LORD acted for me
when I came out of Egypt.'"
It was not only our ancestors
whom the Holy One redeemed;
He redeemed us too along with them,
as it is said:
"He took us out of there, *Deut. 6*
to bring us to the land
He promised our ancestors
and to give it to us."

The Netivot explains that there were two things that happened on the night of the Seder. First, we were no longer *avdei Pharaoh,* and second, we became *avdei Hashem.*

What are we really celebrating? That we were freed from Pharaoh, or that we became servants of Hashem?

If the order were *maror, pesah,* and matza, one may think the essence was our freedom from our bondage and servitude to Pharaoh. However, our main celebration is actually the fact that we became *avdei Hashem.* That is why our emphasis is on *korban pesah.*

Leaving Mitzrayim is what facilitated our becoming His nation, but the *korban pesah,* symbolizing our connection to Hashem, is our primary emphasis of the night and thus we place it first.

בְּכָל דּוֹר וָדוֹר

חַיָּב אָדָם לִרְאוֹת אֶת עַצְמוֹ כְּאִלּוּ הוּא יָצָא מִמִּצְרָיִם פסחים קטז:

שֶׁנֶּאֱמַר

וְהִגַּדְתָּ לְבִנְךָ בַּיּוֹם הַהוּא שמות יג

לֵאמֹר

בַּעֲבוּר זֶה

עָשָׂה יהוה לִי בְּצֵאתִי מִמִּצְרָיִם:

לֹא אֶת אֲבוֹתֵינוּ בִּלְבָד

גָּאַל הַקָּדוֹשׁ בָּרוּךְ הוּא

אֶלָּא אַף אוֹתָנוּ גָּאַל עִמָּהֶם

שֶׁנֶּאֱמַר

וְאוֹתָנוּ הוֹצִיא מִשָּׁם דברים ו

לְמַעַן הָבִיא אֹתָנוּ

לָתֶת לָנוּ אֶת־הָאָרֶץ

אֲשֶׁר נִשְׁבַּע לַאֲבֹתֵינוּ:

RABBAN GAMLIEL HAYA OMER

CHRONOLOGICAL ORDER?

The Netivot (*Maaseh Nissim*) asks a relatively well-known question about Rabban Gamliel's statement. We recite these three cardinal items in the following order: *pesah,* matza, and *maror.* Why are they not listed in chronological order? That is, first *maror* to symbolize our servitude, then the *pesah* which we sacrificed before we left Egypt, and finally the matza that we baked as we exited Egypt. Why is *maror* placed last on the list instead?

The matzot are covered and the cup is raised.

לְפִיכָךְ Therefore it is our duty
to thank, praise, laud,
glorify, exalt, honor,
bless, raise high, and acclaim
the One who has performed all these miracles
for our ancestors and for us;
who has brought us out from slavery to freedom,
from sorrow to joy, from grief to celebration;
from darkness to great light
and from enslavement to redemption;
and so we shall sing a new song before Him.

HALLELUYA!

Jews are connected to expressing the praises of God. In fact, we are referred to as *Yehudim* which is derived from *Yehuda*. Yehuda was named by his mother, Leah, to express her appreciation for having given birth to him, her fourth son: *Hapaam odeh et Hashem* (*Bereshit* 29:34), this time I will praise God.

Our very essence, what is most meaningful to us, is this characteristic of praising God. We use various words to describe our appreciation of Hashem. Yet knowing full well that it is impossible to thank God for all he has bestowed upon us, we also include a catch-all phrase at the end, *al kol divrei shirot vetishbahot*. We are Yehudim, and we should always express our gratitude to the Almighty and to those around us.

HALLEL

A BREAK IN THE ACTION?

The *Hallel* that is recited at the Seder is a bit strange. First, we interrupt the recitation of *Hallel* and break for a meal. Second, we do not recite a *berakha* over *Hallel*.

Perhaps

The מצות *are covered and the cup is raised.*

לְפִיכָךְ אֲנַחְנוּ חַיָּבִים
לְהוֹדוֹת, לְהַלֵּל, לְשַׁבֵּחַ, לְפָאֵר
לְרוֹמֵם, לְהַדֵּר, לְבָרֵךְ, לְעַלֵּה וּלְקַלֵּס
לְמִי שֶׁעָשָׂה לַאֲבוֹתֵינוּ וְלָנוּ אֶת כָּל הַנִּסִּים הָאֵלֶּה
הוֹצִיאָנוּ מֵעַבְדוּת לְחֵרוּת
מִיָּגוֹן לְשִׂמְחָה, מֵאֵבֶל לְיוֹם טוֹב
וּמֵאֲפֵלָה לְאוֹר גָּדוֹל
וּמִשִּׁעְבּוּד לִגְאֻלָּה
וְנֹאמַר לְפָנָיו שִׁירָה חֲדָשָׁה
הַלְלוּיָהּ.

The cup is put down.

לְפִיכָךְ אֲנַחְנוּ חַיָּבִים לְהוֹדוֹת –
LEFIKHAKH ANAHNU HAYAVIM LEHODOT

Therefore It Is Our Duty to Praise

In this paragraph, we express several synonyms of "praise," including *lehodot, lehallel, leshabe'ah, lefa'er, leromem*. In the *tefilla* of *Shokhen Ad* we recite similar language yet at the conclusion of the prayer, we have a catch-all phrase, *al kol divrei shirot vetishbahot*, referring to *all* words of praise.

Why are there so many words in the Hebrew language to praise God?

I once heard that in Canada, the native Inuit have many words for describing snow. Likewise, Italians have many words to describe types of pasta, including fettucine, ravioli, penne, linguine, gnocchi, macaroni, and spaghetti. When something is important and meaningful to you, you use different terms to distinguish between the nuances.

The cup is put down.

הַלְלוּיָהּ HALLELUYA! *Ps. 113*
Servants of the LORD, give praise;
praise the name of the LORD.
Blessed be the name of the LORD
now and for evermore.
From the rising of the sun to its setting,
may the LORD's name be praised.
High is the LORD above all nations;
His glory is above the heavens.
Who is like the LORD our God, who sits enthroned so high,
yet turns so low to see the heavens and the earth?
He raises the poor from the dust
and the needy from the refuse heap,
giving them a place alongside princes,
the princes of His people.
He makes the woman in a childless house
a happy mother of children.

HALLELUYA!

בְּצֵאת When Israel came out of Egypt, *Ps. 114*
the house of Yaakov from a people of foreign tongue,
Judah became His sanctuary, Israel His dominion.
The sea saw and fled; the Jordan turned back.
The mountains skipped like rams, the hills like lambs.
Why was it, sea, that you fled? Jordan, why did you turn back?
Why, mountains, did you skip like rams,
and you, hills, like lambs?
It was at the presence of the LORD, Creator of the earth,
at the presence of the God of Yaakov,
who turned the rock into a pool of water,
flint into a flowing spring.

---

hours discussing the exile and Exodus, we should truly feel an outburst of emotion, the desire for spontaneous praise.

Thus, if

תהלים קיג

הַלְלוּיָהּ

הַלְלוּ עַבְדֵי יהוה, הַלְלוּ אֶת־שֵׁם יהוה:
יְהִי שֵׁם יהוה מְבֹרָךְ, מֵעַתָּה וְעַד־עוֹלָם:
מִמִּזְרַח־שֶׁמֶשׁ עַד־מְבוֹאוֹ, מְהֻלָּל שֵׁם יהוה:
רָם עַל־כָּל־גּוֹיִם יהוה, עַל הַשָּׁמַיִם כְּבוֹדוֹ:
מִי כַּיהוה אֱלֹהֵינוּ, הַמַּגְבִּיהִי לָשָׁבֶת:
הַמַּשְׁפִּילִי לִרְאוֹת, בַּשָּׁמַיִם וּבָאָרֶץ:
מְקִימִי מֵעָפָר דָּל, מֵאַשְׁפֹּת יָרִים אֶבְיוֹן:
לְהוֹשִׁיבִי עִם־נְדִיבִים, עִם נְדִיבֵי עַמּוֹ:
מוֹשִׁיבִי עֲקֶרֶת הַבַּיִת, אֵם־הַבָּנִים שְׂמֵחָה

הַלְלוּיָהּ:

תהלים קיד

בְּצֵאת יִשְׂרָאֵל מִמִּצְרָיִם, בֵּית יַעֲקֹב מֵעַם לֹעֵז:
הָיְתָה יְהוּדָה לְקָדְשׁוֹ, יִשְׂרָאֵל מַמְשְׁלוֹתָיו:
הַיָּם רָאָה וַיָּנֹס, הַיַּרְדֵּן יִסֹּב לְאָחוֹר:
הֶהָרִים רָקְדוּ כְאֵילִים, גְּבָעוֹת כִּבְנֵי־צֹאן:
מַה־לְּךָ הַיָּם כִּי תָנוּס, הַיַּרְדֵּן תִּסֹּב לְאָחוֹר:
הֶהָרִים תִּרְקְדוּ כְאֵילִים, גְּבָעוֹת כִּבְנֵי־צֹאן:
מִלִּפְנֵי אָדוֹן חוּלִי אָרֶץ, מִלִּפְנֵי אֱלוֹהַּ יַעֲקֹב:
הַהֹפְכִי הַצּוּר אֲגַם־מָיִם, חַלָּמִישׁ לְמַעְיְנוֹ־מָיִם:

Perhaps we can explain this phenomenon based on a suggestion by Rav Hai Gaon, quoted in the *Ran* at the end of *Masekhet Pesahim*. He explains that this *Hallel* is classified as song, as *shira*, rather than as a reading, a *kriya*. What does Rav Hai Gaon mean by this?

Rav Yosef Dov Soloveitchik explains that after spending two

The cup is raised.

בָּרוּךְ Blessed are You, LORD our God, King of the Universe,
who has redeemed us
and redeemed our ancestors from Egypt,
and brought us to this night to eat matza and bitter herbs.
So may the LORD our God bring us in peace
to other seasons and festivals that are coming to us,
happy in the building of Your city
and rejoicing in Your service;
and there we shall eat of sacrifices and Pesah offerings
[*On Motza'ei Shabbat:* of Pesah offerings and sacrifices],
of which the blood will reach
the side of Your altar to be accepted.
And we shall thank You in a new song
for our redemption and for our lives' salvation.
Blessed are You, LORD, Redeemer of Israel.

Blessed are You, LORD our God, King of the Universe,
who creates the fruit of the vine.

Drink while reclining to the left.

Shira Hadasha

When we recite *Hallel* at the Seder, we introduce it with the words *venomar lefanav shira hadasha,* we will sing before you a new song. With that introduction, one would expect to use new and different words that are uttered only at the Seder. Yet we then reiterate the same *Hallel* that we recite on holidays and on Rosh Hodesh. So why do we refer to it as a new song, a *shira hadasha*?

Rabbi Lamm (*The Royal Table,* pp. 78–79) explains that in Judaism, we take the old and instill it with vigor and newness. The same religion that has been practiced for centuries does not go out of vogue. It crosses the chasm of time.

It is amazing how each year we once again read the same Torah, and yet we uncover new insights on each *parasha*. When we recite

Hallel

The cup is raised.

בָּרוּךְ אַתָּה יהוה אֱלֹהֵינוּ מֶלֶךְ הָעוֹלָם
אֲשֶׁר גְּאָלָנוּ, וְגָאַל אֶת אֲבוֹתֵינוּ מִמִּצְרַיִם
וְהִגִּיעָנוּ הַלַּיְלָה הַזֶּה, לֶאֱכָל בּוֹ מַצָּה וּמָרוֹר.
כֵּן יהוה אֱלֹהֵינוּ וֵאלֹהֵי אֲבוֹתֵינוּ
יַגִּיעֵנוּ לְמוֹעֲדִים וְלִרְגָלִים אֲחֵרִים
הַבָּאִים לִקְרָאתֵנוּ לְשָׁלוֹם
שְׂמֵחִים בְּבִנְיַן עִירֶךָ
וְשָׂשִׂים בַּעֲבוֹדָתֶךָ
וְנֹאכַל שָׁם
מִן הַזְּבָחִים וּמִן הַפְּסָחִים
/On מוצאי שבת: מִן הַפְּסָחִים וּמִן הַזְּבָחִים/
אֲשֶׁר יַגִּיעַ דָּמָם
עַל קִיר מִזְבַּחֲךָ לְרָצוֹן
וְנוֹדֶה לְךָ שִׁיר חָדָשׁ
עַל גְּאֻלָּתֵנוּ וְעַל פְּדוּת נַפְשֵׁנוּ
בָּרוּךְ אַתָּה יהוה, גָּאַל יִשְׂרָאֵל.

בָּרוּךְ אַתָּה יהוה אֱלֹהֵינוּ מֶלֶךְ הָעוֹלָם, בּוֹרֵא פְּרִי הַגָּפֶן.

Drink while reclining to the left.

Thus, if we were to recite a *berakha,* it would diminish the authenticity of our passion. We are praising God at this time because we want to, not because we are commanded. That is why we can interrupt our outpouring of praise, and that is also why we do not recite a blessing over this praise. To do so would dilute its personal authenticity.

RAHTZA / WASHING

In preparation for the meal,
all participants wash their hands and recite the blessing:

בָּרוּךְ Blessed are You, Lord our God,
King of the Universe, who has made us holy
through His commandments,
and has commanded us about washing hands.

MOTZI MATZA

The leader holds all three matzot and recites:

בָּרוּךְ Blessed are You, Lord our God,
King of the Universe,
who brings forth bread from the earth.

The lowermost matza is replaced.

The leader recites the following blessing while
holding the uppermost and middle matzot:

בָּרוּךְ Blessed are You, Lord our God,
King of the Universe, who has made us holy
through His commandments,
and has commanded us to eat matza.

A piece of the uppermost matza, together with a piece of the middle matza, is given to each member of the company.
Eat while reclining to the left.

The second *berakha* is *al akhilat matza,* which is categorized as a *birkat hamitzva,* a blessing recited before performing a mitzva.

The Rambam lists three categories of *berakhot*: for praise, for pleasure, and for mitzvot (*Hilkhot Berakhot* 1:4). However, the Rambam seems to link the blessings of praise with blessings of mitzvot.

וכשם שמברכין על ההניה – כך מברכין על כל מצוה. (הלכות ברכות א:ג)

As one blesses on a pleasure, so too one should bless on the performance of a mitzva. (*Hilkhot Berakhot* 1:3)

Why does

רחצה

In preparation for the meal,
all participants wash their hands and recite the blessing:

בָּרוּךְ אַתָּה יהוה אֱלֹהֵינוּ מֶלֶךְ הָעוֹלָם
אֲשֶׁר קִדְּשָׁנוּ בְּמִצְוֹתָיו, וְצִוָּנוּ עַל נְטִילַת יָדַיִם.

מוציא מצה

The leader holds all three מצות *and recites:*

בָּרוּךְ אַתָּה יהוה אֱלֹהֵינוּ מֶלֶךְ הָעוֹלָם
הַמּוֹצִיא לֶחֶם מִן הָאָרֶץ.

The lowermost מצה *is replaced.*

The leader recites the following blessing
while holding the uppermost and middle מצות*:*

בָּרוּךְ אַתָּה יהוה אֱלֹהֵינוּ מֶלֶךְ הָעוֹלָם
אֲשֶׁר קִדְּשָׁנוּ בְּמִצְוֹתָיו, וְצִוָּנוּ עַל אֲכִילַת מַצָּה.

A piece of the uppermost מצה*, together with a piece of the middle* מצה*,*
is given to each member of the company.
Eat while reclining to the left.

Hallel at the Seder, it may be the same words that have been sung over thousands of years, but it is not outdated. Its words are applicable today and express our appreciation to the Almighty. *Hallel* and Judaism maintain their freshness throughout the generations.

RAHTZA / WASHING

MOTZI MATZA

Prior to eating the matza, we recite two blessings. One is *hamotzi,* categorized as a *birkat hanehenin*. Generally, before receiving enjoyment from ingesting food, a *berakha* is recited.

MAROR / BITTER HERBS

The maror is dipped in the haroset before it is eaten.

בָּרוּךְ Blessed are You, Lord our God,
King of the Universe,
who has made us holy through His commandments,
and has commanded us to eat bitter herbs.

KOREKH / WRAPPING

Bitter herbs are sandwiched between two pieces of matza taken from the lowermost matza.

זֵכֶר In memory of the Temple, in the tradition of Hillel.
This is what Hillel would do when the Temple still stood:
he would wrap [the Pesah offering] up
with matza and bitter herbs
and eat them together, to fulfill what is said:
"You shall eat it with matza and bitter herbs." *Num. 9*

Eat while reclining to the left.

By reciting a *berakha* prior to the performance of these acts, we testify that we are doing so with permission from Hashem. Essentially, the *birkat hamitzva* is also like a *matir*, a statement that permits us to partake in an act in order to get closer to Hashem. Therefore, the Rambam connects the blessing over pleasure with the blessing on the performance of a mitzva.

MAROR / BITTER HERBS
KOREKH / WRAPPING

Before we start the main meal, we first eat a portion, a *kezayit* of matza, and then we eat a portion of *maror*. After we eat each separately, we combine the two by making a matza and *maror* sandwich. What is the purpose of this delicacy? We recite that this was Hillel's custom, but perhaps we can gain a deeper understanding as well.

Rabbi Lamm

מרור

The מרור *is dipped in the* חרוסת *before it is eaten.*

בָּרוּךְ אַתָּה יהוה אֱלֹהֵֽינוּ מֶֽלֶךְ הָעוֹלָם
אֲשֶׁר קִדְּשָֽׁנוּ בְּמִצְוֹתָיו
וְצִוָּֽנוּ עַל אֲכִילַת מָרוֹר.

כורך

Bitter herbs are sandwiched between two pieces of מצה *taken from the lowermost* מצה.

זֵֽכֶר לַמִּקְדָּשׁ כְּהִלֵּל.
כֵּן עָשָׂה הִלֵּל בִּזְמַן שֶׁבֵּית הַמִּקְדָּשׁ הָיָה קַיָּם
הָיָה כּוֹרֵךְ פֶּֽסַח, מַצָּה וּמָרוֹר, וְאוֹכֵל בְּיַֽחַד
לְקַיֵּם מַה שֶּׁנֶּאֱמַר: עַל־מַצּוֹת וּמְרֹרִים יֹאכְלֻֽהוּ: במדבר ט

Eat while reclining to the left.

Why does the Rambam connect these two seemingly mutually exclusive types of blessings?

Rav Yosef Dov Soloveitchik (*Shiurei HaRav on Tefilla* and *Keriat Shema, Siman 7*) explains as follows. The *berakha* recited before eating is not just related to enjoyment. Rather, it is a statement that allows us to partake in a meal. The *gemara* in Berakhot 35a declares that anyone who gets enjoyment from this world without reciting a blessing in advance, in recognition that all is a gift from Hashem, it is as if they are stealing. The *berakha* serves as a statement that permits one to obtain enjoyment from the world.

Similarly, what gives one the right to perform an act such as shaking a *lulav* or eating a piece of matza in order to get closer to Hashem? Isn't it presumptuous to think that a physical action can bring a finite, limited human being to connect with the Infinite?

SHULHAN OREKH / TABLE SETTING

The festive meal is now eaten.

SHULHAN OREKH / TABLE SETTING

AN EGG – CYCLE OF LIFE

The Rema (OH 476:2) quotes a custom to eat an egg at the beginning of the Seder meal. What is the significance of an egg at this juncture?

The Rema reasons that the night of the Seder is always the same night of the week as the upcoming Tisha Be'Av. As we complete the *Maggid* section of the Haggada and reach the apex of celebrating our redemption, we eat an egg, a mourner's food. The egg symbolizes the cycle of life and reminds us that our redemption is not yet complete, as we are still unable to sacrifice the *korban pesah* in the *Beit HaMikdash.*

DOUBLE BIRTH

Another idea is offered by the Itzbitzer Rav and is cited in the *Haggada Hegyonei Halakha* by Rav Yitzchak Mirsky. The egg symbolizes two *geulot,* two redemptions, one physical redemption from our bondage in Egypt, and a second spiritual redemption, which was only consummated at Har Sinai when we received the Torah. How does the egg symbolize these two redemptions?

When most creatures give birth to offspring, it arrives in its complete, final form. Typically, there is only one stage of birthing. However, certain animals, birds in particular, lay an egg that later hatches into its final form of a chick. If the egg does not hatch, there is no bird. For birds, there are two stages of birth.

Bnei Yisrael as a nation was born at *yetzi'at Mitzrayim,* but this birth was not complete. Only after receiving the Torah did we evolve into our final form. *Yetzi'at Mitzrayim* was only the

beginning,

שלחן עורך

The festive meal is now eaten.

Rabbi Lamm (*The Royal Table,* p. 89) offers a creative suggestion. Why do we create a *maror* sandwich? Because life is all about balance. Life is about taking various extremes and blending them together into a balanced unit. Rabbi Lamm beautifully states:

> Any one value, when taken to an extreme, can be corrupted. We need a dialectic of virtues. We need freedom and responsibility, peace and self-defense, love and morality. Patience and toughness, discipline and independent thinking.

Matza and *maror,* matza with its *geula* elements and *maror* with its bitterness teaches us that life is about balance. As the Rambam dictates in *Hilkhot Deot,* extremes are troublesome. The middle path is the golden path.

It is also puzzling that we take the *maror,* a bitter herb, and recite a blessing: *asher kideshanu bemitzvotav vetzivanu al akhilat maror.* That's pretty amazing. Matza is tasty and it symbolizes freedom, so it makes sense to make a blessing over it, but to make a *berakha* on *maror*? Why make a blessing on a symbol of slavery? This teaches us that life is not always rosy, nor is it all bleak. Rather, life has its ups and downs, and it's all part of the divine plan.

We cannot dismiss the challenging times, as they often enhance our strength and perseverance. In Rabbi Lamm's words, "Misery is not meaningless and pain not pointless" (*The Royal Table,* p. 77).

That is why, as optimists, we take the bitter *maror* and coat it with sweet *haroset.* What supported us through thousands of years of exile is the attitude of reciting blessings over our *maror,* our challenging times, while yearning and believing that our sweet *haroset* is soon to follow.

TZAFUN / HIDDEN

At the end of the meal, the remaining piece of the middle matza which had been hidden earlier (the afikoman), is eaten.

BAREKH / BLESSING

The third cup of wine is poured.

שִׁיר הַמַּעֲלוֹת A song of ascents. Ps. 126
When the LORD brought back the exiles of Zion
we were like people who dream.
Then were our mouths filled with laughter,
and our tongues with songs of joy.
Then was it said among the nations,
"The LORD has done great things for them."
The LORD did do great things for us and we rejoiced.

---

as "toward the hiding place" (which is similar to the meaning of *tzafun* in the Haggada, referring to the hiding of the afikomen). The Kli Yakar offers an incisive thought: If a Jew finds himself in *galut* (exile), and HaKadosh Barukh Hu provides him with financial success, he should be careful not to flaunt it. He should keep it hidden. Flaunting it could kindle the jealousy and wrath of others. When other nations see our success, it increases their jealousy and animosity toward us. Best not to excessively display our blessings, but rather to keep them hidden.

BAREKH / BLESSING

BIRKAT HAMAZON

There is only one *berakha* that is an obligation of biblical origin. The Torah declares (*Devarim* 8:10): *Ve'akhalta vesavata uverakhta*: eat, be satiated, and bless Hashem. Unfortunately, we sometimes rush through *benching*. After completing our meal, we do not have time to focus and we swallow our words.

It is told

צפון

At the end of the meal, the remaining piece of the middle מצה *which had been hidden earlier (the* אפיקומן*), is eaten.*

ברך

The third cup of wine is poured.

שִׁיר הַמַּעֲלוֹת תהלים קכו
בְּשׁוּב יהוה אֶת־שִׁיבַת צִיּוֹן, הָיִינוּ כְּחֹלְמִים:
אָז יִמָּלֵא שְׂחוֹק פִּינוּ וּלְשׁוֹנֵנוּ רִנָּה
אָז יֹאמְרוּ בַגּוֹיִם הִגְדִּיל יהוה לַעֲשׂוֹת עִם־אֵלֶּה:
הִגְדִּיל יהוה לַעֲשׂוֹת עִמָּנוּ, הָיִינוּ שְׂמֵחִים:

---

beginning, not an end in itself. Perhaps that is why the Rambam does not count *zekhirat yetzi'at Mitzrayim* as a separate mitzva. It is a means to achieving something, not an end in itself. Its purpose was to enable us to receive the Torah, part one of a two-step process, similar to an egg being laid and later hatched.

This is why we eat an egg specifically after completing the *Maggid* section of the Haggada. Following our intense discussion about *yetzi'at Mitzrayim,* when we feel like we are on top of the world, we recognize that this is not the end of the process. Only in another seven weeks, at Shavuot, will we experience complete happiness.

TZAFUN / HIDDEN

HIDING SUCCESS

Tzafun, meaning "hidden," is picked up by the Kli Yakar in a different context. On the *pasuk "pnu lakhem tzafona"*– turn northward (*Devarim* 2:2), the Kli Yakar derives a lesson as to how we should behave in exile. While we are living among the other nations, we need to turn "*tzafona,*" which means "northward" but can be interpreted

Bring back our exiles, Lord, like streams in a dry land.
May those who sowed in tears, reap in joy.
May one who goes out weeping, carrying a bag of seed,
come back with songs of joy, carrying his sheaves.

Some say:

תְּהִלַּת My mouth shall speak the praise of God, and Ps. 145
all creatures shall bless His holy name for ever and all
time. We will bless God now and for ever. Halleluya! Ps. 115
Thank the Lord for He is good: His loving-kindness Ps. 136
is for ever. Who can tell of the Lord's mighty acts and Ps. 106
make all His praise be heard?

One might have thought the opposite would be more appropriate. With respect to a fruit, I had little to do with creating it. I simply picked it off the tree, and it was ready for me. Therefore, the blessing after eating a fruit should be longer and more detailed, so I can express my gratitude to Hashem for doing the work for me. With respect to the bread, I worked hard to turn the grain into bread. Since I had to perform the activity that made the bread edible, one would imagine the blessing can be shorter.

However, *Birkat HaMazon* is precisely where we need to be reminded to offer our appreciation to Hashem for having provided us with our food. We may erroneously take credit for creating our bread, and lack true gratitude to Hashem for having provided us with the ingredients. Therefore, a much longer and more detailed *berakha* is required after eating bread.

With respect to a fruit, it is crystal clear that it was provided by Hashem. As there is no risk of forgetting its source, a concise blessing is sufficient.

Another possibility is that the goal of life is to actually partner with Hashem in achieving accomplishments and not simply to receive divine gifts. Thus, when we merit to share in God's work, that is when we offer the most praise.

שׁוּבָה יהוה אֶת־שְׁבִיתֵנוּ, כַּאֲפִיקִים בַּנֶּגֶב:
הַזֹּרְעִים בְּדִמְעָה, בְּרִנָּה יִקְצֹרוּ:
הָלוֹךְ יֵלֵךְ וּבָכֹה נֹשֵׂא מֶשֶׁךְ־הַזָּרַע
בֹּא־יָבֹא בְרִנָּה נֹשֵׂא אֲלֻמֹּתָיו:

Some say:

תְּהִלַּת יהוה יְדַבֶּר פִּי, וִיבָרֵךְ כָּל־בָּשָׂר שֵׁם קָדְשׁוֹ לְעוֹלָם תהלים קמה
וָעֶד: וַאֲנַחְנוּ נְבָרֵךְ יָהּ מֵעַתָּה וְעַד־עוֹלָם, הַלְלוּיָהּ: תהלים קטו
הוֹדוּ לַיהוה כִּי־טוֹב, כִּי לְעוֹלָם חַסְדּוֹ: מִי יְמַלֵּל גְּבוּרוֹת תהלים קלו תהלים קו
יהוה, יַשְׁמִיעַ כָּל־תְּהִלָּתוֹ:

It is told that on one of Rav Shakh's later birthdays, his *talmidim* inquired as to what the Rav would take upon himself in the coming year. Would it be another *siyum hashas*? Some act of kindness? The Rav replied, I will seek to recite *Birkat HaMazon* from a *bencher*. It is obvious that Rav Shakh knew the *benching* by heart, but he knew that without the use of a *bencher,* it is possible to not recite the *berakhot* properly.

At the Seder, one of the *simanim* is *barekh*. This section of the Haggada directs us to *bench* properly. Let's take it upon ourselves to fulfill this one biblical blessing appropriately daily, undertaking to recite it while viewing the text, rather than by heart.

RECOGNIZING THE SOURCE

Rav Yosef Dov Soloveitchik (*Mo'adei HaRav*, p. 170) compares the *berakha* we make after eating fruit against the *Birkat HaMazon* we recite after bread. After we eat fruit, which is easily obtained from a tree, we recite the short *berakha, borei nefashot*. However, bread required us to toil. It went through several processes of production, from cultivating the grain to producing flour and ultimately baking; for bread, we recite a long *berakha, Birkat HaMazon*. The Rav asks, given these differences, why do we recite a short *berakha* after the fruit and *Birkat HaMazon* after the bread?

ZIMMUN / INVITATION

When three or more men say Birkat haMazon together, the following zimmun is said. When three or more women say Birkat haMazon, substitute "Friends" for "Gentlemen." The leader should ask permission from those with precedence to lead the Birkat haMazon.

Leader Gentlemen, let us say grace.

Others May the name of the Lord be blessed from now and for ever. *Ps. 113*

Leader May the name of the Lord be blessed from now and for ever.
With your permission, (my father and teacher / my mother and teacher / the Kohanim present / our teacher the Rabbi / the master of this house / the mistress of this house)
my masters and teachers,
let us bless (*in a minyan:* our God,) the One
from whose food we have eaten.

Others Blessed be (*in a minyan:* our God,) the One
from whose food we have eaten,
and by whose goodness we live.

**People present who have not taken part in the meal say:*

*Blessed be (*in a minyan:* our God,) the One
whose name is continually blessed for ever and all time.

Leader Blessed be (*in a minyan:* our God,) the One
from whose food we have eaten, and by whose goodness we live.
Blessed be He, and blessed be His name.

BLESSING OF NOURISHMENT

בָּרוּךְ Blessed are You, Lord our God, King of the Universe,
who in His goodness feeds the whole world
with grace, kindness and compassion.
He gives food to all living things, for His kindness is for ever.
Because of His continual great goodness,
we have never lacked food,
nor may we ever lack it, for the sake of His great name.
For He is God who feeds and sustains all, does good to all,
and prepares food for all creatures He has created.
Blessed are You, Lord, who feeds all.

סדר הזימון

When three or more men say ברכת המזון *together, the following* זימון *is said.*
When three or more women say ברכת המזון*, substitute* חַבְרוֹתַי *for* רַבּוֹתַי.
The leader should ask permission from those with precedence to lead the ברכת המזון.

Leader רַבּוֹתַי, נְבָרֵךְ.

Others יְהִי שֵׁם יהוה מְבֹרָךְ מֵעַתָּה וְעַד־עוֹלָם: תהלים קיג

Leader יְהִי שֵׁם יהוה מְבֹרָךְ מֵעַתָּה וְעַד־עוֹלָם:
בִּרְשׁוּת (אָבִי מוֹרִי / אִמִּי מוֹרָתִי / כֹּהֲנִים / מוֹרֵנוּ הָרַב /
בַּעַל הַבַּיִת הַזֶּה / בַּעֲלַת הַבַּיִת הַזֶּה)

מָרָנָן וְרַבָּנָן וְרַבּוֹתַי
נְבָרֵךְ (במניין: אֱלֹהֵינוּ) שֶׁאָכַלְנוּ מִשֶּׁלּוֹ.

Others בָּרוּךְ (במניין: אֱלֹהֵינוּ) שֶׁאָכַלְנוּ מִשֶּׁלּוֹ וּבְטוּבוֹ חָיִינוּ.

**People present who have not taken part in the meal say:*

*בָּרוּךְ (במנין: אֱלֹהֵינוּ) וּמְבֹרָךְ שְׁמוֹ תָּמִיד לְעוֹלָם וָעֶד.

Leader בָּרוּךְ (במניין: אֱלֹהֵינוּ) שֶׁאָכַלְנוּ מִשֶּׁלּוֹ וּבְטוּבוֹ חָיִינוּ.
בָּרוּךְ הוּא וּבָרוּךְ שְׁמוֹ.

ברכת הזן

בָּרוּךְ אַתָּה יהוה אֱלֹהֵינוּ מֶלֶךְ הָעוֹלָם
הַזָּן אֶת הָעוֹלָם כֻּלּוֹ בְּטוּבוֹ בְּחֵן בְּחֶסֶד וּבְרַחֲמִים
הוּא נוֹתֵן לֶחֶם לְכָל בָּשָׂר כִּי לְעוֹלָם חַסְדּוֹ.
וּבְטוּבוֹ הַגָּדוֹל, תָּמִיד לֹא חָסַר לָנוּ
וְאַל יֶחְסַר לָנוּ מָזוֹן לְעוֹלָם וָעֶד, בַּעֲבוּר שְׁמוֹ הַגָּדוֹל.
כִּי הוּא אֵל זָן וּמְפַרְנֵס לַכֹּל וּמֵטִיב לַכֹּל
וּמֵכִין מָזוֹן לְכָל בְּרִיּוֹתָיו אֲשֶׁר בָּרָא.
בָּרוּךְ אַתָּה יהוה, הַזָּן אֶת הַכֹּל.

BLESSING OF LAND

נוֹדֶה We thank You, Lord our God,
for having granted as a heritage to our ancestors
a desirable, good and spacious land;
for bringing us out, Lord our God, from the land of Egypt,
freeing us from the house of slavery;
for Your covenant which You sealed in our flesh;
for Your Torah which You taught us;
for Your laws which You made known to us;
for the life, grace and kindness You have bestowed on us;
and for the food by which You continually feed and sustain us,
every day, every season, every hour.

For all this, Lord our God,
we thank and bless You.
May Your name be blessed continually
by the mouth of all that lives, for ever and all time –
for so it is written:
"You will eat and be satisfied, then you shall bless the Lord *Deut. 8*
your God for the good land He has given you." Blessed are You,
Lord, for the land and for the food.

BLESSING FOR JERUSALEM

רַחֵם נָא Have compassion,
please, Lord our God,
on Israel Your people,
on Jerusalem Your city,
on Zion the dwelling place of Your glory,
on the royal house of David Your anointed,
and on the great and holy House
that bears Your name.

ברכת הארץ

נוֹדֶה לְּךָ יהוה אֱלֹהֵינוּ
עַל שֶׁהִנְחַלְתָּ לַאֲבוֹתֵינוּ
אֶרֶץ חֶמְדָּה טוֹבָה וּרְחָבָה
וְעַל שֶׁהוֹצֵאתָנוּ יהוה אֱלֹהֵינוּ מֵאֶרֶץ מִצְרַיִם
וּפְדִיתָנוּ מִבֵּית עֲבָדִים
וְעַל בְּרִיתְךָ שֶׁחָתַמְתָּ בִּבְשָׂרֵנוּ
וְעַל תּוֹרָתְךָ שֶׁלִּמַּדְתָּנוּ, וְעַל חֻקֶּיךָ שֶׁהוֹדַעְתָּנוּ
וְעַל חַיִּים חֵן וָחֶסֶד שֶׁחוֹנַנְתָּנוּ
וְעַל אֲכִילַת מָזוֹן שָׁאַתָּה זָן וּמְפַרְנֵס אוֹתָנוּ תָּמִיד
בְּכָל יוֹם וּבְכָל עֵת וּבְכָל שָׁעָה.

וְעַל הַכֹּל, יהוה אֱלֹהֵינוּ
אֲנַחְנוּ מוֹדִים לָךְ וּמְבָרְכִים אוֹתָךְ
יִתְבָּרַךְ שִׁמְךָ בְּפִי כָּל חַי תָּמִיד לְעוֹלָם וָעֶד
כַּכָּתוּב: וְאָכַלְתָּ וְשָׂבָעְתָּ, וּבֵרַכְתָּ אֶת־יהוה אֱלֹהֶיךָ דברים ח
עַל־הָאָרֶץ הַטֹּבָה אֲשֶׁר נָתַן־לָךְ:
בָּרוּךְ אַתָּה יהוה, עַל הָאָרֶץ וְעַל הַמָּזוֹן.

ברכת ירושלים

רַחֶם נָא יהוה אֱלֹהֵינוּ
עַל יִשְׂרָאֵל עַמֶּךָ
וְעַל יְרוּשָׁלַיִם עִירֶךָ
וְעַל צִיּוֹן מִשְׁכַּן כְּבוֹדֶךָ
וְעַל מַלְכוּת בֵּית דָּוִד מְשִׁיחֶךָ
וְעַל הַבַּיִת הַגָּדוֹל וְהַקָּדוֹשׁ שֶׁנִּקְרָא שִׁמְךָ עָלָיו.

Our God, our Father,
tend us, feed us, sustain us and support us,
relieve us and send us relief,
Lord our God, swiftly from all our troubles.
Please, Lord our God, do not make us dependent
on the gifts or loans of other people,
but only on Your full, open, holy and generous hand
so that we may suffer neither shame nor humiliation
for ever and all time.

On Shabbat, say:
רְצֵה Favor and strengthen us, Lord our God,
through Your commandments,
especially through the commandment of the seventh day,
this great and holy Shabbat.
For it is, for You, a great and holy day.
On it we cease work and rest in love
in accord with Your will's commandment.
May it be Your will, Lord our God,
to grant us rest without distress,
grief, or lament on our day of rest.
May You show us the consolation of Zion Your city,
and the rebuilding of Jerusalem Your holy city,
for You are the Master of salvation and consolation.

אֱלֹהֵינוּ Our God and God of our ancestors,
may there rise, come, reach, appear,
be favored, heard, regarded
and remembered before You,
our recollection and remembrance,
as well as the remembrance of our ancestors,
and of the Messiah son of David Your servant,
and of Jerusalem Your holy city,
and of all Your people the house of Israel –
for deliverance and well-being, grace, loving-kindness and
compassion, life and peace, on this day of the festival of Matzot.

אֱלֹהֵינוּ, אָבִינוּ
רְעֵנוּ, זוּנֵנוּ, פַּרְנְסֵנוּ וְכַלְכְּלֵנוּ
וְהַרְוִיחֵנוּ, וְהַרְוַח לָנוּ יהוה אֱלֹהֵינוּ מְהֵרָה מִכָּל צָרוֹתֵינוּ.
וְנָא אַל תַּצְרִיכֵנוּ, יהוה אֱלֹהֵינוּ
לֹא לִידֵי מַתְּנַת בָּשָׂר וָדָם וְלֹא לִידֵי הַלְוָאָתָם
כִּי אִם לְיָדְךָ הַמְּלֵאָה, הַפְּתוּחָה, הַקְּדוֹשָׁה וְהָרְחָבָה
שֶׁלֹּא נֵבוֹשׁ וְלֹא נִכָּלֵם לְעוֹלָם וָעֶד.

On שבת, say:

רְצֵה וְהַחֲלִיצֵנוּ, יהוה אֱלֹהֵינוּ, בְּמִצְוֹתֶיךָ
וּבְמִצְוַת יוֹם הַשְּׁבִיעִי
הַשַּׁבָּת הַגָּדוֹל וְהַקָּדוֹשׁ הַזֶּה
כִּי יוֹם זֶה גָּדוֹל וְקָדוֹשׁ הוּא לְפָנֶיךָ
לִשְׁבָּת בּוֹ, וְלָנוּחַ בּוֹ בְּאַהֲבָה כְּמִצְוַת רְצוֹנֶךָ
וּבִרְצוֹנְךָ הָנִיחַ לָנוּ, יהוה אֱלֹהֵינוּ
שֶׁלֹּא תְהֵא צָרָה וְיָגוֹן וַאֲנָחָה בְּיוֹם מְנוּחָתֵנוּ
וְהַרְאֵנוּ, יהוה אֱלֹהֵינוּ, בְּנֶחָמַת צִיּוֹן עִירֶךָ
וּבְבִנְיַן יְרוּשָׁלַיִם עִיר קָדְשֶׁךָ
כִּי אַתָּה הוּא בַּעַל הַיְשׁוּעוֹת וּבַעַל הַנֶּחָמוֹת.

אֱלֹהֵינוּ וֵאלֹהֵי אֲבוֹתֵינוּ

יַעֲלֶה וְיָבוֹא וְיַגִּיעַ, וְיֵרָאֶה וְיֵרָצֶה וְיִשָּׁמַע, וְיִפָּקֵד
וְיִזָּכֵר זִכְרוֹנֵנוּ וּפִקְדוֹנֵנוּ, וְזִכְרוֹן אֲבוֹתֵינוּ
וְזִכְרוֹן מָשִׁיחַ בֶּן דָּוִד עַבְדֶּךָ
וְזִכְרוֹן יְרוּשָׁלַיִם עִיר קָדְשֶׁךָ
וְזִכְרוֹן כָּל עַמְּךָ בֵּית יִשְׂרָאֵל
לְפָנֶיךָ, לִפְלֵיטָה לְטוֹבָה, לְחֵן וּלְחֶסֶד וּלְרַחֲמִים
לְחַיִּים וּלְשָׁלוֹם בְּיוֹם חַג הַמַּצּוֹת הַזֶּה.

On it remember us, Lord our God, for good;
recollect us for blessing, and deliver us for life.
In accord with Your promise of salvation and compassion,
spare us and be gracious to us;
have compassion on us and deliver us,
for our eyes are turned to You because You are God,
gracious and compassionate.

And may Jerusalem the holy city be rebuilt soon, in our time.
Blessed are You, Lord, who in His compassion
will rebuild Jerusalem. Amen.

BLESSING OF GOD'S GOODNESS

בָּרוּךְ Blessed are You, Lord our God, King of the Universe –
God our Father, our King, our Sovereign,
our Creator, our Redeemer, our Maker,
our Holy One, the Holy One of Yaakov.
He is our Shepherd, Israel's Shepherd,
the good King who does good to all.
Every day He has done, is doing, and will do good to us.
He has acted, is acting,
and will always act kindly toward us for ever,
granting us grace, kindness and compassion, relief and rescue,
prosperity, blessing, redemption and comfort,
sustenance and support, compassion, life,
peace and all good things,
and of all good things may He never let us lack.

ADDITIONAL REQUESTS

הָרַחֲמָן May the Compassionate One reign over us
for ever and all time.

May the Compassionate One be blessed
in heaven and on earth.

זָכְרֵנוּ יהוה אֱלֹהֵינוּ בּוֹ לְטוֹבָה וּפָקְדֵנוּ בוֹ לִבְרָכָה
וְהוֹשִׁיעֵנוּ בוֹ לְחַיִּים.
וּבִדְבַר יְשׁוּעָה וְרַחֲמִים
חוּס וְחָנֵּנוּ וְרַחֵם עָלֵינוּ, וְהוֹשִׁיעֵנוּ
כִּי אֵלֶיךָ עֵינֵינוּ, כִּי אֵל חַנּוּן וְרַחוּם אָתָּה.

וּבְנֵה יְרוּשָׁלַיִם עִיר הַקֹּדֶשׁ בִּמְהֵרָה בְיָמֵינוּ.
בָּרוּךְ אַתָּה יהוה, בּוֹנֵה בְרַחֲמָיו יְרוּשָׁלָיִם, אָמֵן.

ברכת הטוב והמטיב

בָּרוּךְ אַתָּה יהוה אֱלֹהֵינוּ מֶלֶךְ הָעוֹלָם
הָאֵל אָבִינוּ, מַלְכֵּנוּ, אַדִּירֵנוּ
בּוֹרְאֵנוּ, גּוֹאֲלֵנוּ, יוֹצְרֵנוּ, קְדוֹשֵׁנוּ, קְדוֹשׁ יַעֲקֹב
רוֹעֵנוּ, רוֹעֵה יִשְׂרָאֵל, הַמֶּלֶךְ הַטּוֹב וְהַמֵּטִיב לַכֹּל
שֶׁבְּכָל יוֹם וָיוֹם
הוּא הֵטִיב, הוּא מֵטִיב, הוּא יֵיטִיב לָנוּ
הוּא גְמָלָנוּ, הוּא גוֹמְלֵנוּ, הוּא יִגְמְלֵנוּ לָעַד
לְחֵן וּלְחֶסֶד וּלְרַחֲמִים, וּלְרֶוַח, הַצָּלָה וְהַצְלָחָה
בְּרָכָה וִישׁוּעָה, נֶחָמָה, פַּרְנָסָה וְכַלְכָּלָה
וְרַחֲמִים וְחַיִּים וְשָׁלוֹם וְכָל טוֹב
וּמִכָּל טוּב לְעוֹלָם אַל יְחַסְּרֵנוּ.

בקשות נוספות

הָרַחֲמָן הוּא יִמְלֹךְ עָלֵינוּ לְעוֹלָם וָעֶד.

הָרַחֲמָן הוּא יִתְבָּרַךְ בַּשָּׁמַיִם וּבָאָרֶץ.

May the Compassionate One be praised
from generation to generation,
be glorified by us to all eternity,
and honored among us for ever and all time.

May the Compassionate One
grant us an honorable livelihood.

May the Compassionate One
break the yoke from our neck
and lead us upright to our land.

May the Compassionate One
send us many blessings to this house
and this table at which we have eaten.

May the Compassionate One
send us Elijah the prophet –
may he be remembered for good –
to bring us good tidings
of salvation and consolation.

Some say:
May the Compassionate One
bless the State of Israel,
first flowering of our redemption.

May the Compassionate One
bless the members of Israel's Defense Forces,
who stand guard over our land.

A guest says:

יְהִי רָצוֹן May it be Your will that the master of this house shall not suffer shame in this world, nor humiliation in the World to Come. May all he owns prosper greatly, and may his and our possessions be successful and close to hand. Let not the Accuser hold sway over his deeds or ours, and may no thought of sin, iniquity or transgression enter him or us from now and for evermore.

הָרַחֲמָן הוּא יִשְׁתַּבַּח לְדוֹר דּוֹרִים
וְיִתְפָּאַר בָּנוּ לָעַד וּלְנֵצַח נְצָחִים
וְיִתְהַדַּר בָּנוּ לָעַד וּלְעוֹלְמֵי עוֹלָמִים.

הָרַחֲמָן הוּא יְפַרְנְסֵנוּ בְּכָבוֹד.

הָרַחֲמָן הוּא יִשְׁבֹּר עֻלֵּנוּ מֵעַל צַוָּארֵנוּ
וְהוּא יוֹלִיכֵנוּ קוֹמְמִיּוּת לְאַרְצֵנוּ.

הָרַחֲמָן הוּא יִשְׁלַח לָנוּ
בְּרָכָה מְרֻבָּה בַּבַּיִת הַזֶּה
וְעַל שֻׁלְחָן זֶה שֶׁאָכַלְנוּ עָלָיו.

הָרַחֲמָן הוּא יִשְׁלַח לָנוּ
אֶת אֵלִיָּהוּ הַנָּבִיא זָכוּר לַטּוֹב
וִיבַשֶּׂר לָנוּ בְּשׂוֹרוֹת טוֹבוֹת יְשׁוּעוֹת וְנֶחָמוֹת.

Some say:

הָרַחֲמָן הוּא יְבָרֵךְ
אֶת מְדִינַת יִשְׂרָאֵל
רֵאשִׁית צְמִיחַת גְּאֻלָּתֵנוּ.

הָרַחֲמָן הוּא יְבָרֵךְ
אֶת חַיָּלֵי צְבָא הַהֲגָנָה לְיִשְׂרָאֵל
הָעוֹמְדִים עַל מִשְׁמַר אַרְצֵנוּ.

A guest says:

יְהִי רָצוֹן שֶׁלֹּא יֵבוֹשׁ בַּעַל הַבַּיִת בָּעוֹלָם הַזֶּה, וְלֹא יִכָּלֵם לָעוֹלָם הַבָּא, וְיִצְלַח מְאֹד בְּכָל נְכָסָיו, וְיִהְיוּ נְכָסָיו וּנְכָסֵינוּ מֻצְלָחִים וּקְרוֹבִים לָעִיר, וְאַל יִשְׁלֹט שָׂטָן לֹא בְּמַעֲשֵׂה יָדָיו וְלֹא בְּמַעֲשֵׂה יָדֵינוּ. וְאַל יִזְדַּקֵּק לֹא לְפָנָיו וְלֹא לְפָנֵינוּ שׁוּם דְּבַר הִרְהוּר חֵטְא, עֲבֵירָה וְעָוֹן, מֵעַתָּה וְעַד עוֹלָם.

הָרַחֲמָן May the Compassionate One bless –

When eating at one's own table, say (include the words in parentheses that apply):

me, (my wife / husband / my father, my teacher / my mother, my teacher / my children) and all that is mine,

A guest at someone else's table says (include the words in parentheses that apply):

the master of this house, him (and his wife, the mistress of this house / and his children) and all that is his,

Children at their parents' table say (include the words in parentheses that apply):

my father, my teacher (master of this house), and my mother, my teacher (mistress of this house), them, their household, their children, and all that is theirs.

For all other guests, add:

and all the diners here,

אוֹתָנוּ – together with us and all that is ours. Just as our forefathers Avraham, Yitzhak, and Yaakov were blessed in all, from all, with all, so may He bless all of us together with a complete blessing, and let us say: Amen.

בַּמָּרוֹם On high, may grace be invoked for them and for us,
as a safeguard of peace.
May we receive a blessing from the Lord
and a just reward from the God of our salvation,
and may we find grace and good favor in the eyes of God and man.

On Shabbat: May the Compassionate One let us inherit the time, that will be entirely Shabbat and rest for life everlasting.

May the Compassionate One let us inherit the day that is all good.

הָרַחֲמָן הוּא יְבָרֵךְ

When eating at one's own table, say (include the words in parentheses that apply):

אוֹתִי (וְאֶת אִשְׁתִּי / וְאֶת בַּעֲלִי / וְאֶת אָבִי מוֹרִי / וְאֶת אִמִּי מוֹרָתִי / וְאֶת זַרְעִי) וְאֶת כָּל אֲשֶׁר לִי.

A guest at someone else's table says (include the words in parentheses that apply):

אֶת בַּעַל הַבַּיִת הַזֶּה, אוֹתוֹ (וְאֶת אִשְׁתּוֹ בַּעֲלַת הַבַּיִת הַזֶּה / וְאֶת זַרְעוֹ) וְאֶת כָּל אֲשֶׁר לוֹ.

Children at their parents' table say (include the words in parentheses that apply):

אֶת אָבִי מוֹרִי (בַּעַל הַבַּיִת הַזֶּה), וְאֶת אִמִּי מוֹרָתִי (בַּעֲלַת הַבַּיִת הַזֶּה), אוֹתָם וְאֶת בֵּיתָם וְאֶת זַרְעָם וְאֶת כָּל אֲשֶׁר לָהֶם

For all other guests, add:

וְאֶת כָּל הַמְּסֻבִּין כָּאן

אוֹתָנוּ וְאֶת כָּל אֲשֶׁר לָנוּ כְּמוֹ שֶׁנִּתְבָּרְכוּ אֲבוֹתֵינוּ אַבְרָהָם יִצְחָק וְיַעֲקֹב, בַּכֹּל, מִכֹּל, כֹּל כֵּן יְבָרֵךְ אוֹתָנוּ כֻּלָּנוּ יַחַד בִּבְרָכָה שְׁלֵמָה, וְנֹאמַר אָמֵן.

בַּמָּרוֹם יְלַמְּדוּ עֲלֵיהֶם וְעָלֵינוּ זְכוּת שֶׁתְּהֵא לְמִשְׁמֶרֶת שָׁלוֹם וְנִשָּׂא בְרָכָה מֵאֵת יהוה וּצְדָקָה מֵאֱלֹהֵי יִשְׁעֵנוּ וְנִמְצָא חֵן וְשֵׂכֶל טוֹב בְּעֵינֵי אֱלֹהִים וְאָדָם.

בשבת: הָרַחֲמָן הוּא יַנְחִילֵנוּ יוֹם שֶׁכֻּלּוֹ שַׁבָּת וּמְנוּחָה לְחַיֵּי הָעוֹלָמִים.

הָרַחֲמָן הוּא יַנְחִילֵנוּ יוֹם שֶׁכֻּלּוֹ טוֹב.

הָרַחֲמָן May the Compassionate One make us worthy
of the messianic age and life in the World to Come.
He is a tower of salvation to His king, *II Sam. 22*
showing kindness to His anointed,
to David and his descendants for ever.
He who makes peace in His high places,
may He make peace for us and all Israel, and let us say: Amen.

יְראוּ Fear the LORD, you His holy ones; *Ps. 34*
those who fear Him lack nothing.
Young lions may grow weak and hungry,
but those who seek the LORD lack no good thing.
Thank the LORD for He is good: *Ps. 118*
His loving-kindness is for ever.
You open Your hand and satisfy the desire of every living thing. *Ps. 145*
Blessed is the person who trusts in the LORD, *Jer. 17*
whose trust is in the LORD alone.
Once I was young, and now I am old, *Ps. 37*
yet I have never watched a righteous man forsaken
or his children begging for bread.
The LORD will give His people strength. *Ps. 29*
The LORD will bless His people with peace.

Blessed are You, LORD our God, King of the Universe,
who creates the fruit of the vine.

Drink while reclining to the left.

---

and stand idly by and not do anything about it? (*Esther* 8:6). *Ra'iti* means to see something and not react to it. Therefore, perhaps the verse above can be understood in this fashion as well: I've grown old, and I have experienced a lot in my life, but I never stood idly by when I saw somebody else in need.

When we express our appreciation to Hashem after consuming our meal, we declare that we will *also* provide for others, as Hashem

has provided

הָרַחֲמָן הוּא יְזַכֵּנוּ לִימוֹת הַמָּשִׁיחַ וּלְחַיֵּי הָעוֹלָם הַבָּא
מִגְדּוֹל יְשׁוּעוֹת מַלְכּוֹ וְעֹשֶׂה־חֶסֶד לִמְשִׁיחוֹ שמואל ב׳ כב
לְדָוִד וּלְזַרְעוֹ עַד־עוֹלָם:
עֹשֶׂה שָׁלוֹם בִּמְרוֹמָיו הוּא
יַעֲשֶׂה שָׁלוֹם עָלֵינוּ וְעַל כָּל יִשְׂרָאֵל, וְאִמְרוּ אָמֵן.

יְראוּ אֶת־יהוה קְדֹשָׁיו כִּי־אֵין מַחְסוֹר לִירֵאָיו: תהלים לד
כְּפִירִים רָשׁוּ וְרָעֵבוּ וְדֹרְשֵׁי יהוה לֹא־יַחְסְרוּ כָל־טוֹב:
הוֹדוּ לַיהוה כִּי־טוֹב כִּי לְעוֹלָם חַסְדּוֹ: תהלים קיח
פּוֹתֵחַ אֶת־יָדֶךָ וּמַשְׂבִּיעַ לְכָל־חַי רָצוֹן: תהלים קמה
בָּרוּךְ הַגֶּבֶר אֲשֶׁר יִבְטַח בַּיהוה ירמיה יז
וְהָיָה יהוה מִבְטַחוֹ:
נַעַר הָיִיתִי גַּם־זָקַנְתִּי וְלֹא־רָאִיתִי צַדִּיק נֶעֱזָב וְזַרְעוֹ מְבַקֶּשׁ־לָחֶם: תהלים לז
יהוה עֹז לְעַמּוֹ יִתֵּן יהוה יְבָרֵךְ אֶת־עַמּוֹ בַשָּׁלוֹם: תהלים כט

בָּרוּךְ אַתָּה יהוה אֱלֹהֵינוּ מֶלֶךְ הָעוֹלָם
בּוֹרֵא פְּרִי הַגָּפֶן.

Drink while reclining to the left.

נַעַר הָיִיתִי – NAAR HAYITI

In *Birkat HaMazon,* we recite *naar hayiti, gam zakanti, velo ra'iti tzaddik ne'ezav* (*Tehillim* 37:25). Do we ever think about the meaning of this *pasuk*? It is, I have lived many days and I've never seen a *tzaddik* that was forsaken. Is this statement accurate? Are there no righteous people that suffer?

Rabbi Lord Jonathan Sacks *z"l,* in his Haggada (p. 118), says that the key phrase here is *lo ra'iti*. Think back to *Megillat Esther*. Esther says, *eikhakha ukhal vera'iti be'avedon moladeti,* how could I see

A cup of wine is now poured in honor of Elijah, and the door opened.

שְׁפֹךְ **POUR OUT** Your rage *Ps. 79*
upon the nations that do not know You,
and on regimes that have not called upon Your name.
For Yaakov is devoured;
they have laid his places waste.
Pour out Your great anger upon them, *Ps. 69*
and let Your blazing fury overtake them.
Pursue them in Your fury and destroy them *Lam. 3*
from under the heavens of the Lord.

---

goal. This happened at the time of the flood. Representatives of all of the animals gathered together for survival because they had no other choice.

There is, however, another type of *ahdut*. The prophet Yeshayahu states that in the future days, the wolf shall dwell with the lamb (*Yeshayahu* 11:6). This type of unity is not out of necessity, but of true comradery.

Unfortunately, what usually unites the other nations is their common goal of destroying the Jews. It is a unity based on a common goal, not out of true love for each other. Bilam explained that at Har Sinai, it was not similar to the flood. At Har Sinai, we experienced true unity, *ke'ish ehad belev ehad*, like one people with one heart.

The nations of the world unite against us. The common denominator is their hatred of Israel. The UN has consistently enacted more resolutions against Israel than it has against any other country. Corrupt regimes around the world unite to condemn Israel, notwithstanding all the human rights violations that are being conducted in their respective countries.

That is the meaning of *ki akhal* in the singular. We ask Hashem to pour out His wrath on those nations that unjustifiably unite against our people and our country, so that true peace and justice can prevail.

A cup of wine is now poured in honor of Elijah, and the door opened.

שְׁפֹךְ חֲמָתְךָ אֶל־הַגּוֹיִם אֲשֶׁר לֹא־יְדָעוּךָ תהלים עט
וְעַל מַמְלָכוֹת אֲשֶׁר בְּשִׁמְךָ לֹא קָרָאוּ:
כִּי אָכַל אֶת־יַעֲקֹב, וְאֶת־נָוֵהוּ הֵשַׁמּוּ:
שְׁפָךְ־עֲלֵיהֶם זַעְמֶךָ וַחֲרוֹן אַפְּךָ יַשִּׂיגֵם: תהלים סט
תִּרְדֹּף בְּאַף וְתַשְׁמִידֵם מִתַּחַת שְׁמֵי יהוה: איכה ג

---

has provided for us. Essentially, I never witnessed a *tzaddik* lacking, because I cared for him. We must always focus on other people's physical needs.

I once heard that in Judaism, the right side of the body is always more significant. Why then did Hashem create our heart on our left side? Perhaps because it is on the right side of the person facing you, so our heart will be focused on that of the other.

שְׁפֹךְ חֲמָתְךָ – SHEFOKH HAMATEKHA

Following the meal, we open our doors and declare, *shefokh hamatekha el hagoyim,* pour out your wrath unto other nations, *ki akhal et Yaakov,* because they have eaten Yaakov.

It is interesting to note that the language shifts from plural to singular. We refer to *goyim,* which are many nations, and then we state *ki akhal* in the singular, rather than *ki akhlu* in the plural.

The *gemara* in Zevahim 116 records that when the Torah was given, the nations of the world reached out to Bilam to inquire as to what was transpiring. They felt the world shaking, panicked, and wondered if another flood was about to ensue. Bilam calmed them down and explained that the commotion was related to momentous occasion of *matan Torah.*

What exactly is the connection between the flood and *matan Torah*?

Rav Meir Shapiro explains that there are two types of *ahdut,* two types of unity. One type of *ahdut* occurs because of a common

HALLEL / PRAISING

The fourth cup of wine is poured, and Hallel is completed.

לֹא לָנוּ Not to us, Lord, not to us, Ps. 115
but to Your name give glory,
for Your love, for Your faithfulness.
Why should the nations say, "Where now is their God?"
Our God is in heaven; whatever He wills He does.
Their idols are silver and gold, made by human hands.
They have mouths but cannot speak; eyes but cannot see.
They have ears but cannot hear; noses but cannot smell.
They have hands but cannot feel; feet but cannot walk.
No sound comes from their throat.
Those who make them become like them;
so will all who trust in them.
Israel, trust in the Lord –
He is their Help and their Shield.
House of Aaron, trust in the Lord –
He is their Help and their Shield.
You who fear the Lord,
trust in the Lord –
He is their Help and their Shield.

The Maharal in the beginning of *Pirkei Avot,* in his *sefer Derekh Haim,* asks an interesting question. We know that there are three cardinal sins for which one is obligated to sacrifice his life. These are *avoda zara* (idolatry), *gilui arayot* (prohibited relations), and *shefikhut damim* (murder). Why are these three selected over all other prohibitions?

The Maharal

הלל

The fourth cup of wine is poured, and הלל *is completed.*

תהלים קטו

לֹא לָנוּ יהוה לֹא לָנוּ
כִּי־לְשִׁמְךָ תֵּן כָּבוֹד
עַל־חַסְדְּךָ עַל־אֲמִתֶּךָ:
לָמָּה יֹאמְרוּ הַגּוֹיִם אַיֵּה־נָא אֱלֹהֵיהֶם:
וֵאלֹהֵינוּ בַשָּׁמָיִם, כֹּל אֲשֶׁר־חָפֵץ עָשָׂה:
עֲצַבֵּיהֶם כֶּסֶף וְזָהָב, מַעֲשֵׂה יְדֵי אָדָם:
פֶּה־לָהֶם וְלֹא יְדַבֵּרוּ, עֵינַיִם לָהֶם וְלֹא יִרְאוּ:
אָזְנַיִם לָהֶם וְלֹא יִשְׁמָעוּ, אַף לָהֶם וְלֹא יְרִיחוּן:
יְדֵיהֶם וְלֹא יְמִישׁוּן, רַגְלֵיהֶם וְלֹא יְהַלֵּכוּ, לֹא־יֶהְגּוּ בִּגְרוֹנָם:
כְּמוֹהֶם יִהְיוּ עֹשֵׂיהֶם, כֹּל אֲשֶׁר־בֹּטֵחַ בָּהֶם:
יִשְׂרָאֵל בְּטַח בַּיהוה
עֶזְרָם וּמָגִנָּם הוּא:
בֵּית אַהֲרֹן בִּטְחוּ בַיהוה
עֶזְרָם וּמָגִנָּם הוּא:
יִרְאֵי יהוה בִּטְחוּ בַיהוה
עֶזְרָם וּמָגִנָּם הוּא:

HALLEL / PRAISING

לֹא לָנוּ – LO LANU

Lo lanu contains several statements related to idolatry. “They have eyes but cannot see, ears but cannot hear.”

יהוה זְכָרָנוּ The LORD remembers us and will bless us.
He will bless the house of Israel.
He will bless the house of Aaron.
He will bless those who fear the LORD, small and great alike.
May the LORD give you increase: you and your children.
May you be blessed by the LORD, Maker of heaven and earth.
The heavens are the LORD's,
but the earth He has given over to mankind.
It is not the dead who praise the LORD,
nor those who go down to the silent grave.
But we will bless the LORD, now and for ever.

HALLELUYA!

אָהַבְתִּי I love the LORD, *Ps. 116*
for He hears my voice, my pleas.
He turns His ear to me whenever I call.
The bonds of death encompassed me,
the anguish of the grave came upon me,
I was overcome by trouble and sorrow.
Then I called on the name of the LORD:
"LORD, I pray, save my life."

- *Gemilut hasadim* corresponds with murder, as murder is the antithesis of an act of kindness one can perform for another.

The connection between Torah and *gilui arayot,* however, is not so obvious. The Maharal suggests that *gilui arayot* is the most animalistic, mundane, and physical activity in which one might engage. Torah is the opposite. It offers the most sublime, heavenly, and uplifting activity.

As we recite this paragraph in *Hallel* and denounce idolatry, we should be reminded that we are engaging in prayer, one of the greatest pillars upon which this world stands.

Ana Hashem

יהוה זְכָרָנוּ יְבָרֵךְ
יְבָרֵךְ אֶת־בֵּית יִשְׂרָאֵל, יְבָרֵךְ אֶת־בֵּית אַהֲרֹן:
יְבָרֵךְ יִרְאֵי יהוה, הַקְּטַנִּים עִם־הַגְּדֹלִים:
יֹסֵף יהוה עֲלֵיכֶם, עֲלֵיכֶם וְעַל־בְּנֵיכֶם:
בְּרוּכִים אַתֶּם לַיהוה, עֹשֵׂה שָׁמַיִם וָאָרֶץ:
הַשָּׁמַיִם שָׁמַיִם לַיהוה, וְהָאָרֶץ נָתַן לִבְנֵי־אָדָם:
לֹא הַמֵּתִים יְהַלְלוּ־יָהּ, וְלֹא כָּל־יֹרְדֵי דוּמָה:
וַאֲנַחְנוּ נְבָרֵךְ יָהּ, מֵעַתָּה וְעַד־עוֹלָם
הַלְלוּיָהּ:

תהלים קטז

אָהַבְתִּי
כִּי־יִשְׁמַע יהוה, אֶת־קוֹלִי תַּחֲנוּנָי:
כִּי־הִטָּה אָזְנוֹ לִי, וּבְיָמַי אֶקְרָא:
אֲפָפוּנִי חֶבְלֵי־מָוֶת, וּמְצָרֵי שְׁאוֹל מְצָאוּנִי
צָרָה וְיָגוֹן אֶמְצָא:
וּבְשֵׁם־יהוה אֶקְרָא, אָנָּה יהוה מַלְּטָה נַפְשִׁי:

The Maharal suggests that they are the opposite of the three pillars upon which the world stands. Torah, *avoda,* which is prayer, and *gemilut hasadim,* which is acts of kindness (*Pirkei Avot* 1:2). Therefore, if one commits one of the three cardinal sins, it is as if they are uprooting the pillars upon which the world stands.

Two of these comparisons are quite straightforward:

- *Avoda zara* corresponds with *avoda* of prayer, as one who worships idolatry uproots the prayer through which we communicate with our Creator.

Gracious is the Lord, and righteous;
our God is full of compassion.
The Lord protects the simple hearted.
When I was brought low, He saved me.
My soul, be at peace once more,
for the Lord has been good to you.
For You have rescued me from death,
my eyes from weeping, my feet from stumbling.
I shall walk in the presence of the Lord
in the land of the living.
I had faith, even when I said, "I am greatly afflicted,"
even when I said rashly, "All men are liars."

מָה־אָשִׁיב How can I repay the Lord for all His goodness to me?
I will lift the cup of salvation and call on the name of the Lord.
I will fulfill my vows to the Lord
in the presence of all His people.
Grievous in the Lord's sight is the death of His devoted ones.
Truly, Lord, I am Your servant;
I am Your servant, the son of Your maidservant.
You set me free from my chains.
To You I shall bring a thanksgiving-offering
and call on the Lord by name.
I will fulfill my vows to the Lord in the presence of all His people,
in the courts of the House of the Lord,
in your midst, Jerusalem.

HALLELUYA!

The Rebbe responded that it was neither. He was referring to *ana Hashem ki ani avdekha*, please Hashem, for I am your servant. This is the key to being a Jew: understanding that we are here to serve Hashem. Tonight, we should state this verse with special concentration, special *kavana*, as we are proclaiming that we went from being servants of Pharaoh to being *avdei Hashem*!

חַנּוּן יהוה וְצַדִּיק, וֵאלֹהֵינוּ מְרַחֵם:
שֹׁמֵר פְּתָאִים יהוה, דַּלּוֹתִי וְלִי יְהוֹשִׁיעַ:
שׁוּבִי נַפְשִׁי לִמְנוּחָיְכִי, כִּי־יהוה גָּמַל עָלָיְכִי:
כִּי חִלַּצְתָּ נַפְשִׁי מִמָּוֶת, אֶת־עֵינִי מִן־דִּמְעָה, אֶת־רַגְלִי מִדֶּחִי:
אֶתְהַלֵּךְ לִפְנֵי יהוה, בְּאַרְצוֹת הַחַיִּים:
הֶאֱמַנְתִּי כִּי אֲדַבֵּר, אֲנִי עָנִיתִי מְאֹד:
אֲנִי אָמַרְתִּי בְחָפְזִי, כָּל־הָאָדָם כֹּזֵב:

מָה־אָשִׁיב לַיהוה, כָּל־תַּגְמוּלוֹהִי עָלָי:
כּוֹס־יְשׁוּעוֹת אֶשָּׂא, וּבְשֵׁם יהוה אֶקְרָא:
נְדָרַי לַיהוה אֲשַׁלֵּם, נֶגְדָה־נָּא לְכָל־עַמּוֹ:
יָקָר בְּעֵינֵי יהוה, הַמָּוְתָה לַחֲסִידָיו:
אָנָּה יהוה כִּי־אֲנִי עַבְדֶּךָ, אֲנִי־עַבְדְּךָ בֶּן־אֲמָתֶךָ
פִּתַּחְתָּ לְמוֹסֵרָי:
לְךָ־אֶזְבַּח זֶבַח תּוֹדָה, וּבְשֵׁם יהוה אֶקְרָא:
נְדָרַי לַיהוה אֲשַׁלֵּם, נֶגְדָה־נָּא לְכָל־עַמּוֹ:
בְּחַצְרוֹת בֵּית יהוה, בְּתוֹכֵכִי יְרוּשָׁלָםִ
הַלְלוּיָהּ:

אָנָּה יהוה כִּי־אֲנִי עַבְדֶּךָ – ANA HASHEM KI ANI AVDEKHA

A story is told that the Lev Simha, one of the Gerer rebbeim, told his *hasidim* to have special *kavana* when reciting the words *ana Hashem* during *Hallel*. There was an argument among the *hasidim* as to whether the Rebbe was referring to *ana Hashem hoshia na,* or *ana Hashem hatzliha na.* The Rebbe's son approached Rav Simha to resolve the debate among the *hasidim*.

הַלְלוּ Praise the Lord, all nations; acclaim Him, all you peoples; *Ps. 117*
for His loving-kindness to us is strong,
and the Lord's faithfulness is everlasting.
HALLELUYA!

הוֹדוּ Thank the Lord for He is good, *Ps. 118*
His loving-kindness is for ever.
Let Israel say
His loving-kindness is for ever.
Let the house of Aaron say
His loving-kindness is for ever.
Let those who fear the Lord say
His loving-kindness is for ever.

מִן־הַמֵּצַר In my distress I called on the Lord.
The Lord answered me and set me free.
The Lord is with me; I will not be afraid.
What can man do to me? The Lord is with me.
He is my Helper. I will see the downfall of my enemies.
It is better to take refuge in the Lord than to trust in man.

---

protect us. That is to say, you may plan to blow up a bridge and destroy a caravan of Jews, but Hashem causes your explosive device to jam, and the Jewish caravan is saved. Only you are aware of this compassionate act of the Almighty, and therefore, only you can praise Him for His *hesed* toward us.

Even in those generations where there appears to be tranquility, the other nations either plot unsuccessfully against us or seek to annihilate us not through physical means but by doing all they can to degrade us spiritually.

תהלים קיז

הַלְלוּ אֶת־יהוה כָּל־גּוֹיִם, שַׁבְּחוּהוּ כָּל־הָאֻמִּים:
כִּי גָבַר עָלֵינוּ חַסְדּוֹ, וֶאֱמֶת־יהוה לְעוֹלָם
הַלְלוּיָהּ:

תהלים קיח

הוֹדוּ לַיהוה כִּי־טוֹב כִּי לְעוֹלָם חַסְדּוֹ:
יֹאמַר־נָא יִשְׂרָאֵל כִּי לְעוֹלָם חַסְדּוֹ:
יֹאמְרוּ־נָא בֵית־אַהֲרֹן כִּי לְעוֹלָם חַסְדּוֹ:
יֹאמְרוּ־נָא יִרְאֵי יהוה כִּי לְעוֹלָם חַסְדּוֹ:

מִן־הַמֵּצַר קָרָאתִי יָּהּ, עָנָנִי בַמֶּרְחָב יָהּ:
יהוה לִי לֹא אִירָא, מַה־יַּעֲשֶׂה לִי אָדָם:
יהוה לִי בְּעֹזְרָי, וַאֲנִי אֶרְאֶה בְשֹׂנְאָי:
טוֹב לַחֲסוֹת בַּיהוה, מִבְּטֹחַ בָּאָדָם:

הַלְלוּ אֶת־יהוה כָּל־גּוֹיִם – HALLELU ET HASHEM KOL GOYIM

A priest once asked Rav Chaim of Volozhin a question regarding a *pasuk* in *Tehillim* that we recite in *Hallel*. It says in *Tehillim* (117), *Hallelu et Hashem kol goyim, shabehuhu kol ha'umim,* all the nations of the world will praise God. Why? *Ki gavar aleinu hasdo,* because God showered us Jews with compassion. The priest did not comprehend why gentiles would praise God for showing compassion to the Jews.

Rav Chaim Volozhin explained to the priest that we are not cognizant of all the evil schemes that you plotted against us. Only you know exactly what you have planned for us, and Hashem acts to

It is better to take refuge in the LORD than to trust in princes.
The nations all surrounded me,
but in the LORD's name I drove them off.
They surrounded me on every side,
but in the LORD's name I drove them off.
They surrounded me like bees, they attacked me as fire attacks
brushwood, but in the LORD's name I drove them off.
They thrust so hard against me, I nearly fell,
but the LORD came to my help.
The LORD is my strength and my song;
He has become my salvation.
Sounds of song and salvation resound in the tents of the righteous:
"The LORD's right hand has done mighty deeds.
The LORD's right hand is lifted high.
The LORD's right hand has done mighty deeds."
I will not die but live, and tell what the LORD has done.
The LORD has chastened me severely,
but He has not given me over to death.
Open for me the gates of righteousness
that I may enter them and thank the LORD.
This is the gateway to the LORD; through it,
the righteous shall enter.

אוֹדְךָ I will thank You,
for You answered me, and became my salvation.
I will thank You, for You answered me, and became my salvation.

The stone the builders rejected has become the main cornerstone.
The stone the builders rejected has become the main cornerstone.

This is the LORD's doing. It is wondrous in our eyes.
This is the LORD's doing. It is wondrous in our eyes.

This is the day the LORD has made. Let us rejoice and be glad in it.
This is the day the LORD has made. Let us rejoice and be glad in it.

טוֹב לַחֲסוֹת בַּיהוה, מִבְּטֹחַ בִּנְדִיבִים:
כָּל־גּוֹיִם סְבָבוּנִי, בְּשֵׁם יהוה כִּי אֲמִילַם:
סַבּוּנִי גַם־סְבָבוּנִי, בְּשֵׁם יהוה כִּי אֲמִילַם:
סַבּוּנִי כִדְבֹרִים, דֹּעֲכוּ כְּאֵשׁ קוֹצִים
בְּשֵׁם יהוה כִּי אֲמִילַם:
דָּחֹה דְחִיתַנִי לִנְפֹּל, וַיהוה עֲזָרָנִי:
עָזִּי וְזִמְרָת יָהּ, וַיְהִי־לִי לִישׁוּעָה:
קוֹל רִנָּה וִישׁוּעָה בְּאָהֳלֵי צַדִּיקִים
יְמִין יהוה עֹשָׂה חָיִל:
יְמִין יהוה רוֹמֵמָה, יְמִין יהוה עֹשָׂה חָיִל:
לֹא־אָמוּת כִּי־אֶחְיֶה, וַאֲסַפֵּר מַעֲשֵׂי יָהּ:
יַסֹּר יִסְּרַנִּי יָּהּ, וְלַמָּוֶת לֹא נְתָנָנִי:
פִּתְחוּ־לִי שַׁעֲרֵי־צֶדֶק, אָבֹא־בָם אוֹדֶה יָהּ:
זֶה־הַשַּׁעַר לַיהוה, צַדִּיקִים יָבֹאוּ בוֹ:

אוֹדְךָ כִּי עֲנִיתָנִי, וַתְּהִי־לִי לִישׁוּעָה:
אוֹדְךָ כִּי עֲנִיתָנִי, וַתְּהִי־לִי לִישׁוּעָה:

אֶבֶן מָאֲסוּ הַבּוֹנִים, הָיְתָה לְרֹאשׁ פִּנָּה:
אֶבֶן מָאֲסוּ הַבּוֹנִים, הָיְתָה לְרֹאשׁ פִּנָּה:

מֵאֵת יהוה הָיְתָה זֹּאת, הִיא נִפְלָאת בְּעֵינֵינוּ:
מֵאֵת יהוה הָיְתָה זֹּאת, הִיא נִפְלָאת בְּעֵינֵינוּ:

זֶה־הַיּוֹם עָשָׂה יהוה, נָגִילָה וְנִשְׂמְחָה בוֹ:
זֶה־הַיּוֹם עָשָׂה יהוה, נָגִילָה וְנִשְׂמְחָה בוֹ:

אָנָּא LORD, PLEASE, SAVE US.
LORD, PLEASE, SAVE US.
LORD, PLEASE, GRANT US SUCCESS.
LORD, PLEASE, GRANT US SUCCESS.

בָּרוּךְ Blessed is one who comes in the name of the LORD;
we bless you from the House of the LORD.
Blessed is one who comes in the name of the LORD;
we bless you from the House of the LORD.

The LORD is God; He has given us light. Bind the festival offering
with thick cords [and bring it] to the horns of the altar.
The LORD is God; He has given us light. Bind the festival offering
with thick cords [and bring it] to the horns of the altar.

You are my God and I will thank You;
You are my God, I will exalt You.
You are my God and I will thank You; You are my God, I will exalt You.

Thank the LORD for He is good, His loving-kindness is for ever.
Thank the LORD for He is good, His loving-kindness is for ever.

---

kot, expressing that we know Hashem is in charge, no matter what we are experiencing.

In addition, twice in Tanakh the statement *yehi shem Hashem mevorakh,* blessed be the name of Hashem, appears. Once in *Tehillim* (113:2) which is cited in *Hallel* and the other at the beginning of *Iyov* (1:21) when it states *Hashem natan veHashem lakah, yehi shem Hashem mevorakh* – "The Lord has given and the Lord has taken; may the Lord's name be blessed." Thus, we recognize and turn to Hashem in times of difficulty, as well as in times of celebration.

HODU

אָנָּא יהוה הוֹשִׁיעָה נָּא:
אָנָּא יהוה הוֹשִׁיעָה נָּא:
אָנָּא יהוה הַצְלִיחָה נָא:
אָנָּא יהוה הַצְלִיחָה נָא:

בָּרוּךְ הַבָּא בְּשֵׁם יהוה, בֵּרַכְנוּכֶם מִבֵּית יהוה:
בָּרוּךְ הַבָּא בְּשֵׁם יהוה, בֵּרַכְנוּכֶם מִבֵּית יהוה:

אֵל יהוה וַיָּאֶר לָנוּ, אִסְרוּ־חַג בַּעֲבֹתִים עַד־קַרְנוֹת הַמִּזְבֵּחַ:
אֵל יהוה וַיָּאֶר לָנוּ, אִסְרוּ־חַג בַּעֲבֹתִים עַד־קַרְנוֹת הַמִּזְבֵּחַ:

אֵלִי אַתָּה וְאוֹדֶךָּ, אֱלֹהַי אֲרוֹמְמֶךָּ:
אֵלִי אַתָּה וְאוֹדֶךָּ, אֱלֹהַי אֲרוֹמְמֶךָּ:

הוֹדוּ לַיהוה כִּי־טוֹב, כִּי לְעוֹלָם חַסְדּוֹ:
הוֹדוּ לַיהוה כִּי־טוֹב, כִּי לְעוֹלָם חַסְדּוֹ:

אָנָּא יהוה הוֹשִׁיעָה נָּא – ANA HASHEM HOSHIA NA

As we recite *Hallel* and feel like we are on top of the world, it seems a bit strange that we are also asking for a *yeshua,* for salvation. Similarly, on Sukkot, we perform *Hoshanot* at a time of tremendous celebration. We cry out *hoshia na,* save us! It would seem more appropriate to conduct *Hoshanot* on Rosh HaShana or Yom Kippur rather than on Sukkot, which is *zman simhatenu,* a time of joy.

The Shemen HaTov explains that calling out to Hashem should not be limited to an *eit tzara,* to challenging times. We should turn to Hashem even at times of celebration, during *Hallel* and on Suk-

יְהַלְלוּךָ ALL YOUR WORKS WILL PRAISE YOU,
LORD our God, and Your devoted ones –
the righteous who do Your will,
together with all Your people
the house of Israel –
will joyously thank, bless, praise,
glorify, exalt, revere, sanctify,
and proclaim the sovereignty of Your name, our King.
For it is good to thank You
and fitting to sing psalms to Your name,
for from eternity to eternity You are God.

הוֹדוּ Thank the LORD, for He is good, His loving-kindness is for ever. *Ps. 136*
Thank the God of gods, His loving-kindness is for ever.
Thank the LORD of lords, His loving-kindness is for ever.
To the One who alone
works great wonders, His loving-kindness is for ever.

Yehuda in typical, natural childbirth. Thousands of babies are born each day. What was the great miracle of Yehuda's birth?

It was a normal birth. No great miracle occurred. Leah recognized Hashem's greatness and kindness, and thanked Him for what most of us view as simple childbearing. Leah was the first to thank Hashem for something natural, recognizing that it's truly miraculous, that there's nothing natural about it.

What appears to be mundane is often a great miracle performed by Hashem on our behalf. We have to internalize this message and remember it in our lives.

Rav Dessler in his *sefer Mikhtav Me'Eliyahu* offers a *mashal* to emphasize the miraculous acts of Hashem that occur on a daily basis. Imagine gazing out a window and suddenly witnessing a hand coming out of the ground. After taking a closer look, a face begins to appear, then another, and soon, several others follow. The excitement begins to build as it becomes clear that *tehiat hametim* is occurring before our very eyes.

Yet on

יְהַלְלוּךָ

יהוה אֱלֹהֵינוּ כָּל מַעֲשֶׂיךָ
וַחֲסִידֶיךָ צַדִּיקִים עוֹשֵׂי רְצוֹנֶךָ
וְכָל עַמְּךָ בֵּית יִשְׂרָאֵל
בְּרִנָּה יוֹדוּ וִיבָרְכוּ וִישַׁבְּחוּ
וִיפָאֲרוּ וִירוֹמְמוּ וְיַעֲרִיצוּ
וְיַקְדִּישׁוּ וְיַמְלִיכוּ אֶת שִׁמְךָ מַלְכֵּנוּ
כִּי לְךָ טוֹב לְהוֹדוֹת וּלְשִׁמְךָ נָאֶה לְזַמֵּר
כִּי מֵעוֹלָם וְעַד עוֹלָם אַתָּה אֵל.

הוֹדוּ לַיהוה כִּי־טוֹב כִּי לְעוֹלָם חַסְדּוֹ: תהלים קלו
הוֹדוּ לֵאלֹהֵי הָאֱלֹהִים כִּי לְעוֹלָם חַסְדּוֹ:
הוֹדוּ לַאֲדֹנֵי הָאֲדֹנִים כִּי לְעוֹלָם חַסְדּוֹ:
לְעֹשֵׂה נִפְלָאוֹת גְּדֹלוֹת לְבַדּוֹ כִּי לְעוֹלָם חַסְדּוֹ:

הוֹדוּ לַיהוה כִּי־טוֹב – HODU LAHASHEM KI TOV

We recite the paragraph of *hodu LaHashem ki tov,* offering our gratitude to Hashem for the kindness He bestowed upon us.

Expressing gratitude is something that is engrained in us as Yehudim. We are referred to as Yehudim, being descendants of the Kingdom of Yehuda. Leah gave birth to her fourth son and named him Yehuda to acknowledge her gratitude to Hashem.

The Gemara (Berakhot 7b) states that Leah was the first person to thank Hashem. This is surprising. Did Adam, Noah, and Avraham never express gratitude to Hashem?

The *avot* certainly praised and thanked Hashem, but they lived a life of tremendous miracles, so their praise may not be viewed on the highest level of *hoda'a*. Leah, on the other hand, gave birth to

Who made the heavens with wisdom, His loving-kindness is for ever.
Who spread the earth
upon the waters, His loving-kindness is for ever.
Who made the great lights, His loving-kindness is for ever.
The sun to rule by day, His loving-kindness is for ever.
The moon and the stars
to rule by night; His loving-kindness is for ever.
Who struck Egypt
through their firstborn, His loving-kindness is for ever.
And brought out Israel
from their midst, His loving-kindness is for ever.
With a strong hand
and outstretched arm, His loving-kindness is for ever.
Who split the Reed Sea into parts, His loving-kindness is for ever.
And made Israel pass through it, His loving-kindness is for ever.
Casting Pharaoh and his army
into the Reed Sea; His loving-kindness is for ever.
Who led His people
through the wilderness; His loving-kindness is for ever.
Who struck down great kings, His loving-kindness is for ever.
And slew mighty kings, His loving-kindness is for ever.
Sihon, king of the Amorites, His loving-kindness is for ever.
And Og, king of Bashan, His loving-kindness is for ever.
And gave their land as a heritage, His loving-kindness is for ever.
A heritage for His servant Israel; His loving-kindness is for ever.
Who remembered us
in our lowly state, His loving-kindness is for ever.
And rescued us from our tormentors, His loving-kindness is for ever.
Who gives food to all flesh, His loving-kindness is for ever.
Give thanks to the God of heaven. His loving-kindness is for ever.

May we express our appreciation to Hashem for all the daily miracles we encounter.

NISHMAT

לְעֹשֵׂה הַשָּׁמַיִם בִּתְבוּנָה   כִּי לְעוֹלָם חַסְדּוֹ:
לְרֹקַע הָאָרֶץ עַל־הַמָּיִם   כִּי לְעוֹלָם חַסְדּוֹ:
לְעֹשֵׂה אוֹרִים גְּדֹלִים   כִּי לְעוֹלָם חַסְדּוֹ:
אֶת־הַשֶּׁמֶשׁ לְמֶמְשֶׁלֶת בַּיּוֹם   כִּי לְעוֹלָם חַסְדּוֹ:
אֶת־הַיָּרֵחַ וְכוֹכָבִים לְמֶמְשְׁלוֹת בַּלָּיְלָה   כִּי לְעוֹלָם חַסְדּוֹ:
לְמַכֵּה מִצְרַיִם בִּבְכוֹרֵיהֶם   כִּי לְעוֹלָם חַסְדּוֹ:
וַיּוֹצֵא יִשְׂרָאֵל מִתּוֹכָם   כִּי לְעוֹלָם חַסְדּוֹ:
בְּיָד חֲזָקָה וּבִזְרוֹעַ נְטוּיָה   כִּי לְעוֹלָם חַסְדּוֹ:
לְגֹזֵר יַם־סוּף לִגְזָרִים   כִּי לְעוֹלָם חַסְדּוֹ:
וְהֶעֱבִיר יִשְׂרָאֵל בְּתוֹכוֹ   כִּי לְעוֹלָם חַסְדּוֹ:
וְנִעֵר פַּרְעֹה וְחֵילוֹ בְיַם־סוּף   כִּי לְעוֹלָם חַסְדּוֹ:
לְמוֹלִיךְ עַמּוֹ בַּמִּדְבָּר   כִּי לְעוֹלָם חַסְדּוֹ:
לְמַכֵּה מְלָכִים גְּדֹלִים   כִּי לְעוֹלָם חַסְדּוֹ:
וַיַּהֲרֹג מְלָכִים אַדִּירִים   כִּי לְעוֹלָם חַסְדּוֹ:
לְסִיחוֹן מֶלֶךְ הָאֱמֹרִי   כִּי לְעוֹלָם חַסְדּוֹ:
וּלְעוֹג מֶלֶךְ הַבָּשָׁן   כִּי לְעוֹלָם חַסְדּוֹ:
וְנָתַן אַרְצָם לְנַחֲלָה   כִּי לְעוֹלָם חַסְדּוֹ:
נַחֲלָה לְיִשְׂרָאֵל עַבְדּוֹ   כִּי לְעוֹלָם חַסְדּוֹ:
שֶׁבְּשִׁפְלֵנוּ זָכַר לָנוּ   כִּי לְעוֹלָם חַסְדּוֹ:
וַיִּפְרְקֵנוּ מִצָּרֵינוּ   כִּי לְעוֹלָם חַסְדּוֹ:
נֹתֵן לֶחֶם לְכָל־בָּשָׂר   כִּי לְעוֹלָם חַסְדּוֹ:
הוֹדוּ לְאֵל הַשָּׁמָיִם   כִּי לְעוֹלָם חַסְדּוֹ:

Yet on a daily basis we see grass growing, vegetables sprouting, and flowers blossoming, and we take it for granted. We attribute this miraculous phenomenon to "mother nature." What we seem to ignore is that mother nature indeed has a father!

THE SOUL

of all that lives shall bless Your name,
Lord our God,
and the spirit of all flesh shall always glorify
and exalt Your remembrance, our King.
From eternity to eternity You are God.
Without You, we have no King, Redeemer or Savior,
who liberates, rescues, sustains
and shows compassion in every time of trouble and distress.
We have no King but You,
God of the first and last,
God of all creatures,
Master of all ages,
extolled by a multitude of praises,
who guides His world with loving-kindness
and His creatures with compassion.
The Lord neither slumbers nor sleeps.
He rouses the sleepers and wakens the slumberers.
He makes the dumb speak, sets the bound free,
supports the fallen,
and raises those bowed down.
To You alone we give thanks:
If our mouths were as full of song as the sea,

The last *berakha* of *birkhot hashahar* is *hamaavir shena me'einai*, that He removes sleep from our eyes. First, why is this at the end of the morning *berakhot*? The other *berakhot* are in a specific order, corresponding to the acts we perform each morning. This, then, should have been the first blessing, as we initially open our eyes when we first awaken.

Second, why do we go from there right into *yehi ratzon* without pause? Isn't that paragraph a different theme?

Third, why

נִשְׁמַת

כָּל חַי תְּבָרֵךְ אֶת שִׁמְךָ, יהוה אֱלֹהֵינוּ
וְרוּחַ כָּל בָּשָׂר תְּפָאֵר וּתְרוֹמֵם זִכְרְךָ מַלְכֵּנוּ תָּמִיד.
מִן הָעוֹלָם וְעַד הָעוֹלָם אַתָּה אֵל
וּמִבַּלְעָדֶיךָ אֵין לָנוּ מֶלֶךְ
גּוֹאֵל וּמוֹשִׁיעַ פּוֹדֶה וּמַצִּיל וּמְפַרְנֵס וּמְרַחֵם
בְּכָל עֵת צָרָה וְצוּקָה אֵין לָנוּ מֶלֶךְ אֶלָּא אָתָּה.
אֱלֹהֵי הָרִאשׁוֹנִים וְהָאַחֲרוֹנִים, אֱלוֹהַּ כָּל בְּרִיּוֹת
אֲדוֹן כָּל תּוֹלָדוֹת, הַמְהֻלָּל בְּרֹב הַתִּשְׁבָּחוֹת
הַמְנַהֵג עוֹלָמוֹ בְּחֶסֶד וּבְרִיּוֹתָיו בְּרַחֲמִים.
וַיהוה לֹא יָנוּם וְלֹא יִישָׁן
הַמְעוֹרֵר יְשֵׁנִים וְהַמֵּקִיץ נִרְדָּמִים
וְהַמֵּשִׂיחַ אִלְּמִים וְהַמַּתִּיר אֲסוּרִים
וְהַסּוֹמֵךְ נוֹפְלִים וְהַזּוֹקֵף כְּפוּפִים.
לְךָ לְבַדְּךָ אֲנַחְנוּ מוֹדִים.
אִלּוּ פִינוּ מָלֵא שִׁירָה כַּיָּם
וּלְשׁוֹנֵנוּ רִנָּה כַּהֲמוֹן גַּלָּיו

נִשְׁמַת – NISHMAT

AWAKENING THE SLEEPY

In *Nishmat,* we find the statement *hameorer yeshenim*. Hashem awakens those who are sleeping.

What is the definition of sleep? The Rambam tells us in *Hilkhot Teshuva* (3:4) that the *shofar* wakes us up from our slumber. Therefore, it seems that sleep is not just physical, since we are awake in synagogue when we hear the *shofar*.

and our tongue with jubilation as its myriad waves,
if our lips were full of praise like the spacious heavens,
and our eyes shone like the sun and moon,
if our hands were outstretched like eagles of the sky,
and our feet as swift as hinds –
still we could not thank You enough,
LORD our God and God of our ancestors,
or bless Your name
for even one of the thousand thousands
and myriad myriads of favors
You did for our ancestors and for us.
You redeemed us from Egypt, LORD our God,
and freed us from the house of bondage.
In famine You nourished us; in times of plenty You sustained us.
You delivered us from the sword, saved us from the plague,
and spared us from serious and lasting illness.
Until now Your mercies have helped us.
Your love has not forsaken us.
May You, LORD our God, never abandon us.
Therefore the limbs You formed within us,
the spirit and soul You breathed into our nostrils,
and the tongue You placed in our mouth –
they will thank and bless, praise and glorify, exalt and esteem,
hallow and do homage to Your name, O our King.
For every mouth shall give thanks to You,
every tongue vow allegiance to You, every knee shall bend to You,
every upright body shall bow to You,

Rabbi Norman Lamm in his *sefer Torah Beloved* (chapter 17) explains that being awake, for a Jew, means being connected to Torah. That is our lifeline supply of oxygen.

Rabbi Lamm quotes a story of a dispute between the *hasidim* and the Gra regarding the significance of having a dream of learning

Torah.

וְשִׂפְתוֹתֵינוּ שֶׁבַח כְּמֶרְחֲבֵי רָקִיעַ
וְעֵינֵינוּ מְאִירוֹת כַּשֶּׁמֶשׁ וְכַיָּרֵחַ
וְיָדֵינוּ פְרוּשׂוֹת כְּנִשְׁרֵי שָׁמָיִם
וְרַגְלֵינוּ קַלּוֹת כָּאַיָּלוֹת
אֵין אֲנַחְנוּ מַסְפִּיקִים לְהוֹדוֹת לְךָ, יהוה אֱלֹהֵינוּ וֵאלֹהֵי אֲבוֹתֵינוּ
וּלְבָרֵךְ אֶת שְׁמֶךָ
עַל אַחַת מֵאֶלֶף אֶלֶף אַלְפֵי אֲלָפִים וְרִבֵּי רְבָבוֹת פְּעָמִים הַטּוֹבוֹת
שֶׁעָשִׂיתָ עִם אֲבוֹתֵינוּ וְעִמָּנוּ.
מִמִּצְרַיִם גְּאַלְתָּנוּ, יהוה אֱלֹהֵינוּ, וּמִבֵּית עֲבָדִים פְּדִיתָנוּ
בְּרָעָב זַנְתָּנוּ וּבְשָׂבָע כִּלְכַּלְתָּנוּ
מֵחֶרֶב הִצַּלְתָּנוּ וּמִדֶּבֶר מִלַּטְתָּנוּ
וּמֵחֳלָיִים רָעִים וְנֶאֱמָנִים דִּלִּיתָנוּ.
עַד הֵנָּה עֲזָרוּנוּ רַחֲמֶיךָ, וְלֹא עֲזָבוּנוּ חֲסָדֶיךָ
וְאַל תִּטְּשֵׁנוּ, יהוה אֱלֹהֵינוּ, לָנֶצַח.
עַל כֵּן אֵבָרִים שֶׁפִּלַּגְתָּ בָּנוּ
וְרוּחַ וּנְשָׁמָה שֶׁנָּפַחְתָּ בְּאַפֵּנוּ, וְלָשׁוֹן אֲשֶׁר שַׂמְתָּ בְּפִינוּ
הֵן הֵם יוֹדוּ וִיבָרְכוּ וִישַׁבְּחוּ וִיפָאֲרוּ
וִירוֹמְמוּ וְיַעֲרִיצוּ וְיַקְדִּישׁוּ וְיַמְלִיכוּ אֶת שִׁמְךָ מַלְכֵּנוּ
כִּי כָל פֶּה לְךָ יוֹדֶה וְכָל לָשׁוֹן לְךָ תִשָּׁבַע
וְכָל בֶּרֶךְ לְךָ תִכְרַע וְכָל קוֹמָה לְפָנֶיךָ תִשְׁתַּחֲוֶה

Third, why do we end this *berakha* with *hagomel hasadim tovim le'amo Yisrael,* who bestows loving-kindness on His people Israel? Only two other *berakhot* mention Yisrael: *oter Yisrael betifara* and *ozer Yisrael bigvura*. Others refer to the entire world, such as *matir asurim,* freeing prisoners, and *malbish arumim,* clothing the naked.

all hearts shall fear You,
and our innermost being sing praises to Your name,
as is written:
"All my bones shall say: LORD, who is like You? *Ps. 35*
You save the poor from one stronger than him,
the poor and needy from one who would rob him."
Who is like You? Who is equal to You?
Who can be compared to You?
O great, mighty and awesome God, God Most High,
Maker of heaven and earth.
We will laud, praise and glorify You and bless Your holy name,
as it is said:
"Of David. Bless the LORD, O my soul, *Ps. 103*
and all that is within me bless His holy name."
God – in Your absolute power,
Great – in the glory of Your name,
Mighty – for ever,
Awesome – in Your awe-inspiring deeds,
The King – who sits on a throne.
High and lofty
He inhabits eternity; exalted and holy is His name.

---

it includes a reference to Yisrael and is not universal. Lastly, this *berakha* is connected and an integral part of the final paragraph of *yehi ratzon*, since that paragraph references the study of Torah. Hashem wakes up those that are sleeping by providing us with Torah.

שׁוֹכֵן עַד – SHOKHEN AD

Yesharim

In the *tefilla* of *Shokhen Ad*, we reference individuals who are *yesharim*. We have heard of *tzadikim* (righteous individuals) and people who are *kadosh* (holy), but what does it mean to be *yashar* (literally, straightforward)?

The Netziv

וְכָל לְבָבוֹת יִירָאוּךָ וְכָל קֶרֶב וּכְלָיוֹת יְזַמְּרוּ לִשְׁמֶךָ
כַּדָּבָר שֶׁכָּתוּב
כָּל עַצְמֹתַי תֹּאמַרְנָה יהוה מִי כָמוֹךָ תהלים לה
מַצִּיל עָנִי מֵחָזָק מִמֶּנּוּ, וְעָנִי וְאֶבְיוֹן מִגֹּזְלוֹ:
מִי יִדְמֶה לָּךְ וּמִי יִשְׁוֶה לָּךְ וּמִי יַעֲרָךְ לָךְ.
הָאֵל הַגָּדוֹל, הַגִּבּוֹר וְהַנּוֹרָא
אֵל עֶלְיוֹן, קוֹנֵה שָׁמַיִם וָאָרֶץ.
נְהַלֶּלְךָ וּנְשַׁבֵּחֲךָ וּנְפָאֶרְךָ וּנְבָרֵךְ אֶת שֵׁם קָדְשֶׁךָ
כָּאָמוּר
לְדָוִד, בָּרְכִי נַפְשִׁי אֶת־יהוה, וְכָל־קְרָבַי אֶת־שֵׁם קָדְשׁוֹ: תהלים קג
הָאֵל בְּתַעֲצוּמוֹת עֻזֶּךָ
הַגָּדוֹל בִּכְבוֹד שְׁמֶךָ
הַגִּבּוֹר לָנֶצַח וְהַנּוֹרָא בְּנוֹרְאוֹתֶיךָ
הַמֶּלֶךְ הַיּוֹשֵׁב עַל כִּסֵּא.
רָם וְנִשָּׂא
שׁוֹכֵן עַד מָרוֹם וְקָדוֹשׁ שְׁמוֹ

Torah. The Gra felt that there isn't real learning taking place in such a dream. The *hasidim* claimed that learning while sleeping is proof that one is not really sleeping. Both seem to agree that sleep and learning cannot exist simultaneously. Only when we are awake are we connected to Torah.

Rav Shimon Schwab in his *sefer* on the siddur (*Rav Schwab on Prayer*), provides an answer to our three questions using a similar thought to that expressed by Rabbi Lamm. The *berakha* of *hamaavir shena me'einai* appears at the end of *birkhot hashahar* because it is about our connection to Torah, not about waking up from our sleep. Our connection to Torah is unique to Am Yisrael. Therefore,

And it is written:

Sing joyfully to the LORD, you righteous, *Ps. 33*
for praise from the upright is seemly
By the mouth of the upright You shall be praised.
By the words of the righteous You shall be blessed.
By the tongue of the devout You shall be extolled,
And in the midst of the holy You shall be sanctified.

וּבְמַקְהֲלוֹת And in the assemblies
of tens of thousands of Your people, the house of Israel,
with joyous song shall Your name, our King,
be glorified in every generation.
For this is the duty of all creatures before You,
LORD our God and God of our ancestors:
to thank, praise, laud, glorify, exalt,
honor, bless, raise high and acclaim –
even beyond all the words of song and praise
of David, son of Jesse, Your servant, Your anointed.

יִשְׁתַּבַּח May Your name be praised for ever, our King,
the great and holy God, King in heaven and on earth.
For to You, LORD our God and God of our ancestors,
it is right to offer song and praise,
hymn and psalm, strength and dominion,
eternity, greatness and power,
song of praise and glory,
holiness and kingship,
blessings and thanks, from now and for ever.

The *avot* respected others even if their *hashkafot* differed. The *avot* knew how to distinguish between the person and the idea. One can argue with a view while respecting the individual. That is the definition of an *adam yashar*!

וְכָתוּב

רַנְּנוּ צַדִּיקִים בַּיהוה, לַיְשָׁרִים נָאוָה תְהִלָּה: תהלים לג

בְּפִי	יְשָׁרִים	תִּתְהַלָּל
וּבְדִבְרֵי	צַדִּיקִים	תִּתְבָּרַךְ
וּבִלְשׁוֹן	חֲסִידִים	תִּתְרוֹמָם
וּבְקֶרֶב	קְדוֹשִׁים	תִּתְקַדָּשׁ

וּבְמַקְהֲלוֹת רִבְבוֹת עַמְּךָ בֵּית יִשְׂרָאֵל
בְּרִנָּה יִתְפָּאַר שִׁמְךָ מַלְכֵּנוּ בְּכָל דּוֹר וָדוֹר
שֶׁכֵּן חוֹבַת כָּל הַיְצוּרִים
לְפָנֶיךָ יהוה אֱלֹהֵינוּ וֵאלֹהֵי אֲבוֹתֵינוּ
לְהוֹדוֹת, לְהַלֵּל, לְשַׁבֵּחַ, לְפָאֵר, לְרוֹמֵם
לְהַדֵּר, לְבָרֵךְ, לְעַלֵּה וּלְקַלֵּס
עַל כָּל דִּבְרֵי שִׁירוֹת וְתִשְׁבְּחוֹת
דָּוִד בֶּן יִשַׁי, עַבְדְּךָ מְשִׁיחֶךָ.

יִשְׁתַּבַּח שִׁמְךָ לָעַד מַלְכֵּנוּ
הָאֵל הַמֶּלֶךְ הַגָּדוֹל וְהַקָּדוֹשׁ בַּשָּׁמַיִם וּבָאָרֶץ
כִּי לְךָ נָאֶה, יהוה אֱלֹהֵינוּ וֵאלֹהֵי אֲבוֹתֵינוּ
שִׁיר וּשְׁבָחָה, הַלֵּל וְזִמְרָה
עֹז וּמֶמְשָׁלָה, נֶצַח, גְּדֻלָּה וּגְבוּרָה
תְּהִלָּה וְתִפְאֶרֶת, קְדֻשָּׁה וּמַלְכוּת
בְּרָכוֹת וְהוֹדָאוֹת, מֵעַתָּה וְעַד עוֹלָם.

The Netziv in his introduction to *Sefer Bereshit* cites the *gemara* Avoda Zara 25 that states that the forefathers, the *avot*, were *yesharim*.

Many follow Hashem through what they believe to be the correct path and reject others who follow a different approach. They disrespect people with other views, and it causes hatred among the various groups.

Blessed are You, Lord, God and King, exalted in praises,
God of thanksgivings, Master of wonders,
who delights in hymns of song,
King, God, Giver of life to the worlds.

Blessed are You, Lord our God, King of the Universe,
who creates the fruit of the vine.

Drink the fourth cup while reclining to the left.

בָּרוּךְ Blessed are You, Lord our God,
King of the Universe,
for the vine and the fruit of the vine,
and for the produce of the field;
for the desirable, good
and spacious land that You willingly gave as heritage to our
ancestors, that they might eat of its fruit
and be satisfied with its goodness.
Have compassion, Lord our God,
on Israel Your people, on Jerusalem,
Your city, on Zion the home of Your glory,
on Your altar and Your Temple.
May You rebuild Jerusalem,
the holy city swiftly in our time,
and may You bring us back there,
rejoicing in its rebuilding, eating from its fruit,
satisfied by its goodness,
and blessing You for it in holiness and purity.
(*On Shabbat:* Be pleased to refresh us on this Shabbat Day.)
Grant us joy on this festival of Matzot.
For You, God, are good and do good to all
and we thank You for the land
and for the fruit of the vine.
Blessed are You, Lord,
for the land and for the fruit of the vine.

בָּרוּךְ אַתָּה יהוה, אֵל מֶלֶךְ גָּדוֹל בַּתִּשְׁבָּחוֹת
אֵל הַהוֹדָאוֹת אֲדוֹן הַנִּפְלָאוֹת
הַבּוֹחֵר בְּשִׁירֵי זִמְרָה, מֶלֶךְ, אֵל, חֵי הָעוֹלָמִים.

בָּרוּךְ אַתָּה יהוה אֱלֹהֵינוּ מֶלֶךְ הָעוֹלָם
בּוֹרֵא פְּרִי הַגָּפֶן.

Drink the fourth cup while reclining to the left.

בָּרוּךְ אַתָּה יהוה אֱלֹהֵינוּ מֶלֶךְ הָעוֹלָם
עַל הַגֶּפֶן וְעַל פְּרִי הַגֶּפֶן
וְעַל תְּנוּבַת הַשָּׂדֶה
וְעַל אֶרֶץ חֶמְדָּה טוֹבָה וּרְחָבָה
שֶׁרָצִיתָ וְהִנְחַלְתָּ לַאֲבוֹתֵינוּ
לֶאֱכֹל מִפִּרְיָהּ וְלִשְׂבֹּעַ מִטּוּבָהּ.
רַחֵם נָא יהוה אֱלֹהֵינוּ עַל יִשְׂרָאֵל עַמֶּךָ
וְעַל יְרוּשָׁלַיִם עִירֶךָ, וְעַל צִיּוֹן מִשְׁכַּן כְּבוֹדֶךָ
וְעַל מִזְבְּחֶךָ וְעַל הֵיכָלֶךָ.
וּבְנֵה יְרוּשָׁלַיִם עִיר הַקֹּדֶשׁ בִּמְהֵרָה בְיָמֵינוּ
וְהַעֲלֵנוּ לְתוֹכָהּ וְשַׂמְּחֵנוּ בְּבִנְיָנָהּ
וְנֹאכַל מִפִּרְיָהּ וְנִשְׂבַּע מִטּוּבָהּ
וּנְבָרֶכְךָ עָלֶיהָ בִּקְדֻשָּׁה וּבְטָהֳרָה.
(בשבת: וּרְצֵה וְהַחֲלִיצֵנוּ בְּיוֹם הַשַּׁבָּת הַזֶּה)
וְשַׂמְּחֵנוּ בְּיוֹם חַג הַמַּצּוֹת הַזֶּה
כִּי אַתָּה יהוה טוֹב וּמֵטִיב לַכֹּל וְנוֹדֶה לְּךָ
עַל הָאָרֶץ וְעַל פְּרִי הַגָּפֶן/ *If from* ארץ ישראל: גַּפְנָהּ/.
בָּרוּךְ אַתָּה יהוה
עַל הָאָרֶץ וְעַל פְּרִי הַגָּפֶן/ *If from* ארץ ישראל: גַּפְנָהּ/.

NIRTZA / PARTING

חֲסַל סִדּוּר פֶּסַח The Pesah service is finished,
as it was meant to be performed,
in accordance with all its rules and laws.
Just as we have been privileged to lay out its order,
so may we be privileged to perform it [in the Temple].
Pure One, dwelling in Your heaven,
raise up this people, too abundant to be counted.
Soon, lead the shoots of [Israel's] stock,
redeemed, into Zion with great joy.

NEXT YEAR IN JERUSALEM REBUILT!

Outside Israel, the Omer is counted on the second night of the festival.

בָּרוּךְ Blessed are You, Lord our God, King of the Universe,
who has made us holy through His commandments,
and has commanded us about counting the Omer.
Today is the first day of the Omer.

---

references the *Beit HaMikdash,* it includes Jerusalem, so that *medina* refers to all locations outside of Jerusalem. Rav Soloveitchik explains the Rambam's opinion by suggesting that the city of Jerusalem is an extension of the *kedusha* of the *Mikdash*. It radiates and makes the entire city holy.

JERUSALEM UNITES

Jerusalem is the place of unity of Am Yisrael. In *Tehillim* (122:3) it is referred to as *ir shehubra la yahdav,* a city joined together. All Jews come together to Jerusalem on the festivals, but this verse does not refer only to a geographical unity. It goes much deeper.

There were

נרצה

חֲסַל סִדּוּר פֶּסַח כְּהִלְכָתוֹ
כְּכָל מִשְׁפָּטוֹ וְחֻקָּתוֹ
כַּאֲשֶׁר זָכִינוּ לְסַדֵּר אוֹתוֹ
כֵּן נִזְכֶּה לַעֲשׂוֹתוֹ
זָךְ שׁוֹכֵן מְעוֹנָה
קוֹמֵם קְהַל עֲדַת מִי מָנָה
קָרֵב נַהֵל נִטְעֵי כַנָּה, פְּדוּיִם לְצִיּוֹן בְּרִנָּה.

לְשָׁנָה הַבָּאָה בִּירוּשָׁלָיִם הַבְּנוּיָה.

Outside ארץ ישראל*, the* עומר *is counted on the second night of the festival.*

בָּרוּךְ אַתָּה יהוה אֱלֹהֵינוּ מֶלֶךְ הָעוֹלָם
אֲשֶׁר קִדְּשָׁנוּ בְּמִצְוֹתָיו, וְצִוָּנוּ עַל סְפִירַת הָעֹמֶר.
הַיּוֹם יוֹם אֶחָד בָּעֹמֶר.

NIRTZA / PARTING
LESHANA HABAAH BIYERUSHALAYIM

THE HOLY CITY

Jerusalem is the center of our existence in a number of ways. First, it is the center of our spiritual existence. We see this in a fascinating Rambam.

The Mishna in Rosh HaShana (29) states that there are different rules for blowing a *shofar* on Shabbat in the *Beit HaMikdash* and in the *medina*.

Rashi explains that *medina* refers to all locations outside the *Mikdash*. The Rambam differs and claims that when the Mishna

The phrase could have been included in the *ani maamin* that relates to the fact that God does not have a body. The principle could have been, "*Even though* the Torah refers to God's hand, we believe He does not have a body."

It also could have been included in the *ani maamin* about reward and punishment, so it would have been, "I believe in punishment and reward, *even though* I see wicked people flourishing and pious individuals suffering."

Why isn't *ve'af al pi* included in these other principles?

The Griz (R. Yitzhak Ze'ev Soloveitchik) answers that the reason the term *af al pi* appears only in connection with a statement about *Mashiah* is to emphasize that it is not enough to believe that *Mashiah* exists. We have to yearn for his arrival and expect it.

In *Hilkhot Melakhim* 11:1, the Rambam states that we have to believe in the *Mashiah,* and we have to wait with bated breath and anticipation for his arrival. In addition, in *Hilkhot Para,* at the end of the third chapter, the Rambam speaks of ten red heifers and says the tenth will come in the time of the *Mashiah meheira yegaleh*. Why does the Rambam add those last two words *meheira yegaleh,* that it should be revealed speedily?

The Lubavitcher Rebbe suggests that when one mentions the *Mashiah,* one should feel a knee-jerk reaction to include a statement that it should quickly come upon us. This illustrates one's sincere desire that the *Mashiah* arrive. This is the faith one needs to exhibit, that no matter what challenges one may be experiencing, there is a wholehearted belief that the *Mashiah* can appear at any moment.

VAYEHI

There were several miracles that occurred on a daily basis in the *Mikdash*. The smoke from sacrifices went straight up, the meat never spoiled, and no one ever said, It is too narrow here, there is not enough space. The Barukh She'amar on *Pirkei Avot* sharply points out that although it was likely crowded, Jerusalem is a place that brings everyone together so no one complained about the crowded conditions.

CLOSENESS TO GOD AND MAN

The midrash tells us that Avraham called the *Akeda*'s location *Hashem Yera'eh,* and Malkitzedek called the same location *Shalem*. Not to insult either of them, Hashem combined the two names and called the city Yerushalem: the name *Yera'eh,* referencing fear of God, and the name *shalem,* referencing peace among the people. Jerusalem is the city that combines both closeness with God and peace with our fellow man.

YEARNING FOR *MASHIAH*

We say, *Next year in Jerusalem,* expressing our hope and desire that the *Mashiah* will arrive.

The Brisker Rav asked the following question. The Rambam established the thirteen principles of faith, which form the basis for *Ani Maamin*. Only one of the thirteen principles, the one that relates to *Mashiah,* includes the term *af al pi,* "even though": *Ve'af al pi sheyitmame'ah,* "And even though he may tarry...." Why is this the only one of the thirteen that includes that phrase?

Outside Israel, this poem is recited on the first night of the festival only.

וּבְכֵן וַיְהִי בַּחֲצִי הַלַּיְלָה AND SO – IT HAPPENED AT MIDNIGHT. *Ex. 12*

Many were the miracles You performed long ago, at night.
At the beginning of the watch, on this night,
You won [Avraham]'s battle, when [his men were] split, and the night
IT HAPPENED AT MIDNIGHT.

You judged the king of Gerar in his dream at night.
You put dread into [Lavan] the Aramean's heart that night.
And Israel struggled with an angel and overcame him at night
IT HAPPENED AT MIDNIGHT.

You crushed the firstborns of Patros [Egypt] in the middle of the night.
They could not find their strength, when they rose up [against Israel] at night.
You flung [Sisera] the commander of Haroshet off course with the stars of night
IT HAPPENED AT MIDNIGHT.

[Sennacherib] the blasphemer thought to raise his hand against the beloved [city]; but You dried up the bodies of his fallen in the night.
You overthrew Bel, idol and pedestal together, in the dead of night.
To [Daniel] the beloved man were revealed the secrets of that vision of the night
IT HAPPENED AT MIDNIGHT.

Why is Yisrael an appropriate name? True, he fought with an angel, but what was most significant is that he prevailed! It might be more appropriate to name Yaakov after his victory rather than after his fight. Perhaps *tukhal*, for example. We would be *Tukhalim* rather than *Yisraelim*!

The answer is that Yaakov Avinu was not called Yisrael because he won, but rather, because he put up a fight. Life is full of challenges, and we are not always victorious. The important factor is that we give it our all and put up the best fight we can!

Haman the

Outside ארץ ישראל, this poem is recited on the first night of the festival only.

שמות יב וּבְכֵן וַיְהִי בַּחֲצִי הַלַּיְלָה

אָז רֹב נִסִּים הִפְלֵאתָ בַּלַּיְלָה
בְּרֹאשׁ אַשְׁמוּרוֹת זֶה הַלַּיְלָה
גֵּר צֶדֶק נִצַּחְתּוֹ, כְּנֶחֱלַק לוֹ לַיְלָה
וַיְהִי בַּחֲצִי הַלַּיְלָה

דַּנְתָּ מֶלֶךְ גְּרָר בַּחֲלוֹם הַלַּיְלָה
הִפְחַדְתָּ אֲרַמִּי בְּאֶמֶשׁ לַיְלָה
וְיִשְׂרָאֵל יָשַׂר לָאֵל, וַיּוּכַל לוֹ לַיְלָה
וַיְהִי בַּחֲצִי הַלַּיְלָה

זֶרַע בְּכוֹרֵי פַתְרוֹס מָחַצְתָּ בַּחֲצִי הַלַּיְלָה
חֵילָם לֹא מָצְאוּ בְּקוּמָם בַּלַּיְלָה
טִיסַת נְגִיד חֲרֹשֶׁת סִלִּיתָ בְכוֹכְבֵי לַיְלָה
וַיְהִי בַּחֲצִי הַלַּיְלָה

יָעַץ מְחָרֵף לְנוֹפֵף אִוּוּי, הוֹבַשְׁתָּ פְגָרָיו בַּלַּיְלָה
כָּרַע בֵּל וּמַצָּבוֹ בְּאִישׁוֹן לַיְלָה
לְאִישׁ חֲמוּדוֹת נִגְלָה רָז חֲזוֹת לַיְלָה
וַיְהִי בַּחֲצִי הַלַּיְלָה

VAYEHI BAHATZI HALAYLA

וְיִשְׂרָאֵל יָשַׂר לָאֵל, וַיּוּכַל לוֹ –
And Israel struggled with the angel and overcame him

One of the events that occurred in the middle of the night is when Yaakov Avinu fought with the angel of Esav. After the battle, the angel named him Yisrael, *ki sarita im Elokim ve'im anashim vatukhal,* because you have struggled with [an angel of] God and with men and you have prevailed (*Bereshit* 32:29). The name Yisrael is derived from the word *sarita,* underscoring that Yaakov fought with the angel.

[Belshazzar], who drank himself merry
from the holy vessels, was killed on that same night.
[Daniel] was brought out unharmed from the
lions' den; he who had explained those terrors of the night.
[Haman] the Agagite bore his hatred and wrote his orders at night
IT HAPPENED AT MIDNIGHT.

You awakened Your might against him, disturbing
[King Ahashverosh's] sleep at night.
You shall tread the winepress of [Se'ir],
who asks anxiously, "What of the night?"
You will cry out like the watchman, calling,
"Morning is come, and also night"
IT HAPPENED AT MIDNIGHT.

Draw near the day that will be neither day nor night.
Highest One, make known that day is Yours and also night.
Appoint watchmen [to guard] Your city all day long and all night,
Light up like daylight the darkness of night
IT HAPPENED AT MIDNIGHT.

The Jews of Persia were victorious, but they could not assert their independence as openly as the Maccabees were able to, generations later. They were still in exile, and so the victory had to be subdued. The *Megilla* had to be written with such finesse that it could be understood on two levels: revealed and concealed, open and hidden, with an outer and inner tale.

As Mordekhai himself states, the words of the *Megilla* are *divrei shalom ve'emet*, words of peace and truth. They were indeed words of truth for the Jews, while simultaneously toned down to ensure that they were words of peace, so as not to offend the ruling authority in the empire. Ahashverosh felt that he was in command, but we know that he was merely a puppet whose strings were being manipulated from above.

The message of the *Megilla* for us is that often, we feel as if we are in charge, but we are all just actors in a great, divine drama. As the end of the paragraph of *vayehi bahatzi halayla* reminds us, even in the darkest of times, God sheds His light. Ultimately, He alone is in control of our destiny.

מִשְׁתַּכֵּר בִּכְלֵי קֹדֶשׁ נֶהֱרַג בּוֹ בַּלַּיְלָה
נוֹשַׁע מִבּוֹר אֲרָיוֹת, פּוֹתֵר בִּעֲתוּתֵי לַיְלָה
שִׂנְאָה נָטַר אֲגָגִי, וְכָתַב סְפָרִים בַּלַּיְלָה
וַיְהִי בַּחֲצִי הַלַּיְלָה

עוֹרַרְתָּ נִצְחֲךָ עָלָיו בְּנֶדֶד שְׁנַת לַיְלָה
פּוּרָה תִדְרֹךְ לְשׁוֹמֵר מַה מִּלַּיְלָה
צָרַח כַּשּׁוֹמֵר, וְשָׂח אָתָא בֹקֶר וְגַם לַיְלָה
וַיְהִי בַּחֲצִי הַלַּיְלָה

קָרֵב יוֹם אֲשֶׁר הוּא לֹא יוֹם וְלֹא לַיְלָה
רָם הוֹדַע כִּי לְךָ הַיּוֹם אַף לְךָ הַלַּיְלָה
שׁוֹמְרִים הַפְקֵד לְעִירְךָ כָּל הַיּוֹם וְכָל הַלַּיְלָה
תָּאִיר כְּאוֹר יוֹם חֶשְׁכַת לַיְלָה
וַיְהִי בַּחֲצִי הַלַּיְלָה

שִׂנְאָה נָטַר אֲגָגִי, וְכָתַב סְפָרִים בַּלַּיְלָה – Haman the Agagite bore his hatred and wrote his orders at night

This is a reference to Purim, regarding which there is an intriguing thought offered by Rabbi Norman Lamm in his book *Majesty and Mystery*.

In *Megillat Esther,* there is one character that is mentioned over and over again. Ahashverosh seems to be a central personality. He is involved in every event, and everything seems to revolve around him. Rabbi Lamm states, "The king is happy, the king is angry, the king is restless, the king is upset, the king is fuming, the king is drunk, the king commands, the king consents" (*Majesty and Mystery,* p. 58). He is a central figure, yet he seems somewhat weak, always seeking advice from others. Not one act of importance is initiated by Ahashverosh. How are we to account for this paradox?

The answer is that the *Megilla* promulgated by Mordekhai and Esther was addressed to two distinct audiences. Primarily, it was written to and for their fellow Jews of that era and beyond. However, secondarily, its content could not offend Ahashverosh and his royal court.

Outside Israel, this poem is recited on the second night of the festival only.

וּבְכֵן וַאֲמַרְתֶּם זֶבַח פֶּסַח TELL [your children]: "THIS IS THE PESAH." *Ex. 12*

You showed Your immense power in wonders on Pesah;
to the head of all seasons You have raised up Pesah.
You revealed to [Avraham] the Ezrahi what would come
at midnight on Pesah.
TELL [your children]: "THIS IS THE PESAH."

You knocked at his doors in the heat of the day on Pesah;
he gave Your shining [messengers] unleavened cakes to eat on Pesah;
and he ran to the herd, hinting at the ox in the Torah reading of Pesah.
TELL [your children]: "THIS IS THE PESAH."

The men of Sodom raged and burned in fire on Pesah.
Lot was saved; he baked matzot at the end of Pesah.
You swept bare the land of Mof and Nof [Egypt]
in Your great rage on Pesah.
TELL [your children]: "THIS IS THE PESAH."

The firstborns of [Egypt's] vigor You crushed, Lord,
on the night of guarding, on Pesah.
[But,] Mighty One, You passed over Your firstborn son
when You saw the blood of the Pesah,
allowing no destruction through my doors on Pesah.
TELL [your children]: "THIS IS THE PESAH."

The walled city [of Jericho] was closed [for fear] when it was Pesah.
Midian was destroyed in the din, [after a dream of]
Omer barley on Pesah.
The fat ones of [Assyria; of] Pul and Lud were
burned away in fires on Pesah.
TELL [your children]: "THIS IS THE PESAH."

This day [Sennacherib] halted at Nob [and laid siege]
until the time of Pesah.
A hand wrote Babylonia's doom on the wall at Pesah:
the lamp was lit, the table was laid on Pesah.
TELL [your children]: "THIS IS THE PESAH."

Outside ארץ ישראל*, this poem is recited on the second night of the festival only.*

שמות יב

וּבְכֵן וַאֲמַרְתֶּם זֶבַח פֶּסַח

אֹמֶץ גְּבוּרוֹתֶיךָ הִפְלֵאתָ בַּפֶּסַח
בְּרֹאשׁ כָּל מוֹעֲדוֹת נִשֵּׂאתָ פֶּסַח
גִּלִּיתָ לְאֶזְרָחִי חֲצוֹת לֵיל פֶּסַח
וַאֲמַרְתֶּם זֶבַח פֶּסַח

דְּלָתָיו דָּפַקְתָּ כְּחֹם הַיּוֹם בַּפֶּסַח
הִסְעִיד נוֹצְצִים עֻגוֹת מַצּוֹת בַּפֶּסַח
וְאֶל הַבָּקָר, רָץ זֵכֶר לְשׁוֹר עֵרֶךְ פֶּסַח
וַאֲמַרְתֶּם זֶבַח פֶּסַח

זֹעֲמוּ סְדוֹמִים, וְלֹהֲטוּ בָּאֵשׁ בַּפֶּסַח
חֻלַּץ לוֹט מֵהֶם, וּמַצּוֹת אָפָה בְּקֵץ פֶּסַח
טִאטֵאתָ אַדְמַת מֹף וְנֹף בְּעָבְרְךָ בַּפֶּסַח
וַאֲמַרְתֶּם זֶבַח פֶּסַח

יָהּ, רֹאשׁ כָּל אוֹן מָחַצְתָּ בְּלֵיל שִׁמּוּר פֶּסַח
כַּבִּיר, עַל בֵּן בְּכוֹר פָּסַחְתָּ בְּדַם פֶּסַח
לְבִלְתִּי תֵּת מַשְׁחִית לָבֹא בִּפְתָחַי בַּפֶּסַח
וַאֲמַרְתֶּם זֶבַח פֶּסַח

מְסֻגֶּרֶת סֻגָּרָה בְּעִתּוֹתֵי פֶּסַח
נִשְׁמְדָה מִדְיָן בִּצְלִיל שְׂעוֹרֵי עֹמֶר פֶּסַח
שֹׂרְפוּ מִשְׁמַנֵּי פּוּל וְלוּד, בִּיקַד יְקוֹד פֶּסַח
וַאֲמַרְתֶּם זֶבַח פֶּסַח

עוֹד הַיּוֹם בְּנֹב לַעֲמֹד, עַד גָּעָה עוֹנַת פֶּסַח
פַּס יַד כָּתְבָה לְקַעֲקֵעַ צוּל בַּפֶּסַח
צָפֹה הַצָּפִית עָרוֹךְ הַשֻּׁלְחָן בַּפֶּסַח
וַאֲמַרְתֶּם זֶבַח פֶּסַח

Hadassa gathered the people to fast three days at Pesah;
You crushed [Haman,] the head of that evil family,
on a gallows fifty cubits high on Pesah.
[Loss and widowhood –] You will bring these two
in a moment to [Edom, which rules us now,] on Pesah.
Strengthen Your hand, raise Your right hand,
as on the night first sanctified as Pesah.
TELL [your children]: "THIS IS THE PESAH."

כִּי לוֹ נָאֶה FOR HIM IT IS FITTING

Majestic in Kingship, truly chosen: His legions say to Him:
"Yours and Yours; Yours, for it is Yours; Yours, only Yours;
Yours, LORD, is the Kingdom." *1 Chron. 29*
FOR HIM IT IS FITTING, FOR HIM IT IS RIGHT.

Unmistakable in His Kingship, truly glorious:
His venerable ones say to Him:
"Yours and Yours; Yours, for it is Yours; Yours, only Yours;
Yours, LORD, is the kingdom."
FOR HIM IT IS FITTING, FOR HIM IT IS RIGHT.

Worthy of Kingship, truly mighty: His officers say to Him:
"Yours and Yours; Yours, for it is Yours; Yours, only Yours;
Yours, LORD, is the kingdom."
FOR HIM IT IS FITTING, FOR HIM IT IS RIGHT.

---

from the tent" (*Shemot* 33:11). Yehoshua was at the time likely 56 years old. (He died at 110, was in the desert for 40 years, and it took 14 years to divide Eretz Yisrael.) Why is he referred to as a lad?!

Rav Yisrael Salanter explains that it was because of his youthful attitude. He shadowed Moshe and served him, so that he could learn and constantly improve.

As people

קָהָל כִּנְסָה הֲדַסָּה, צוֹם לְשַׁלֵּשׁ בַּפֶּסַח
רֹאשׁ מִבֵּית רָשָׁע מָחַצְתָּ בְּעֵץ חֲמִשִּׁים בַּפֶּסַח
שְׁתֵּי אֵלֶּה, רֶגַע תָּבִיא לְעוּצִית בַּפֶּסַח
תָּעֹז יָדְךָ, תָּרוּם יְמִינְךָ, כְּלֵיל הִתְקַדֵּשׁ חַג פֶּסַח
וַאֲמַרְתֶּם זֶבַח פֶּסַח

כִּי לוֹ נָאֶה, כִּי לוֹ יָאֶה
אַדִּיר בִּמְלוּכָה בָּחוּר כַּהֲלָכָה גְּדוּדָיו יֹאמְרוּ לוֹ
לְךָ וּלְךָ, לְךָ כִּי לְךָ, לְךָ אַף לְךָ, לְךָ יהוה הַמַּמְלָכָה דברי הימים א׳ כט
כִּי לוֹ נָאֶה, כִּי לוֹ יָאֶה

דָּגוּל בִּמְלוּכָה הָדוּר כַּהֲלָכָה וָתִיקָיו יֹאמְרוּ לוֹ
לְךָ וּלְךָ, לְךָ כִּי לְךָ, לְךָ אַף לְךָ, לְךָ יהוה הַמַּמְלָכָה
כִּי לוֹ נָאֶה, כִּי לוֹ יָאֶה

זַכַּאי בִּמְלוּכָה חָסִין כַּהֲלָכָה טַפְסְרָיו יֹאמְרוּ לוֹ
לְךָ וּלְךָ, לְךָ כִּי לְךָ, לְךָ אַף לְךָ, לְךָ יהוה הַמַּמְלָכָה
כִּי לוֹ נָאֶה, כִּי לוֹ יָאֶה

KI LO NA'EH

בָּחוּר כַּהֲלָכָה – *Truly chosen*

Hashem is referred to as *bahur kahalakha*. Why is a *bahur*, a reference to being young, a positive attribute?

In *Parashat Ki Tissa*, Yehoshua is referred to as a *naar*, a youth or lad: "His attendant, Yehoshua bin Nun, a lad, would not depart

One in Kingship, truly omnipotent: His learned ones say to Him:
"Yours and Yours; Yours, for it is Yours; Yours, only Yours;
Yours, LORD, is the kingdom."
FOR HIM IT IS FITTING, FOR HIM IT IS RIGHT.

King in His Kingship, truly awesome:
those surrounding Him say to Him:
"Yours and Yours; Yours, for it is Yours; Yours, only Yours;
Yours, LORD, is the kingdom."
FOR HIM IT IS FITTING, FOR HIM IT IS RIGHT.

Humble in Kingship, truly the Redeemer, His righteous ones say to Him:
"Yours and Yours; Yours, for it is Yours; Yours, only Yours;
Yours, LORD, is the kingdom."
FOR HIM IT IS FITTING, FOR HIM IT IS RIGHT.

Holy in Kingship, truly compassionate, His angels say to Him:
"Yours and Yours; Yours, for it is Yours; Yours, only Yours;
Yours, LORD, is the kingdom."
FOR HIM IT IS FITTING, FOR HIM IT IS RIGHT.

Powerful in Kingship, truly our Support, His perfect ones say to Him:
"Yours and Yours; Yours, for it is Yours; Yours, only Yours;
Yours, LORD, is the kingdom."
FOR HIM IT IS FITTING, FOR HIM IT IS RIGHT.

Similarly, with learning Torah, a knowledgeable person is referred to as a *talmid hakham*, a smart student, who can continue to attain greater knowledge.

HaKadosh Barukh Hu is referred to as a *bahur* because He is constantly active and moving forward. May we keep this in mind and constantly strive to be productive and to enhance our learning and commitment to Torah.

יָחִיד בִּמְלוּכָה כַּבִּיר כַּהֲלָכָה לִמּוּדָיו יֹאמְרוּ לוֹ
לְךָ וּלְךָ, לְךָ כִּי לְךָ, לְךָ אַף לְךָ, לְךָ יהוה הַמַּמְלָכָה
כִּי לוֹ נָאֶה, כִּי לוֹ יָאֶה

מֶלֶךְ בִּמְלוּכָה נוֹרָא כַּהֲלָכָה סְבִיבָיו יֹאמְרוּ לוֹ
לְךָ וּלְךָ, לְךָ כִּי לְךָ, לְךָ אַף לְךָ, לְךָ יהוה הַמַּמְלָכָה
כִּי לוֹ נָאֶה, כִּי לוֹ יָאֶה

עָנָו בִּמְלוּכָה פּוֹדֶה כַּהֲלָכָה צַדִּיקָיו יֹאמְרוּ לוֹ
לְךָ וּלְךָ, לְךָ כִּי לְךָ, לְךָ אַף לְךָ, לְךָ יהוה הַמַּמְלָכָה
כִּי לוֹ נָאֶה, כִּי לוֹ יָאֶה

קָדוֹשׁ בִּמְלוּכָה רַחוּם כַּהֲלָכָה שִׁנְאַנָּיו יֹאמְרוּ לוֹ
לְךָ וּלְךָ, לְךָ כִּי לְךָ, לְךָ אַף לְךָ, לְךָ יהוה הַמַּמְלָכָה
כִּי לוֹ נָאֶה, כִּי לוֹ יָאֶה

תַּקִּיף בִּמְלוּכָה תּוֹמֵךְ כַּהֲלָכָה תְּמִימָיו יֹאמְרוּ לוֹ
לְךָ וּלְךָ, לְךָ כִּי לְךָ, לְךָ אַף לְךָ, לְךָ יהוה הַמַּמְלָכָה
כִּי לוֹ נָאֶה, כִּי לוֹ יָאֶה

As people grow older, they often retire and are not interested in changing anything in their lives. Judaism does not have that attitude. Regardless of our stage in life, we focus on future growth. We need to constantly seek to accomplish more. A person can be 110 years old and have the attitude of a *naar*. Age is a number, and it may change annually, but our youthful attitude of constant growth and self-improvement should remain with us throughout life.

אַדִּיר הוּא HE IS MAJESTIC
may He build His house soon,
soon, speedily in our days.
Build, O God, build, O God,
build Your house soon.

He is chosen, He is great, He is unmistakable,
may He build His house soon, soon, speedily in our days.
Build, O God, build, O God,
build Your house soon.

He is glorious, He is venerable, He is worthy, He is kind,
may He build His house soon, soon, speedily in our days.
Build, O God, build, O God,
build Your house soon.

He is pure, He is One, He is mighty,
He is learned, He is King, He is awesome,
He is elevated, He is strong, He is Savior, He is righteous,
may He build His house soon, soon, speedily in our days.
Build, O God, build, O God,
build Your house soon.

He is holy, He is compassionate, He is Almighty,
He is powerful,

may He build His house soon,
soon, speedily in our days.
Build, O God, build, O God,
BUILD YOUR HOUSE SOON.

Mishkan was designed to embody the continuation of the Har Sinai experience. Its purpose was *hasraat haShekhina*, providing a dwelling place, figuratively, for God among Am Yisrael.

The Rambam

אַדִּיר הוּא

יִבְנֶה בֵיתוֹ בְּקָרוֹב
בִּמְהֵרָה בִּמְהֵרָה, בְּיָמֵינוּ בְּקָרוֹב
אֵל בְּנֵה אֵל בְּנֵה בְּנֵה בֵיתְךָ בְּקָרוֹב

בָּחוּר הוּא גָּדוֹל הוּא דָּגוּל הוּא
יִבְנֶה בֵיתוֹ בְּקָרוֹב בִּמְהֵרָה בִּמְהֵרָה, בְּיָמֵינוּ בְּקָרוֹב
אֵל בְּנֵה אֵל בְּנֵה בְּנֵה בֵיתְךָ בְּקָרוֹב

הָדוּר הוּא וָתִיק הוּא זַכַּאי הוּא חָסִיד הוּא
יִבְנֶה בֵיתוֹ בְּקָרוֹב בִּמְהֵרָה בִּמְהֵרָה, בְּיָמֵינוּ בְּקָרוֹב
אֵל בְּנֵה אֵל בְּנֵה בְּנֵה בֵיתְךָ בְּקָרוֹב

טָהוֹר הוּא יָחִיד הוּא כַּבִּיר הוּא לָמוּד הוּא
מֶלֶךְ הוּא נוֹרָא הוּא סַגִּיב הוּא עִזּוּז הוּא
פּוֹדֶה הוּא צַדִּיק הוּא
יִבְנֶה בֵיתוֹ בְּקָרוֹב בִּמְהֵרָה בִּמְהֵרָה, בְּיָמֵינוּ בְּקָרוֹב
אֵל בְּנֵה אֵל בְּנֵה בְּנֵה בֵיתְךָ בְּקָרוֹב

קָדוֹשׁ הוּא רַחוּם הוּא שַׁדַּי הוּא תַּקִּיף הוּא

יִבְנֶה בֵיתוֹ בְּקָרוֹב
בִּמְהֵרָה בִּמְהֵרָה, בְּיָמֵינוּ בְּקָרוֹב
אֵל בְּנֵה אֵל בְּנֵה

בְּנֵה בֵיתְךָ בְּקָרוֹב

ADIR HU

יִבְנֶה בֵיתוֹ בְּקָרוֹב – *May He build His house soon*

The Ramban at the beginning of *Parashat Teruma* states that the

אֶחָד מִי יוֹדֵעַ WHO KNOWS ONE?

Who knows one?
I know one:
our God is One, in heaven and on earth.

EHAD MI YODE'A?

THROUGH A SPIRITUAL LENS

Why do we include this song towards the end of the Haggada? What is so significant about counting these specific items: *luhot*, the forefathers, the foremothers, Mishna, Shabbat, and others?

Rav Avraham Schorr (*HaLekah VeHalibuv*) notes that there seems to be a contradiction with respect to two ideas expressed by *Hazal*. We are told not to look at women's colored clothing lest it may lead to inappropriate thoughts (Avoda Zara 20b). Yet we are told that the color blue, *tekhelet*, should remind us of the heavens, of God's throne (Menahot 43b).

Rav Schorr suggests that the type of influence a vision will have upon us depends on what we are involved in throughout the day. If we are involved in the study of Torah and the performance of mitzvot, then we will view the items around us in a positive light.

Therefore, at this juncture in the Seder, after being engaged in Torah discussion for several hours, we relate to every number through Torah-inspired lenses! Each number reminds us of something connected to Torah.

A *talmid* once visited Rav Shlomo Zalman Auerbach after returning from a trip to America. Rav Shlomo Zalman asked him, "Did you see the skyscrapers?" The *talmid* replied, "What?" Rav Shlomo Zalman asked again. "Did you see the skyscrapers?" The *talmid*, a bit surprised by the inquiry, responded in the affirmative.

Rav Shlomo Zalman then continued, "Do you know that if a child is born on the third floor of a skyscraper, and another child is born

on the 130th

אֶחָד מִי יוֹדֵעַ

אֶחָד אֲנִי יוֹדֵעַ

אֶחָד אֱלֹהֵינוּ שֶׁבַּשָּׁמַיִם וּבָאָרֶץ

The Rambam at the beginning of *Hilkhot Beit HaBekhira* suggests that the purpose of the *Mishkan* was to gather and offer sacrifices.

How are we to explain this debate? Perhaps their differing opinions in another area can shed some light on their opposing views with respect to the purpose of the *Mishkan*.

What makes *lashon hakodesh*, biblical Hebrew, so holy? The Rambam in *Moreh Nevukhim*, quoted in the Ramban at the beginning of *Parashat Ki Tisa*, states that what is unique about biblical Hebrew is that it does not contain any inappropriate words. Essentially, *kedusha* comes from below, from man's use of the language. The Ramban (*Shemot* 30:13) states otherwise, that biblical Hebrew derives its sanctification due to the fact that God wrote the Torah and spoke to the prophets in that language. In that case, the sanctification comes from above.

Perhaps this logic applies to the purpose of the *Mishkan* as well. The Rambam is of the opinion that the sanctification of the *Mishkan* is derived from below, from our offering of sacrifices. The Ramban, who states its purpose is to serve as a dwelling place for God, believes that the sanctity of the *Mishkan* comes from God's presence, from above.

The Bnei Yissakhar offers a related insight with respect to two *rabbinic* holidays. On Hanukka, we spin the dreidel from the top. On Purim, we shake a grogger from the bottom. This may be symbolic of the way in which the miracles transpired. On Hanukka, it all stemmed from above, so we spin the dreidel from above. On Purim, we took action, and Hashem acted in hidden ways. It was initiated from below, so we shake a grogger from below.

Who knows two?
I know two:
two Tablets of the Covenant;
but our God is One, in heaven and on earth.

---

is limping along, then one of his legs is weak, symbolizing a lacking in his *bein adam laMakom* or his *bein adam lehaveiro.*

The Gemara (Hulin 90b) cites a *mahloket* with respect to what transpired when the angel hit Yaakov in his *gid hanasheh.* The *hakhamim* hold that the prohibition of *gid hanasheh* applies to both the right and left sciatic nerves. Rav Yehuda argues that it applies only to the right nerve. The *Be'er Yosef* brings this *mahloket* alive. He explains the depth of the wording of the Gemara to teach us its hidden message. Since the angel of Esav could not harm Yaakov, he went for Yaakov's descendants, which was symbolized by the location of the *gid hanasheh.* He tried to hurt them in two aspects. What did he do to them? According to Rav Yehuda, he weakened them in the right leg, the area of *bein adam laMakom.* To beat the Jew, one must severe his relationship with God. When we excel in our interpersonal *middot,* but neglect Hashem's Torah, we have a limp on our right side. That is the explanation of Rav Yehuda.

The *hakhamim* contend with Rav Yehuda and state that the angel came from behind Yaakov and knocked both sides out of commission. What do they mean? The *hakhamim* are teaching us that you cannot knock out the *bein adam laMakom* and still have a perfectly healthy *bein adam lehaveiro.* If you're limping on the right side, if your *bein adam laMakom* is stained and faulty, then the left side, the *bein adam lehaveiro,* will have problems too, and be faulty and misguided.

Perhaps this can be connected to a fundamental thought expressed by Rav Ovadiah of Bartenura on *Pirkei Avot.* He asks why *Pirkei Avot* begins with a description of the transmission of the Torah from Moshe at Sinai to the time of the *Tanna'im.* It would have

שְׁנַיִם מִי יוֹדֵעַ
שְׁנַיִם אֲנִי יוֹדֵעַ
שְׁנֵי לוּחוֹת הַבְּרִית
אֶחָד אֱלֹהֵינוּ שֶׁבַּשָּׁמַיִם וּבָאָרֶץ

---

on the 130th floor of the skyscraper at the same exact moment, and they're born two minutes before the sundown, it could be that one of the boys will have his *brit mila* one day and the other will have a *brit mila* on the next day?" When Rav Shlomo Zalman thought of skyscrapers, he viewed them in light of his other thoughts. He contemplated that from a halakhic perspective, the exact time of sundown may differ at varies altitudes. This led him to hypothesize a unique *pesak*!

By the end of the Seder, we should be on a level that, whatever number we hear, we associate it with spirituality. That's the goal of the Seder, to reach such a level. That's also the goal of our lives: to see everything through spiritual spectacles.

THE TWO *LUHOT*

For the number two, we refer to the two *luhot*. Many commentators explain that the right side of the *luhot* represents the commandments *bein adam laMakom*, and the left side represents the commandments *bein adam lehaveiro*.

The Gemara (Shabbat 31) relates a story of a potential convert who came to Hillel and asked Hillel to teach him the entire Torah while standing on one foot. This is interpreted as the convert asking for an explanation of just one side of the *luhot*. Hillel taught him the root of *bein adam lehaveiro*. Then Hillel sent him to go learn the other half, the *bein adam laMakom*.

The Be'er Yosef (*Parashat Vayishlah*) explains that a person who is complete in his *avodat Hashem*, both in *bein adam laMakom* and *bein adam lehaveiro*, is referred to as a person who walks on two feet. He is complete with no blemishes. On the other hand, if someone

Who knows three?
I know three:
three fathers,
two Tablets of the Covenant;
but our God is One, in heaven and on earth.

Who knows four?
I know four:
four mothers, three fathers,
two Tablets of the Covenant;
but our God is One, in heaven and on earth.

Who knows five?
I know five:
five books of the Torah,
four mothers, three fathers,
two Tablets of the Covenant;
but our God is One, in heaven and on earth.

---

of *Pirkei Avot* were God-given, received by Moshe at Mount Sinai, and transmitted to subsequent generations. These are precepts that cannot be adapted or compromised. As we have witnessed all too often, leaving morality to be defined by mortal beings can lead to tragedy. When defining moral and ethical principles and behaviors, it is our duty and obligation to answer to a Higher Authority.

We always have to remember that there are two sides to the *luhot*. One represents commandments *bein adam laMakom*, and the other, *bein adam lehaveiro*. These are interconnected, and for completeness, they cannot be separated. If one is compromised, there is a blemish in the observance of the other.

SEVEN AND

שְׁלוֹשָׁה מִי יוֹדֵעַ
שְׁלוֹשָׁה אֲנִי יוֹדֵעַ
שְׁלוֹשָׁה אָבוֹת
שְׁנֵי לוּחוֹת הַבְּרִית
אֶחָד אֱלֹהֵינוּ שֶׁבַּשָּׁמַיִם וּבָאָרֶץ

אַרְבַּע מִי יוֹדֵעַ
אַרְבַּע אֲנִי יוֹדֵעַ
אַרְבַּע אִמָּהוֹת
שְׁלוֹשָׁה אָבוֹת שְׁנֵי לוּחוֹת הַבְּרִית
אֶחָד אֱלֹהֵינוּ שֶׁבַּשָּׁמַיִם וּבָאָרֶץ

חֲמִשָּׁה מִי יוֹדֵעַ
חֲמִשָּׁה אֲנִי יוֹדֵעַ
חֲמִשָּׁה חֻמְשֵׁי תוֹרָה
אַרְבַּע אִמָּהוֹת שְׁלוֹשָׁה אָבוֹת שְׁנֵי לוּחוֹת הַבְּרִית
אֶחָד אֱלֹהֵינוּ שֶׁבַּשָּׁמַיִם וּבָאָרֶץ

---

made more sense for this description to come at the beginning of the first tractate, *Masekhet Berakhot,* to illustrate the transition from the Written Torah to the Oral Torah, but not to introduce *Pirkei Avot,* which is at the end in *Seder Nezikin* and contains no mitzvot!

Rav Ovadiah suggests that this is exactly the point. It is not necessary to be told that Moshe received the Torah from Sinai at the beginning of *Eiruvin* or *Temura.* Where else would such laws come from? One may hypothesize, however, that ethics, such as those that are found in *Pirkei Avot,* are from humans. The grave danger with such a belief is that man may feel that he can redefine ethical and moral behaviors and adapt them to current societal norms.

It is critical for us to understand that the ethical and moral precepts

Who knows six?
I know six:
six divisions of the Mishna, five books of the Torah,
four mothers, three fathers,
two Tablets of the Covenant;
but our God is One, in heaven and on earth.

Who knows seven?
I know seven:
seven days from Shabbat to Shabbat,
six divisions of the Mishna, five books of the Torah,
four mothers, three fathers,
two Tablets of the Covenant;
but our God is One, in heaven and on earth.

Similarly, we are designated guards. A *brit mila* is the stamp that we have all our lives, symbolizing our connection to HaKadosh Barukh Hu, *ot hi beini u'beineikhem. A brit mila* continues perpetually throughout our lives.

Similarly, Shabbat is not just about one day. In fact, we refer to each day of the week as connected to Shabbat. *Rishon Le'Shabbat, Sheni Le'Shabbat*... all week, we are preparing for and anticipating Shabbat. Shabbat must permeate the entire week, just like a *brit mila* and all that it symbolizes permeates our entire lives. That is why Shabbat is referred to as *shiva yemei shabbata* – we need to contemplate the Shabbat throughout the entire week.

SHABBAT – A TIME FOR INTIMACY WITH HASHEM

There is a custom to sing *Shalom Aleikhem* when one returns home from *shul* on Friday night. It is based on a *gemara* in Shabbat (119) that states that the angels follow us home from synagogue that evening.

If we are

שִׁשָּׁה מִי יוֹדֵעַ
שִׁשָּׁה אֲנִי יוֹדֵעַ
שִׁשָּׁה סִדְרֵי מִשְׁנָה
חֲמִשָּׁה חֻמְשֵׁי תוֹרָה אַרְבַּע אִמָּהוֹת שְׁלוֹשָׁה אָבוֹת
שְׁנֵי לוּחוֹת הַבְּרִית
אֶחָד אֱלֹהֵינוּ שֶׁבַּשָּׁמַיִם וּבָאָרֶץ

שִׁבְעָה מִי יוֹדֵעַ
שִׁבְעָה אֲנִי יוֹדֵעַ
שִׁבְעָה יְמֵי שַׁבַּתָּא
שִׁשָּׁה סִדְרֵי מִשְׁנָה חֲמִשָּׁה חֻמְשֵׁי תוֹרָה
אַרְבַּע אִמָּהוֹת שְׁלוֹשָׁה אָבוֹת שְׁנֵי לוּחוֹת הַבְּרִית
אֶחָד אֱלֹהֵינוּ שֶׁבַּשָּׁמַיִם וּבָאָרֶץ

SEVEN AND EIGHT, OR SEVENTH AND EIGHTH?

When referencing items for numbers seven and eight, we refer to *shivah yemei shabbata* and *shemoneh yemei mila* – seven days of Shabbat and eight days of circumcision. However, isn't Shabbat just one day, and *brit mila* just one moment?

Rav Moshe Feinstein quotes the midrash (Menahot 43b) that tells how Dovid HaMelekh once went into the bath house, and he was crying because he was *arum mimitzvot*: he wasn't engaged in the performance of a mitzva while bathing. All of a sudden, he remembered his *brit mila*. He said, oh, I'm not *arum*. Rav Moshe asks, what relevance did his *brit mila* have at that juncture? The actual act was performed years prior!

Rav Moshe offers a *mashal* to explain. If someone is hired to guard a building to ensure that no one enters the building all night, then if no one attempts to enter the building, the guard might have had a boring night, but he has still fulfilled his duty. He gets paid no less than if he had successfully thwarted an unlawful entrance.

Who knows eight?
I know eight:
eight days to a *brit*,
seven days from Shabbat to Shabbat,
six divisions of the Mishna, five books of the Torah,
four mothers, three fathers,
two Tablets of the Covenant;
but our God is One, in heaven and on earth.

Who knows nine?
I know nine:
nine months until birth, eight days to a *brit*,
seven days from Shabbat to Shabbat,
six divisions of the Mishna,
five books of the Torah, four mothers, three fathers,
two Tablets of the Covenant;
but our God is One, in heaven and on earth.

---

be like the *hasidim harishonim* who sit with anticipation preparing for *tefilla* (Berakhot 30b).

The Rav cites Rav Chaim Soloveitchik (*Hilkhot Tefilla* 4:1), who suggests that it is not enough to understand the meaning of the words one recites during prayer. It is essential that one recognize that they are about to engage in an intimate communication with the Almighty.

Since we prepare in a similar way for Shabbat, it must be because Shabbat is a similar experience, a day when we can engage in an intimate relationship with God. Therefore, the Shem MiShmuel posits, we kindly see off the angels, because on Shabbat we need to be alone with our Creator.

NINE MONTHS OF PREGNANCY

All references enumerated in *Ehad Mi Yode'a* seem to have a religious

connotation:

שְׁמוֹנָה מִי יוֹדֵעַ
שְׁמוֹנָה אֲנִי יוֹדֵעַ
שְׁמוֹנָה יְמֵי מִילָה
שִׁבְעָה יְמֵי שַׁבְּתָא שִׁשָּׁה סִדְרֵי מִשְׁנָה
חֲמִשָּׁה חֻמְשֵׁי תוֹרָה אַרְבַּע אִמָּהוֹת שְׁלוֹשָׁה אָבוֹת
שְׁנֵי לוּחוֹת הַבְּרִית
אֶחָד אֱלֹהֵינוּ שֶׁבַּשָּׁמַיִם וּבָאָרֶץ

תִּשְׁעָה מִי יוֹדֵעַ
תִּשְׁעָה אֲנִי יוֹדֵעַ
תִּשְׁעָה יַרְחֵי לֵדָה
שְׁמוֹנָה יְמֵי מִילָה שִׁבְעָה יְמֵי שַׁבְּתָא
שִׁשָּׁה סִדְרֵי מִשְׁנָה חֲמִשָּׁה חֻמְשֵׁי תוֹרָה
אַרְבַּע אִמָּהוֹת שְׁלוֹשָׁה אָבוֹת
שְׁנֵי לוּחוֹת הַבְּרִית
אֶחָד אֱלֹהֵינוּ שֶׁבַּשָּׁמַיִם וּבָאָרֶץ

If we are inviting the angels into our homes, then why in the last stanza of the song do we state *tzetkhem leshalom*? Why would we want them to leave? Wouldn't it be better to have the angels remain with us throughout the Shabbat?

Rav Yosef Dov Soloveitchik in a *yahrzeit shiur* explained as follows. Based on the Rambam (*Shabbat,* chapter 30) there are four ways that one ought to prepare for Shabbat: (i) washing, (ii) gathering in groups, (iii) sitting with bated anticipation, and (iv) wrapping ourselves in a *tallit*.

Isn't it interesting that there is another experience that we prepare for in a similar fashion? We do these very same acts when preparing for *tefilla*. We wash our hands, gather as a congregation, and try to

Who knows ten?
I know ten:
Ten Commandments,
nine months until birth, eight days to a *brit,*
seven days from Shabbat to Shabbat,
six divisions of the Mishna, five books of the Torah,
four mothers, three fathers,
two Tablets of the Covenant;
but our God is One, in heaven and on earth.

Who knows eleven?
I know eleven:
eleven stars [in Joseph's dream],
Ten Commandments,
nine months until birth, eight days to a *brit,*
seven days from Shabbat to Shabbat,
six divisions of the Mishna, five books of the Torah,
four mothers, three fathers,
two Tablets of the Covenant;
but our God is One, in heaven and on earth.

---

a religious context and to recognize its miraculous nature. As the Gemara states in Kiddushin 31b, there are three partners in the creation of man: the father, the mother, and God.

עֲשָׂרָה מִי יוֹדֵעַ
עֲשָׂרָה אֲנִי יוֹדֵעַ
עֲשָׂרָה דִבְּרַיָּא
תִּשְׁעָה יַרְחֵי לֵדָה   שְׁמוֹנָה יְמֵי מִילָה
שִׁבְעָה יְמֵי שַׁבַּתָּא   שִׁשָּׁה סִדְרֵי מִשְׁנָה
חֲמִשָּׁה חֻמְשֵׁי תוֹרָה   אַרְבַּע אִמָּהוֹת   שְׁלֹשָׁה אָבוֹת
שְׁנֵי לֻחוֹת הַבְּרִית
אֶחָד אֱלֹהֵינוּ שֶׁבַּשָּׁמַיִם וּבָאָרֶץ

אַחַד עָשָׂר מִי יוֹדֵעַ
אַחַד עָשָׂר אֲנִי יוֹדֵעַ
אַחַד עָשָׂר כּוֹכְבַיָּא
עֲשָׂרָה דִבְּרַיָּא   תִּשְׁעָה יַרְחֵי לֵדָה
שְׁמוֹנָה יְמֵי מִילָה   שִׁבְעָה יְמֵי שַׁבַּתָּא
שִׁשָּׁה סִדְרֵי מִשְׁנָה   חֲמִשָּׁה חֻמְשֵׁי תוֹרָה
אַרְבַּע אִמָּהוֹת   שְׁלֹשָׁה אָבוֹת
שְׁנֵי לֻחוֹת הַבְּרִית
אֶחָד אֱלֹהֵינוּ שֶׁבַּשָּׁמַיִם וּבָאָרֶץ

---

connotation: *luhot, imahot, avot, humash,* Mishna, etc. But why is nine months of pregnancy included in this list?

Perhaps it is included to teach us that we are to view this too in

Who knows twelve?
I know twelve:
twelve tribes, eleven stars,
Ten Commandments,
nine months until birth, eight days to a *brit,*
seven days from Shabbat to Shabbat,
six divisions of the Mishna, five books of the Torah,
four mothers, three fathers,
two Tablets of the Covenant;
but our God is One, in heaven and on earth.

Who knows thirteen?
I know thirteen:
thirteen attributes [of God's compassion],
twelve tribes, eleven stars,
Ten Commandments,
nine months until birth,
eight days to a *brit,*
seven days from Shabbat to Shabbat,
six divisions of the Mishna,
five books of the Torah,
four mothers,
three fathers,
two Tablets of the Covenant;

BUT OUR GOD IS ONE,
IN HEAVEN AND ON EARTH.

שְׁנֵים עָשָׂר מִי יוֹדֵֽעַ
שְׁנֵים עָשָׂר אֲנִי יוֹדֵֽעַ
שְׁנֵים עָשָׂר שִׁבְטַיָּא
אַחַד עָשָׂר כּוֹכְבַיָּא עֲשָׂרָה דִבְּרַיָּא
תִּשְׁעָה יַרְחֵי לֵדָה שְׁמוֹנָה יְמֵי מִילָה
שִׁבְעָה יְמֵי שַׁבַּתָּא שִׁשָּׁה סִדְרֵי מִשְׁנָה
חֲמִשָּׁה חֻמְשֵׁי תוֹרָה אַרְבַּע אִמָּהוֹת
שְׁלוֹשָׁה אָבוֹת שְׁנֵי לוּחוֹת הַבְּרִית
אֶחָד אֱלֹהֵֽינוּ שֶׁבַּשָּׁמַֽיִם וּבָאָֽרֶץ

שְׁלוֹשָׁה עָשָׂר מִי יוֹדֵֽעַ
שְׁלוֹשָׁה עָשָׂר אֲנִי יוֹדֵֽעַ
שְׁלוֹשָׁה עָשָׂר מִדַּיָּא
שְׁנֵים עָשָׂר שִׁבְטַיָּא
אַחַד עָשָׂר כּוֹכְבַיָּא
עֲשָׂרָה דִבְּרַיָּא
תִּשְׁעָה יַרְחֵי לֵדָה
שְׁמוֹנָה יְמֵי מִילָה
שִׁבְעָה יְמֵי שַׁבַּתָּא
שִׁשָּׁה סִדְרֵי מִשְׁנָה
חֲמִשָּׁה חֻמְשֵׁי תוֹרָה
אַרְבַּע אִמָּהוֹת
שְׁלוֹשָׁה אָבוֹת
שְׁנֵי לוּחוֹת הַבְּרִית

אֶחָד אֱלֹהֵֽינוּ שֶׁבַּשָּׁמַֽיִם וּבָאָֽרֶץ

חַד גַּדְיָא ONE LITTLE GOAT

one little goat
my father bought for two zuzim;
one little goat, one little goat.

Along came a cat and ate the goat
my father bought for two zuzim;
one little goat, one little goat.

Then came a dog and bit the cat who ate the goat
my father bought for two zuzim;
one little goat, one little goat.

Then came a stick and hit the dog
who bit the cat who ate the goat
my father bought for two zuzim;
one little goat, one little goat.

In every generation, in every situation we are in, we are able to visualize only certain pieces of a larger puzzle. We see the water, the cat, and the goat. Sometimes, we witness the *malakh hamavet*. Yet we are unable to picture the complete puzzle.

In Mitzrayim, while being oppressed, we were unable to see the larger picture: that this was a necessary step toward achieving salvation. This was a required step in order to build a nation that would be sympathetic to less fortunate individuals. Clearly, life can only be understood retrospectively.

Rabbi Lau cites an encounter that a friend of his had with Colin Powell, a former Secretary of State of the United States. When Rabbi Lau's friend, who was part of the Israeli lobby in Washington, met Colin Powell, he was greeted with a warm *vus makht a yid?* This is Yiddish for *how are you, my friend?* The Jewish man almost fainted on the spot. He inquired as to how Colin Powell knew Yiddish.

חַד גַּדְיָא חַד גַּדְיָא

דְּזַבִּן אַבָּא בִּתְרֵי זוּזֵי
חַד גַּדְיָא חַד גַּדְיָא

וַאֲתָא שׁוּנְרָא וְאָכְלָה לְגַדְיָא
דְּזַבִּן אַבָּא בִּתְרֵי זוּזֵי
חַד גַּדְיָא חַד גַּדְיָא

וַאֲתָא כַלְבָּא וְנָשַׁךְ לְשׁוּנְרָא דְּאָכְלָה לְגַדְיָא
דְּזַבִּן אַבָּא בִּתְרֵי זוּזֵי
חַד גַּדְיָא חַד גַּדְיָא

וַאֲתָא חֻטְרָא וְהִכָּה לְכַלְבָּא דְּנָשַׁךְ לְשׁוּנְרָא
דְּאָכְלָה לְגַדְיָא
דְּזַבִּן אַבָּא בִּתְרֵי זוּזֵי
חַד גַּדְיָא חַד גַּדְיָא

HAD GADYA

PIECES OF A PUZZLE

At the end of the Seder, we sing our beloved tune of *Had Gadya*. Upon exploring the text, it seems a bit strange that a legend about various animals and objects overcoming one another serves as the epilogue of our Haggada. Rabbi Israel Meir Lau offers a meaningful lesson that is to be derived from this final chapter.

Life is a puzzle, and many times, we see only part of the puzzle. It is hard for us to comprehend why a specific event transpired, given our limited perspective. As with a puzzle, when one opens the box, several independent pieces appear, but the whole picture is visible only after all pieces are connected.

Then came a fire and burned the stick
that hit the dog who bit the cat who ate the goat
my father bought for two zuzim;
one little goat, one little goat.

Then came water and put out the fire
that burned the stick that hit the dog
who bit the cat who ate the goat
my father bought for two zuzim;
one little goat, one little goat.

Then came an ox
and drank the water that put out the fire
that burned the stick that hit the dog
who bit the cat who ate the goat
my father bought for two zuzim;
one little goat, one little goat.

At the conclusion of the Seder, when we've spoken about everything and we've had ups and downs, we've cried, we've laughed, and we've been through all the emotions, we sing to HaKadosh Barukh Hu the *Had Gadya*. We recognize that life is a puzzle and have faith in God's greater plan.

We know that *ve'asa HaKadosh Barukh Hu veshahat lemalakh hamavet* – the Holy One, blessed be He, came and smote the angel of death. That's the last piece, the last missing piece to complete the puzzle. That's the generation we are in now. We are missing HaKadosh Barukh Hu's redemption.

That's what we daven for, for the day that HaKadosh Barukh Hu redeems us. At the end of the Seder, we declare to HaKadosh Barukh Hu and we pray that He complete the puzzle, so that we can see a clear and complete picture. At next year's Seder, may we merit partaking in the actual *korban pesah* in Yerushalayim!

WHAT'S THE

וַאֲתָא נוּרָא וְשָׂרַף לְחֻטְרָא דְּהִכָּה לְכַלְבָּא
דְּנָשַׁךְ לְשׁוּנְרָא דְּאָכְלָה לְגַדְיָא
דִּזְבַן אַבָּא בִּתְרֵי זוּזֵי
חַד גַּדְיָא חַד גַּדְיָא

וַאֲתָא מַיָּא וְכָבָה לְנוּרָא דְּשָׂרַף לְחֻטְרָא דְּהִכָּה לְכַלְבָּא
דְּנָשַׁךְ לְשׁוּנְרָא דְּאָכְלָה לְגַדְיָא
דִּזְבַן אַבָּא בִּתְרֵי זוּזֵי
חַד גַּדְיָא חַד גַּדְיָא

וַאֲתָא תוֹרָא וְשָׁתָה לְמַיָּא דְּכָבָה לְנוּרָא דְּשָׂרַף לְחֻטְרָא
דְּהִכָּה לְכַלְבָּא דְּנָשַׁךְ לְשׁוּנְרָא דְּאָכְלָה לְגַדְיָא
דִּזְבַן אַבָּא בִּתְרֵי זוּזֵי
חַד גַּדְיָא חַד גַּדְיָא

Colin Powell explained that when he was a youth growing up in the Bronx, he earned some extra money by serving as a delivery boy. There was one Jewish couple that was very friendly to him. Over time, they began speaking with him, and impressed with his wisdom and potential, they paid for Colin Powell's education.

Due to this generous act that provided him with unlimited opportunity, he made a promise to himself that he would never forget the Jewish people. Later in life, when he became Secretary of State and Saddam Hussein attacked Israel with long- range missiles, Colin Powell said, "I had to do all in my power to protect the Jewish homeland."

We see only one part of the puzzle. In fifty, sixty, or a hundred years from now, what we will see is the groundwork being laid by Hashem for a significant event in the future.

Then came a slaughterer and slew the ox
who drank the water that put out the fire
that burned the stick that hit the dog
who bit the cat who ate the goat
my father bought for two zuzim;
one little goat, one little goat.

Then came the angel of death
and slew the slaughterer who slew the ox
who drank the water that put out the fire
that burned the stick that hit the dog
who bit the cat who ate the goat
my father bought for two zuzim;
one little goat, one little goat.

---

*Ve'asa HaKadosh Barukh Hu veshahat lemalakh hamave*t. The just reward and punishment will be attributed to each and every person in history. Then, truth and justice will prevail.

CONCLUDING WITH HOPE

We conclude the Haggada with *Had Gadya*. On a deeper level, this is an allegory about Jewish history, and it all starts with a goat.

When we think of the imagery of a goat in Jewish history, we think of the sale of Yosef and the dipping of his multicolored garment in the blood of a goat. Throughout the twenty-two years that Yaakov mourned Yosef's absence, we are told that he resisted being comforted (*vayima'en lehitnahem, Bereshit* 37:35). Why was Yaakov so reluctant to be comforted? Because one does not accept *nehama* for somebody who is alive. Subconsciously, he would not give up

hope

וַאֲתָא הַשּׁוֹחֵט וְשָׁחַט לְתוֹרָא
דְּשָׁתָא לְמַיָּא דְּכָבָה לְנוּרָא
דְּשָׂרַף לְחֻטְרָא דְּהִכָּה לְכַלְבָּא
דְּנָשַׁךְ לְשׁוּנְרָא
דְּאָכְלָה לְגַדְיָא
דִּזְבַן אַבָּא בִּתְרֵי זוּזֵי
חַד גַּדְיָא חַד גַּדְיָא

וַאֲתָא מַלְאַךְ הַמָּוֶת וְשָׁחַט לְשׁוֹחֵט דְּשָׁחַט לְתוֹרָא
דְּשָׁתָא לְמַיָּא דְּכָבָה לְנוּרָא דְּשָׂרַף לְחֻטְרָא
דְּהִכָּה לְכַלְבָּא דְּנָשַׁךְ לְשׁוּנְרָא דְּאָכְלָה לְגַדְיָא
דִּזְבַן אַבָּא בִּתְרֵי זוּזֵי
חַד גַּדְיָא חַד גַּדְיָא

WHAT'S THE MESSAGE OF *HAD GADYA*?

Rabbi Yitzchak Sender suggests a *mashal*. If someone enters in the middle of the song *Had Gadya* and reads that the dog attacks the cat, he sympathizes with the cat. The cat is the victim, and the dog is the aggressor. Yet the cat himself was the aggressor a short while earlier.

Had Gadya is about not seeing the entire picture. So often our enemies create "fake news" and manipulate public opinion by turning themselves into the apparent victims, even though they are the aggressors. They state their poor economic situation was caused by the Jews, as if they are the victims of our wrongdoing, and in order to justify actions against us.

Had Gadya is actually a prayer for the day when everything becomes clear, when the victims are really shown to be the victims, and the attackers are really shown to be the attackers.

Then came the Holy One
and slew the angel of death,
who slew the slaughterer
who slew the ox
who drank the water that put out the fire
that burned the stick that hit the dog
who bit the cat
who ate the goat
my father bought for two zuzim;
ONE LITTLE GOAT, ONE LITTLE GOAT.

Upon hearing that the crying and weeping was in connection with a temple that was destroyed centuries ago, Napoleon responded, "If this temple is so ingrained in the people that it cannot be forgotten, it will surely be rebuilt in the future."

As Rabbi Sacks in his Haggada (p. 164) so eloquently states:

> *Had Gadya* expresses the Jewish refusal to give up hope. Though history is full of man's inhumanity to man – dog bites cat, stick hits dog – that is not the final verse. The Haggada ends with the death of death in eternal life, a fitting end for the story of a people dedicated to Moses' great command, "choose life" (*Devarim* 30:19).

וַאֲתָא הַקָּדוֹשׁ בָּרוּךְ הוּא
וְשָׁחַט לְמַלְאַךְ הַמָּוֶת
דְּשָׁחַט לְשׁוֹחֵט
דְּשָׁחַט לְתוֹרָא
דְּשָׁתָא לְמַיָּא
דְּכָבָה לְנוּרָא
דְּשָׂרַף לְחֻטְרָא
דְּהִכָּה לְכַלְבָּא
דְּנָשַׁךְ לְשׁוּנְרָא
דְּאָכְלָה לְגַדְיָא
דִּזְבַן אַבָּא בִּתְרֵי זוּזֵי

חַד גַּדְיָא חַד גַּדְיָא

---

hope of one day being reunited with his son Yosef. Yaakov continued to mourn throughout the twenty-two years. So long as we cry, that means we still have hope.

We still cry for the *Beit HaMikdash* because we know one day, it will be rebuilt. We end the Seder by saying that we have hope. We do not stop crying, and we do not stop yearning. Because we know, *ve'asa HaKadosh Barukh Hu veshahat lemalakh hamavet.* HaKadosh Barukh Hu is in charge.

A story is told about Napoleon who saw Jews mourning on Tisha Be'Av and inquired about it. He was told that the Jews were mourning the destruction of their temple. Napoleon was puzzled, since he did not hear of any recent destruction of a Jewish temple.

Introduction to *Shir HaShirim*

There is a custom to read *Shir HaShirim* on Pesah, and so it is included at the end of the Haggada.

Shir HaShirim is like no other book in Tanakh. On the surface it seems like a song between two lovers, yet *Hazal* inform us that it is to be understood on a deeper level as an allegory reflecting the special relationship between Hashem and Am Yisrael. We will provide some background on this unique *sefer* in order to better appreciate its content.

KODESH KODASHIM

The Mishna *in Masekhet Yadayim* (3:5) declares that *Shir HaShirim veKohelet metamei et hayadayim* (*Shir HaShirim* and *Kohelet* can make one's hands impure).[1] Including *Shir HaShirim* as a scroll that can make something else impure highlights its inherent sanctity

---

1. The Mishna in *Yadayim* 3 states: *Kol kitvei hakodesh metamin et hayadayim* (All holy writings can make one's hands impure). This highlights that these books (the *Ketuvim*) are inherently *kodesh* (holy), as they are considered a part of Tanakh. Why would a holy scroll cause one's hands to become impure? This was a *gezera,* a dictum established by *Hazal,* for the following reason: *Kohanim* would place their *teruma* in the same closet as their scrolls to prevent the *teruma* from becoming impure by being touched by impure family members. But this would then lead animals to gain access to the *teruma,* thereby also nibbling on the scrolls. *Hazal* enacted a *gezera* that if a Torah scroll comes into contact with *teruma,* the *teruma* becomes impure, so that *kohanim* would avoid storing *teruma* with their scrolls and prevent the scrolls from being desecrated by the animals.

◂ and solid

and solid footing as a book in *Kitvei HaKodesh* (Holy Scripture). It is interesting to note that *Shir HaShirim* is one of only a few books singled out, perhaps because one may have questioned whether it should be categorized with such *kedusha* (sanctity).

The mishna continues and explains that according to Rabbi Akiva, there is no controversy as to whether or not *Shir HaShirim* should be included in Tanakh: *She'ein kol ha'olam kulo kedai keyom shenitan bo Shir HaShirim leYisrael* (The most amazing day in the history of the whole world was the day that *Shir HaShirim* was given to Am Yisrael).

Rabbi Akiva continues and says: *Shekol haketuvim kodesh, veShir HaShirim kodesh kodashim* (Every book included in Tanakh is holy, yet *Shir HaShirim* is holy of holies). What exactly does it mean that it is *kodesh kodashim*?

This *Targum* at the beginning of *Shir HaShirim* quotes that there are ten songs in Tanakh:

1. "Mizmor Shir LeYom HaShabbat," sung by Adam
2. "Az Yashir," sung by Moshe
3. "Shirat HaBe'er," in *Parashat Hukat*.[2]
4. "Shirat Haazinu"
5. "The Shira of Yehoshua Bin Nun"[3]
6. "Shirat Devora"
7. "Shirat Hanna"
8. "Shirat David"
9. *Shir HaShirim*
10. The *shira* that will be sung in the time of the *Mashiah*, after the battle of Gog U'Magog.

Rav Shimshon Pincus, in his Haggada, points out that all but one

2. Rashi explains that they sang *shira* at this juncture because the Emorites were hiding in caves, and Hashem moved the mountains and crushed those hiding in the caves.
3. In Givon when the sun stood still in one of Yehoshua's battles.

◂ of the

of the ten songs are sung as an expression of gratitude for having been saved from an enemy. Even Adam sings about overcoming evil. The only exception *is Shir HaShirim,* which is all about the pure love between HaKadosh Barukh Hu and Am Yisrael. That is what makes *Shir HaShirim kodesh kodashim.*

The Torah Temima in his commentary on *Shir HaShirim* (in the back of *Sefer Vayikra*) suggests that all the other songs have a *peshat* (can be taken literally), and then perhaps a deeper way of understanding the text. However, *Shir HaShirim* may not be understood literally. It is not a story of human lovers but *must* be interpreted at a deeper level as a story about the relationship between God and His chosen nation.

In addition, the Torah Temima states, all the other songs are unidirectional; we are praising HaKadosh Barukh Hu. But *Shir HaShirim* is bidirectional. There are verses that express our love toward Hashem and there are verses that express God's love for Am Yisrael. That is why *Shir HaShirim* is referred to as *kodesh kodashim*. It possesses *kedusha mukhpelet,* a double *kedusha,* due to its bidirectional praise of God and Am Yisrael.

The Gemara in Berakhot (57b) provides a list of dreams and their meaning. If one dreams about *Shir HaShirim,* the Gemara explains, *metzapeh leHasidut* (one aspires to piety). It is something unique. Rashi interprets this to mean that it will lead one to *ahavat Hashem* (love God) because it's on one's mind.

NOT TO BE TAKEN LITERALLY

The Gemara tells us (Shabbat 63a) that the rule is: *Ein hamikra yotzei midei peshuto,* there's always a level of *peshat,* the literal way of understanding the text. However, Rashi, in his introduction to *Shir HaShirim,* cites a *pasuk* in *Tehillim* (62:12): *Akhat dibber Elokim shetayim zu shamati,* "'God has spoken once, twice have I heard it': A single verse of Scripture may bear multiple interpretations." Rashi intends that with respect to *Shir HaShirim,* there is more than one way to interpret the text.

◂ Rashi suggests

Rashi suggests that Shlomo HaMelekh saw through prophecy that we will experience an elongated exile *(hurban ahar hurban)*, and we will need to recall the earlier times and remember the initial love God exhibited toward Am Yisrael, when we were a light unto the nations. That's why he wrote *Shir HaShirim*, which is a two-sided yearning, like a woman whose husband is alive somewhere, but she's like a widow. She realizes her mistakes, and they yearn for each other. This is what *Shir HaShirim* is all about, the yearning of Am Yisrael for a close relationship with HaKadosh Barukh Hu.

The Rambam tells us (*Peirush HaMishnayot*, Sanhedrin), that one of the Thirteen Principles of Faith is *ein lo guf*, that HaKadosh Barukh Hu does not have a body. We cannot attribute physical or human attributes to God. If so, then how are we to understand *Shir HaShirim*, which is full of graphic physical descriptions of God in its depiction of Hashem's relationship with Am Yisrael?

The Shelah HaKadosh has a beautiful idea which he expresses several times in his writings.[4] The Shelah explains that our world is connected to the upper worlds, and terms used on earth are interpreted differently above. For example, *ayin* refers to an eye. Yet when we express that Hashem has an eye, we don't mean a physical eye. Rather, the word "eye" is a reference to the power of sight. Hashem has the power of seeing, of comprehending, and of experiencing a vision of the future. We call it an "eye" in this world because the eye is what the power of seeing is in this world.

When we state that God has an ear, it refers to the power of hearing, and understanding. That Hashem has a *yad* (hand) refers to His control over the world. Hashem has the world in His hands. He controls rain, the power of enabling growth. Hashem is in charge. At the beginning of *Masekhet Taanit*, it states that Hashem doesn't give the keys of rain to anyone else because He retains the power of enabling growth.

This idea applies to all body parts. A number of times in

4. In Pesahim and *Parashat Kedoshim*.

Shir HaShirim, we find the reference to *shadayim,* the breasts of a woman. This refers to the ability to give nourishment. The Midrash says that *shadayim* refer to Moshe and Aharon. They provide spiritual nourishment. This is the way in which one needs to understand the language in *Shir HaShirim* as it relates to certain physical descriptions.

One might be curious as to why Shlomo HaMelekh wrote *Shir HaShirim* in this manner, which risks being misunderstood. Rav Dessler in his Haggada explains that we are not on the level of Shlomo HaMelekh, who was the wisest of all men (*hakham mikol adam*). For example, at times a student may not comprehend all that a teacher is relaying, understanding that he or she is not at the same level as the teacher. We too must recognize that Shlomo HaMelekh had an understanding beyond that which we are capable of comprehending. We have to try to understand his writings, in particular *Shir HaShirim,* at a deeper level.

The Netziv in his commentary distinguishes between two books written by Shlomo HaMelekh. Shlomo first wrote *Kohelet,* which is recited on Sukkot, when all the nations gathered together.[5] Kohelet has universal messages. *Shir HaShirim* is recited on Pesah, a holiday that relates only to Am Yisrael as they were formed into a nation. This is when the unique relationship between Am Yisrael and HaKadosh Barukh Hu is to be encapsulated.

It is stated that Rabbi Akiva cried when he recited *Shir HaShirim* because he knew the heights these words could achieve.[6] Rav Shalom Schwadron in his Haggada explains this statement. When one writes a letter to a king, he is careful how he articulates his thoughts, knowing that it will be read by such a distinguished and important individual. Rabbi Akiva understood that the words

5. On Sukkot the sacrifices offered in the *Beit HaMikdash* represented the seventy nations.
6. For a fascinating discussion of this type of crying on Shabbat, see the Rema, *Orah Hayim* 288:2 and the Taz, *Mishna Berura,* ibid. 4.

of *Shir HaShirim* reach Hashem, and so one must be careful and attentive when reciting these precious words.

AUTHORSHIP

With respect to authorship, many understand, and we have referenced above, that Shlomo HaMelekh wrote *Shir HaShirim* along with *Mishlei* and *Kohelet*. However, a Gemara in Bava Batra (14b–15a) lists all the books of Tanakh and their respective authors, and there *Shir HaShirim* is attributed to Hizkiyahu HaMelekh. Who is the true author? One explanation offered is that Hizkiyahu edited what Shlomo HaMelekh initially scripted.

Generally, it's understood that Shlomo wrote *Shir HaShirim* in his younger years; it's more of a youthful song. *Mishlei* was composed in his middle years, and *Kohelet* in his later years, after reflecting on his experiences.

שיר השירים

SHIR HASHIRIM / SONG OF SONGS

1 1 2 *Shlomo's Song of Songs.* [*She*] Would that he would kiss me with
3 that mouth. Better than any wine is your love, the fragrance of
your oils finer; your very name flows forth like fragrant oil; what
4 wonder that all the maidens love you? Come, draw me after you;
come, let us run – the king has brought me into his chambers. In
you our joy, our happiness: your love possesses us more than any
5 wine; flowing freely falls this love. [*She*] I am dark yet

---

Torah, as one would share a tasty wine with his comrades (Rav Pam Haggada).

1:4 מָשְׁכֵנִי אַחֲרֶיךָ נָּרוּצָה הֱבִיאַנִי הַמֶּלֶךְ חֲדָרָיו נָגִילָה וְנִשְׂמְחָה בָּךְ Following *yetzi'at Mitzrayim,* You brought us to Your private chambers – Har Sinai – and we rejoiced with You (Rashi).

Rav Pincus writes in his Haggada regarding the phrase *heviani haMelekh hadarav,* "the king has brought me into his chambers" – going into HaKadosh Barukh Hu's inner chamber is a reference to the *Amida* prayer. A king has a private life and a communal life. In his private life, he is responsible for his family as a father, husband, or grandfather. Then there's the king as the governmental official, caring for the nation.

Rav Pincus explains that it is similar with respect to *tefilla.* We begin our morning prayers praising God as a King who cares for His people in general. Then we get to the *Amida* prayer, which is more intimate. There we refer to our relationship with God in a more personal manner. He is no longer the King, but rather He is our Father. That is where we refer to God solely as *Barukh Ata Hashem* (You are God) without mentioning that He is *Elokenu Melekh ha'olam* (the King of the universe).

1:5 שְׁחוֹרָה אֲנִי וְנָאוָה Our outer appearance may be blackened, but inside we are beautiful. Perhaps this is a statement to the other nations of the world. We may have transgressed, but we have not been rejected by Hashem (Rashi).

Although

א א ב שִׁיר הַשִּׁירִים אֲשֶׁר לִשְׁלֹמֹה: יִשָּׁקֵנִי מִנְּשִׁיקוֹת פִּיהוּ כִּי־טוֹבִים
ג דֹדֶיךָ מִיָּיִן: לְרֵיחַ שְׁמָנֶיךָ טוֹבִים שֶׁמֶן תּוּרַק שְׁמֶךָ עַל־כֵּן עֲלָמוֹת
ד אֲהֵבוּךָ: מָשְׁכֵנִי אַחֲרֶיךָ נָּרוּצָה הֱבִיאַנִי הַמֶּלֶךְ חֲדָרָיו נָגִילָה וְנִשְׂמְחָה
ה בָּךְ נַזְכִּירָה דֹדֶיךָ מִיַּיִן מֵישָׁרִים אֲהֵבוּךָ: שְׁחוֹרָה אֲנִי

PEREK ALEF

1:1 שִׁיר הַשִּׁירִים אֲשֶׁר לִשְׁלֹמֹה Many commentators attribute the use of the name *Shlomo* in this book to God – *Melekh shehashalom shelo* (King who controls peace).

Shir HaShirim was one of many songs Shlomo HaMelekh composed (Metzudat David), based on the *pasuk* (*I Melakhim* 5:12) *Vayehi shiro hamisha vaalef.* That is why this book is referred to as Shir HaShirim – it is the greatest of all songs composed by Shlomo HaMelekh.

1:2 יִשָּׁקֵנִי מִנְּשִׁיקוֹת פִּיהוּ The Megilla commences with Bnei Yisrael yearning to achieve closeness to Hashem.

Shlomo HaMelekh is talking by way of prophecy, of what will transpire in the future when we are exiled. Bnei Yisrael ask for a kiss from God. The graphic imagery is to provide us with a deeper insight. There are different types of kisses. There is a kiss on the cheek, a kiss on the forehead, and a kiss on the lips, which is the ultimate connection. Am Yisrael are requesting that intimate connection with Hashem (Rashi), or that close bond we had at Har Sinai – the divine kiss (Metzudat David).

כִּי־טוֹבִים דֹּדֶיךָ מִיָּיִן Our relationship with God is more satisfying than any physical pleasure.

If we really appreciate the closeness of Hashem and the awesomeness of the Torah, we should want to share it with others. One who enjoys a good meal or a good wine delights all the more by sharing it with others. So too with Torah, one should desire to share the joy of Torah with others so they too can experience a closeness to the Creator. Love for Torah should translate into a love for sharing

fair, daughters of Jerusalem, like the tents of Kedar, like the
6 curtains of Shlomo. Do not look at me: I am scorched black; the
sun has stared at me. My mother's sons were furious: they made
me a keeper of the vineyards; my own vineyard I did not keep.
7 Tell me, you whom I have loved, where will you pasture; where
will you rest your flock at noon? Do not make me swathe my face
8 and wander among all the herds of your friends. [*He*] If you do
not know, most beautiful of women, go out in the tracks of the
flock; bring your own young goats to pasture beside the shepherds'
9 huts. [*He*] A mare among Pharaoh's chariots, that is what
10 you are to me, my love, your cheeks fair in their strands of beads,
11 your neck bejeweled; I would make you strands of gold – with
12 silver flecks. [*She*] As long as my king reclined to drink, my musk

---

to apply the Torah's age-old principles to new situations, but never to change them.

Our *mesora* is crucial to our survival. That's why Hashem says, You want to come back to Me? You want to be safe? *Tze'i lakh be'ikvei hatzon*, follow in the path of the *mesora*.

In *Mesillat Yesharim* (chapter 3), life is referred to as a maze, and if we don't know where to go, we need to ask someone who has experience to guide us through. A maze has several paths but most of them lead to a dead end. While traveling through a maze one cannot know if he is on the correct path. Only someone who has been through the maze can guide others to the finish line successfully. That is the *mesora*. We must trust those that have experienced the path before us and have received the correct instructions from their predecessors.

1:12 עַד־שֶׁהַמֶּלֶךְ בִּמְסִבּוֹ נִרְדִּי נָתַן רֵיחוֹ While the king was still at the party, my odor escaped. According to Hazal, this refers to the sin of the golden calf, which transpired at the foot of Har Sinai following the momentous transmission of the Torah.

Rav Pam

ו וְנָאוָה בְּנוֹת יְרוּשָׁלָ͏ִם כְּאָהֳלֵי קֵדָר כִּירִיעוֹת שְׁלֹמֹה׃ אַל־תִּרְאֻנִי
שֶׁאֲנִי שְׁחַרְחֹרֶת שֶׁשְּׁזָפַתְנִי הַשָּׁמֶשׁ בְּנֵי אִמִּי נִחֲרוּ־בִי שָׂמֻנִי נֹטֵרָה
ז אֶת־הַכְּרָמִים כַּרְמִי שֶׁלִּי לֹא נָטָרְתִּי׃ הַגִּידָה לִּי שֶׁאָהֲבָה נַפְשִׁי
אֵיכָה תִרְעֶה אֵיכָה תַּרְבִּיץ בַּצָּהֳרָיִם שַׁלָּמָה אֶהְיֶה כְּעֹטְיָה עַל עֶדְרֵי
ח חֲבֵרֶיךָ׃ אִם־לֹא תֵדְעִי לָךְ הַיָּפָה בַּנָּשִׁים צְאִי־לָךְ בְּעִקְבֵי הַצֹּאן
ט וּרְעִי אֶת־גְּדִיֹּתַיִךְ עַל מִשְׁכְּנוֹת הָרֹעִים׃ לְסֻסָתִי בְּרִכְבֵי
יא פַרְעֹה דִּמִּיתִיךְ רַעְיָתִי׃ נָאווּ לְחָיַיִךְ בַּתֹּרִים צַוָּארֵךְ בַּחֲרוּזִים׃ תּוֹרֵי
יב זָהָב נַעֲשֶׂה־לָּךְ עִם נְקֻדּוֹת הַכָּסֶף׃ עַד־שֶׁהַמֶּלֶךְ בִּמְסִבּוֹ נִרְדִּי נָתַן

Although at times we distance ourselves from God, we always have the ability to return. Every Jew deep down inside has that inner beauty, even though there are so many layers of darkness (Metzudat David).

The Rambam refers to a similar concept in *Hilkhot Gerushin* (2:20). Deep down, every Jew wants to do the right thing. It's the *shehora* (darkness), the *yetzer hara*, the negative forces within us that are causing us to transgress. That is why, says the Rambam, one could force a man to give a *get*, even though the halakha requires that it be willfully delivered. *Kofin oto ad sheyomar rotzeh ani*. We persuade such an individual to reach deep inside and overcome those dark influences that were inhibiting proper behavior.

1:8 בְּעִקְבֵי הַצֹּאן This is a reference to following the *mesora* (tradition); if you do this, then you will be safe.

It may be a reference to the *avot*: *hitboneni bedarkhei avotekha,* follow in the ways of your forefathers (Rashi).

In the introduction to his *sefer Be'Ikvei HaTzon,* Rav Hershel Schachter emphasizes the importance of passing on the *mesora*. The concept of staying true to our *mesora* doesn't mean merely mimicking what was done in the past. *Mesora* means following. We have to be a *mehadesh* but not a *meshaneh*. We have to be able

13 root gave its scent, my beloved a bundle of myrrh to me, resting
14 between my breasts; my beloved a cluster of henna to me in the
15 vineyards of Ein Gedi. [*He*] How beautiful you are, my
16 love, how beautiful, your eyes like doves. [*She*] How beautiful you
17 are, beloved, and how good. Our bed is green, luscious; our house
2 1 is roofed with cedars; its rafters are juniper trees. I am a dune
2 flower of the coast, I am a lily of the valleys. [*He*] A lily among
3 thorn weeds is my love among the maidens. [*She*] An apple tree

---

not allow the sacrifice of a tainted animal or sentence the instigator to death, thinking he was acting in a pious manner, yet that led to the destruction of the *Beit HaMikdash*.

1:16 הִנְּךָ יָפֶה דוֹדִי אַף נָעִים This is a love story. Each party is stressing that the other is more beautiful.

This is one of the examples where the commentators point out that we praise Hashem and Hashem praises us. The Gemara in Berakhot 6a states that in our tefillin we include a statement that there is but one God. In Hashem's tefillin it states, *Mi ke'amkha Yisrael* – There is no other nation like Israel. Similarly, we refer to the holiday as Pesah, because Hashem passed over our homes – stressing the act God performed to save us. Conversely, in the Torah, the holiday is called Hag HaMatzot, because He remembers our act, that we quickly left and followed Him to the desert.

PEREK BET

2:3 כְּתַפּוּחַ בַּעֲצֵי הַיַּעַר, כֵּן דּוֹדִי בֵּין הַבָּנִים "An apple tree in the forest is my beloved among young men." The comparison to fruit may be on several levels. First, trees provide shade, which is a temporary benefit, like other nations seeking pleasures of the moment. Bnei Yisrael, by contrast, are willing to wait for the tree to bear fruit, which is a reference to the longer-term benefit – that of the World to Come (Metzudat David).

Rashi,

יג יד רֵיחוֹ: צְרוֹר הַמֹּר ׀ דּוֹדִי לִי בֵּין שָׁדַי יָלִין: אֶשְׁכֹּל הַכֹּפֶר ׀ דּוֹדִי לִי
טו בְּכַרְמֵי עֵין גֶּדִי: הִנָּךְ יָפָה רַעְיָתִי הִנָּךְ יָפָה עֵינַיִךְ יוֹנִים:
טז יז הִנְּךָ יָפֶה דוֹדִי אַף נָעִים אַף־עַרְשֵׂנוּ רַעֲנָנָה: קֹרוֹת בָּתֵּינוּ אֲרָזִים
ב א ב רחיטנו בְּרוֹתִים: אֲנִי חֲבַצֶּלֶת הַשָּׁרוֹן שׁוֹשַׁנַּת הָעֲמָקִים: כְּשׁוֹשַׁנָּה רָהִיטֵנוּ
ג בֵּין הַחוֹחִים כֵּן רַעְיָתִי בֵּין הַבָּנוֹת: כְּתַפּוּחַ בַּעֲצֵי הַיַּעַר כֵּן דּוֹדִי בֵּין

Rav Pam explains what was so tragic about the sin of the golden calf: It's one thing for a person to sin, but when he deceives himself into believing that by sinning he's actually fulfilling Hashem's will, and he calls his sin *avodat Hashem*, it becomes a sin of an entirely different magnitude.

Am Yisrael thought they were acting in God's name, although they were engaged in idolatry. The Hafetz Hayim explains this phenomenon in his commentary to the *haftara* on *Parashat Behaalotekha*, where he talks about the *pasuk* in *Zekharya*, that references the *satan* (*yetzer hara*) being on our right. The Hafetz Hayim points out that usually the *yetzer tov* is on the right, and the *yetzer hara* is on the left. However, often the *yetzer hara* realizes he can't succeed in getting one to commit a transgression. Therefore, he dresses it up like a mitzva. He says, Stay in the *beit midrash* until late at night. Then you can sleep late and miss *tefilla* with a minyan! A person has to be careful to ensure that he is not being tricked by the *yetzer hara* into performing a mitzva that will lead to a different transgression. That's exactly what happened with the golden calf. The people felt they needed a vehicle through which to serve Hashem, something to replace Moshe.

The Ramhal writes, in *Mesillat Yesharim* (chapter 20), that this was the mistake of Gedalya ben Ahikam. He thought he was engaging in a mitzva by not accepting *lashon hara* about someone who was planning to kill him.

Similarly, he explains that this was the mistake of Zekharya ben Avkules, in the story of Kamtza and Bar Kamtza (Gittin 55b). He did

in the forest is my beloved among young men. I yearn for his
shade; there I rest, and his fruit fills my mouth with sweetness.
4 [*She*] He has brought me to the wine house, and his ensign flying
5 over me is love. Sustain me with raisin cakes; spread a bed for me
6 among apples – for I am sick with love. My head rests in his left

---

therefore not interested in eating more, they will despise even the honeycomb, even the sweetest item. By contrast, when someone desires and loves to learn Torah, he is willing to toil to decipher the more difficult tractates. The more one invests in Torah, the more one appreciates it.

2:4 הֱבִיאַנִי אֶל־בֵּית הַיָּיִן Hashem brought me to the house of wine. Rashi interprets the *pasuk* as referring to the *Ohel Mo'ed*, the *Mishkan*, for that is from where the clarity of the Torah was disseminated. The Gra adds – *yayin* in *gematria* (numerical value of its letters) is seventy, representing the seventy faces (*panim*) of the Torah. In other words, Hashem brought us close to the *beit hayayin* – He gave us the secrets of the Torah. As is stated, *Nikhnas yayin, yatza sod* (Sanhedrin 38a) – when one drinks wine, secrets are revealed.

There are many comparisons between wine and Torah. For example, if one adds preservatives, it dilutes the quality of the wine. Similarly, if one adds other values to the Torah, the Torah gets diluted. A cup of wine upon which one blesses (*kos shel berakha*) has to be full; likewise, we have to learn with overflowing enthusiasm. The more one drinks, the greater the desire for more; so too, the more one studies Torah, the more one thirsts to delve deeper into it (Rav Zilberstein, *Haggada Hashukei Hemed*).

2:5 סַמְּכוּנִי, בָּאֲשִׁישׁוֹת, רַפְּדוּנִי בַּתַּפּוּחִים - כִּי־חוֹלַת אַהֲבָה אָנִי We turn to Hashem: Sustain me with raisin cakes; spread a bed for me among apples – for I am sick with love.

The Rambam at the end of *Hilkhot Teshuva* talks about the ultimate love toward HaKadosh Barukh Hu and being lovesick. This

ד הַבָּנִים בְּצִלּוֹ חִמַּדְתִּי וְיָשַׁבְתִּי וּפִרְיוֹ מָתוֹק לְחִכִּי: הֱבִיאַנִי אֶל־בֵּית
ה הַיָּיִן וְדִגְלוֹ עָלַי אַהֲבָה: סַמְּכוּנִי בָּאֲשִׁישׁוֹת רַפְּדוּנִי בַּתַּפּוּחִים
ו כִּי־חוֹלַת אַהֲבָה אָנִי: שְׂמֹאלוֹ תַּחַת לְרֹאשִׁי וִימִינוֹ תְּחַבְּקֵנִי:

Rashi, citing a midrash, explains this metaphor differently. In *Shir HaShirim Rabba* it states: *Hatapuah hazeh hakol borhim mimenu*, “This fruit – everyone runs away from it,” *lefi she’ein lo tzel*, “because fruit trees don’t provide shade.” *Kakh barhu kol ha’umot me’al HaKadosh Barukh Hu bematan Torah*, “All the other nations ran away from HaKadosh Barukh Hu when He inquired if they would accept the gift of the Torah.” Bnei Yisrael remained to partake of the fruit.

This reminds us of the *Sifrei* in *Vezot Haberakha*. HaKadosh Barukh Hu offered the Torah to all the nations, but they rejected it. They asked what was written in it. Hashem responded: “Do not kill,” “Do not steal,” “Do not commit adultery.” After learning of its contents, the other nations rejected the Torah. It would be too difficult to abide by all those restrictions and limitations.

The *baalei mussar* ask why Hashem chose to highlight the seemingly more difficult restrictions rather than more simple and noncontroversial mitzvot, like returning lost objects, not placing a stumbling block in front of a blind person, or other similar mitzvot *bein adam lehavero*. The answer they provide is that once the nations asked, *Ma katuv bah*? (What is written in it?), they made it clear that their commitment would be subject to the content. If Hashem wrote the Torah, they should have accepted it without question. We stated, *Naaseh venishma*. We will fulfill the precepts of the Torah unconditionally! That is true faith and loyalty.

בְּצִלּוֹ חִמַּדְתִּי וְיָשַׁבְתִּי, וּפִרְיוֹ מָתוֹק לְחִכִּי Rav Pincus in his Haggada discusses this idea, *betzilo himadeti*, that the more one learns, the more one loves to learn. The Vilna Gaon states, based on a *pasuk* in *Mishlei* (chapter 27), that when an individual is satiated, and

7 arm; his right embraces me. Swear to me, daughters of Jerusalem,
by the she-gazelles, by the does of the field, swear that you will
8 not waken, will not rouse, this love before its time. The
voice of my beloved – I hear him coming, springing over the hills,
9 leaping the slopes; he is like a gazelle, my beloved; he is like a
young deer – here he stands behind our wall, gazing through the

---

2:9 הִנֵּה־זֶה עוֹמֵד אַחַר כָּתְלֵנוּ, מַשְׁגִּיחַ מִן־הַחַלֹּנוֹת, מֵצִיץ מִן־הַחֲרַכִּים He's there, we don't realize it, but He's standing behind the wall, He's looking, He's peeking in through the cracks.

Just like in Mitzrayim, they weren't prepared, they thought it would take longer to be redeemed, and it happened so fast. That's how the future exile will end as well (Metzudat David). The Hafetz Hayim highlights this point in *Torah Ohr* (chapter 12), in his introduction to the commentary on *kodshim*. The *Mashiah* will arrive suddenly. As it says in *Behaalotekha,* when Hashem appeared *pitom* (suddenly) to Aharon and Miriam and they weren't prepared. Hashem did this to teach them that Moshe had to separate from his wife and be in a state of purity at all times, since God could appear to him at any moment. In the future Hashem will appear to Am Yisrael in this sudden manner as well, in an unexpected manner, as He did in Egypt. Therefore, we have to be prepared for the future redemption because it will come suddenly. We have to be familiar with the laws relating to sacrifices so that at any moment we will be able to offer sacrifices. The Hafetz Hayim emphasized on several occasions that we need to be familiar with *kodshim* and *taharot,* since we may be required at any moment to reinitiate the sacrifices in the Temple.

Omed ahar kotlenu, "Here he stands behind our wall," may be a hint to the Kotel, highlighting that the *Shekhina* never left the Kotel. This is truly amazing that a midrash written two thousand years ago promised that the Kotel would always be standing. Hashem promised that this wall and its *kedusha* will always remain there.

It's springtime

ז הִשְׁבַּעְתִּי אֶתְכֶם בְּנוֹת יְרוּשָׁלַםִ בִּצְבָאוֹת אוֹ בְּאַיְלוֹת הַשָּׂדֶה אִם־
ח תָּעִירוּ ׀ וְאִם־תְּעוֹרְרוּ אֶת־הָאַהֲבָה עַד שֶׁתֶּחְפָּץ׃ קוֹל
ט דּוֹדִי הִנֵּה־זֶה בָּא מְדַלֵּג עַל־הֶהָרִים מְקַפֵּץ עַל־הַגְּבָעוֹת׃ דּוֹמֶה
דוֹדִי לִצְבִי אוֹ לְעֹפֶר הָאַיָּלִים הִנֵּה־זֶה עוֹמֵד אַחַר כָּתְלֵנוּ מַשְׁגִּיחַ

---

pasuk specifically refers to a Jew in exile, who yearns for the closeness of HaKadosh Barukh Hu, who seeks support from Hashem to help get through the difficult and challenging times.

2:7 הִשְׁבַּעְתִּי אֶתְכֶם בְּנוֹת יְרוּשָׁלַםִ...אִם־תָּעִירוּ וְאִם־תְּעוֹרְרוּ אֶת־הָאַהֲבָה עַד שֶׁתֶּחְפָּץ This is a difficult *pasuk* to translate literally. The Midrash interprets this *pasuk* as follows: We make the other nations swear: Don't try to divert our loyalty to HaKadosh Barukh Hu, nor affect the love HaKadosh Barukh Hu exhibits toward us.

Many quote the Ramban (in his sefer *Emuna U'Bitahon*), on this *pasuk*: *Im ta'iru ve'im te'oreru*, if you get a moment of inspiration, a flash of light from above, you feel inspired – *ad shetehpatz*, you have to concretize it. You can't let it last for just a fleeting moment. You have to internalize it. When a person is inspired by a *shiur*, song, or other religious experience, they should immediately engage in the performance of a mitzva.

Perhaps that is why there is a custom to refer to the holiday of Shavuot as Atzeret (as referenced in the Oral Torah). When Bnei Yisrael felt inspired at *matan Torah*, they desired to engage in a mitzva. They even stated, *Naaseh venishma*, "We will act and then we will listen." They wanted to perform an act to concretize their inspiration. What act could they perform? At this moment the only command they received was not to come close to the mountain. That is why it is referred to as Atzeret – to halt. That is the "mitzva" they performed at Har Sinai. Therefore, Shavuot commemorating *matan Torah* is referred to as Atzeret.

10 windows, catching glimpses through every gap. My beloved
spoke; he said to me, "Come, rise, my love, my beautiful one, let
11 12 us leave. Winter is over; the rains have passed and left us. On the
land, buds have appeared. The songbirds' time has come, and the
13 turtle dove's call sounds over our land. The fig has put out her
buds, and the flowering vines give scent – so come, rise, my love,
14 my beautiful one, let us leave." [*He*] My dove in the rock's
cleft, in the cliff's shadow – show me your face; let me hear your
15 voice, for lovely is your voice; your face so fair. [*She*]
Catch the foxes, the little foxes ravaging the vineyards just as our
16 vineyard is in flower. My beloved is mine, and I am his who
17 pastures among lilies. Until the day has breathed its last and the
shadows have flown, turn like a gazelle, my beloved, turn like a

---

Parashat Beshallah, explains that they prayed at that juncture – *tafsu be'umnot avotam*.

Rav Yeruham asks, They didn't daven all the years? They davened plenty! The hidden message, Hazal explain, is that at that moment they realized that it's an *et tzara*, a severely dangerous moment. Davening always has to come out of a feeling of *et tzaras*. All *Rishonim* agree that there is a definite obligation to pray when one is in danger. They differ on their understanding of the definition of an *et tzara*. (Rav Yosef Dov Soloveitchik makes a distinction and asks whether an *et tzara* is at the point of a specific hardship, or if each moment is considered a potential *et tzara* and therefore one is obligated to pray daily.)

That this *perek* expresses so much longing is fascinating, given that Shlomo HaMelekh wrote it at a time when the *Beit HaMikdash* stood and Bnei Yisrael were at the height of their glory; nevertheless, he was able to envision a time when we would be in exile yearning to return.

י מִן־הַחַלֹּנוֹת מֵצִיץ מִן־הַחֲרַכִּים: עָנָה דוֹדִי וְאָמַר לִי קוּמִי לָךְ רַעְיָתִי
יא יב יָפָתִי וּלְכִי־לָךְ: כִּי־הִנֵּה הַסְּתָו עָבָר הַגֶּשֶׁם חָלַף הָלַךְ לוֹ: הַנִּצָּנִים
יג נִרְאוּ בָאָרֶץ עֵת הַזָּמִיר הִגִּיעַ וְקוֹל הַתּוֹר נִשְׁמַע בְּאַרְצֵנוּ: הַתְּאֵנָה
חָנְטָה פַגֶּיהָ וְהַגְּפָנִים ׀ סְמָדַר נָתְנוּ רֵיחַ קוּמִי לְכִי רַעְיָתִי יָפָתִי וּלְכִי־ לָךְ
יד לָךְ: יוֹנָתִי בְּחַגְוֵי הַסֶּלַע בְּסֵתֶר הַמַּדְרֵגָה הַרְאִינִי
אֶת־מַרְאַיִךְ הַשְׁמִיעִנִי אֶת־קוֹלֵךְ כִּי־קוֹלֵךְ עָרֵב וּמַרְאֵיךְ
טו נָאוֶה: אֶחֱזוּ־לָנוּ שׁוּעָלִים שֻׁעָלִים קְטַנִּים מְחַבְּלִים
טז יז כְּרָמִים וּכְרָמֵינוּ סְמָדַר: דּוֹדִי לִי וַאֲנִי לוֹ הָרֹעֶה בַּשּׁוֹשַׁנִּים: עַד
שֶׁיָּפוּחַ הַיּוֹם וְנָסוּ הַצְּלָלִים סֹב דְּמֵה־לְךָ דוֹדִי לִצְבִי אוֹ לְעֹפֶר

2:12 עֵת הַזָּמִיר הִגִּיעַ, וְקוֹל הַתּוֹר נִשְׁמַע בְּאַרְצֵנוּ It's springtime, and there are lots of birds singing.

The winter, representing the dark and cold exile, has passed; the blossoms, representing the redemption (*geula*), are sprouting. The Gemara in Sanhedrin 98a cites Rabbi Aba, who believes that when the fields of Eretz Yisrael begin to blossom it is evidence of the *geula*.

2:14 יוֹנָתִי בְּחַגְוֵי הַסֶּלַע, בְּסֵתֶר הַמַּדְרֵגָה Hashem compares us to a dove; we were stuck between the crevices of the rock. The Midrash tells us that at the Yam Suf, we had nowhere to go. In front of us was the sea and behind us we were being chased by Pharaoh. This is being compared to a dove that is stuck between the crevices of a rock trying to avoid a hawk. Yet there is a snake awaiting the dove between the cracks. There is no escape. The only alternative is to look up and pray!

Why did Hashem place us into such a trap? Because Hashem wanted us to pray to Him and exhibit our *emuna*, our belief in Him.

הַרְאִינִי אֶת־מַרְאַיִךְ, הַשְׁמִיעִנִי אֶת־קוֹלֵךְ Show me your true colors; I want to hear your voice of prayer. This is the ultimate *tefilla*. Rashi, in

3 1 young deer to the riven hills. Upon my bed at night
2 I sought the one I love; I sought him, I did not find him. I shall
rise, I shall go all around the town – through the streets, across
the squares – searching for the one I love. I searched for him but
3 did not find him. The guards found me, those who go around the
4 town: "The one whom I love – have you seen him?" I had scarcely
moved away from them when I found the one I love. I caught hold
of him; I will not let him go until I have brought him to my

---

by the Smak (*Sefer Mitzvot Katan*), one of the *Baalei HaTosafot,* in mitzva *alef,* where he discusses the source of *tzipita liyeshua*. The sources of the other inquiries are easily found in the Torah. There is a clear imperative to learn Torah. There is a commandment not to lie, cheat, or steal. Yet what is the source of yearning for the redemption?

The Smak explains that it's part of the mitzva of *emuna,* of believing in HaKadosh Barukh Hu. It's the first mitzva. Just as we have to believe that Hashem took us out of Mitzrayim once, as it says, *Anokhi Hashem Elokekha asher hotzeitikha miMitzrayim*. Just like I want you to believe in Me, that I took you out of Mitzrayim, I want you to believe in Me, that I will take you out in the future. *Ani maamin be'emuna sheleima,* a Jew always hopes for a better tomorrow.

Rav Nebenzahl posits that this is why during Minha on Shabbat we read from the following week's *parasha*. We just completed the prior *parasha;* why move on to next week's already? This is to highlight that there is always another week. No matter what is happening in a Jew's life, there is another *parasha,* a future on the horizon. That is reflected in this *pasuk*. Klal Yisrael say *Bikashtiv,* we search for the beloved, even though we don't always find Him.

3:4 כִּמְעַט שֶׁעָבַרְתִּי מֵהֶם עַד שֶׁמָּצָאתִי אֵת שֶׁאָהֲבָה נַפְשִׁי; אֲחַזְתִּיו וְלֹא אַרְפֶּנּוּ עַד־שֶׁהֲבֵיאתִיו אֶל־בֵּית אִמִּי וְאֶל־חֶדֶר הוֹרָתִי I almost missed him, but I found him. He returned. I'll grab him tight, and won't let him

go, until

ג א הָאַיָּלִים עַל־הָרֵי בָתֶר׃ עַל־מִשְׁכָּבִי בַּלֵּילוֹת בִּקַּשְׁתִּי
ב אֵת שֶׁאָהֲבָה נַפְשִׁי בִּקַּשְׁתִּיו וְלֹא מְצָאתִיו׃ אָקוּמָה נָּא וַאֲסוֹבְבָה
בָעִיר בַּשְּׁוָקִים וּבָרְחֹבוֹת אֲבַקְשָׁה אֵת שֶׁאָהֲבָה נַפְשִׁי בִּקַּשְׁתִּיו
ג וְלֹא מְצָאתִיו׃ מְצָאוּנִי הַשֹּׁמְרִים הַסֹּבְבִים בָּעִיר אֵת שֶׁאָהֲבָה נַפְשִׁי
ד רְאִיתֶם׃ כִּמְעַט שֶׁעָבַרְתִּי מֵהֶם עַד שֶׁמָּצָאתִי אֵת שֶׁאָהֲבָה נַפְשִׁי
אֲחַזְתִּיו וְלֹא אַרְפֶּנּוּ עַד־שֶׁהֲבֵיאתִיו אֶל־בֵּית אִמִּי וְאֶל־חֶדֶר הוֹרָתִי׃

PEREK GIMEL

This perek continues with a cryptic description of our longing for a relationship with Hashem, using the metaphor of a woman waiting for her beloved to arrive.

3:1 עַל־מִשְׁכָּבִי בַּלֵּילוֹת בִּקַּשְׁתִּי אֵת שֶׁאָהֲבָה נַפְשִׁי Bnei Yisrael are seeking Hashem, as a woman would inquire of her beloved, whom she misses and with whom she looks forward to reuniting.

בִּקַּשְׁתִּיו וְלֹא מְצָאתִיו I searched for Him, but I couldn't find Him. I yearn for the closeness.

This may be referring to the thirty-eight years in the desert following the transgression of the spies, when Bnei Yisrael had no communication with HaKadosh Barukh Hu (Rashi; see *Shalom Rav, Parashat Korah,* citing Rav Soloveitchik on the silent [blackout] years in the desert).

Others suggest that this *pasuk* refers to the Babylonian exile (*galut Bavel,* Alsheikh). We hope and we yearn, we never lose hope. A Jew is always *bikashtiv,* always searching for HaKadosh Barukh Hu, even though He may not be responsive at that moment.

The Gemara in Shabbat (31a) discusses the six questions that will be asked of us in heaven, three of which are: *Kavata itim laTorah, nasata venatata be'emuna, tzipita liyeshua*? Did one set aside time to learn Torah, did one conduct business in an honest manner, did one yearn for the redemption? There is an interesting thought suggested

5 mother's house, to the chamber where I was conceived. Swear to
me, daughters of Jerusalem, by the she-gazelles, by the does of the
field, swear that you will not waken, will not rouse, this love before
6 its time. [*Friends*] Who is this rising from the
wilderness like plumes of smoke, perfumed with myrrh and
frankincense more fragrant than all the merchants' powders?

---

alternatively, he desires to befriend him, to be like brothers and live together. Yaakov was afraid of both scenarios; he feared the hatred of his brother, and he feared the love of his brother. Even Esav's love would be tainted and would cause trouble for Yaakov. Yaakov requests assistance in the event of either scenario – *miyad ahi, miyad Esav.*

The Beit Halevi continues, *Maaseh avot siman labanim.* The other nations act in a similar fashion toward Am Yisrael. First they seek to annihilate us. When that is unsuccessful, they seek to befriend us to get us to assimilate and renounce our faith and commitment to our religion. Their common intention is to divert us away from Hashem. We must be cognizant of both of these dangers.

Based on this interpretation, the Rinat Yitzhak explains why this *pasuk* is repeated. It is a warning to other nations not to use either tactic in trying to divert us from Hashem. Don't try to kill us or assimilate us.

3:6 מִי זֹאת עֹלָה מִן־הַמִּדְבָּר When we left Egypt the other nations inquired, Who is arising from the desert? In particular, when they learned of all the miracles that transpired in the desert, the other nations were startled and questioned who is behind all these miracles (Rashi).

כְּתִימְרוֹת עָשָׁן, מְקֻטֶּרֶת מֹר וּלְבוֹנָה מִכֹּל אַבְקַת רוֹכֵל Like smoke that goes straight up, it smells sweeter than any spice collection.

We think back to the time when they were in shock and wonderment over the acts of *hesed* that Hashem performs for us.

ה הִשְׁבַּ֨עְתִּי אֶתְכֶ֜ם בְּנ֤וֹת יְרֽוּשָׁלִַ֨ם֙ בִּצְבָא֔וֹת א֖וֹ בְּאַיְל֣וֹת הַשָּׂדֶ֑ה אִם־
ו תָּעִ֧ירוּ ׀ וְֽאִם־תְּעֽוֹרְר֛וּ אֶת־הָאַהֲבָ֖ה עַ֥ד שֶׁתֶּחְפָּֽץ׃ מִ֣י
זֹ֗את עֹלָה֙ מִן־הַמִּדְבָּ֔ר כְּתִֽימְר֖וֹת עָשָׁ֑ן מְקֻטֶּ֤רֶת מֹר֙ וּלְבוֹנָ֔ה מִכֹּ֖ל

---

go, until he takes me to my mother's house, to the room where I was conceived.

This room is a reference to the *Mishkan,* the *Ohel Mo'ed,* the location of the ultimate *hashraat haShekhina* (Rashi).

The Ramban labels the book of *Shemot Sefer HaGeula. Sefer HaGeula* does not end with *yetzi'at Mitzrayim. Sefer HaGeula* does not end with *maamad Har Sinai. Sefer HaGeula* ends with *Vayakhel Pekudei,* with Hashem's presence resting among Klal Yisrael. The Ramban also states in his introduction to *Parashat Teruma* that the purpose of the *Mishkan* is to enable the Shekhina, which was revealed at Har Sinai, to reside in the *Ohel Mo'ed.*

3:5 **הִשְׁבַּעְתִּי אֶתְכֶם בְּנוֹת יְרוּשָׁלַםִ** We again turn to the other nations, referred to as *bnot Yerushalayim,* and demand that they do not interfere with our special relationship with HaKadosh Barukh Hu.

בִּצְבָאוֹת אוֹ בְּאַיְלוֹת הַשָּׂדֶה If you interfere, you will end up being a gazelle that will be attacked by other animals.

אִם־תָּעִירוּ וְאִם־תְּעוֹרְרוּ אֶת־הָאַהֲבָה עַד שֶׁתֶּחְפָּץ Don't do anything that may adversely affect our connection to Hashem.

These *pesukim* seem to appear in an identical manner in chapter 2. Why the repetition? The Rinat Yitzhak, Rav Avraham Yitzhak Sorotzkin, suggests an explanation based on an interpretation of the Beit Halevi in *Parashat Vayishlah.* In anticipation of the reunion between Yaakov and Esav, Yaakov asks for Hashem's assistance: *Hatzileini na miyad ahi miyad Esav.* Yaakov asks to be saved from his brother, from Esav. Why the double language? A reference to his only brother would suffice. The Beit Halevi explains that Yaakov is unsure of Esav's motive. Either Esav is seeking to kill Yaakov, or

7 Here is Shlomo's bed, sixty soldiers all around it, heroes of Israel,
8 each bearing his sword, each schooled in war, each with his sword
9 at his thigh for fear at night. King Shlomo built a
10 palanquin of Lebanon wood; he ordered its pillars of silver, its
seat of gold; its cushions are purple, its space is lined with love by
11 the daughters of Jerusalem. Go out now and see, daughters of
Zion; look at Shlomo the king, at the crown his mother gave him
4 1 on this his wedding day, on the day his heart rejoiced. [*He*]
How beautiful you are, my love, how beautiful, your eyes like

---

an influencer – like a mother, who is *mashpia* on the other nations of the world.

The Vilna Gaon posits that there are three levels of learning Torah. First, one is like a daughter, a *mekabel* (recipient). Then one evolves into a partner with HaKadosh Barukh Hu, where one is able to decipher the intricacies of the Torah. Finally, one becomes a *talmid hakham*, a scholar, where one is able to spread Torah and impact others in the realm of spirituality.

PEREK DALET

In this chapter we encounter Hashem talking to Bnei Yisrael. The relationship is compared to the relationship of a man and a woman, in particular a bride and groom or husband and wife.

4:1 הִנָּךְ יָפָה רַעְיָתִי, הִנָּךְ יָפָה – עֵינַיִךְ יוֹנִים You are beautiful, your eyes are like doves.

Why the comparison to doves? A dove is monogamous, and when it's slaughtered it doesn't fight; it relinquishes its power and allows itself to be taken. So too, Hashem says to Am Yisrael, you accepted the yoke of Torah and mitzvot, the responsibility of being a Jew (Rashi).

The Gemara in Shabbat 49a cites a story of Elisha Baal Kenafayim. He received this title because he wore tefillin in a time of religious

subjugation,

ז אֲבָקַת רוֹכֵל: הִנֵּה מִטָּתוֹ שֶׁלִּשְׁלֹמֹה שִׁשִּׁים גִּבֹּרִים סָבִיב לָהּ
ח מִגִּבֹּרֵי יִשְׂרָאֵל: כֻּלָּם אֲחֻזֵי חֶרֶב מְלֻמְּדֵי מִלְחָמָה אִישׁ חַרְבּוֹ עַל־
ט יְרֵכוֹ מִפַּחַד בַּלֵּילוֹת: אַפִּרְיוֹן עָשָׂה לוֹ הַמֶּלֶךְ שְׁלֹמֹה
י מֵעֲצֵי הַלְּבָנוֹן: עַמּוּדָיו עָשָׂה כֶסֶף רְפִידָתוֹ זָהָב מֶרְכָּבוֹ אַרְגָּמָן תּוֹכוֹ
יא רָצוּף אַהֲבָה מִבְּנוֹת יְרוּשָׁלָםִ: צְאֶינָה ׀ וּרְאֶינָה בְּנוֹת צִיּוֹן בַּמֶּלֶךְ
שְׁלֹמֹה בָּעֲטָרָה שֶׁעִטְּרָה־לּוֹ אִמּוֹ בְּיוֹם חֲתֻנָּתוֹ וּבְיוֹם שִׂמְחַת
ד א לִבּוֹ: הִנָּךְ יָפָה רַעְיָתִי הִנָּךְ יָפָה עֵינַיִךְ יוֹנִים מִבַּעַד

The Meshekh Hokhma in *Parashat Kedoshim* posits on the *pasuk Ve'ahavta lere'akha kamokha*: *ketimrot ashan*, that the *ashan* (smoke) of the *Ohel Mo'ed* in the desert went straight up. This is like a Jew in *galut* yearning for HaKadosh Barukh Hu. Throughout the exile, we stay together as Jews. We create communities of Torah*, avoda*, and *gemilut hasadim*. Jews take care of Jews. The other nations are bewildered. They see that Jews remain together and care for one another.

3:11 צְאֶינָה וּרְאֶינָה בְּנוֹת צִיּוֹן בַּמֶּלֶךְ שְׁלֹמֹה - בָּעֲטָרָה שֶׁעִטְּרָה־לּוֹ אִמּוֹ בְּיוֹם חֲתֻנָּתוֹ, וּבְיוֹם שִׂמְחַת לִבּוֹ We remember the *bnot Tzion,* the crown that Shlomo's mother crowned him with.

What is the *atara* with which his mother crowned him? There's an amazing midrash on this *pasuk*. The midrash says that HaKadosh Barukh Hu refers to Am Yisrael first as a daughter, then as a sister, then as a mother. How could HaKadosh Barukh Hu call us "mother"?

Rav Dessler explains that HaKadosh Barukh Hu loves us in three different ways. Number one, as a daughter, a recipient – we are recipients of His goodness. Number two, as a partner, like a sister. We are partners in making this world a better place. Finally, we act as a *mashpia* (influencer). When we behave in a proper way and are *mekadesh shem Shamayim* in the world, that is when we act as

doves seen through your tresses; your hair like a flock of goats
2 flowing down from Mount Gilad. Your teeth are like a perfect
flock rising up from washing: each mother ewe bore twins, not
3 one among them lost. Your lips are a scarlet ribbon, and your
speech is fair; your forehead like a pomegranate glows through

---

The Hida is curious as to why the Gemara specifically singles out Teveria over all other cities. What is so special about Teveria that the simple residents there had an abundance of mitzvot? The Gemara in Shabbat (118b) tells us that Teveria is a valley, and its residents brought in Shabbat early. They were viewed favorably for *tosefet Shabbat* (extending the length of Shabbat), so much so that they were considered as if they had fulfilled numerous mitzvot, like the multitude of seeds in a pomegranate.

In *Hasidic Tales of the Holocaust* (Yaffa Eliach, pp. 155–158), the following story is told that highlights the idea of a Jew being full of mitzvot like the seeds of a pomegranate:

Yom Kippur in the Janowska Work Camp

"This particular story is one of those stories that deserves to be published in a book," said the Rabbi of Bluzhov, Rabbi Israel Spira.

In the Janowska camp there was a Jewish foreman from Lvov by the name of Schneeweiss, one of those people that one stays away from if he values his life.

Yom Kippur was nearing and fears in the camp mounted; everyone knew that the Germans especially liked to use Jewish holidays as days for inflicting terror and death. Nevertheless, a group of Hasidim asked the Rabbi of Bluzhov to approach Schneeweiss and request that on Yom Kippur his group not be assigned to any of the thirty-nine main categories of work, so that their transgression of the law by working on Yom Kippur would not be a major one.

The rabbi

ב לְצַמָּתֵךְ שַׂעְרֵךְ כְּעֵדֶר הָעִזִּים שֶׁגָּלְשׁוּ מֵהַר גִּלְעָד: שִׁנַּיִךְ כְּעֵדֶר
הַקְּצוּבוֹת שֶׁעָלוּ מִן־הָרַחְצָה שֶׁכֻּלָּם מַתְאִימוֹת וְשַׁכֻּלָה אֵין בָּהֶם:
ג כְּחוּט הַשָּׁנִי שִׂפְתוֹתַיִךְ וּמִדְבָּרֵיךְ נָאוֶה כְּפֶלַח הָרִמּוֹן רַקָּתֵךְ מִבַּעַד

---

subjugation, even though he was risking his life. One day, he was caught by the authorities, and he placed his tefillin in his hand behind his back. They asked him to reveal what he had hidden in his hand. He assured the inquirers that it was the wings of a dove. He opened up his hands, and indeed – there were wings of a dove. The Gemara asks, Why wings of a dove, rather than any other bird? The Gemara explains that it is because Bnei Yisrael are compared to a *yona*, a dove, as it says in *Tehillim* (68:14), *Kanfei yona nehpa vakesef*. Just as a dove needs wings to protect her, so too, with respect to Bnei Yisrael, the performance of our mitzvot protect us.

Tosafot suggest that with respect to all other birds, when they're tired, they rest. But the *yona* keeps on flying. It uses one wing to fly while the other rests. Even after being persecuted, Am Yisrael persevere.

This story is the basis of some who have the custom to wrap the straps of the tefillin around the box on both sides is so that it appears like wings of a bird, in commemoration of the story of Elisha Baal Kenafayim.

4:3 כְּפֶלַח הָרִמּוֹן רַקָּתֵךְ מִבַּעַד לְצַמָּתֵךְ Your forehead like a pomegranate glows through your tresses.

What does the pomegranate allude to? The Gemara relates in several places, including Berakhot and Sanhedrin, that even the *reikanim*, the emptiest of Jews, are filled with mitzvot like a pomegranate.

The Gemara in Megilla (6a) refers to this idea regarding the people in Teveria: *Reket zu Teveria*. Why is Teveria nicknamed *reket*? *She'afilu reikanim shebakhem mele'im bemitzvot* (Even the simplest of men there are full of mitzvot).

The room was filled with the aroma of freshly cooked food, such as they had not seen since the German occupation: white bread, steaming hot vegetable soup, and huge portions of meat.

The tall SS soldier commanded, "You must eat immediately or you will be shot on the spot!" No one moved. The rabbi and the Hasidim remained in their places. The German repeated the orders. The Jews remained glued to their places. The SS men called in Schneeweiss. "Schneeweiss, if the dirty dogs refuse to eat, I will kill you along with them!"

Schneeweiss pulled himself to attention, looked the German directly in the eyes, and said in a quiet tone, "We Jews do not eat today. Today is Yom Kippur, our most holy day, the Day of Atonement."

"You don't understand, Jewish dog," roared the SS soldier. "I command you in the name of the Fuhrer and the Third Reich – *fress*!"

Schneeweiss, composed, his head high, repeated the same answer. "We Jews obey the law of our tradition. Today is Yom Kippur, a day of fasting."

The German took out his revolver from its holster and pointed it at Schneeweiss's temple. Schneeweiss remained calm. He stood still, at attention, his head high. A shot pierced the room. Schneeweiss fell.

The rabbi and the Hasidim remained frozen in their places, not believing what their eyes had just witnessed. Schneeweiss, the man who in the past had publicly transgressed against Jewish tradition, had sanctified G-d's Name publicly and died a martyr's death for the sake of Jewish honor.

"Only then, on that Yom Kippur day in Janowska," said the rabbi, "did I understand the meaning of the statement in the Talmud: 'Even the transgressors in Israel are as full of good deeds as a pomegranate is filled with seeds' (Berachot 57a)."

The rabbi knew that the foreman had little respect for Jewish tradition. Before the war, Schneeweiss had publicly violated the Jewish holidays, and in Janowska, he was a merciless man. Despite his fears, the rabbi agreed to speak with him.

"You probably remember me. I am the Rabbi of Pruchnik, Rabbi Israel Spira." Schneeweiss did not respond. "Tonight is Kol Nidrei night," the rabbi continued. "There is a small group of Jews who do not want to transgress any of the major prohibitions of the day. It means everything to them. It is the essence of their existence. Can you do something about it? Can you help?"

The rabbi noticed a hidden shiver went through Schneeweiss. He took his hand and said, "I beg you to do this for us so that we may still find some dignity in our humiliating existence."

The stern face of Schneeweiss changed. For the first time, the rabbi saw in it a human spark. "Tonight I cannot help you," Schneeweiss replied. "But tomorrow, on Yom Kippur, I will do whatever I can."

Even the Transgressors in Israel

The following day, the rabbi and a small group of young Hasidim were summoned to the foreman's cottage. He arranged for them to clean in a way that would not transgress any of the thirty-nine major categories of work.

The rabbi was standing on a ladder with rags in his hand, cleaning the huge windows while chanting prayers, and his companions were on the floor polishing the wood and praying with him. "The floor was wet with our tears. You can imagine the prayers of that Yom Kippur..."

At about twelve o'clock noon, the door opened wide. Into the room stormed two angels of death, SS men in their black uniforms. They were followed by a food cart filled to capacity.

4 your tresses. Your neck is like the Tower of David, built in splendor,
a thousand shields adorning it, the shields of all the heroes.
5 Your two breasts are like young twins of a she-gazelle, pasturing

---

Rav Pam in his Haggada discusses Aharon's transgression when he didn't recognize the uniqueness of Moshe. That is a major issue today. Rav Pam states:

Rav Chaim Soloveitchik was once asked if someone who disputes the views of the *Rishonim* is an *apikores* (heretic). Rav Chaim said, No, just a fool, a *shoteh*. A person who even entertains the belief that his view is comparable to the *Rishonim* and doesn't comprehend the vast difference is not a *hoteh* (sinner), but a *shoteh* (fool). Unfortunately, this type of [idiocy] is quite common today. There are those who are like midgets in their knowledge of Torah. They do not even reach the ankles of the true Torah giants, yet they proclaim their own opinions and criticize the views of *gedolei haTorah*.

We have to recognize who the *shadayim* of Am Yisrael are and realize that they really nourish us.

Rashi's second explanation of the term *shnei shadayim* is that it represents the two *luhot*. That is what provides us with nourishment. Rashi draws a parallel between each commandment on the right side of the *dibrot* with its similarly numbered commandment on the left side of the *dibrot*.

1. *Anokhi/Lo Tirtzah*: I am God and don't kill – murder diminishes one created in the image of God.
2. *Lo Yiheye/Lo Tinaf:* There shall be no other gods and do not commit adultery – both depict disloyalty.
3. *Lo Tisa/Lo Tignov*: Do not use God's name in vain and do not steal – one who steals will end up falsely swearing in God's name to cover it up.
4. *Zakhor/Lo Taaneh*: Remember the Shabbat and do not bear false testimony – Shabbat is testimony that God created the world.

5. Kabed/Lo

ד לְצַמָּתֵךְ: כְּמִגְדַּל דָּוִיד צַוָּארֵךְ בָּנוּי לְתַלְפִּיּוֹת אֶלֶף הַמָּגֵן תָּלוּי עָלָיו
ה כֹּל שִׁלְטֵי הַגִּבֹּרִים: שְׁנֵי שָׁדַיִךְ כִּשְׁנֵי עֳפָרִים תְּאוֹמֵי צְבִיָּה הָרוֹעִים
ו בַּשּׁוֹשַׁנִּים: עַד שֶׁיָּפוּחַ הַיּוֹם וְנָסוּ הַצְּלָלִים אֵלֶךְ לִי אֶל־הַר הַמּוֹר

The Metzudat David believes that the statement "Your forehead like a pomegranate" refers to the Sanhedrin. They are full of every wisdom, like a pomegranate is full of seeds. In his introduction to *Pe'at HaShulhan*, Rav Yisrael Mishkelov says that his rebbe the Gra was an expert in every field, including math, music, and botany. The Gra considered studying medicine, but his father did not allow it, reasoning that if his son would study medicine, he would have to become a doctor since he would certainly be the most skilled practitioner in the world. This is but one example of how *rabbanim* are full of wisdom, like a pomegranate is full of seeds.

4:4 אֶלֶף הַמָּגֵן תָּלוּי עָלָיו כֹּל שִׁלְטֵי הַגִּבֹּרִים The term *shiltei hagibborim* reminds us of a story in the Gemara where Torah scholars are called *baalei trisin* (those who bear shields): "He said to the other, wait until they enter, the *baalei trisin*, into the *beit midrash*" (Berakhot 27b).

Rav Kook in *Ein Aya* explains that a *tris* is a shield. Why are scholars referred to as "shield bearers"? Sages don't win disputes by merely finding fault in the other side's argument; rather, they do so by defending and shielding their position. When one seeks the truth, he does not need to attack another. However, he must be able to defend his ideals and beliefs.

We should always do what we can to increase peace and avoid conflicts. As it states, *Talmidei hakhamim marbim shalom ba'olam* (Wise men spread peace in the world).

4:5 שְׁנֵי שָׁדַיִךְ כִּשְׁנֵי עֳפָרִים Breasts are symbolic of nourishment, as they nourish an infant. This is a reference to Moshe and Aharon, who brought nourishment to Am Yisrael. Moshe merited the *mann* and Aharon merited the *ananei hakavod* (Rashi).

6 in lilies. Until the day has breathed its last, and the shadows have
flown, I am going to the hill of myrrh, to the slopes of frankincense.
7 8 And all of you is beauty, my love, is flawless, wholly. Come
with me from Lebanon, bride; come down with me from Lebanon;
from the peak of Amana come, from the peaks of Senir and
9 Hermon, from the lions' haunts, the leopards' hills. You have
taken my heart, my sister, my bride; one glance of your eyes could
10 take my heart, any strand of the necklace you wear. How beautiful

---

the Jew that was problematic or faulty. Therefore, he couldn't curse them.

4:8 תָּשׁוּרִי מֵרֹאשׁ אֲמָנָה, מֵרֹאשׁ שְׂנִיר וְחֶרְמוֹן, מִמְּעֹנוֹת אֲרָיוֹת, מֵהַרְרֵי נְמֵרִים The Midrash in *Shir HaShirim Rabba* interprets this *pasuk* as referring to our *emuna*, our belief in Hashem that causes God to remain with us throughout the generations and that will bring the redemption. Which kind of *emuna* are we talking about that will bring about the *geula*?

The first opinion is: *Vayaaminu baHashem u'veMoshe avdo* (*Shemot* 14:31). The *emuna* we exhibited at Keriat Yam Suf, our belief in Moshe and Hashem, will provide the merit to bring the *geula*. The Midrash asks, Why is that worthy of a reward? Who would witness such a miracle and not believe in Hashem? The Midrash then suggests that the *emuna* through which we will merit the *geula* refers to an earlier time, when Bnei Yisrael were in Mitzrayim, based on the *pasuk Vayaamen haam*" (*Shemot* 4:31). To have *emuna* when things are going smoothly is no great feat. We had *emuna* when things were tough, while experiencing the oppression in Mitzrayim, and that is why we merited to be redeemed. Redemption came due to our retaining our *emuna* even in the darkest of times.

4:9 לִבַּבְתִּנִי באחד (בְּאַחַת) מֵעֵינַיִךְ One glance.

You accepted all of My mitzvot, but even if you would have accepted only one of the mitzvot surely I would have loved you. This

reminds

ח וְאֶל־גִּבְעַת הַלְּבוֹנָה׃ כֻּלָּךְ יָפָה רַעְיָתִי וּמוּם אֵין בָּךְ׃ אִתִּי
מִלְּבָנוֹן כַּלָּה אִתִּי מִלְּבָנוֹן תָּבוֹאִי תָּשׁוּרִי ׀ מֵרֹאשׁ אֲמָנָה מֵרֹאשׁ
ט שְׂנִיר וְחֶרְמוֹן מִמְּעֹנוֹת אֲרָיוֹת מֵהַרְרֵי נְמֵרִים׃ לִבַּבְתִּנִי אֲחֹתִי כַלָּה
י לִבַּבְתִּנִי באחד מֵעֵינַיִךְ בְּאַחַד עֲנָק מִצַּוְּרֹנָיִךְ׃ מַה־יָּפוּ דֹדַיִךְ אֲחֹתִי בְּאַחַת

---

5. *Kabed/Lo Tahmod*: Honor parents and do not be jealous – a jealous person will bring up a child in an environment that will cause the child to disrespect his parents.

The Meiri in his introduction to *Shas* offers a similar analogy, with an interesting twist on the connection between *Lo Tisa* and *Lo Tignov*. If someone dresses like a pious Jew and appears to fulfill all of the mitzvot on the outside but transgresses in the area of business and deceives others, such an individual is bearing God's name falsely.

4:7 כֻּלָּךְ יָפָה רַעְיָתִי וּמוּם אֵין בָּךְ Hashem acknowledges our sins and faults, yet He still recognizes our beauty.

Most of Klal Yisrael are righteous (*tzaddikim*). We may have deficiencies as individuals, yet when we are all together, we are beautiful and our faults are not visible.

When Bilam wanted to curse the Jews, he saw that the openings of their tents did not face one another (Bava Batra 60a). This highlights their modesty, that they maintained their privacy in the desert by ensuring that the openings of their tents were not visible to another.

It's difficult to understand why their modesty was considered such a great characteristic that it made them worthy of not being cursed. Rav Isser Zalman offers a profound insight. The opening of the tent, the *petah*, refers to the *petah hatat rovetz*, the source of all sin. Bilam saw that there wasn't one root problem that he could latch onto and curse the Jews. Everyone may have sinned because of their desires and faults, but there wasn't something inherent in

your love is, my sister, my bride; how much better than wine your
11 love, and finer than all perfumes the scent of your oils. Your lips
drip nectar, my bride; honey and milk lie under your tongue, and
12 on your dress lingers Lebanon's scent. A locked garden
13 is my sister, my bride, a locked well, a spring sealed up – yet your
dry ground is a pomegranate grove of sweetest fruits, henna plants,
14 musk root; musk root and saffron, calamus, cinnamon, fragrant
trees of every kind, with myrrh plants and aloe, with all the finest
15 spices, with a spring to water gardens, a well of living waters,
16 waters flowing down from Lebanon. [*She*] Wake
now, north wind; south wind, come; breathe life into my garden;
let its perfumes flow. Let my beloved come to his garden and eat
5 1 his sweetest fruits. [*He*] I have come into my garden, my sister, my
bride; I have gathered my myrrh and my balsam; I have eaten my

---

One does not need an acquired taste for ice cream. Similarly, with respect to Torah, one does not need an acquired taste. That's *devash vehalav*. It is inherently delicious.

The Rambam (*Yesodei HaTorah*, ch. 4), based on the Gemara in Hagiga (13a), relates *devash* to the *maaseh merkava*, the secrets of the Torah. The secrets of the Torah cannot be taught in public because they're so deep and may be misunderstood. *Aleihen amar devash vehalav tahat leshonekh*. Keep it under your tongue; it's not supposed to be publicized.

PEREK HEH

This is known as the *kol dodi dofek* chapter.

The story is told of a woman who's in bed, and she hears her beloved knocking on the door. She responds to the knocking by stating that she is not able to answer the door, she first has to get dressed. Finally, she rises from her bed, but by that time the *dod* (her beloved), the guest at the door, has left. She leaves her home

יא כַּלָּה מַה־טֹּבוּ דֹדַיִךְ מִיַּיִן וְרֵיחַ שְׁמָנַיִךְ מִכָּל־בְּשָׂמִים: נֹפֶת תִּטֹּפְנָה
שִׂפְתוֹתַיִךְ כַּלָּה דְּבַשׁ וְחָלָב תַּחַת לְשׁוֹנֵךְ וְרֵיחַ שַׂלְמֹתַיִךְ כְּרֵיחַ
יב יג לְבָנוֹן: גַּן ׀ נָעוּל אֲחֹתִי כַלָּה גַּל נָעוּל מַעְיָן חָתוּם: שְׁלָחַיִךְ
יד פַּרְדֵּס רִמּוֹנִים עִם פְּרִי מְגָדִים כְּפָרִים עִם־נְרָדִים: נֵרְדְּ ׀ וְכַרְכֹּם קָנֶה
וְקִנָּמוֹן עִם כָּל־עֲצֵי לְבוֹנָה מֹר וַאֲהָלוֹת עִם כָּל־רָאשֵׁי בְשָׂמִים:
טו טז מַעְיַן גַּנִּים בְּאֵר מַיִם חַיִּים וְנֹזְלִים מִן־לְבָנוֹן: עוּרִי צָפוֹן וּבוֹאִי תֵימָן
ה א הָפִיחִי גַנִּי יִזְּלוּ בְשָׂמָיו יָבֹא דוֹדִי לְגַנּוֹ וְיֹאכַל פְּרִי מְגָדָיו: בָּאתִי לְגַנִּי
אֲחֹתִי כַלָּה אָרִיתִי מוֹרִי עִם־בְּשָׂמִי אָכַלְתִּי יַעְרִי עִם־דִּבְשִׁי שָׁתִיתִי

---

reminds us of the question the Rambam asks: Why did HaKadosh Barukh Hu give us so many mitzvot? *Ratza HaKadosh Barukh Hu lezakot et Yisrael.* Wouldn't it be better if we had less to focus on? The Rambam explains that every Jew has a different personality. Of course we must fulfill all of the mitzvot, but there are certain mitzvot that speak to us in a very deep and intense way. Each individual can latch onto the mitzva that fits their personality and fulfill it wholeheartedly. That is what will enable one to merit the World to Come.

Others explain the one eye as referring to the wink a person gives his spouse as an expression of affection; that is how Hashem views us (Metzudat David).

4:11 נֹפֶת תִּטֹּפְנָה שִׂפְתוֹתַיִךְ, כַּלָּה; דְּבַשׁ וְחָלָב תַּחַת לְשׁוֹנֵךְ Your lips drip nectar, my bride; honey and milk lie under your tongue.

This relates to the taste of Torah, which is dripping with goodness. As it states, *Devash vehalav tahat leshonekh,* "The sweetness of Torah is like honey and milk under your tongue" (Rashi).

The connection between Torah and *devash vehalav* may be understood as follows. There are sweet foods that are not healthy, and there are healthy foods that are not sweet or tasty. Torah has both characteristics; it is both sweet and good for you!

honeycomb with honey; I have drunk my wine with milk.
[*Friends*] Eat, loved ones, eat; drink, drink deep of
2 love. [*She*] I am asleep; my heart is awake – my beloved's
voice, he is knocking – "Open for me, my sister, my love, my dove,
my perfection, for my head is covered with dew, my locks with
3 drops of the night." "I have taken off my dress; how can I put it on
4 again? I have already washed my feet; how can I dirty them?" My

---

This is a reference to the prophets. When Bnei Yisrael are sleeping – in other words, not abiding by the mitzvot – Hashem sends prophets knocking on the door for a wake-up call, warning of the dire consequences of our transgressions.

In *Shir HaShirim Rabba* 5:2 there is a famous midrash on the words *Pit'hi li*. Hashem declares: Just open up a little for Me; I'll do the rest. *Pit'hi li petah kehudo shel mahat, ve'ani eftah lahem petah she'afilu agalot u'kronot nihnasim bo*, you give Me a little opening like the eye of a needle, and I'll open it up all the way. Many commentators cite this midrash to teach us that we need to take the first step in *teshuva* to return to God and He will assist us with the remainder.

5:3 **פָּשַׁטְתִּי אֶת־כֻּתָּנְתִּי, אֵיכָכָה אֶלְבָּשֶׁנָּה** The woman states: I already disrobed so I cannot answer the door – now I have to get dressed to open the door?

רָחַצְתִּי אֶת־רַגְלַי, אֵיכָכָה אֲטַנְּפֵם I already washed my feet; how can I get them dirty?

This is a statement Bnei Yisrael make in exile: We are so distant from Hashem; is there any way back? Metzudat David explains that this is referring to the period of *galut Bavel*, before the rebuilding of the second *Beit HaMikdash*. Ezra sought to solicit those in Bavel to return to Eretz Yisrael, but they were too comfortable where they were to join him.

Rav Hershel Schachter

ב יֵינִי עִם־חֲלָבִי אִכְלוּ רֵעִים שְׁתוּ וְשִׁכְרוּ דּוֹדִים׃ אֲנִי
יְשֵׁנָה וְלִבִּי עֵר קוֹל ׀ דּוֹדִי דוֹפֵק פִּתְחִי־לִי אֲחֹתִי רַעְיָתִי יוֹנָתִי תַמָּתִי
ג שֶׁרֹּאשִׁי נִמְלָא־טָל קְוֻצּוֹתַי רְסִיסֵי לָיְלָה׃ פָּשַׁטְתִּי אֶת־כֻּתָּנְתִּי
ד אֵיכָכָה אֶלְבָּשֶׁנָּה רָחַצְתִּי אֶת־רַגְלַי אֵיכָכָה אֲטַנְּפֵם׃ דּוֹדִי שָׁלַח יָדוֹ

---

to search for her lover but to no avail. This is all a *mashal* (allegory). It depicts Hashem knocking at our door, yet we delay our response.

Rav Yosef Dov Soloveitchik has a famous article entitled "Kol Dodi Dofek," where he discusses the Holocaust and the period of the 1940s and '50s. He talks about six knocks. He talks about that secretive, magical night, when all of a sudden, the woman is surprised to hear knocking. She's been waiting for this knock. The *dod,* her beloved, is begging for her to open the door.

She has waited, yet it comes as a surprise. He reaches in and tries opening the door. She starts shaking; it's happening, it's happening! She could open the door in a moment. But suddenly she becomes lazy; she is stubborn. Within seconds, the fire of yearning is extinguished in her, and her dreams destroyed. He begs, please open the door! But she does not respond.

The Rav relates this allegory to modern times, to the creation of the State of Israel. It is as if Hashem is knocking on our door, fulfilling our hope and desire to return to our homeland after two thousand years, and yet many remain in the Diaspora, ignoring the call to return.

5:2 אֲנִי יְשֵׁנָה וְלִבִּי עֵר I am asleep, but my heart is awake.

Rav Pincus interprets *libi* to depict that every Jew has a connection to HaKadosh Barukh Hu. Even though it may appear as if an individual is asleep, inside, his connection to God is very much alive; it just needs to be awakened.

קוֹל דּוֹדִי דוֹפֵק, פִּתְחִי־לִי אֲחֹתִי רַעְיָתִי יוֹנָתִי תַמָּתִי Her beloved is knocking on the door, open up the door...

beloved withdrew his hand from the door, and my being longed
5 for him. I rose to open the door for my beloved; my hands were
dripping with myrrh, my fingers streaming myrrh oil over the
6 handles of the latch. I opened for my beloved – he had slipped
away, gone. I fainted for him as he spoke – I searched for him but
7 could not find him; I called out but he did not answer. The guards
found me, those who go around the town; they beat me, they
wounded me, they pulled my shawl from me, those guardians of

Rav Shimshon Pincus emphasizes this in his Haggada. Seize the moment when inspired. If you wait, you'll lose the moment. He quotes a story that when Rav Aharon Kotler died, a number of *talmidim* went to Israel to attend his funeral. The rest of the yeshiva held *hespedim* every day. The boys who came for the funeral asked the *rosh yeshiva* if they could visit Tzfat and Meron before returning home. The *rosh yeshiva* replied that they should return immediately. Right then they were inspired by the eulogies they heard about Rav Kotler. If they were to delay their return, even for a good reason, they risked losing the momentum from such inspiration. That's *dodi hamak avar*.

5:7 מְצָאֻנִי הַשֹּׁמְרִים הַסֹּבְבִים בָּעִיר The guards found me.

Rashi suggests that the guards are Nevukhadnetzar and his soldiers, sent by Hashem.

הִכּוּנִי פְצָעוּנִי They beat me and wounded me.

Rav Zilberstein notes in the *Hashukei Hemed* that one would have expected this *pasuk* to appear in *Eikha* rather than in *Shir HaShirim*. Perhaps this refers to pains of love. Parents sometimes scold children out of love and concern for their well-being. HaKadosh Barukh Hu scolds Klal Yisrael out of love. It's the same father that hugs and scolds to teach a lesson; both come from love and concern.

ה מִן־הַחוֹר וּמֵעַי הָמוּ עָלָיו׃ קַמְתִּי אֲנִי לִפְתֹּחַ לְדוֹדִי וְיָדַי נָטְפוּ־מוֹר
ו וְאֶצְבְּעֹתַי מוֹר עֹבֵר עַל כַּפּוֹת הַמַּנְעוּל׃ פָּתַחְתִּי אֲנִי לְדוֹדִי וְדוֹדִי
חָמַק עָבָר נַפְשִׁי יָצְאָה בְדַבְּרוֹ בִּקַּשְׁתִּיהוּ וְלֹא מְצָאתִיהוּ קְרָאתִיו
ז וְלֹא עָנָנִי׃ מְצָאֻנִי הַשֹּׁמְרִים הַסֹּבְבִים בָּעִיר הִכּוּנִי פְצָעוּנִי נָשְׂאוּ

Rav Hershel Schachter often cites the Maharal Diskin (*Parashat Mishpatim*) regarding piercing the ear of a slave. The Gemara in Kiddushin explains that we pierce his ear to indicate that this *ear* heard at Har Sinai that it is prohibited to steal, yet this individual did not *listen* and is now being sold as a slave to repay the cost of the stolen object. That is why we pierce his ear.

The Maharal Diskin asks an insightful question. Why wait six years to pierce this thief's ear, only after he declines to go free? We should punish him immediately. He answers that the punishment the thief receives immediately is to become a slave. After six years, when he states *ahavti et adoni,* I like my boss and wish to remain, we see that he did not view these six years as a punishment. Therefore, we need to perform another act to highlight that he is being punished for his transgression.

To be exiled to Bavel was a punishment for violating the precepts of the Torah. When the people of that generation did not recognize that *galut* was a punishment but rather were happy where they were, they needed to be reminded of their distorted sense of reality.

5:6 פָּתַחְתִּי אֲנִי לְדוֹדִי וְדוֹדִי חָמַק עָבָר I opened for my beloved – he had slipped away.

When the maiden finally opens the door, it is too late, her beloved is gone. She calls out but there is no answer.

We often put off changing our ways and improving our spiritual lives. Unfortunately, we have learned that sometimes it can be too late. The destruction of the *Beit HaMikdash* occurred after we ignored the many warnings of the prophets. The message is that we cannot delay or procrastinate.

8 the walls. Swear to me, daughters of Jerusalem: if you find my
beloved, swear that you will tell him – tell him I am sick with love.
9 [*Friends*] What makes your lover more than other lovers, most
beautiful of women? What makes your lover more than other
10 men, that this is what you have us swear? [*She*] He is bright, my
beloved; he is glowing; you would know him among ten thousand.
11 His head shines like gold, fine gold, his hair cascading curls, raven
12 black; his eyes are like doves at springs of water, washed in milk,
13 at rest by the stream. His cheeks are like beds of balsam, like
towers of perfume herbs. His lips smell like lilies flowing with
14 myrrh oil. His arms are like golden bars set with stones of
aquamarine, his stomach like solid ivory inlaid with lapis lazuli.
15 His legs stand firm as marble pillars fixed on gold foundations. To
see him is like looking upon Lebanon, and he is as choice as its
16 cedars. His mouth is filled with sweetness; for all of him my
longing. This is my beloved, this is my love, daughters of Jerusalem.
6 1 [*Friends*] Where has your beloved gone, most beautiful of women?
Where has your beloved turned? We shall search for him with you.
2 [*She*] My beloved has gone to his garden, down to the beds of
3 balsam to pasture in the gardens, to gather in lilies. I am my
beloved's – my beloved is mine – who pastures among lilies.

---

to us and inquire, What is so special about our beloved? What makes our God so special? The other nations are bewildered by our willingness to sacrifice our lives on His behalf (Rashi).

PEREK VAV

6:3 אֲנִי לְדוֹדִי וְדוֹדִי לִי, הָרֹעֶה בַּשּׁוֹשַׁנִּים This is a famous *pasuk*, from which we derive the acronym for the month of Elul. In this verse we declare a relationship: "I am to my *dod* and my *dod* is to me."

In the context of the chapter, Rashi emphasizes, *ani ledodi*, I am to my *dod*. You, the nations, are not *ledodi*. I have a special relationship

with Hashem.

ח אֶת־רְדִידִי מֵעָלַי שֹׁמְרֵי הַחֹמוֹת: הִשְׁבַּעְתִּי אֶתְכֶם בְּנוֹת יְרוּשָׁלָ͏ִם
ט אִם־תִּמְצְאוּ אֶת־דּוֹדִי מַה־תַּגִּידוּ לוֹ שֶׁחוֹלַת אַהֲבָה אָנִי: מַה־דּוֹדֵךְ
י מִדּוֹד הַיָּפָה בַּנָּשִׁים מַה־דּוֹדֵךְ מִדּוֹד שֶׁכָּכָה הִשְׁבַּעְתָּנוּ: דּוֹדִי צַח
יא וְאָדוֹם דָּגוּל מֵרְבָבָה: רֹאשׁוֹ כֶּתֶם פָּז קְוֻצּוֹתָיו תַּלְתַּלִּים שְׁחֹרוֹת
יב כָּעוֹרֵב: עֵינָיו כְּיוֹנִים עַל־אֲפִיקֵי מָיִם רֹחֲצוֹת בֶּחָלָב יֹשְׁבוֹת עַל־
יג מִלֵּאת: לְחָיָו כַּעֲרוּגַת הַבֹּשֶׂם מִגְדְּלוֹת מֶרְקָחִים שִׂפְתוֹתָיו
יד שׁוֹשַׁנִּים נֹטְפוֹת מוֹר עֹבֵר: יָדָיו גְּלִילֵי זָהָב מְמֻלָּאִים בַּתַּרְשִׁישׁ
טו מֵעָיו עֶשֶׁת שֵׁן מְעֻלֶּפֶת סַפִּירִים: שׁוֹקָיו עַמּוּדֵי שֵׁשׁ מְיֻסָּדִים עַל־
טז אַדְנֵי־פָז מַרְאֵהוּ כַּלְּבָנוֹן בָּחוּר כָּאֲרָזִים: חִכּוֹ מַמְתַקִּים וְכֻלּוֹ
ו א מַחֲמַדִּים זֶה דוֹדִי וְזֶה רֵעִי בְּנוֹת יְרוּשָׁלָ͏ִם: אָנָה הָלַךְ דּוֹדֵךְ הַיָּפָה
ב בַּנָּשִׁים אָנָה פָּנָה דוֹדֵךְ וּנְבַקְשֶׁנּוּ עִמָּךְ: דּוֹדִי יָרַד לְגַנּוֹ לַעֲרוּגוֹת
ג הַבֹּשֶׂם לִרְעוֹת בַּגַּנִּים וְלִלְקֹט שׁוֹשַׁנִּים: אֲנִי לְדוֹדִי וְדוֹדִי לִי הָרוֹעֶה
בַּשּׁוֹשַׁנִּים:

Bnei Yisrael turn to the nations of the world and declare:

5:8 הִשְׁבַּעְתִּי אֶתְכֶם, בְּנוֹת יְרוּשָׁלָ͏ִם: אִם־תִּמְצְאוּ אֶת־דּוֹדִי מַה־תַּגִּידוּ לוֹ, שֶׁחוֹלַת אַהֲבָה אָנִי Swear to me, if you find my beloved, what should you tell him? That I am sick with love.

As a nation we remained loyal to Hashem throughout all the oppression, at times paying with our lives. This is a statement to the nations of the world. They think God has rejected us in exile. However, they witness the miracles that have transpired. Nevukhadnetzar witnessed the miracle of Hananya, Mishael, and Azarya, who were thrown into the fiery oven and came out alive, as well as Daniel, who was thrown to the lion's den and survived. On Purim we recall Mordekhai's triumph over Haman. *Hishabati et'hem,* just open up your eyes, and recognize that Hashem is with us and has a special relationship with us, even during the darkest of times in exile.

5:9 מַה־דּוֹדֵךְ מִדּוֹד הַיָּפָה בַּנָּשִׁים; מַה־דּוֹדֵךְ מִדּוֹד שֶׁכָּכָה הִשְׁבַּעְתָּנוּ They turn

4 [*He*] My love, you are as beautiful as Tirtza, as lovely as Jerusalem, as
5 terrifying as the ensigned armies. Turn your eyes from me for they
have overwhelmed me. Your hair is like a flock of goats streaming
6 down from Gilad. Your teeth are like a flock of ewes rising up from
washing; each mother ewe bore twins, not one among them lost.
7 Your forehead like a pomegranate glows through your tresses.
8 Queens there are sixty, eighty concubines, and maidens there
9 are without number. But my dove, my perfection, is one – one,
unique to her mother – the shining one she bore. All the girls gaze

---

there were no other people in the world. This is the kind of love felt between God and Am Yisrael.

Another idea on the love between a bride and groom: The Gemara explains in Kiddushin (2a) that we learn about how to conduct a marriage transaction from the acquisition of property by Avraham from Efron. Doesn't it seem a bit peculiar to derive a lesson about a marriage transaction from the acquisition of a burial plot? Couldn't the Gemara have selected a more positive parallel? Perhaps the connection is as follows. If you had asked Efron who got the better deal, he would have said, What do you mean? He gave me four hundred shekel for a cave. I completed the deal of the century. I sold an empty plot of land for the highest price per square meter ever! If you had asked Avraham, he would have said, I was able to acquire the entrance to Gan Eden for a few shekels. What a bargain!

Each party felt that they got the best deal of their life. And that's what marriage is about. Each spouse should look at the other and say, What a deal I got! That's what Hashem expresses: Out of all of the nations, the only one I have eyes for is you.

אַחַת הִיא לְאִמָּהּ There are many arguments in *batei midrash,* but it is all to be able to arrive at the truth. The Maharal in *Be'er HaGola* explains that if you ask people what causes a tree to grow so beautifully, one individual might suggest that it was the sunlight, another

ד ה יָפָה אַתְּ רַעְיָתִי כְּתִרְצָה נָאוָה כִּירוּשָׁלָםִ אֲיֻמָּה כַּנִּדְגָּלוֹת׃ הָסֵבִּי
עֵינַיִךְ מִנֶּגְדִּי שֶׁהֵם הִרְהִיבֻנִי שַׂעְרֵךְ כְּעֵדֶר הָעִזִּים שֶׁגָּלְשׁוּ מִן־
ו הַגִּלְעָד׃ שִׁנַּיִךְ כְּעֵדֶר הָרְחֵלִים שֶׁעָלוּ מִן־הָרַחְצָה שֶׁכֻּלָּם
ז מַתְאִימוֹת וְשַׁכֻּלָה אֵין בָּהֶם׃ כְּפֶלַח הָרִמּוֹן רַקָּתֵךְ מִבַּעַד לְצַמָּתֵךְ׃
ח שִׁשִּׁים הֵמָּה מְלָכוֹת וּשְׁמֹנִים פִּילַגְשִׁים וַעֲלָמוֹת אֵין מִסְפָּר׃
ט אַחַת הִיא יוֹנָתִי תַמָּתִי אַחַת הִיא לְאִמָּהּ בָּרָה הִיא לְיוֹלַדְתָּהּ

---

with Hashem. Only Am Yisrael received the Torah as a *morasha*, an heirloom, that solidifies our special relationship with Hashem.

Rav Moshe Feinstein, cited in the Haggada *Arzei HaLevanon*, points out that one would have expected this *pasuk* to be in a different book of Tanakh. Why does it appear in *Shir HaShirim*? If this is a reference to Elul, wouldn't it be better placed in a more awe-related context? Rav Moshe explains that that's exactly the point. The highest level of *teshuva* is *teshuva me'ahava*, returning to God out of love rather than out of fear. That's why this *pasuk* appears specifically in *Shir HaShirim*.

6:8 שִׁשִּׁים הֵמָּה מְלָכוֹת וּשְׁמֹנִים פִּילַגְשִׁים, וַעֲלָמוֹת אֵין מִסְפָּר This *pasuk* relates to the many different opinions in the Torah (Rashi). Rav Chaim Kanievsky posits that the word *shishim*, sixty, refers to the sixty *masekhtot* in the Oral Torah and the word *shemonim*, eighty, refers to the eighty *parashot* in the Written Torah.

6:9 אַחַת הִיא יוֹנָתִי תַמָּתִי I have eyes only for one.

It is interesting to note that we allude to Adam and Hava in the *sheva berakhot* when we say: *kesamehakha yetzirkha beGan Eden mikedem*, "like the happiness experienced in the Garden of Eden." What relevance do Adam and Hava have to the bride and groom? Perhaps this expresses the wish that just as Adam and Hava focused solely on one another, since they were the only couple in the world, so should the new couple's love for each other be exclusive, as if

at her – declare that she is blessed – the queens and concubines –
10 and speak her praise. Who is this, like dawn to gaze
upon, beautiful as the moon, shining like the sun, as terrifying as
11 the ensigned armies? [*She*] I went down to the nut garden to see
the spring growth by the stream, to see whether the vines were in
12 flower, whether the pomegranate buds had burst. I did not know
myself – I found myself amid the chariots of my princely people.

---

covers the nut inside. On the outside they all appear simple and similar, but on the inside, each is full of life and has so much to offer.

Rashi offers another idea. When a nut falls into the mud, nothing happens to it. You just wash off the mud, and the nut is clean. So too, when Am Yisrael go into exile, they are covered in mud, but retain their inner beauty.

The Shemen HaTov offers an alternative explanation. There are different kinds of nuts, which are opened with varying degrees of difficulty. Some are opened easily, while others require more effort to crack. Sometimes you need to have a special tool to crack a nut. Similarly, some Jews are inspired easily, while others require a bit more effort to inspire. Others even need to experience tragedy. Yet once all the covers are removed, their insides are all the same in that they are all beautiful people.

One last thought: When you remove one nut from a mound of nuts, all the nuts in the heap move, because everything is connected. Rav Hershel Schachter, in his introduction to his *sefer Ginat Egoz*, explains that similarly, all the parts of the Torah are interconnected. You could explain one Gemara at the end of *Shas* based on another Gemara at the beginning. That is one of the incredibly beautiful aspects of the Torah.

י רָאוּהָ בָנוֹת וַיְאַשְּׁרוּהָ מְלָכוֹת וּפִילַגְשִׁים וַיְהַלְלוּהָ׃ מִי־
זֹאת הַנִּשְׁקָפָה כְּמוֹ־שָׁחַר יָפָה כַלְּבָנָה בָּרָה כַּחַמָּה אֲיֻמָּה כַּנִּדְגָּלוֹת׃
יא אֶל־גִּנַּת אֱגוֹז יָרַדְתִּי לִרְאוֹת בְּאִבֵּי הַנָּחַל לִרְאוֹת הֲפָרְחָה
יב הַגֶּפֶן הֵנֵצוּ הָרִמֹּנִים׃ לֹא יָדַעְתִּי נַפְשִׁי שָׂמַתְנִי מַרְכְּבוֹת עַמִּי נָדִיב׃

---

might state it was the water it received, while yet a third might declare it was the fertile soil in which it was planted. The truth is that each of these factors played a role. All the suggestions are correct, yet each provides a different perspective. So too with Torah. We seek to derive a true understanding through various perspectives, but the goal is to arrive at the one truth – *ahat hi le'imah*.

בָּרָה הִיא לְיוֹלַדְתָּהּ; רָאוּהָ בָנוֹת וַיְאַשְּׁרוּהָ, מְלָכוֹת וּפִילַגְשִׁים וַיְהַלְלוּהָ All the other nations see her, and they praise her.

Our mandate in life is to be a light unto the nations. The tragedy of our generation is that we have become attracted by foreign cultures that compromise our Torah values. This is the antithesis of our mission. We are to act as the *rosh* (the head; the influencer) and not as the *zanav* (literally the tail, depicting a follower). In that way we will earn the praise and respect of the other nations.

6:11 **אֶל־גִּנַּת אֱגוֹז יָרַדְתִּי לִרְאוֹת בְּאִבֵּי הַנָּחַל, לִרְאוֹת הֲפָרְחָה הַגֶּפֶן, הֵנֵצוּ הָרִמֹּנִים** I went down to the nut garden, to see the flowers of the river, to see whether the vines had blossomed, whether the pomegranate buds had burst. This is a reference to the time period of the second *Beit HaMikdash*, when Hashem returned to dwell among us (Rashi).

Why is Am Yisrael compared to a nut (*egoz*)? Rashi suggests that from the outside, a nut looks hard. They all look the same. When you crack it open, you see something that is edible and nutritious. So too, Jews are humble; they cover up their actions, like the shell

7 1 [*He*] Turn, turn back, Shulamite; turn back, turn; let us see you.
Why do you gaze at the Shulamite as if she were a Mahanayim
2 dancer? How lovely are your steps in sandals, prince's daughter;

Rav Yosef Dov Soloveitchik describes in *Family Redeemed* (p. 45):

> The *umot ha'olam* say to us, time has changed, history marches on. The covenantal union is no longer beneficial. On the contrary, it has become the source of misery and distress. The interrogators suggest the termination of the old covenantal relationship, binding the *shulamit* (maiden) to her beloved. But the *shulamit,* however, does not even attempt to rationalize her absolute loyalty, and her unqualified dedication to her beloved. She admits that her dedication and loyalty are a mystery even to herself. It is futile to debate or to analyze her unswerving loyalty, because she acts like one who under the sway of ecstatic experience has plunged into a never-ending dance whose very rhythm is intoxicating.

Rav Soloveitchik suggests that our response to the other nations is that we are proud and ecstatic to perform the mitzvot and with our ability to serve our Creator.

The Rambam also quotes this *pasuk* in his *Iggeret Teiman,* a letter that he wrote to the Jews in Teiman to offer them encouragement in a time of persecution. He states that the other nations attempt to convert us; they try to seduce us. We respond by asking, Why are you pulling us away? Can you provide us with something like *simhat hamahanayim*? At *maamad Har Sinai,* we were so close to Hashem. Can you give us something as fulfilling as that?

The Rambam then states that the word *shuvi* appears four times to demonstrate that throughout the four exiles it's been so hard but we have kept our faith. We are still in the fourth exile but we must remain strong and committed.

7:2 מַה־יָּפוּ פְעָמַיִךְ בַּנְּעָלִים, בַּת־נָדִיב How lovely are your steps, with the shoes of the daughter, the princess.

According

ז א שׁ֤וּבִי שׁ֙וּבִי֙ הַשּׁ֣וּלַמִּ֔ית שׁ֥וּבִי שׁ֖וּבִי וְנֶחֱזֶה־בָּ֑ךְ מַה־תֶּֽחֱזוּ֙ בַּשּׁ֣וּלַמִּ֔ית
ב כִּמְחֹלַ֖ת הַֽמַּחֲנָֽיִם׃ מַה־יָּפ֧וּ פְעָמַ֛יִךְ בַּנְּעָלִ֖ים בַּת־נָדִ֑יב חַמּוּקֵ֣י יְרֵכַ֔יִךְ

PEREK ZAYIN

In the seventh chapter we again encounter a discussion between Am Yisrael and the other nations, where they ask us why we remain loyal to HaKadosh Barukh Hu. The chapter describes the sense of amazement the other nations experience over our loyalty to God. Toward the end of the chapter HaKadosh Barukh Hu describes His love for Am Yisrael. Lastly, we have another declaration of loyalty to HaKadosh Barukh Hu.

7:1 שׁוּבִי שׁוּבִי הַשּׁוּלַמִּית The other nations request that we return to them and turn away from Hashem.

שׁוּבִי וְנֶחֱזֶה־בָּךְ The other nations emphasize that if we turn away from Hashem and join them, we will enjoy ourselves. We should free ourselves from the restrictions demanded by the commandments.

מַה־תֶּחֱזוּ בַּשּׁוּלַמִּית, כִּמְחֹלַת, הַמַּחֲנָיִם This part of the *pasuk* is Am Yisrael's response to the other nations. They ask, do you think you understand us so well that you know what satisfies us? Could you possibly offer us the same experience that we had when we traveled in the desert and the *Shekhina* dwelled among us? (Rashi). Other commentaries explain *shuvi* as a statement uttered by the prophets to Am Yisrael, exhorting them to do *teshuva* – to return to Hashem and not to return to the other nations.

What is the meaning of the term *kimholat hamahanayim*? Am Yisrael asks the nations: Could you show us a greatness like a *mehola*? The word *mekhola* refers to a dance. Metzudat Tzion suggests that this is a joyous dance (*rikud shel simha*), likely a reference to Har Sinai. In other words, Can you show us something as fulfilling as what we experienced at Har Sinai?

the turn of your thighs like jewelry, work of the artist's hands;
3 your navel a circular bowl – may it never want for wine; your
4 belly curved like baled wheat, bounded round with lilies. Your

---

בִּטְנֵךְ עֲרֵמַת חִטִּים Your belly is a pile of wheat.

Just like wheat nourishes all those who eat it, so too, the Sanhedrin nourishes the nation through its application of law and order. It's the center of the world, and it protects the whole world.

סוּגָה בַּשּׁוֹשַׁנִּים Surrounded by lilies.

What does this refer to? Even when it may be tempting to sin and there is no iron gate stopping one from transgressing, but only a flowerbed of lilies that can easily be trampled upon, a Jew withstands such temptation. It may also refer to a young groom who is able to withstand temptation on the first night of marriage after learning that his new bride is a *nidda* (Rashi).

Rav Yosef Dov Soloveitchik, in *The Rav Speaks* (pp. 104–105), describes this phenomenon:

> If you ask me who is a Jew? I would answer, one who lives a life of heroism. In my eyes, a Jew is ready to live heroically, to always be in the minority. The observance of mitzvot is itself bound up with heroism. The capacity to break down one's will and the ability to overcome the natural instinctive drive in man, are part of the Jewish talent for living heroically. What compels the young man to move away from his bride, to whom he is drawn? An external force? A physical danger? No! Who would blame him were he to sin? Who would criticize him were he unable to overcome his impulse? Who would know about it? This entire drama takes place in the innermost chamber in the dead of the night. No iron wall shuts him out, but a flowerbed of lilies. He has only to step on the flowerbed and trample the lilies. But the unique strength found in every Jew prevents him from acting rashly, from trampling fresh

and beautiful

ג כְּמוֹ חֲלָאִים מַעֲשֵׂה יְדֵי אָמָּן׃ שָׁרְרֵךְ אַגַּן הַסַּהַר אַל־יֶחְסַר הַמָּזֶג
ד בִּטְנֵךְ עֲרֵמַת חִטִּים סוּגָה בַּשּׁוֹשַׁנִּים׃ שְׁנֵי שָׁדַיִךְ כִּשְׁנֵי עֳפָרִים תָּאֳמֵי

According to *Hazal,* this refers to when Am Yisrael were *oleh regel.* Other nations were inspired by that event. Rav Shimon Schwab in his *sefer Maayan Beit Hasho'eiva* gives a beautiful insight on this *pasuk.* It's a bit strange that when praising Am Yisrael for partaking in *aliya leregel* what is cited in this *pasuk* is a reference to their shoes. When we ascend to the *Beit HaMikdash* we actually remove our shoes, so why associate this activity with wearing them?

Rav Schwab explains that in Musaf of Yom Tov we state: *Vehashev kohanim le'avodatam ulevi'im leshiram ulezimram vehashev Yisrael linveihem.* The *kohanim* return to their sacrifices, the *levi'im* to their song, and Yisrael to their...homes?

The reference to Yisrael returning to their homes is about the end of the *aliya leregel* process. This was a major endeavor equal to the acts of worship of the *kohanim* and *levi'im.* Meaning, did you take *aliya leregel* home with you? Did you let it change you? All your inspiration that you experienced during *aliya leregel* – are you taking that with you to your homes and your daily lives? It is not meant to be a one-off experience that remains in Yerushalayim. That is why there is a reference to shoes. It continues after they complete their journey and are on their way home. The other nations were in awe, because they saw how we were changed individuals from what we experienced during *aliya leregel. Aliya leregel* didn't end when one exited the *Beit HaMikdash.* People internalized the event and carried it with them to their homes and families.

7:3 שָׁרְרֵךְ אַגַּן הַסַּהַר אַל־יֶחְסַר הַמָּזֶג Literally, your navel is [like] a circular bowl, where no wine is lacking.

This refers to the Sanhedrin. This may be a continuation of the compliments the other nations bestow on Yerushalayim. The Sanhedrin sits in a semicircle; therefore it is referenced as a circle.

5 two breasts are like young twins of a she-gazelle, your neck an
ivory tower, your eyes like pools in Heshbon, like pools by the
Bat Rabim Gate, your nose like the Tower of Lebanon gazing out
6 to Damascus, your head rising from you like the Carmel; its curls
7 shine like purple – a king is tangled up among its tresses. How
8 beautiful you are, how good; love with all its joys. Your bearing
9 is like a date palm, your breasts its clustered fruits, but I said, "I
shall climb the date palm; I shall take hold of its branches," and
your breasts will be like clustered grapes, your breath the scent
10 of apples. And your mouth is like good wine, inside – [*She*] It is
11 for my beloved, flowing freely, bringing words to sleeping lips. I
12 am my beloved's, and his longing is for me. Come, my beloved,
13 let us go to the fields; let us lodge in the villages; we will get up
early and go to the vineyards and see if the vine has flowered,
if its blossoms have opened out, and if the pomegranate buds
14 have burst; there I shall give you my love. The mandrakes impart
their scent, and on our own doorstep the sweetest of fruits, new
8 1 and old; my beloved, I have hoarded them for you. If only you
could have been my brother, could have suckled at my mother's

---

one of two lovers. It is not acceptable to show affection between a man and a woman in public. Yet a hug between siblings is different. Therefore, here we desire to be able to show immediate affection even in public as siblings (Metzudat David).

What does it mean to hug and kiss Hashem? This is a reference to publicly serving HaKadosh Barukh Hu, to do all the mitzvot with no fear or shame. In the first *siman* in *Shulhan Arukh,* the Tur quotes the Mishna in *Pirkei Avot* (5:20), citing Rabbi Yehuda ben Teima: *Hevei az kanamer vekal kanesher, ratz katzvi vegibbor kaari, laasot retzon Avikha shebaShamayim,* "Be strong as a leopard, light as an eagle, swift as a gazelle, and brave as a lion, to do the will of your Father in Heaven."

We should

ה צְבִיָּה: צַוָּארֵךְ כְּמִגְדַּל הַשֵּׁן עֵינַיִךְ בְּרֵכוֹת בְּחֶשְׁבּוֹן עַל־שַׁעַר בַּת־
ו רַבִּים אַפֵּךְ כְּמִגְדַּל הַלְּבָנוֹן צוֹפֶה פְּנֵי דַמָּשֶׂק: רֹאשֵׁךְ עָלַיִךְ כַּכַּרְמֶל
ז וְדַלַּת רֹאשֵׁךְ כָּאַרְגָּמָן מֶלֶךְ אָסוּר בָּרְהָטִים: מַה־יָּפִית וּמַה־נָּעַמְתְּ
ח אַהֲבָה בַּתַּעֲנוּגִים: זֹאת קוֹמָתֵךְ דָּמְתָה לְתָמָר וְשָׁדַיִךְ לְאַשְׁכֹּלוֹת:
ט אָמַרְתִּי אֶעֱלֶה בְתָמָר אֹחֲזָה בְּסַנְסִנָּיו וְיִהְיוּ־נָא שָׁדַיִךְ כְּאֶשְׁכְּלוֹת
י הַגֶּפֶן וְרֵיחַ אַפֵּךְ כַּתַּפּוּחִים: וְחִכֵּךְ כְּיֵין הַטּוֹב הוֹלֵךְ לְדוֹדִי לְמֵישָׁרִים
יא יב דּוֹבֵב שִׂפְתֵי יְשֵׁנִים: אֲנִי לְדוֹדִי וְעָלַי תְּשׁוּקָתוֹ: לְכָה דוֹדִי נֵצֵא
יג הַשָּׂדֶה נָלִינָה בַּכְּפָרִים: נַשְׁכִּימָה לַכְּרָמִים נִרְאֶה אִם־פָּרְחָה הַגֶּפֶן
יד פִּתַּח הַסְּמָדַר הֵנֵצוּ הָרִמּוֹנִים שָׁם אֶתֵּן אֶת־דֹּדַי לָךְ: הַדּוּדָאִים
נָתְנוּ־רֵיחַ וְעַל־פְּתָחֵינוּ כָּל־מְגָדִים חֲדָשִׁים גַּם־יְשָׁנִים דּוֹדִי צָפַנְתִּי
ח א לָךְ: מִי יִתֶּנְךָ כְּאָח לִי יוֹנֵק שְׁדֵי אִמִּי אֶמְצָאֲךָ בַחוּץ אֶשָּׁקְךָ גַּם לֹא־

> and beautiful flowers, which cannot protect itself, and can complain against no one.

This is silent heroism and strength.

The Rav also writes about a similar idea in *Yemei Zikaron* (pp. 47–48), the idea of *tzimtzum*. HaKadosh Barukh Hu created the world in an act of *tzimtzum* – He somehow minimized Himself, and withheld Himself. That is how a Jew at times has to conduct himself. To be able to withdraw or withhold himself from temptation, even when there is no one physically policing him.

The nations of the world recognize our discipline and allegiance to adhering to God's commandments even behind closed doors, and they admire it.

PEREK HET

8:1 *מִי יִתֶּנְךָ כְּאָח לִי* Bnei Yisrael wish that Hashem could be like a brother. Why the sudden change? Until now the relationship was

breast. I would find you outside, I would kiss you, yet none would
2 shame me. I would lead you; I would bring you to my mother's
house; you would teach me. I would give you to drink spiced
3 wine, juice of my pomegranate tree. My head rests on his left arm,
4 his right embraces me. Swear to me, daughters of Jerusalem; tell
me, why do you seek to waken, why to rouse, this love before its
5 time? [*Friends*] Who is this rising from the wilderness,
entwined with her beloved? [*She*] Beneath the apple tree I roused
you where your mother bore you, where in suffering she gave

Then, in the next verse, we turn to the other nations and assure them that Hashem has not rejected us:

8:3 שְׂמֹאלוֹ תַּחַת רֹאשִׁי וִימִינוֹ תְּחַבְּקֵנִי His left hand is supporting my head and His right hand is embracing me. It may appear as if we are forlorn and forgotten. For thousands of years, many nations sought to destroy us, but we have outlasted all of those nations. It is clear that Hashem protects us – He hugs us with His right hand.

8:5 תַּחַת הַתַּפּוּחַ עוֹרַרְתִּיךָ, שָׁמָּה חִבְּלַתְךָ אִמֶּךָ, שָׁמָּה חִבְּלָה יְלָדַתְךָ What is the meaning of this reference to apple trees? Perhaps it relates to the Gemara in Sota (11b) that depicts what transpired when we were enslaved in Mitzrayim. It was the faith of the Jewish women that enabled the Jews to merit *geula*. Due to the slave labor, the men were not motivated to maintain intimacy with their wives. In order to procreate and ensure the future of Am Yisrael, the women dressed up and enticed their husbands in the fields. They would later give birth in those fields under the apple trees to prevent their newborns from being killed by the Egyptians. Miraculously, Hashem would care for those children. This portrays Hashem's love and acts of kindness for Am Yisrael in a time of crisis. This idea relates to the last phrase in the verse about the early days, when we had birthing pains, likely a reference to *yetzi'at Mitzrayim*, the beginning of our relationship with Hashem as a nation.

The jealousy

ב יָבֻזוּ לִי׃ אֶנְהָגְךָ אֲבִיאֲךָ אֶל־בֵּית אִמִּי תְּלַמְּדֵנִי אַשְׁקְךָ מִיַּיִן הָרֶקַח
ג ד מֵעֲסִיס רִמֹּנִי׃ שְׂמֹאלוֹ תַּחַת רֹאשִׁי וִימִינוֹ תְּחַבְּקֵנִי׃ הִשְׁבַּעְתִּי
אֶתְכֶם בְּנוֹת יְרוּשָׁלָ͏ִם מַה־תָּעִירוּ ׀ וּמַה־תְּעֹרְרוּ אֶת־הָאַהֲבָה עַד
ה שֶׁתֶּחְפָּץ׃ מִי זֹאת עֹלָה מִן־הַמִּדְבָּר מִתְרַפֶּקֶת עַל־דּוֹדָהּ
תַּחַת הַתַּפּוּחַ עוֹרַרְתִּיךָ שָׁמָּה חִבְּלַתְךָ אִמֶּךָ שָׁמָּה חִבְּלָה יְלָדַתְךָ׃

We should mimic the characteristics of these strong animals for worshipping Hashem. The first *is az kanamer* – strong as a leopard. At times an individual seeks to perform a mitzva, but he holds himself back because other people may scoff at him. Rabbi Yehuda ben Teima teaches his students to withstand such fear and fulfill mitzvot. As Rabbi Yohanan ben Zakkai told his students, *Yehi mora Shamayim aleihem kemora basar vedam,* "Your fear of HaKadosh Barukh Hu should be like your fear of people."

יוֹנֵק שְׁדֵי אִמִּי Rashi suggests that nursing here is portrayed as a comforting act. Taken in the context of the fraternal relationship mentioned earlier in the verse, we are reminded of how Yosef comforted his brothers when he revealed his identity to them in Mitzrayim. We reach out to Hashem and admit that we may have acted inappropriately as well and that we yearn for the day when we will be forgiven, as Yosef forgave his brothers.

8:2 אֶנְהָגְךָ, אֲבִיאֲךָ אֶל־בֵּית אִמִּי תְּלַמְּדֵנִי, אַשְׁקְךָ מִיַּיִן הָרֶקַח מֵעֲסִיס רִמֹּנִי This verse can be paraphrased according to Rashi's understanding: I will bring you back to the *Beit HaMikdash* and there you will teach me. I will offer you wine, a reference to sacrifices.

The Beit Halevi, citing the Brisker Rav, believes the word *ashkekha* (I would give you to drink) refers to prophecy, as in the verse *Yishakeini mineshikot pihu* (1:2). We yearn to return to the *Mikdash,* to abide by the Torah with the assistance of the prophets, whom we had previously ignored.

6 you birth. Set me like a seal upon your heart, like the seal upon
your arm – for love is as powerful as death itself, and jealousy
unyielding as Sheol; it burns with sparks of fire, with the LORD's
7 own flame. Great waters cannot quench love, nor torrents
sweep it by. If a man offered all his wealth for love – they would
8 laugh him to shame. [*Brothers*] We have a little sister;
her breasts are not yet grown. What shall we do for our sister

---

overflow, caused by an external source, symbolizes the decrees that the other nations establish to forbid us from practicing our religion. Both phenomena will be unsuccessful in extinguishing the love between Am Yisrael and Hashem.

Even after we transgress, or as the Beit Halevi describes above, Heaven forbid, assimilate, Hashem still loves us. To highlight this point, Rav Yosef Dov Soloveitchik asks why on the afternoon of Tisha Be'Av, specifically when the *Beit HaMikdash* began to burn, we start to ease our mourning and are able to sit on chairs and put on tefillin. As the flames spread, shouldn't we engage in stricter mourning?

The Rav explains that until that point, nobody knew whether Hashem would destroy Am Yisrael for their transgressions or take a *mashkon* (collateral) in their place, that is, take out His anger on the wood and stones of the *Mikdash* rather than annihilate the nation. Once we understood that the *Mikdash* would be destroyed and we would essentially survive, it became somewhat of a consolation within this tragic event. Therefore, we ease our mourning a bit. We realize that Hashem will never leave us. Nothing can extinguish our relationship. This is something that the other nations will never fathom.

As a response

ו שִׂימֵ֨נִי כַחוֹתָ֜ם עַל־לִבֶּ֗ךָ כַּחוֹתָם֙ עַל־זְרוֹעֶ֔ךָ כִּֽי־עַזָּ֤ה כַמָּ֙וֶת֙ אַהֲבָ֔ה
ז קָשָׁ֥ה כִשְׁא֖וֹל קִנְאָ֑ה רְשָׁפֶ֕יהָ רִשְׁפֵּ֖י אֵ֥שׁ שַׁלְהֶבֶתְיָֽה׃ מַ֣יִם רַבִּ֗ים
לֹ֤א יֽוּכְלוּ֙ לְכַבּ֣וֹת אֶת־הָֽאַהֲבָ֔ה וּנְהָר֖וֹת לֹ֣א יִשְׁטְפ֑וּהָ אִם־יִתֵּ֨ן אִ֜ישׁ
ח אֶת־כׇּל־ה֤וֹן בֵּיתוֹ֙ בָּאַהֲבָ֔ה בּ֖וֹז יָב֥וּזוּ לֽוֹ׃ אָח֥וֹת
לָ֙נוּ֙ קְטַנָּ֔ה וְשָׁדַ֖יִם אֵ֣ין לָ֑הּ מַֽה־נַּעֲשֶׂה֙ לַאֲחֹתֵ֔נוּ בַּיּ֖וֹם שֶׁיְּדֻבַּר־בָּֽהּ׃

8:6 קָשָׁה כִשְׁאוֹל קִנְאָה The jealousy the other nations feel is deep rooted.

Rav Dessler in his Haggada distinguishes between two types of jealousy. One type is characterized by wanting an object in another's possession. A second type of jealousy is characterized by having no tolerance for another's very existence. It is threatening, and it will not subside until the other person does not exist. This is the type of jealousy exhibited by the other nations toward us.

That's the *kina* we talk about, that the other nations have an inherent hatred and jealousy toward us.

Next comes one of the most beautiful of *pesukim* in all of Tanakh.

8:7 מַיִם רַבִּים לֹא יוּכְלוּ לְכַבּוֹת אֶת־הָאַהֲבָה All the greatest waters in the world cannot extinguish the love that Hashem feels toward us. This connects to the comparison of our love to heated coals in verse 6. Water may refer to the nations of the world that seek unsuccessfully to extinguish Am Yisrael's loyalty to Hashem.

וּנְהָרוֹת, לֹא יִשְׁטְפוּהָ And the rivers can't sweep it away.

The Beit Halevi in his Haggada distinguishes between great waters, and rivers which can overflow and flood. Great water symbolizes natural assimilation as we mix with other nations. The river

9 when a suitor comes for her? If she is a wall, we will build a silver
10 watchtower; if a door, we will bar her up with cedar. [*She*] But I am
a wall; my breasts are like towers. It was then that I found peace in
11 his eyes. [*He*] Once, Shlomo had a vineyard at Baal Hamon. He
gave the vineyard over to the keepers; each keeper brought him
12 in a thousand in silver from the fruits. My vineyard stands before
me, my own: Shlomo, keep your thousand; pay two hundred to

8:12 כַּרְמִי שֶׁלִּי לְפָנָי, הָאֶלֶף לְךָ שְׁלֹמֹה וּמָאתַיִם לְנֹטְרִים אֶת־פִּרְיוֹ Hashem declares, There will come a time when the vineyard will be in front of Me. This may relate to the day of judgment, when justice will be served to the other nations that oppressed and taxed the Jewish people (Rashi).

This reminds us of the Gemara in the beginning of Avoda Zara (2b–3a). The nations of the world try to defend themselves before HaKadosh Barukh Hu. They claim that everything they did was for the good of Am Yisrael. They built markets and so forth. HaKadosh Barukh Hu calls them fools; it is clear that all they did was for their own benefit. They ask for a second chance and Hashem tells them to fulfill the simple mitzva of sukka, which they cannot fulfill due to the heat, and they subsequently kick the sukka, destroying it.

Please

ט אִם־חוֹמָה הִיא נִבְנֶה עָלֶיהָ טִירַת כָּסֶף וְאִם־דֶּלֶת הִיא נָצוּר עָלֶיהָ

י לוּחַ אָרֶז: אֲנִי חוֹמָה וְשָׁדַי כַּמִּגְדָּלוֹת אָז הָיִיתִי בְעֵינָיו כְּמוֹצְאֵת שָׁלוֹם:

יא כֶּרֶם הָיָה לִשְׁלֹמֹה בְּבַעַל הָמוֹן נָתַן אֶת־הַכֶּרֶם לַנֹּטְרִים אִישׁ יָבִא

יב בְּפִרְיוֹ אֶלֶף כָּסֶף: כַּרְמִי שֶׁלִּי לְפָנָי הָאֶלֶף לְךָ שְׁלֹמֹה וּמָאתַיִם לְנֹטְרִים

8:10 אֲנִי חוֹמָה וְשָׁדַי כַּמִּגְדָּלוֹת, אָז הָיִיתִי בְעֵינָיו כְּמוֹצְאֵת שָׁלוֹם As a response to the angels' inquiry as to how to save their sister (Am Yisrael) in exile, Hashem states that whether the exile will last for a short or long period all depends on their level of *emuna*. If they have *emuna* that is firm like a wall, then Am Yisrael will be able to build a *Beit Mikdash* out of silver and it will last an eternity. However, if their faith is like a shaky door that sways open and shut (meaning, it constantly changes its state), then they will build a house of wood, which is subject to rotting and is only a temporary edifice (Rashi).

The Gemara in Yoma (9b) references this *pasuk*. Reish Lakish tells Rava bar Hana that Hashem is angry with the Jews in Bavel. Had they returned with Ezra, the *Beit HaMikdash* would have been made of silver and consequently would have been everlasting. Since so few people (roughly twenty-two thousand) returned, the second *Beit HaMikdash* was only temporary.

13 the keepers of the fruits. "You who still sit in the gardens, friends
14 listen for your voice. Have me hear." [*She*] Away with you, my
beloved, like a gazelle or a young deer over perfumed hills.

> The story of religious complacency of Diaspora Jewry is an old story. Not only did the midrash predict it and Rashi quote it, but unfortunately the last of several generations practice it.
>
> Jews must remember in their religious life and practice that they are in *galut*. They must be reminded by the observance of that extra day, that Holiday of the Exiles (*Yom Tov Sheni*), to know and realize and remind themselves, that they are indeed in exile, sweet as it is, and that no exile, no matter how pleasant, is permanently desirable.
>
> Perhaps we Orthodox American Jews are delinquent in Aliyah.... The fact is that a great majority will remain here [in America] for the foreseeable future.... But we must never lose sight of the profound distinction between a temporary stay, even for a few generations, and the fixing of our destiny permanently in exile.... We must never abandon the vision of *shivat Zion* and redemption.

Perhaps this is one of the main reasons that we recite *Shir HaShirim* at the end of the Seder and on *Shabbat Hol HaMo'ed Pesah*. In addition to highlighting the special relationship that we share with Hashem, which all began on Pesah as we became His nation, we are to yearn for the future redemption, when we can all gather from the four corners of the earth and unite in Yerushalayim as His chosen nation.

יג אֶת־פִּרְיוֹ: הַיּוֹשֶׁבֶת בַּגַּנִּים חֲבֵרִים מַקְשִׁיבִים לְקוֹלֵךְ הַשְׁמִיעִנִי:
יד בְּרַח ׀ דּוֹדִי וּדְמֵה־לְךָ לִצְבִי אוֹ לְעֹפֶר הָאַיָּלִים עַל הָרֵי בְשָׂמִים:

8:14 בְּרַח דּוֹדִי, וּדְמֵה־לְךָ לִצְבִי אוֹ לְעֹפֶר הָאַיָּלִים עַל הָרֵי בְשָׂמִים Please run with me, Hashem. Hashem, who's in *galut* (exile) with me, *Shekhinta begaluta*. Run with me, take me back, be like a quick hind, returning to Yerushalayim.

Rabbi Norman Lamm expresses a beautiful idea with respect to the ending of Shir HaShirim. The penultimate *pasuk* speaks of Torah and *tefilla*. That would have been a strong ending. It is the essence of our relationship with Hashem and the basis of our religion. Why not end the book with that *pasuk*?

Often we have well-established spiritual comforts in *galut*. We have shuls, yeshivot, an abundance of kosher restaurants. We feel as if we have achieved our goal. We forget that Eretz Yisrael is the true endgame for every Jew. That's why the second-to-last *pasuk* deals with Torah and *tefilla*, but the last *pasuk* voices our yearning to return to Eretz Yisrael. Rabbi Lamm (*The Royal Table*, pp. 189–92) states:

> Our companions, the angels, cluster about our synagogues and yeshivas, to listen to the pure voice of our spiritual accomplishments. And yet, despite all this, despite the angelic approbation of our Yiddishkeit in Diaspora, it's only the next to last verse. The last verse changes all that. The song of songs of the Jewish life ends on a different note.... Despite the physical comforts and the spiritual convenience of the Diaspora, we ask God to flee from it and to take us out of it with him.

מגיד
MAGGID